PART TWO – THE GROUP

Chapter 4 – Leadership Across the Lifespan

Chapter 5 – The Dynamics of Leadership in Groups

Chapter 6 – Leadership and Motivation

PART THREE – THE SETTING

Chapter 10 – Leadership in Social Settings

Chapter 11 – Leadership and Event Management

PREFACE

Two decades have passed since the initial edition of this book was written focusing on the topic of leadership in recreation, parks, and leisure services. Scanning the introductions to the previous editions of this current effort entitled *Leadership for Recreation, Parks, and Leisure Services* reveals the importance of the topic to our professional field. In previous prefaces to the book, we have described leadership as "the single most important factor in the success" of any recreation, parks, and leisure service organization. We have also described it as a "vital element and the cornerstone to successful programs." Leadership has been defined in the preface of other editions as a "central activity" in all recreation, parks and leisure service organizations. The primacy of leadership has not been diminished over the past 20 years in the recreation, parks, and leisure service field. Leadership is as critical a component today as it was when this book was first written.

Much has been written about leadership over the past 100 years. Without question, we have a clearer understanding of leadership and its importance. However, understanding leadership can be elusive. When individuals are asked to define leadership, the responses are varied and wide-ranging. We have posited leadership as a process that assists individuals and groups in achieving their goals. We have called leadership a transformational process wherein individuals use their knowledge, skills, and abilities, as well as their creative insight and common sense to assist individuals, groups, and organizations to move forward. Nonetheless, when professionals are asked the question "What comes to mind when you think of leadership?" their responses are mixed and diverse. We are left with the feeling that leadership can be defined and viewed from many different perspectives. However, one thing is clear: everyone has some view as to the value and importance of leadership.

Without question, leadership is pervasive in recreation, parks, and leisure service organizations. We find it at all levels within organizations—direct service, supervisory, and administration. Successful recreation, parks, and leisure service organizations are ones that recognize this fact and build the capacity for leadership within all individuals at all levels. Leadership, at the face-to-face or direct service level, is as important as the leadership provided by individuals in supervisory or managerial roles. As indicated in the previous edition of this book, leadership "exists at all levels of service provision. It is evident in the transmission of skills to individual participants, in the process of coaching or mentoring individuals, and in the encouragement and nurturing of others with responsibilities as program managers or executives." Leadership is the force that enables individuals to unleash their creative energies, seek their full potential, and unlock and use their knowledge, skills, and abilities to advance their individual interests while pursuing organizational goals.

Our study of leadership over the past two decades has confirmed that it is a complex and sophisticated topic. Many different theoretical perspectives and research studies, both qualitative and quantitative, require examination. A great deal of popular literature on the topic of leadership offers simplistic explanations that have limited applications to the recreation, parks, and leisure service field. The examination of leadership and its centrality to the work of recreation, parks, and leisure service professionals at all levels requires ongoing attention. The perspectives that one forms as a student may very well be tempered in the future with the experience gained from actual practice of the profession. Continuous and ongoing reflection is required on what works as a leader, what is most appropriate, and how one's influence as a leader is measured. It is our intent that *Leadership for Recreation, Parks, and Leisure Services* will be a starting point for continuous discussion that will occur throughout one's professional life.

The third edition of *Leadership for Recreation, Parks, and Leisure Services* is unique from many different perspectives. In the first edition, entitled *Leadership in Recreation and Leisure Service Organizations*, we organized the effort into separate theoretical and practical applications sections that covered a variety of direct service areas. The second edition found us splitting the book into two textbooks, one entitled *Leadership in Recreation and Leisure Service Organizations* and the other entitled *Leadership for Recreation and Leisure Programs and Settings*. The current effort is focused on bringing together a number of interrelated elements that influence leadership in recreation, parks, and leisure service organizations. Thus, we have focused the effort on three important elements contributing to the interactive process of leadership. The first part of the book discusses of the work of leaders and includes presentation of theoretical and foundational information. The second part focuses on leaders in groups. Finally, the third part is dedicated to leadership elements in a number of recreation, parks, and leisure service settings.

Leadership for Recreation, Parks, and Leisure Services also features many distinctive pedagogical elements. We have identified learning objectives and key terms at the beginning of each chapter. This will be useful in helping students focus their attention to the intent of each chapter. In addition, we have included within each chapter marginal quotations featuring perspectives from notable individuals. These quotations will provide heightened awareness and understanding of the subject matter. We have also featured in each chapter an outstanding leader in the recreation, parks, and leisure service field. These vignettes, known as "A Legacy of Leadership," feature historic and current figures in the recreation, parks, and leisure service field. Further, leadership perspectives from professionals across the United States are included in each chapter in a section entitled "Leadership: A Point of View from the Profession." Each chapter is concluded with discussion questions, a case study, and experiential learning experiences from which students can explore and analyze their own thinking, engage in problem-solving strategies, and reflect upon their own thinking regarding leadership.

Note: Although the terms recreation, parks, and leisure services are thought to be redundant by many, we have employed all three terms in both the title of this book and throughout our discussion. We feel they capture the breadth and diversity of the field. Furthermore, the lay person may relate better to one of these terms than the others, depending on his or her previous experience, background, or knowledge of the field. Until philosophers of our field clarify precisely the points of distinction between these terms, and until the perceptions of the public are more clearly focused on one term or another, we feel that the use of the terms interchangeably is appropriate.

Acknowledgments

Professional knowledge, the basis for *Leadership for Recreation, Parks, and Leisure Services*, is typically thought of as integrating both theoretical knowledge and applied information drawn directly from professional practice. We were fortunate to have the contributions of a number of practicing professionals as a part of this edition of *Leadership for Recreation, Parks, and Leisure Services*. Their professional contributions were significant in adding meaningful and relevant information to our effort. We would like to extend our appreciation and thanks to Sara L. Hensley, Director, Department of Parks, Recreation and Neighborhood Services for the City of San Jose, California; Marco A. "Tony" Cisneros, Director, Park and Recreation Department, City of Mesquite, Texas; Ronald "Ron" H. Dodd, Executive Director, Joliet Park District, Joliet, Illinois; Terry G. Trueblood, Director, Parks and Recreation, Iowa City, Iowa; James (Jim) A. Donahue, Recreation Director, Perinton Recreation & Parks Department, Fairport, New York; Michelle Park, Executive Director, Ohio Parks and Recreation Association, Westerville, Ohio; Ronald A. Olson; Associate City Administrator/ Superintendent, Parks and Recreation, Ann Arbor, Michigan; James R. Hall, Director, Parks and Recreation Department, Boise, Idaho; Dr. Kenneth Gladish, National Executive Director, National YMCA of the USA; Dr. Kala Stroup, President, American Humanics, Inc.

In addition, we would like to acknowledge our conversations and exchange of information with Frances Hesselbein, formerly the Chief Executive Office of the Girl Scouts of the USA, and currently Chairman, Board of Governors, Leader to Leader Institute (formerly the Peter F. Drucker Foundation). Hesselbein has provided great insight into the management of nonprofit organizations. She is a beacon for leadership and an inspiration to our field.

At the University of Northern Iowa, Karen Peterson was responsible for providing clerical and administrative support to this effort. Karen is an outstanding clerical staff member who formerly served as the secretary to the Director of the School of Health, Physical Education and Leisure Services at the University of Northern Iowa. Her great patience, understanding, and exemplary technical skills were essential to this project. Karen possesses great dedication and determination and as a result, this project was moved forward in a timely and well-organized fashion. The environment at the University of Northern Iowa promotes great exploration, intellectual curiosity and productivity, as is reflected in our contributions to the body of knowledge. We would like to acknowledge the support we receive from our colleagues, including Dean of the College of Education, Jeffrey Cornett, and Associate Deans Bill Callahan and Sandy Alper. Within the School of Health, Physical Education and Leisure Services at the University of Northern Iowa, we are appreciative of the support we receive from our close colleagues in the Division of Leisure, Youth and Human Services, including Sam Lankford, Rod Dieser, Betty van der Smissen, Allison Stringer, Chris Kowalski, Stacy Van Gorp, Juli Gassman, Diane Engbretson, Jason Lau, Angie Noll, Heather Olsen, Gordon Mack, and Sarah Stille. In addition, we would like to acknowledge and thank Donna Thompson, Rip Marston, and Mick Mack in the Division of Physical Education.

Our colleagues at Sagamore Publishing have provided steadfast support to this endeavor. In particular, we would like to acknowledge the great leadership provided by Joseph Bannon, Sr. to the recreation, parks, and leisure service field. Joe serves as an inspiration to us all. His remarkable career as a park and recreation administrator, university educator, and publisher has provided great insights into effective leadership. We would also like to extend our appreciation to Doug Sanders, General Manager, Sagamore Publishing. Doug has served as a great cheerleader for this project, providing encouragement and support for the effort. His commitment to advancing professional knowledge in the recreation, parks, and leisure service field is greatly appreciated. We would also like to thank all of the staff at Sagamore Publishing. Their efforts at editing, designing, and marketing the book are appreciated.

We would also like to acknowledge the support we receive from our family members and close friends. In particular, we would like to thank Susan Edginton. Susan has been supportive of these types of writing endeavors in the 30-year career of the senior author. In addition, he would like to acknowledge the support of his children, Carole and David. Carole is currently pursuing a master's degree at Iowa State University and continues to this day to contribute to the program offerings of the University of Northern Iowa's *Camp Adventure™ Youth Services*. David is now a Foreign Service Officer with the U.S. Department of State following a long time professional career with *Camp Adventure™ Youth Services*. Our grandchildren, Hanna, Jake and Joey, represent tomorrow's leaders. They remind us of the joy of play and the importance of providing leadership to ensure that future generations have appropriate play environments. We would also like to thank Sarah Rich and Sandra Williamson, who have kept us active as participants in various leisure pursuits through the years, making sure that we "practice what we preach." Scott Hudson, husband of Kathy Scholl, has been supportive of this endeavor and of the development of her professional career. She would like to express her love and affection for the journey they have traveled together and for the sacrifices he has made in order for pursue her career opportunities.

PROLOGUE

Leadership:
An Interactive
Process

LEARNING OBJECTIVES

1. To understand leadership as a process of influence.
2. To gain an awareness of the interrelated elements involved in the processof leadership (refer to as the nexus of leadership).
3. To gain an understanding of the hallmarks of leadership.

KEY TERMS

- Leadership
- Leadership as influence
- Nexus of leadership
- Leadership factors
- Group processes
- Leadership setting
- Leadership roles
- Hallmarks of leadership

INTRODUCTION

Leadership is one of
the most endearing,
universal human
responsibilities.

Rosabeth Moss Kanter

We live in a time and a world where leadership is valued. The challenges of living in a contemporary society are reflected in the rate of change, complexity, and interconnectedness of our lives. As Hesselbein and Cohen (1999, p. xi) have written, "Times of great change are always times of great anxiety – but also of great opportunity and hope. That reality has led to an extraordinary hunger for new insights and understandings in all institutions in our society." Gaining an understanding and a knowledge of the processes of leadership is essential to the success of any recreation, parks, or leisure service organization.

Leisure has become a central focus in the lives of North Americans. We seek leisure and increasingly see it as a central element contributing to the quality of our lives. We also increasingly define ourselves through our leisure interests and pursuits. Leisure has become a major force in contemporary society with powerful social, cultural, and economic implications for how we live our lives.

In a society wherein leisure is valued and sought, the leadership provided by individuals in professional roles promoting recreation, parks, and leisure services is increasingly important. This introduction, provides an overview of the basic elements involved in the process of leadership within recreation, parks, and leisure services organizations. Leadership can best be viewed as an interactive process that ties the work of the leader, the group, and the setting in ways that assist individuals to experience leadership.

Leadership in Recreation, Parks, and Leisure Services is organized to emphasize the three elements identified in the interactive process of leadership. Part One—The Leader is focused on basic leadership concepts including foundational underpinnings used in defining leadership (Chapter 1—The Language of Leadership); past and present theories and concepts of leadership (Chapter 2—Leadership: Basic Concepts and Theories); and various roles within which leadership is required in recreation, parks, and leisure services organizations (Chapter 3—Leadership Roles). Part Two—The Group presents information regarding leadership and the lifespan (Chapter 4—Leadership Across the Lifespan); group dynamics (Chapter 5—The Dynamics of Leadership in Groups); motivation (Chapter 6—Leadership and Motivation); and communications (Chapter 7—Leadership and Communication). Part Three—The Setting is dedicated to a discussion of leadership specifics as related to recreation, parks, and leisure services settings. Included is a discussion of risk management (Chapter 8—Risk Management); leisure settings leadership (Chapter 9—Leadership in Leisure Settings); social settings leadership (Chapter 10—Leadership in Social Settings); and event management (Chapter 11—Leadership and Event Management).

This comprehensive, integrated approach to studying leadership in recreation, parks, and leisure services settings provides an overview for individuals seeking professional positions in this area. The text is complemented with learning objectives, identification of key terms, discussion questions, exercises, and a case study at the conclusion of each chapter. Embedded within each chapter are selected quotes, definitions, and key concepts. In addition, we have included research overviews to complement information from the recreation, parks, and leisure services literature. Also embedded are key web resources that students may access to enhance their knowledge and understanding of the concepts presented.

LEADERSHIP AS INFLUENCE

Leadership is about getting extraordinary things done with groups or individuals. It is a process of influencing and assisting others to achieve great things. Leadership involves the building and strengthening of individuals and a commitment to a set of worthwhile ends. The essence of leadership involves inspiring a shared vision, enabling others to act, modeling desired ways of behaving, and recognizing and celebrating the contributions individuals make. Leadership is the process of building commitment amongst individuals and mobilizing them as they struggle for shared aspirations (Kouzes & Posner, 1995, p. 18).

Frances Hesselbein, the former Chief Executive Officer of the Girl Scouts of the USA, and her colleague, Paul M. Cohen, have suggested that leadership in relation to organizational management involves the following:

• Leadership is a matter of how to be, not how to do. We spend most of our lives mastering how to do things, but in the end, it is the quality and character of the individual that defines the performance of great leaders.

• Leaders succeed through the efforts of their people. The basic task of the leader is to build a highly motivated, highly productive [group]. This means moving across the boundaries both within and outside the [group], investing in people and resources, and exemplifying—demanding—personal commitment to a common task.

> When we listen to the spirit within, when we are called to lead—as all effective leaders are—we are leaders of change, not protectors and perpetuators of a cherished, honored past.
>
> *Frances Hesselbein*

- Leaders build bridges. The boundaries between [individuals, groups], sectors, organizations, employees, customers, and others are blurring. The challenge for leaders is to build a cohesive community both within and outside the [group], to invest in relationships, and to communicate a vision that speaks to a richly diverse [group].

Hesselbein and Cohen provide a clear and resonating prescription for quality leadership. As they note, the quality and character of an individual defines great leadership. A leader's basic task is to motivate people to in achieve their desired ends, and to make a personal commitment to the success of others. Leaders are bridge builders. Creating linkages and building networks between and among individuals and other groups is highly essential for successful leadership. As Hesselbein and Cohen note, ". . .leaders today have to be healers and unifiers. They are responsible for what lies outside the walls as well as what lies within. . . " (1999, p. xii). As these authors note, true leaders are energetic and engaged in dispersing leadership across the group in a circular, flexible, and fluid manner.

THE NEXUS OF LEADERSHIP

Leadership involves a number of interrelated elements. The process of leadership involves combining the work of the recreation, parks, and leisure services leader with group members in a setting that encourages individuals to experience leisure. Recreation, parks, and leisure services leaders bring to any given situation or setting their knowledge, skills, and abilities. Likewise, the individuals within the group served by the recreation, parks, and leisure services leader bring their needs as well as their own particular interests and values. Each group has its own particular goals and chemistry that influence the work of the recreation, parks, and leisure services leader and the success of each and every group member. Also, the setting greatly influences the leadership process. Recreation, parks, and leisure settings are unique and distinctive in their construction and intent. All of these three variables—the leader, the group, and the setting—have great influence on the process of leadership.

The figure below outlines the interrelated elements that influence one's approach to leadership. This model incorporates three important factors: the leader, the group, and the setting. Careful consideration should be given to all these elements, for they are interrelated and influence one another. The recreation, parks, and leisure services leader influences group members and the situation, group members influence the setting and the leader, and the setting influences the leader and the group. In reviewing a setting, a

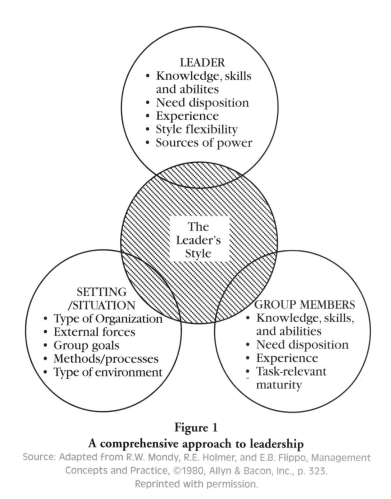

Figure 1
A comprehensive approach to leadership
Source: Adapted from R.W. Mondy, R.E. Holmer, and E.B. Flippo, Management
Concepts and Practice, ©1980, Allyn & Bacon, Inc., p. 323.
Reprinted with permission.

All great teams—and
all great organiza-
tions—are built
around a shared dream
or motivating purpose.

Warren Bennis

recreation, parks, and leisure services leader must evaluate the effects of the type of organization, external forces, group goals, methods and procedures used to achieve group goals, and the type of environment. The members of the group also must be evaluated in order to determine the most appropriate approach to leadership. The recreation, parks, and leisure services leader should analyze the knowledge, skills, and abilities of group members, as well as the members' need disposition, previous experience, and task-relevant maturity. Finally, the recreation, parks, and leisure services leader should be aware of and assess his or her own knowledge, skills and abilities, need disposition, experience, style flexibility, and source of power.

It is important to remember that the purpose of leadership is to influence others to achieve their own or the group's goals. In selecting an appropriate approach to leadership, the leader may have limited or no control over the situation. For example, external social, cultural, and economic forces may not be influenced by the leader in an immediate and direct fashion. Even though the purpose of leadership is to influence the individuals or group being led, the probability of changing the group members' knowledge, need disposition, or even maturity is difficult. Therefore, the key element in selecting an appropriate approach to leadership is the ability of the leader to change his or her own behavior. The recreation, parks, and leisure services leader must do this while being conscious or the other forces and factors that affect the achievement of group and individual goals. For example, the recreation, parks, and leisure services leader may not necessarily be able to change the maturity level of group members, but he or she can employ a leadership that fits this particular factor as it influences the achievement of group goals. Following is a brief analysis of each component of the comprehensive approach to leadership.

THE LEADER

The recreation, parks, and leisure services leader can be the key to meeting individual and group needs. The influence of the recreation, parks, and leisure services leader moves the group as a whole to action. When this action is directed toward meeting the goals of the group, the group succeeds. The following list details some of the factors that are important in developing a successful approach to leadership.

Knowledge, Skills, and Abilities. Like group members, recreation, parks, and leisure services leaders bring their own knowledge, skills, and abilities to the group. The recreation, parks, and leisure services leader's awareness of his or her strengths and weaknesses can be important in the selection of an approach to leadership.

Need Disposition. The expectations of the recreation, parks, and leisure services leader, as well as his or her own needs, wants, and interests, influence the type of approach to leadership that will be employed. Achievement-oriented leaders, for example, have a different motivation from those who are not similarly oriented. One leader's behavior may be characterized by a high degree of risk taking and entrepreneurship, whereas another leader may exhibit a low degree of risk taking.

Experience. The recreation, parks, and leisure services leader who has developed successful patterns of interaction with individuals in a group situation will obviously draw on them in the future. Thus, the previous experience of an individual will greatly influence the approach to leadership that he or she adopts.

Style Flexibility. Style flexibility can be thought of as a behavioral attribute of the recreation, parks, and leisure services leader. Some recreation, parks, and leisure services leaders have the ability to change to meet varying conditions. Other recreation, parks, and leisure services leaders may be rigid lack the ability to adapt their basic approach to leadership to differing situations.

Source of Power. There are five different sources of power: legitimate or formal, reward, coercive, referent, and expert. If a recreation, parks, and leisure services leader's only source of power is, for example, legitimate or formal, he or she may be forced to use a more task-oriented, authoritarian style of leadership. On the other hand, if the recreation, parks, and leisure services leader has a strong basis of attraction with group members, another approach to leadership may emerge.

The ability of a recreation, parks, and leisure services leader to evaluate accurately each of the three components—the situation, group members, and the leader—will influence his or her success. The misinterpretation of these factors can lead to the adoption of an inappropriate approach to leadership.

THE GROUP

Consideration of each group member, as well as the characteristics of the group as a whole, is essential in establishing an appropriate approach to leadership. The recreation, parks, and leisure services leader should perhaps be most sensitive to the needs, desires, and expectations of group members, for these are the individuals the leader wishes to influence. Good listening skills are essential in this process. Four factors related to group members that should be considered by the recreation, parks, and leisure services leader follow.

Knowledge, Skills, and Abilities. Each individual within a group possesses different knowledge, skills, and abilities. It is incumbent upon the recreation, parks, and leisure services leader to gain an awareness of the capabilities of each individual group member. In a sense, the leader must take stock of the resources of the group, as reflected in the abilities of each member. Assessment of the knowledge, skills, and abilities of group members can be useful in the organization of group tasks. Obviously, the recreation, parks, and leisure services leader wants to maximize the group's resources.

Need Disposition. The needs, wants, and interests of individual group members is another essential component in the process of determining one's approach to leadership. Individuals affiliate with or join groups for a variety of reasons. Some individuals are motivated because of the opportunities for social relationships, others because of the oppor-

None of us is as smart as all of us.

Warren Bennis

tunities for achievement and increased self-esteem. Still others become involved in groups in order to learn and grow.

Experience. The level and type of experience of group members should also be considered by the recreation, parks, and leisure services leader in determining his or her approach to leadership. Prior successful experience of group members may allow the leader to be less directive and authoritarian in nature. On the other hand, a lack of experience on the part of group members may prompt the leader to assume the reverse role.

Task-Relevant Maturity. As previously indicated, task-relevant maturity refers to whether an individual has the capacity to set and attain high goals and take responsibility. Viewing maturity on a continuum, the recreation, parks, and leisure services leader will want to vary his or her approach to leadership according to the maturity level of group members. It is important to re-emphasize that the concept of maturity should only be applied to the task at hand.

THE SETTING

When we use the term setting, we are referring to the locale within which leisure experiences are provided. Leadership is required in all of the settings and at all levels in which recreation, parks, and leisure services are found. The range of settings within which these services are provided is staggering. We will focus in this book on a select number of recreation, parks, and leisure services settings, including ones where specific leadership knowledge and skills are required, such as outdoor recreation and aquatics venues. In addition, we will discuss leadership in social settings and the broader area of event management.

In general, there are three basic types of organizations or settings—public governmental, nonprofit or non-governmental and commercial/private enterprises—within which recreation, parks, and leisure services are found. The characteristics of these three general types of organizations or settings are presented in Table 1. Public governmental leisure and recreation organizations have been established in the latter part of the nineteenth century to enhance general community welfare and promote social reform. These types of organizations are generally focused on improving the quality of life and are supported by tax revenues and fees or charges. Nonprofit/non-governmental organizations represent the largest sector of growth in North America, focusing on such goals as enriched community living, character education, and community development; they are supported by membership

> Leaders exist at all levels of an organization.
>
> *John P. Kotter*

A LEGACY OF LEADERSHIP
Frederick Law Olmsted, Sr. (1822-1903)

Frederick Law Olmsted is known as the father of landscape architecture in America. He was an author, public administrator, and noted conservationist. His zest and leadership assisted in establishing the park movement in the United States. His influence was far ranging with some 500 commissions in the areas landscape design work in the areas of urban parks, scenic reservations, parkways, park systems, residential community, university campuses, government building, and country estates. As the co-designer of Central Park in New York City in 1858 and as the site planner of the World's Columbian Exposition in Chicago in 1893, he was noted for his ability to collaborate with others, especially across disciplines.

As a young man, he was a great involved in a number of activities including working at a dry goods store and as a seaman was involved in a year-long voyage to China. He was able to study surveying, chemistry, engineering, and agriculture. For a time, he attempted farming, but was not successful. He traveled to the British Isles as a young man and had the opportunity to observe parks and private estates. In his travels, he was greatly influenced by what he saw and eventually brought ideas back to America. He captured his experiences by publishing a book, *Walks and Talks of an American Farmer in England*. Olmsted also was a social activist and opposed to the expansion of slavery. While reporting for the *New York Times*, he was inspired to write *Seaboard Slave States*, a book detailing his experiences witnessing slavery while traveling in southern states. He served as the managing editor of *Putnam's Monthly Magazine* and co-founder of *Nation*. These literary connections assisted him in achieving his position as superintendent of Central Park in New York City.

As the superintendent of Central Park in New York City and later the architect and chief in charge of construction, Olmsted supervised the largest public works project to date in America. He supervised as many as 3,600 workers and was known as considerate and fair in his dealing with co-workers. However, Olmsted was perceived as being an autocrat. He disliked second-guessing or grumbling from his subordinates. When reflecting on his own managerial leadership style, Olmsted, writing to his son, said ". . .whenever you see a head, hit it." During the Civil War, Olmsted was appointed director of the U.S. Sanitation Commission, the forerunner of the American Red Cross. In this role he was responsible for ensuring the health and sanitation of the soldiers in the Union Army which was, no doubt, an enormous logistical challenge requiring application of great managerial leadership skills. Olmsted also served as the manager of the Mariposa Estate in California and was involved in the development of early management plans for Yosemite.

Olmsted made remarkable contributions to the founding of the recreation, parks, and leisure services field. His legacy left Americans firmly supportive of incorporating the beauty of the natural environment into the urban landscape. As a social reformer, he encouraged the preservation of scenic beauty as a way to improve civilization. He encouraged the creation of public spaces available to all individuals. He was a passionate, visionary, reform-minded romantic who had enormous influence on American life.

fees or charges and donations. Last, commercial/private enterprises providing leisure and recreational services are profit-oriented, quality- and customer-driven organizations. Commercial leisure and recreational enterprises make up the largest part of the industry.

What types of leadership roles or functions are found in these general types of recreation, parks, and leisure services organizations? Again, viewing Table 1, one can see the myriad of leadership roles found in public, non-profit, and commercial recreation, parks, and leisure services organizations. Edginton, Hudson, and Ford (1999, p. 126) have identified several basic categories of leadership found in recreation, parks and leisure service organizations. They are:

Direct Program Leadership. This type of leadership involves working directly with participants, providing face-to-face leadership for a leisure experience. Functions of a leader in this role vary from planning the program to leading and directing activities.

Team Leadership. Team leadership is found when teams are brought together for competition. We usually think of individuals operating as coaches, instructors, or team captains promoting a cooperative effort, developing strategies, and encouraging team players toward higher performance.

Instructional Leadership. Individuals involved in this type of leadership usually are involved in crafting learning environments for individuals so that they may acquire selective knowledge, skills or values. This may involve providing information, creating simulations or role-playing, and/or a myriad of learning strategies that can be planned and implemented by the leader.

Counselor. Counselors focus on assisting individuals or groups in reviewing their behaviors, value states, and/or ways in which they make decisions about various life activities, including their leisure and recreation. Individuals in this role act with a great deal of confidentiality, assisting individuals to clarify life goals or challenges they have experienced in their life.

Outreach Worker. This type of leadership role involves extending oneself to the participant in environments where they live, work, and play. Detached workers, street gang leaders, roving leaders, and other such titles are often associated with outreach work. Such leaders often engage in what might be called informal education. Informal learning

Table 1

Recreation, Parks and Leisure Program and Setting

Types of Organizations	Goals	Funding Strategies	Typical Settings	Typical Facilities	Common Leadership Roles	Typical Programs
Public Governmental Organizations	General community welfare; improved quality of life; service to the public; enriched community life; wise use of leisure environmental concerns	Tax revenues; feed and charges; donations; trusts; grants; contracts; partnerships; use of volunteers; in-kind contributions	Municipal park and recreation departments; county and state conservation and park systems; museums, art galleries, historical commissions; nature/conservation agencies	Parks, playgrounds; recreational centers; ice rink; tennis complex; youth/teen center; swimming pools; museums; art galleries; band shells; skate parks; golf courses; trails; bike paths; greenways; sports complexes	Instructors; coaches; play leaders; youth workers; outdoor leaders; senior citizens; directors; officials; community developers; hosts; guides; interpreters; swim instructors; life guards; coordinator; supervisor; program manager; director general manager; superintendent; head executive diector	Leisure skill classes; learning to swim; leagues; tournaments; pageants; contests; festival; drop-in programs; outdoor leadership; environmental programs; senior citizen activities; school age care programs; community theatres; youth development activities; community drama productions; social recreation; parties; meetings; nature interpretations; clubs; special events; seminars; workshops; conferences; outreach programs
Non-Profit, Non-governmental Organizations	Social welfare; benefits to members in terms of enriched living; community building; character building; citizenship	Membership fees and charges; donations; grants and contracts, trusts; community enhancements; use of volunteers; in-kind contributions	YMCA, YWCA, Boys & Girls Clubs, Boy Scouts of the USA; Camp Fire; Salvation Army; Big Brothers/Big Sisters of America; Junior Achievement	Gymnasiums; community centers; fitness centers; swimming pools; computer laboratories; game rooms; art and crafs areas; camps; playgrounds; equestrian centers	Instructors; coaches; play leaders; youth workers; outdoor leaders; senior citizens; directors; officials; community developer; hosts; guide; interpreter; swim instructor; life guard; coordinator; supervisor; program manager; director general manager; superintendent; head executive director	Academic enrichment; peer mentoring; outreach; leadership development; violence prevention/conflict resolution; health promotion; special interests groups; learning to swim; leisure skill classes; leagues; tournaments; pageants; contests; festivals; drop-in programs; outdoor leadership; environmental programs; senior citizen activities; school age care programs; community drama productions; social recreation; parties; meetings; nature interpretations; clubs; special events; seminars; workshops; conferences
Commercial/Private Organizations	Profit; market-driven quality services; customer-oriented; community development through enterprise	Fees and charges; partnerships	Amusement parks; hostels; convention cen-ters; race tracks; pro-fessional sports; outdoor orientation businesses; casinos; resorts; theatres; bowling centers; play centers; retail outlets; water parks	Theatres; skate board parks; play centers; tennis complex; ice rinks; swimming pools/slide; bowling centers; roller rinks; equestrian centers; fitness centers; gymnasiums; arcades and video centers	Attendants; hosts; guides; instructors; coaches; dealers; performer; sales representatives; ride operators; outdoor leaders; ticket sellers; concession operators; clerks; coordinator; supervisor; program manager; director general manager; superintendent; head executive diector; vice president; president	Drop-in; self-enrichment activities; instructional classes; school age care programs; preschool activities; equipment and faculty rental; special events

emphasizes conversation and reflection as a means of helping individuals develop a greater awareness of self, solve problems, and build a sense of community.

Host/Guide/Interpreter. Leisure experiences are often enhanced when participants are accompanied by a host, guide, and/or interpreter. Individuals occupying these types of positions provide information, point out items of interest and, in general, enrich the participants' overall experience.

Supervisor/Program Coordinator. This type of position is often responsible for planning, organizing, and directing a program area or facility or complex. Such positions often involve engaging part time or seasonal staff and providing supervisory oversight to their efforts. For example, a supervisor could be responsible for supervising program areas such as sports, arts or outdoor recreation, or for the super-vision of a facility or complex such as an ice rink, recreation center, or athletic complex.

Superintendent/General Manager/Head. Managerial leadership is evident in these types of positions found in recreation, parks, and leisure services organizations. Such individuals provide broad oversight to the entire operation or to a significant portion of the organization's activities. Knowledge and skills required for such positions are conceptual, focusing on the ability to establish a vision for the organization and plan and monitor its work toward the accomplishment of such ends.

These general classifications are not inclusive. There may be other roles and functions or titles that one may find in the recreation, parks, and leisure services field. However, they do capture some of the general types of leadership roles that are common in the field.

All segments of the economy are engaged in providing such services, including the commercial, government, and non-profit sectors. Within these three sectors, we can further differentiate the types of settings within which recreation, parks, and leisure services are found.

In each of these settings, the recreation, parks, and leisure services leader and the group are attempting to accomplish unique goals. The methods and procedures employed to achieve such goals are also often unique and require close examination. Furthermore, there may be external and internal forces that may affect the work of the recreation, parks, and leisure services leader and the group. In analyzing any setting within which recreation, parks, and leisure services are provided, the recreation, parks, and leisure services leader must be sensitive to both the obvious and the sub-rosa factors that exist in the environment.

Type of Organization. This refers to the type of setting that recreation, park and leisure services are delivered. As we have indicated in Table 1, recreation, parks and leisure services are found in three types of organizations: 1) public governmental organizations; 2) non-profit, non governmental organizations; and 3) commercial/private organizations. Each one of these types of organizations has unique goals, funding strategies, leadership roles and program services that influence the type of leadership strategies that need to be employed.

External Forces. External forces refer to those factors in the environment that affect the organization and are beyond the direct control of the recreation, parks, and leisure services leader and the group. For example, if the recreation, parks, and leisure services leader is organizing a picnic in the park and it rains, he or she must respond to this factor. The recreation, parks, and leisure services leader will have no control over external variables. Knowledge of such influences as the political structure of a community, social norms and customs, cultural preferences, and the prevailing economic conditions can be essential in achieving group goals and suggesting a relevant approach to leadership.

Group Goals. Goals can be thought of as the ends or aims of an organization. The recreation, parks, and leisure services leader should not assume that groups really have a clear understanding of what their goals are. Some groups have seemingly well-stated goals, but in reality they pursue other ends. Group goals provide a framework for decision making within groups. The formulation of group goals also helps the recreation, parks, and leisure services leader determine the methods and procedures that will be necessary to achieve them.

Methods and Processes. There are numerous methods and processes that can be used in achieving group goals. A recreation, parks, and leisure services leader may have to use a process or procedure that is already in place. Other times, he or she will be able to use his or her discretion in choosing methods or processes. Each situation is unique in terms of the particular processes that can be adapted to the local conditions of the group. A coach, for example, may be required to adapt a drill that may have been used for another type of team.

Type of Environment. When viewing the environment, the recreation, parks, and leisure services leader must consider

The dearth of leadership is apparent through society.

James F. Bolt

two dimensions. The first is the relative stability or instability of the environment. Some environments are very stable, encouraging a more task oriented approach to leadership. The second dimension to be considered by the recreation, parks, and leisure services leader is the unique conditions found in the environment. There may be specific norms, roles, and social conditions that the leader must respond to in choosing an approach to leadership.

THE HALLMARKS OF LEADERSHIP

The delivery of recreation, parks, and leisure services usually involves some interaction between a leader and a participant. Thus it may be implied that recreation, parks, and leisure services organizations are very labor intensive. As such, recreation, parks, and leisure services organizations focus their efforts on building a service-oriented organizational culture. Often, such terms that are used to describe service-oriented organizations include quality, reliability, consistency, empathy, and caring. The challenge is to make the organization responsive to participants.

An example of a service-oriented, customer-focused organization is *Camp Adventure™ Youth Services*. This organization is dedicated to providing high-quality, high-impact programs for children and youth. With a focus on its leadership corps, the organization has built a service culture of excellence, caring, quality, innovation, creativity, and enthusiastic and energetic leadership. A review of its "Values and Traditions" statement reflects its efforts at crafting an effective culture directed toward building a service-oriented culture. One of the organization's primary foci is to place great emphasis on those individuals involved in face-to-face leadership positions serving as counselors, instructors, or program directors. *Camp Adventure™ Youth Services* strongly proclaims that "[their] bottom line is [their] frontline leaders," and that "positive, caring child/leader interactions" based on "sincerity, genuineness and caring" are hallmarks of the organization.

How do we build a service orientation? What is the role of the leader? Kouzes and Posner (1995, p. 18) have suggested that leadership involves helping individuals to get extraordinary things done within organizations. They suggest that there are ten basic commitments of leadership:

1. Search out challenging opportunities to change, grow, innovate, and improve.
2. Experiment, take risks, and learn from the accompanying mistakes.

LEADERSHIP: A POINT OF VIEW FROM THE PROFESSION

Sara L. Hensley

 Sara L. Hensley is Director, Department of Parks, Recreation and Neighborhood Services for the City of San Jose, California. A results-oriented leader, she is responsible for overseeing a department with more than 850 employees and a budget of $49 million. She has oversight of an array of parks, facilities, and programs, including more than 100 neighborhood parks, 19 community centers, 11 senior centers, 10 youth centers, the City's very successful Anti-Graffiti Program, and its new Animal Services Program. Sara has served as the Department of Parks and Recreation's Director in Virginia Beach, Virginia. Sara has also served as the Director of Recreation for the Champaign Park District in Champaign, Illinois and, worked for the Parks and Recreation Department in Austin, Texas. She holds a master's degree and bachelor's degree from the University of Arkansas. Sara has served as the past president of the American Park and Recreation Society and is a member of the American Academy for Park and Recreation Administration.

On leadership. . . . A steering of the way, setting the pace, course, direction from which to travel. Setting the example.

Leadership and success. . . .Without integrated leadership at all levels, opportunities will be missed! Our organization thrives/benefits from leadership at all levels, including the community.

The exemplary leader. . . . is a quiet, reliable, effective leader . . .works well with staff and is truly a TEAM PLAYER AND LEADER . . . speaks softly and when necessary, carries a big stick!

leadership in action. . . Good communication skills, good follow through, sets the example, walk-the-talk, good listener, friendly, good supervisory skills, change agent, fair, flexible, sense of humor.

3. Envision an uplifting and ennobling future.
4. Enlist others in a common vision by appealing to their values, interests, hopes, and dreams.
5. Foster collaboration by promoting cooperative goals and building trust.
6. Strengthen people by giving power away, providing choice, developing competence, assigning critical tasks, and offering visible support.
7. Set the example by behaving in ways that are consistent with shared values.
8. Achieve small wins that promote consistent progress and build commitment.

9. Recognize individual contributions to the success of each project.
10. Celebrate team accomplishments regularly.

How might these concepts relate to service quality? What are the hallmarks of professionals operating recreation, parks, and leisure services? What ends should leaders strive toward? What factors should guide their actions and behavior?

Marty Johnson-Evans, former National Executive Director of the Girl Scouts of the U.S.A. and current president and chief executive officer of the American Red Cross, has provided seven action steps to more effective leadership. Formerly a distinguished Rear Admiral in the United States Navy, Evans has suggested the following elements are important in exercising effective leadership (we have presented them with our interpretation of their meaning):

Strive for Excellence. Leaders should strive for excellence in all their endeavors. Excellence can be thought of as doing things the very best that they can be done. This often involves raising or surpassing the expectations of individuals. To excel means to be superior. Individuals and organizations wedded to excellence will outperform those who are focused elsewhere. A commitment to excellence is a commitment to seek the best that is possible for those we serve.

Earn Trust. Leaders must earn the trust of their followers. This means that leaders work to build confidence between themselves and those with whom they work. To trust another person means to have faith in their abilities and to know with confidence that you can depend on their honesty, integrity and reliability.

Communicate Vision. Vision is the power of forward thinking. Strong visions provide an attractive, creditable future scenario for individuals. At the core of leadership, effective leaders communicate their vision in a meaningful and encouraging fashion on a consistent basis. As Father Theodore Hesburgh (former president of Notre Dame University) said, "You can't blow an uncertain trumpet."

Mentor Others. Recreation, parks, and leisure services leaders serve as role models for others. They mentor or coach others through their behaviors, as others look to their actions for meaning and guidance. It is through their actions, behaviors, and deeds that a framework is established for others to compare their behaviors or emulate their own actions. A mentor is a loyal friend, advisor, and teacher and coach. Likewise, coaching involves providing guidance, assistance, knowledge, support, and encouragement to others.

At the heart of every great group is a shared dream.

Warren Bennis

Reflect Optimism and Enthusiasm. Recreation, parks, and leisure services leaders reflect a positive outlook on life. They believe that the goodness of their work and efforts will prevail. Leaders are often filled with enthusiasm, cheerful, zestful, exuberant, energetic, jubilant, and operate with great passion. Optimistic leaders expect the best outcome and look for the bright side of life.

Practice Ethical Decision-Making Every Day. Leaders are called to serve others and to change the lives of others in positive and meaningful ways. Their profession is value driven. They are committed to the protection and promotion of human dignity, the value of improving life through wise use of leisure, and the promotion and protection of the environment. These values guide their actions as professionals and provide a framework for making ethical decisions to guide their actions.

Keep Hope Alive. Hope is the feeling that something good is going to happen to you. Leaders are dedicated to the profession of hope. They are committed to transforming individuals and society in such a way as to promote human happiness, joy in life, and greater well-being. Their role as recreation, parks, and leisure services leaders is to keep hope alive for today and tomorrow's generations.

As one can see, the leadership strategies outlined above effectively link one's leadership effort to creating a service- and quality-oriented recreation and leisure organization.

SUMMARY

Leadership is a key factor in assisting individuals, groups, and organizations in achieving their goals in an ever changing and complex society. Energized, motivated, and personally committed leaders are central factors in providing high quality, high-impact recreation, parks, and leisure services. Leadership can be thought of as a process of influence. It is a process of assisting individuals, groups, and organizations by helping them focus their goals, helping them develop and clarify tasks, and encouraging individuals to put forth effort in pursuit of worthwhile ends.

The creation of leisure experiences does not occur through happenstance. It requires great planning, coordination, and the movement of resources in order to provide quality recreation, parks, and leisure programs and services. Individuals occupying roles as leaders at the direct service, supervisory, and managerial levels all play important roles in crafting quality leisure experiences, whether it be an event or activity or the creation of an area such as a park or a facility.

> What we need is optimism, humanism, enthusiasm, intuition, curiosity, love, humor, magic, fun, and that secret ingredient— euphoria.
>
> Anita Roddick

In developing one's approach to leadership, we have suggested the use of a three-dimensional model. The individual must be aware of the role of the leader, the group, and the setting. In developing an approach to leadership, especially in reviewing one's own capabilities, the leader must be conscious of a variety of elements including: 1) knowledge, skills, and abilities; 2) needs disposition; 3) experience; 4) style flexibility; and 5) sources of power. In addition, the leader must understand the characteristics of each member of the group that he or she is working with, including their: 1) knowledge, skills, and abilities; 2) needs disposition; 3) experience; and 4) task-relevant maturity. Last, every setting or situation brings new a unique set of circumstances that need to be dealt with. These include: 1) type of organization; 2) external forces; 3) group goals; 4) methods and processes; and 5) type of environment. A key process in deciding on an approach to leadership is the ability of the recreation, parks, and leisure services leader to understand his or her behavior consciously and change it to meet the needs of group members and the dictates of the setting and situation.

> Great leaders are almost always great simplifiers, who can cut through argument, debate, and doubt, to offer a solution everyone can understand.
>
> *Colin Powell*

Discussion Questions

1. Explain the statement, "leadership is one of the most endearing, universal human responsibilities."

2. Identify and describe the basic elements of leadership within recreation, parks, and leisure services.

3. What does the statement "leadership is influence" involve?

4. What factors must a leader consider in developing an approach to one's leadership?

5. What factors must a leader consider when viewing the group he/she is working with in developing an approach to one's leadership?

6. What does the term task-relevant maturity mean? What implications does this have for one's approach to leadership?

7. What factors must a leader consider when viewing the setting he/she is working with in developing an approach to one's leadership?

8. What categories of leadership are found in recreation, parks, and leisure services organizations?

9. What variables must one consider when developing an approach to leadership?

10. Identify and discuss "hallmarks of leadership."

THE CASE FOR LEADERSHIP
The Cedar Center Equation for Development

Points of Consideration

Cedar Center is a community of 65,000 located in the heartland of America. The community includes a mix of small industrial companies, retail outlets, and a few biotechnology-related businesses. The community offers a variety of education, recreation, and cultural opportunities. Although the community has an extensive park system, its leisure resources have declined and are in need of repair. Cedar College, a private, religiously affiliated institution, has an enrollment of 2,500 students and offers a number of activities to the community including athletic and cultural events. The community was named one of America's "Best Heartland Communities" two decades ago.

Recent economic challenges have resulted in a loss of industrial jobs and a decline in population. Further, the tax base has been eroded, forcing reductions in government services on a consistent basis over the past ten years. Community members are increasingly concerned about the long-term viability of the community. Not only are they concerned about insuring the there is a vibrant economic environment within the community, but they are also concerned with issues related to their quality of life, especially the livability of the community. A community task force has been established to review this situation and make recommendations regarding future directions. You have been asked to serve as the chair and facilitator of this task force.

At the first meeting, many voices were heard. However, the group coalesced into two factions. One faction felt very strongly that future development efforts should focus on building a people climate in the community as a priority rather than focusing on building a business climate. All participants express the need to build a vibrant community. The major question posed was what should come first? Should it be economic development? Or should community members focus on enhancing the livability of the environment? Half of the group felt strongly that the community should subsidize and support the start-up of new companies and develop more contemporary retail centers. The other group felt strongly that the focus should be on enhancing the leisure and cultural amenities of the community as a way of attracting more talented people to the community.

Questions of Consideration

Leadership is an important function for recreation, parks, and leisure services professionals.
- How does community leadership factor into the equation? As a community leader, what would you do to reconcile differences between community members?
- What criteria should be used in making decisions about the future of a communi-ty?
- How can you harness the resources of the community to advance it as a leader?
- Do you think that developing a people climate or developing a business climate are mutually exclusive?
- Can you do both?
- Does one support the other?
- If you had limited resources, which of the two perspectives would you emphasize?
- How important are recreation, parks, and leisure services resources in building vibrant communities?
- What leadership role do you play in advancing the development of a community by promoting the enhancement of amenities such as recreation, parks, and leisure services?

REFLECTING ON LEADERSHIP
Leaving Your Legacy

What legacy will you leave?

As a recreation, parks, and leisure services professional, you have the opportunity to make a significant impact on the lives of others. What will you pass on to others as your legacy? How will your actions as a professional influence the future? Joseph Lee is known as the father of the playground. Stephen T. Mather is the father of the National Park Service. John Muir advanced the cause of preservation through his efforts with the Sierra Club. Jane Addams's contributions of social reform continue to influence our profession today.

Leadership in the recreation, parks, and leisure services field is found at all levels—direct service, supervisory, and administrative levels. Your legacy may be made at any one or at all of these levels. It might be measured in the social innovations that you may bring about as a result of your professional efforts or as a result of the enduring relationships that you build with others. What will you pass on to others? What contributions do you want to make to others and to the profession? How do you want to be remembered? What will your legacy be? Personally? Professionally? What will you pass on to future generations?

References

Edginton, C. R., Hudson, S. D., & Ford, P. F. (1999). *Leadership in recreation and leisure services organizations*. Champaign, IL: Sagamore Publishing.

Hesselbein, F,. & Cohen, P. M. (eds.). (1999). *Leader to leader*. San Francisco, CA: Jossey-Bass.

Kouzes, J., & Posner, B. (1995). *The leadership challenge: How to keep getting extraordinary things done in organizations*. San Francisco: Jossey Bass.

CHAPTER

1

The
Language of
Leadership

LEARNING OBJECTIVES

1. To gain an understanding and awareness of recreation and leisure in contemporary society.
2. To obtain knowledge of leadership roles and theory.
3. To understand the relationship between leadership, influence, empowerment, power, and followers.
4. To understand the role that leadership plays in recreation, parks, and leisure services.

KEY TERMS

- Leisure
- Recreation
- Leaders
- Leadership
- Leadership Roles
- Leadership Theory
- Influence and Empowerment
- Power
- Followers
- Types of Leadership
- Goal-Directed Behavior
- Standard Seeker

INTRODUCTION

Leadership is about getting extraordinary things done with groups of individuals. It is a process of influencing and assisting others to achieve great things. Leadership involves the building and strengthening of individuals and a commitment to a set of worthwhile ends. The essence of leadership involves inspiring a shared vision, enabling others to act, modeling desired ways of behaving, and recognizing and celebrating the contributions individuals make. Leadership is the process of building commitment amongst individuals and mobilizing them as they struggle for shared aspirations (Kouzes & Posner, 1995, p. 18).

In the recreation, parks, and leisure services field, leadership is about helping individuals achieve meaningful leisure experiences. It often involves challenging individuals to take risks, seek new opportunities, develop patterns that promote collaboration and cooperation or even competition, and encouraging individuals both when they have succeeded and when they have failed. Leadership in leisure experiences is about helping people discover and find themselves, relate to other people, and often better understand themselves in context with their environmental surroundings.

The recreation, parks, and leisure services field has been involved in building, developing and creating hope for individuals, groups and communities over the past 150 years (Edginton, 1998). Recreation, parks, and leisure services professionals have created opportunities for individuals by providing meaningful leisure opportunities that result in a multitude of benefits aimed at improving quality of life. Leisure provides a great medium that brings hope to those served by recreation, parks, and leisure services organizations. The work of the profession involves keeping hope alive. As Kouzes and Posner (2004, p.128) have written:

Leaders keep hope alive. They keep hope alive by demonstrating the courage of their convictions. They keep hope alive by painting positive images of the future. They keep hope alive by taking charge of change. They keep hope alive by trusting the abilities of others. They keep hope alive by recognizing the dedication of others as they get extraordinary things done.

Hope is attitude in action. It enables people to mobilize their healing and their achieving powers. It helps them to transcend the difficulties of today and envision the potential of tomorrow. Hope enables people to find the will and the way to aspire to greatness. Hope is testimony to the power of the human spirit. Leadership is often a struggle, and the only way to thrive is to keep hope alive.

Thus it might be inferred that recreation, park and leisure service professionals provide great leadership to individuals, groups and communities by instilling hope that they may have a more complete life through participation in the leisure areas, facilities, programs and activities.

As the amount of leisure available to individuals has increased, there has been a corresponding growth in the organization and provision of recreation, parks, and leisure services activities in the form of programs and services by public, private, and commercial agencies. These types of organizations require the involvement of professionally trained individuals to provide leadership for the host of functions that take place within them. Leadership is found at all levels of organization within agencies providing recreation, parks, and leisure services. It is required of individuals serving in management, supervisory, and direct, face-to-face roles.

The responsibilities of individuals providing leadership are varied and diverse. For the individual working as a counselor in a camp setting, leadership may involve teaching and leading songs; for the playground leader, it may require coaching skills; for the aerobics dance instructor, it may demand knowledge of motivation techniques; for the supervisor, it may focus on his or her ability to resolve conflict; and for the manager, it may be reflected in his or her skills to promote and interpret effectively the program of the agency to the community as a whole. In any case, leadership, leadership styles, communications, group dynamics, and motivational techniques and processes are essential general skills or concepts that should be mastered by the leader. Furthermore, the leader should have a knowledge of the specific technical skills that can be used in select recreation, parks, and leisure services settings. For example, the step-by-step processes involved in organizing a campfire program, leading an organized game or song, organizing a tournament, or planning a retreat are specific technical skills that must be acquired and applied by the leader.

In the end, leadership is about valuing relationships, about valuing people.

Frances Hesselbein

RECREATION, PARKS, AND LEISURE SERVICES IN NORTH AMERICAN SOCIETY

I believe that service—whether it is serving the community or your family or the people you love or whatever—is fundamental to what life is about.

Anita Roddick

Opportunities for recreation, parks, and leisure services experiences are pervasive within North American society. Increased affluence, expansion of technology, and changing attitudes toward work and play have dramatically affected the lifestyles of North Americans. Economically, expenditures for the consumption of recreation, parks, and leisure services products and services exceed hundreds of billions of dollars per year (U.S. Bureau of the Census, 2004). This dramatic outlay of money for recreation, parks, and leisure services may be directly tied to the changing concept of the nature of work and leisure. Today individuals use recreation, parks, and leisure services in order to seek self-fulfillment, satisfaction, and self-expression. More and more, individuals are defining themselves and their roles through their leisure. This is a dramatic reversal from a time when individuals identified themselves solely by their occupations or professions. Individuals often identify themselves today according to what they do or experience during their leisure. In other words, the answer to the old question "What do you do?" is not as interesting as asking "How do you play?" (Jones, 1980, p. 4).

Leisure: What Is It? There is no universally accepted concept of leisure. It has been defined as a block of time, as a state of mind, and as an activity. When defining leisure as a block of time, we think of it as a time when individuals are free to pursue those things that are of interest to them. Within this block of time, individuals choose what they want to do; they may be active or passive. When leisure is viewed as time, it has been suggested that one's life routine can be divided into three parts: existence, subsistence, and leisure or discretionary time. The second approach to defining leisure is to view it as a state of mind. This approach is advocated by many contemporary philosophers and researchers. Viewing leisure as a state of mind suggests that the individual's perception of what constitutes a leisure experience is the central determinant of whether or not a leisure experience has occurred. In other words, if individuals think or feel that they are experiencing leisure, then, in fact, they are. This opens up the possibility for leisure to occur at various times and places and in a variety of circumstances. The last approach to defining leisure is dependent upon an analysis of the types of activities in which individuals engage. Leisure is described or defined in terms of such activities as arts, sports, games, volunteering, traveling, reading, swimming, and so on.

If we view leisure as a state of mind or something that one experiences, criteria exist that can be used in order to measure and define it. Commonly, these are considered to be precursors to the leisure experience. Four specific criteria have been identified by social psychologists studying this topic: perceived freedom, intrinsic motivation, perceived competence, and positive affect.

Perceived freedom refers to the notion that individuals must feel that they have independence and latitude in order for the leisure experience to occur. An individual who does not feel forced or constrained to participate has a higher degree of perceived freedom than one who is compelled to participate. Also, the individual who does not feel inhibited or limited by the environment has a higher degree of perceived freedom. Individuals who perceive that they have control over their own behavior, as opposed to those who attribute events in their lives to chance, fate, or luck, also have a higher degree of perceived freedom.

When individuals are motivated from within, they are said to be intrinsically motivated. Intrinsically motivated individuals are unable to reward themselves and are not dependent on external rewards. The intrinsically motivated individual has a greater sense of perceived freedom, hence, has a greater opportunity to experience leisure. Individuals who are intrinsically motivated achieve feelings of satisfaction, enjoyment, and gratification that are inwardly defined and controlled. Finally, the perception an individual has of his or her competence while engaging in an activity will affect the leisure experience. Individuals who are intrinsically motivated achieve feelings of satisfaction, enjoyment, and gratification that are inwardly defined and controlled.

The perception an individual has of his or her competence while engaging in an activity will affect the leisure experience. Individuals must have a perception of competence in order to attain a leisure "state of mind." This is not to say that they must be competent, but only that they must perceive themselves as such. Knowledge of these three precursors to leisure (perceived freedom, intrinsic motivation, and perceived competence) can be used by the leader to provide a motivating environment that enables individuals to achieve positive leisure experiences.

Positive affect is the idea that individuals will have some influence as the leisure experience unfolds. In other words, choice becomes a critical element influencing the success of a person's ability to gain a satisfying leisure experience. Positive affect occurs when an individual can make decisions

> Leadership skill is the preservation of core skills and values.
>
> *Kenichi Ohmae*

A LEGACY OF LEADERSHIP
Jane Addams (1860-1935)

Jane Addams was one of America's foremost social reformers. Her legacy of leadership lifted the American spirit, resulting in numerous social innovations that mark our landscape today. Addams was both criticized and acknowledged for her significant contributions to the welfare of humankind. Following her denunciation of America's involvement in WWI, Addams was identified by the U.S. War Department as "a destructive and dangerous" force in 1919. She was dubbed the "most dangerous woman in America." In 1931, she was acclaimed for her great contributions to world peace, reform, and her concern for human suffering with the awarding of the Nobel Peace Prize. She became known as "Saint Jane" and the "Angel of Halstead Street."

Addams is known principally for her advancements in applied sociology and as the framer of social work in America. Founder of the world famous social settlement known as Hull House in Chicago, Illinois, she pioneered work in the areas of social settlements, public playgrounds, public baths, public gymnasiums, theater, citizenship preparation, college extension coursework, public art exhibits, public swimming pools, youth work, summer camps, and the establishment of labor laws. Addams was one of the founders of the Playground Association of America and served as its first vice president. In addition, she was a charter member of the National Association for the Advancement of Colored People (NAACP).

A prolific writer, Addams authored numerous works including, *Democracy and Social Ethics* (1902), *The Spirit of Youth and the City Streets* (1909), *Twenty Years at Hull House* (1910), *A New Conscience and a Social Evil* (1912), *The Long Road of a Woman's Memory* (1917), *Peace and Bread in Time of War* (1922), and *The Second Twenty Years at Hull House* (1930). Also she authored more than 500 essays, speeches, editorials, columns, and articles in journals and magazines. Her intellectual powers had great influence and her writing efforts alone made her a major force in American society.

Jane Addams was a genuine American leader. She became a symbol for democratic action, humanitarianism, and the promotion of peace. Addams practiced kindness, charity, and empathy in a life of public service to others. She recognized the importance of personal and cultural worth and value of each individual and the need to promote fellowship amongst people of diverse backgrounds. Addams' contributions to the recreation, parks, and leisure services field brought new awareness of the importance of play, the arts and culture, and other forms of leisure to those individuals whose lives she touched. She lived her life with a passion, zest, and energy that breathed meaning and sympathetic understanding into the lives of others.

that influence the way in which the leisure experience relates to their needs in a more personalized way. This becomes highly important in that leisure experiences are highly individualized; the perception that an individual has some influence in how the leisure experience relates to them as an individual is a key element in this concept.

Recreation: What Is It? A common definition of recreation suggests that it is an activity engaged in voluntarily that is satisfying to the individual. Many definitions of recreation also suggest that it must have some socially redeeming qualities. The term wholesomeness is often used to describe or define this dimension of recreation. Recreation is also frequently viewed as a way of restoring or refreshing oneself for work, or as a balance to work activities.

Organizations Providing Recreation, Parks, and Leisure Services

There are many organizations that create and distribute recreation, parks, and leisure services programs. They range from nonprofit, governmental agencies to profit-oriented, commercial ones. Such organizations may be involved in travel and tourism, entertainment services, food and hospitality services, and the provision of areas and facilities. Some organizations target their services toward one particular age group, whereas others have a broader focus. Organizations may be very specialized in nature, providing a few specific activities and programs, or they may attempt to cater to a broader segment of the population. All organizations depend upon efficient and effective leadership in order to serve those individuals toward whom their services are targeted.

A way of viewing different types of leisure service organizations can be applied from the work of the Drucker Foundation (The Drucker Foundation, 1996). This foundation believes that "a healthy society requires three vital sectors: a public sector of effective governments a private sector of effective businesses and a social sector of effective community organizations. Edginton, Hudson, Dieser, and Edginton (2004) likewise have written that there are three approaches to providing leisure services: the political/governmental system, the voluntary system, and the market system. Still further, Henderson et al. (2001) note that "the leisure service delivery system is comprised of governmental, private (not-for-profit and membership organizations), and commercial interests. Public agencies are funded primarily by taxes and provide recreation, parks, and leisure services at the local, county, state, and federal levels of government. Private agen-

> I believe leadership lies more in character than in technical competence, but these two are interwoven.
>
> *Steven R. Covey*

cies are nonprofit organizations that receive their support from donations, fund-raising activities, and membership fees. Agencies in this category include the Boy Scouts, Girl Scouts of the USA, Camp Fire USA, Boys and Girls Clubs, YMCAs, YWCAs and others. Commercial organizations include those agencies that have profit as their primary motive. This category may include amusement and theme parks, resorts, fitness and tennis centers, racquetball centers, travel agencies, movie theaters, and so on. Professional leadership is found in all these types of agencies and at all levels of organization.

LEADERS AND LEADERSHIP

There are many different types of leaders in our profession. Consider the playground leader, coach, leisure counselor, activity instructor, Boy Scout leader, outreach worker, guide, interpretive naturalist, lifeguard, and others. In organized recreation, parks, and leisure services, the leader plays the key role in assisting individuals to achieve the leisure experience. Leaders serve as facilitators, teachers, moderators, encouragers, and motivators, providing direction to individuals and groups.

What Is a Leader?

A leader can be thought of as an individual who guides, directs, and influences the attitudes and behavior of others. A leader guides participants toward goals that are intended to meet their individual needs, wants, and interests while at the same time achieving the goals of the recreation, parks, and leisure services organization. Providing guidance to individuals may involve presenting, directly or indirectly, the path that the participant should follow in order to achieve desired ends. For example, a leader might suggest that "leisure in one's life provides balance." This is a form of guidance. The leader may also guide an individual by suggesting various activities in which the individual can become involved to meet his or her leisure needs. In this sense, the leader guides others.

As the participant becomes involved in a program or activity, the leader may also provide direction. Direction can be thought of as, or is often equated with, giving commands to others. The leader will give direction to others in the form of instructions and orders, and by example. For example, the lifeguard provides direction to individuals by ordering them not to run on the swimming pool deck. The activity instructor provides direction to class members by assigning and explaining tasks. Direction need not be viewed negatively, but rather can be viewed positively, depending on the perceptions of the participant and his or her willingness to take direction. We also equate directing with the idea that the leader "shows the way." In other words, the leader provides direction by helping individuals determine "what to do, how to do it, and where to do it" in order to accomplish individual and group goals.

The leader influences the behavior of others. In fact, many authors have written that "leadership is influence." Influence is the power to affect the behavior of others without force. For example, a leader may use his or her influence to persuade individuals to engage in a certain activity. Often influence is based on the use of motivational principles. In most recreation, parks, and leisure services settings, the leader must lead by the influence of his or her personality, knowledge, or attractiveness to others rather than by the authority of his or her position within the organization.

Discussing the attributes of a leader, Handy (1996, p. 8), Hesselbein (1996, p. 4) and others have suggested that a unique combination of characteristics is required for successful leadership. These are:

1. **A belief in oneself and a decent doubt.** Leaders create a positive and attractive vision of others for the future, and influence and persuade others to move in a new direction. This takes a fair amount of self-confidence, a belief, and a faith in one's ideas and vision for the future. A decent doubt refers to the humility that a leader must have to be open to the ideas of others as well as the potential for failure. As Hesselbein (1996, p. 4) notes, ". . . leaders succeed through the efforts of other people . . . they build bridges, invest in relationships, . . . are healers and unifiers."

2. **A passion for the job and an awareness of other worlds.** Passionate people bring a great deal of energy and focus to their environments. Passion is a strong feeling or emotion that moves a person to pursue an interest. An awareness of other worlds speaks to the need to have a broad or more global perspective.

3. **A love of people and a capacity for aloneness.** Leaders who enjoy working with others are often successful. Being people-oriented is an important attribute of leadership; however, leaders are often on the cutting edge of new ideas and carry the burden of the success of an endeavor on their shoulders. This places leaders in situations where they are at times very alone because they are out in front.

Lead people and not contain them.

Peter Drucker

4. A vision. Leaders create meaning and structure for others by providing a vision that can be shared by others and that offers a course of action. A vision can be thought of as the power or process of forward thinking. Individuals as leaders who have the capacity to create a realistic, attractive future will be successful.

Specifically, what do leaders do? There are a number of functions and responsibilities that leaders carry out (Sessoms & Stevenson, 1981, p. 67). Some of these include the following:

1. Building Camaraderie and Cohesiveness. Leaders help individuals within the group to feel a part of the group and help the group as a whole to feel like a unit.

2. Identifying and Defining Goals. Leaders help individuals and groups identify, define, and clarify their goals and objectives. This involves helping individuals understand what they are trying to achieve (their aims) as well as their needs, interests, and wants.

3. Developing Methods and Procedures to Achieve Goals. Often the leader will work with individuals and groups to identify and clarify the methods and procedures that can be used to achieve their goals. Frequently, individuals know where they want to go, but not how to get there.

4. Organizing the Work of Others. An important responsibility of the leader is the process of organizing. It involves the establishment and creation of roles and a group or organizational structure, as well as a reward system. Organizing often involves the establishment of a communication network.

5. Motivating Others. The leader is often the energizing or motivating force within the group. In this role, the leader encourages individuals to participate, act, and demonstrate other behavior conducive to the attainment of group goals.

6. Evaluating the Work of Others. The leader is often the individual who determines whether or not goals and objectives have been met. He or she does this by measuring the discrepancy between actual performance and the standards initially established by the group. In the event that there is a discrepancy, the leader would suggest or take corrective action.

7. Representing the Group. The leader may be the individual that represents the group to others, speaking on behalf of group members. The leader may represent the group's needs, interests, and wants to other organizations or to groups within the community.

8. **Developing Group Members.** A key responsibility of the leader is the development of others. In recreation, parks, and leisure services organizations, the development of the leadership capabilities, skills, knowledge, and attitudes of others is consistent with the philosophy of the profession. In this role, the leader encourages self-help, self-direction, and voluntary involvement.

9. **Establishing the Group Atmosphere.** The leader is responsible for establishing the climate of the group. Individuals may sometimes find that their relationships within a group are pleasant and productive, whereas in other situations they may find the reverse to occur. The leader plays a key role in establishing a positive group climate.

10. **Promoting the Ideals of the Profession.** Recreation, parks, and leisure services leaders are often in a position to promote the ideals of the profession. Such ideals as protection of the environment, for example, may be promoted by the leader within the context of his or her role.

As one can see, there are numerous functions and responsibilities that are carried out by the leader. Many are carried out simultaneously, adding to the complexity of the leader's role. A group cannot function effectively or meet goals without a leader. A leader facilitates the achievement of goals by guiding, directing, and influencing the actions and behavior of others.

▙▚▚▚ Assuming the Leadership role

A question that may be asked is "How does the leader assume this role?" Shivers (1980, pp. 103–113) has suggested that there are four possible ways in which a leader assumes his or her position: by appointment, by election, by emergence, or as a result of their charisma. The following list discusses each of these avenues for assumption of the leadership role.

Appointment. Often, individuals will be appointed to positions of leadership. They are usually appointed on the basis of the knowledge they hold or the skills they possess. For example, instructors might be appointed to assume the roles of leaders in instructional classes because of their knowledge of the topic presented. The same could be said for playground directors or lifeguards. Appointed leaders are usually concerned with the maintenance of organizational policy and usually have the sanction and authority of the agency as

> You begin with leaders and the creation of a culture that values personal integrity and empowerment.
>
> *Steven R. Covey*

their primary means of influence. The amount of influence that an individual may possess as an appointed leader can be directly related to the type and level of the appointed position held.

> To succeed as a leader you must be able to articulate a defining position for your organization.
>
> *Noel Tichy*

Election. Individuals also occupy leadership roles with considerable influence because they have been elected by others to fulfill these roles. For example, in the recreation, parks, and leisure services setting, sports groups often elect a member to serve as the captain of the team. This individual would serve to represent the interests of the group in various ways, of which some are prescribed by the rules of the game and others emerge situationally. Individuals are elected to serve in leadership roles for a variety of reasons. Some individuals are elected because they are well thought of or are popular with group members. Others are elected as a result of their past performance and leadership capabilities. Still others may be elected because of their expertise or knowledge. Election of an individual to a leadership role does not necessarily predict his or her success as a leader.

Emergence. The emergent leader is one who, because of certain conditions, assumes the leadership role. We often think of this as a spontaneous event in which existing conditions result in the creation of an opportunity for an individual to lead. To illustrate, picture a group of individuals dropping into a gymnasium on a Saturday afternoon. As they begin to interact, someone may emerge from the group to suggest that they organize to engage in a more structured form of the activity. This emergent leader may suggest a process of dividing group members up, then help establish the rules and help create the social climate. Emergent leaders may have varying perceptions of their roles because they are usually untrained. The emergent leader is more likely to assume a leadership role when his or her skills, abilities, knowledge, and interests complement the needs of the existing situation.

Charisma. The charismatic leader is one who occupies the leadership role as a result of the power of his or her personality. Some individuals are highly attractive to others because of those intangible qualities that have been termed charisma. Charismatic leaders are able to assume the leadership position, not so much by what they say, but rather because of their personal demeanor and behavior that imbues their message with a special quality. In the recreation, parks, and leisure services setting, "charisma may be observed among children's groups, where a counselor, coach, or beloved teacher is the recipient of an adoration almost bordering on love" (Shivers, 1980, p. 114).

In recreation, parks, and leisure services settings, all these different avenues for assuming the leadership role are found. Appointed leaders are selected to organize and deliver programs, services, and activities. They may either be paid or serve on a volunteer basis. Elected leaders are formally elected as board members or commissioners, or informally elected as team captains, group leaders, and group representatives. Emergent leaders are found wherever groups of individuals form. They are especially prevalent in drop-in recreation, parks, and leisure services programs, clubs, citizen task force groups, or advisory groups. The charismatic leader, like the emergent leader, is found wherever groups of individuals form. Because of their personal demeanor and behavior, leaders of this type can have great influence on those around them. It should be noted that individuals might also assume leadership roles as a result of a combination of factors. A charismatic leader, for example, might simultaneously be an appointed, elected, or emergent leader.

What is Leadership?

Leadership is a difficult and complex term to define. The word leadership has many meanings and in fact has come to mean all things to all people (Rost, 1993). Further, leadership is often confused with management. As Bennis and Nanus (1985) have stated, "managers do things right, leaders do the right thing." Today, discussions surrounding the topic of leadership often include the idea that it is a transformational process that empowers individuals to higher levels of performance. Leaders encourage the best in others, inspire them, create hope, and encourage them to accomplish challenging tasks. It is often said that leaders create meaning for others. They create a context, which gives a sense of purpose, direction, and focus for their efforts. Therefore, a discussion of leadership must first begin with an attempt to define or describe the idea.

Definitions of leadership abound. *Webster's New World Dictionary* (1988) defines leadership in the context of the work of a leader. It involves directing, commanding, or guiding. The *Blackwell Dictionary of 20th Century Social Thought* (1994, p. 325) defines leadership simply "as the quality permitting one person to command others . . . [it suggests] . . . a mutual relationship between leader and led [and] suggests action: the leader and the group do something together." This source also suggests that leadership is a relationship based on consent, not coercion. In an even more contemporary sense, Kouzes and Posner (1995, pp. 9-15) have suggested that leadership involves: (1) challenging the process—leaders venture out; (2) inspiring assured vision—

> The very highest leader is barely known by men.
> Then comes the leader they know and love.
> Then the leader they fear.
> Then the leader they despise.
> The leader who does not trust enough will not be trusted.
> When actions are performed without unnecessary speech
> The people say, "We did it ourselves."
>
> *Lao Tsu*

leaders have visions and dreams of what could be; (3) enables others to act—leadership is a team effort involving trust and empowerment; (4) modeling the way—leaders model the way through personal example and dedicated execution, and (5) encouraging the heart—leadership is about commitment, celebration, and encouragement. Northhouse (2004, p. 3) has defined leadership as ". . . a process whereby an individual influences a group of individuals to achieve a common goal." This author goes on to point out that leadership involves influence, occurs in groups, and includes attention to goals. Frances Hesselbein, former CEO of the Girl Scouts of the USA and current chairman and founding president of the Drucker Foundation has written that "leadership is a matter of how to be, not how to do it."(2002, p. 3) As Hesselbein, writes "the leader for today and the future will be focused on how to be—how to develop quality, character, mind-set, values, principles, and courage. The 'how to be' leader knows that people are the organization's greatest asset, and in word, behavior and relationship she or he demonstrates this powerful philosophy," (Hesselbein, 2002, p.8).

Definitions of leadership are numerous in the recreation, parks, and leisure services field. For example, Russell (1986, p.15) has suggested that leadership may be defined as "interpersonal influence exercised by a person or persons, through the process of communication, toward the attainment of a specified goal or goals. Jordan (1996, p. 8) defines leadership as a "dynamic process of interactions between two or more members of a group which involves recognition and acceptance of leader–follower roles by group member within a certain situations." Bannon (1999, pp. 387–388), one of the leading theorists in the application of management and leadership concepts to the recreation, parks, and leisure services field, has suggested that leadership involves influence, persuasion, and moving people by their consent without the use of authority. Edginton, Hudson, and Ford (1999) have written that "leadership is the process employed by the leader to assist individuals and groups in identifying and achieving their goals. Leadership may involve listening, persuading, suggesting, doing, and otherwise exerting influence on others."

Leadership to most involves working with people in group settings. The act of leadership is often viewed as an art or a skilled craft practiced by individuals committed to assisting others in moving forward their agenda, interests, or ideals in some way. Thus, we can think of leadership as an art or craft that involves influencing individuals or groups to work together with enthusiasm, dedication, and skill toward some common goal. Leadership can be thought of as a transformational process. It is transformational in the sense that individuals and groups are empowered to act by their collective action. The relationship that is developed between a leader and group members or followers is a powerful interplay of ideas, motivation, dedication and commitment that leads to action. Leaders work to transform individuals and groups in such a way that they are enabled to collectively achieve their ends or goals.

One may view leadership as a process of directing or conducting. As Rost (1993, p. 97-98) has written, "leadership is equated with what one person does to a group of people." Another may suggest that the function of leadership is to produce excellence, to be number one. Still another may suggest that leadership is a way of defining the collective intent of a group, organization or movement.

The previous definitions of leadership reflect an industrial model of thinking. The industrial model suggests that a transaction occurs between leaders and followers. This transaction is one wherein an individual or group accepts the leadership of an individual in exchange for promised benefits. The newer model of leadership, the transformational model, suggests that in the postindustrial or information/learning society there is a need for individuals to be transformed to higher levels of action based on a commitment to the ideals of the endeavor. Transformational leadership sees people not as commodities in an exchange process, but as partners.

The previous approaches to defining leadership may not help us fully understand the complexities related to the process of leadership. In an attempt to articulate a new concept of leadership more suited to postindustrial society or the information era, Rost (1993, p. 102-103) suggests that leadership can be defined as "an influence relationship among leaders and followers who intend real changes that reflect their mutual purposes." He also suggests that the following four elements are essential.

1. The relationship is based on influence.
    a. The influence relationship is multidirectional.
    b. The influence behaviors are noncoercive.
2. Leaders and followers are people in this relationship.
    a. The followers are active.
    b. There must be more than one follower, and there is typically more than one leader in the relationship.
    c. The relationship is inherently unequal because the influence patterns are unequal.

> I'm a great believer that leadership, in a large part, is moral leadership.
>
> *Thornton Bradshaw*

3. Leaders and followers intend real changes.
   a. "Intended" means that the leaders and followers purposefully desire certain changes.
   b. "Real" means that the changes the leader and followers intend must be substantial and transforming.
   c. Leaders and followers do not have to produce changes in order for leadership to occur. The intend changes in the present; the changes take place in the future, if they take place at all.
   d. Leaders and followers intend several changes at once.
4. Leaders and followers develop mutual purposes.
   a. The mutuality of these purposes is forged in a non-coercive influence relationship.
   b. Leaders and followers develop purposes and not goals.
   c. The intended changes reflect, not realize, their pur poses.
   d. The mutual purposes become common purposes.

Leadership can best be viewed a process whereby the leader uses his or her influence to enable mutually desired change to occur. Leadership is not an act of coercion. It is a way of assisting individuals and others to create, in a purposeful way, the desired ends or changes sought. In this paradigm, leadership is not an act that one can force upon another. In this model, one cannot enforce one's will upon another without willing consent. Such an act is not leadership, but rather an act of force.

Another view is that leadership is the process employed by the leader to assist individuals and groups in identifying and achieving their goals. Leadership may involve listening, persuading, suggesting, doing, and otherwise exerting influence on others. We often think of leadership as the act of influencing others to do "what you want them to do because they want to do it." A key factor in the process of leadership is the leader's style. Leadership style often defines the way in which the leader will interact with the group. Some leaders have a very task-oriented style, whereas others focus on facilitating interaction between individuals.

How does a leader determine whether or not his or her leadership is successful? There are guidelines that may be used by the leader as a measure of his or her effectiveness. A leader may assume that his or her efforts are successful if the participants being led can be influenced to do the following:

1. Choose the leader's interpretation of the processes over opposing views to be employed in achieving individual and group goals.

2. Follow the leader's processes or methods for achieving individual and group goals.

3. Perceive that their individual goals can best be achieved by accepting the guidance, direction, and influence of the leader.

4. Perceive that the leader is open-minded toward their views and willing to change or modify processes and ends in order to meet their individual needs, wants, and interests.

5. Perceive that the leader is consistent in his or her behavior, as well as rational in choosing methods and processes for the achievement of goals.

6. Perceive that the interpretation of the leader concerning the methods and processes for the achievement of goals is consistent with their social norms and customs (Reeser, 1973, p. 270).

By definition, leaders lead change.

Judith M. Bardwick

From a functional standpoint, these guidelines represent a method for measuring the effectiveness of the leader. It should be pointed out that each situation encountered by the leader will result in a new and different challenge. The method or methods used by a leader to help one group achieve its goals may not be appropriate within another group. However, the issue is not only the types of methods chosen to accomplish goals, but also whether or not individuals choose to follow the leader's direction or guidance. In other words, a leader may employ different methods and still reach intended goals by virtue of his or her leadership ability. Conversely, two leaders may employ the same methods, yet only one may reach intended goals because the other leader does not possess sufficient leadership skills.

In using the preceding guidelines to assess one's effectiveness as a leader, the reader should be reminded that the guidelines represent behaviors that are characteristic of a group over the long term when leadership is successful. Not in every situation will the group choose the goals and methods presented by the leader or perceive the leader as open-minded and consistent. Nor would this necessarily be desirable. Furthermore, although leaders in many recreation, parks, and leisure services settings will encourage the group to make its own decisions, that is, to identify and choose its own goals and methods, use of the democratic procedure by the leader does not guarantee the success of the group. If the leader presents democratic decision-making as an alternative and the group wants authoritarian decision making, then one would say that the leader is not successful. (In reality, a group usually chooses a democratic decision-making process.)

Leadership Influence and Empowerment

Empowerment is simply having a voice.

Steven Kerr

Two important concepts related to leadership are influence and empowerment. Leaders and followers often share a relationship of mutual influence. In order for such a shared mutual relationship to be achieved, leaders must find a way to empower followers. Likewise, followers can also empower leaders by enabling their influence to result in action in support of mutual purposes. Influence and empowerment are two elements interrelated in the application of the leadership process.

Leadership and Influence. A critical element in the process of leadership is that of influence. We can think of influence as a process of persuasion. From another perspective, we can think of influence as the impact that the leader has on group members or others. Still another way of looking at the concept of influence, from the leadership perspective, is to think of how an individual affects the behavior of others. One can use the power of one's personality, position, or ability to influence another individual. Thus, as one can see, leadership is a process of influence. It is the power of the individual to produce desired results without using force, coercion, or one's authority to achieve desired results.

Rost (1993, p. 105) suggests that influence of persuasion comes from one's "power resources." In other words, the ability to influence another person or group is derived from some source of power. It doesn't just happen out of thin air. There are many power resources available including: ideas, rational discourse, one's reputation, prestige, personality, purpose, status, content of message, interpersonal and group skills, give-and-take behaviors, authority (or lack of it), symbolic interaction, perception, motivation, gender, race, religion, and choices, among countless other things (Rost, 1993).

Influence in a leadership relationship, according to Rost (1993), is multidirectional. This means that influence can be vertical, horizontal, diagonal, or circular. In other words, influence can come from many different sources. Leaders can influence followers; followers can influence leaders. The process of persuasion comes from many sources, and effective leadership attempts to seek multidirectional influence. An effective leader will provide opportunities for the process of influence or persuasion amongst all individuals. In other words, good leaders seek involvement of their followers in the process of influence, often reflected in the decisions on its goals, methods of achievement, and ways of recognizing rewards and success. A relationship of influence strictly from the leaders to followers that is unidirectional in nature may not imply effective leadership. Unidimensional relationships of influence do not build a sense of mutual purpose and involvement.

Another important factor in the process of influence is that persuasion to be successful, must be noncoercive. In knowledge-based and service-based organizations, leadership is thought of as a shared process. Coercive influence is seen as dictatorial in nature. Effective leaders don't tell people what to do but rather collaborate with them to build mutually subscribed-to goals. Power can be abusive when people use their influence to control others in an abusive fashion. Individuals seek through leisure a sense of freedom and autonomy. In order for individuals to experience leisure, they must have some control in the way the experience unfolds. They must be given freedom to influence their choices. Likewise, in knowledge-based and service-based organizations, effective leaders are those who empower others to make decisions about their work environment in a noncoercive fashion. Again, people want a sense of freedom, involvement, and ability to choose their own work methods and procedures. They also want to use their influence to contribute to the formulation of mutually subscribed organizational goals. As Rost (1993, p. 106) notes, coercion is antithetical to developing relationships of influence.

Leadership and Empowerment. Closely related to the concept of influence is the idea of empowerment. If the leader is to share or give influence to others, then he or she must be empowered. Empowerment means to give power or authority to others, thus enabling others to have influence. Central to the idea of a successful leisure experience is the idea that individuals must be empowered to have some control over the way in which the leisure experience unfolds.

How does the leader empower individuals? One may simply delegate or share responsibility for decision-making to another. Giving away responsibility and authority is the ultimate expression of leadership (McCarthy & Spector, 1985, p. 25). By giving people freedom, they are often motivated in return. Giving people the power and freedom to make decisions, to take risks, and to generate their own pathway results in more satisfied, committed individuals. This is a cyclical pattern in which freedom creates higher levels of satisfaction, greater motivation, and a greater sense of fulfillment through leisure.

We communicate with passion—and passion persuades.

Anita Roddick

Bennis and Townsend (1995, p. 73) suggest that empowerment is a key element in successful organizations. They write:

> Good leaders and good followers share many of the same traits. In fact, the single most important characteristic of a follower may be a willingness to speak out and tell the truth, which is precisely the kind of initiative that makes good leadership. And when a leader creates an atmosphere in which employees feel free to offer contrary views and speak the truth, an empowered work force is created. Given the power to do what they do best, these motivated individuals serve as vital allies in transforming the organization.

As one can see, an empowered work force is one that gives people the freedom to express their views, opening the system to other alternatives that result in more meaningful work opportunities. By delegating, employees are able to make their own decisions and generate and use their own ideas to solve complex organizational challenges. By giving people freedom, individual creativity is unleashed. People are empowered to give the best of themselves in circumstances that they have great influence and control. If creative energy is unleashed in such a way that it focuses on higher levels of customer satisfaction, it in turn fuels greater loyalty to the organization, and brings the organization success. As Bennis and Naus (1995) have written, "When an organization has a clear sense of its purpose, direction, and desired future state and when this image is widely shared, individuals are empowered . . . they are themselves as part of a worthwhile enterprise."

Leadership and Power

There is a direct and close relationship between power and leadership. The recreation, parks, and leisure services leader who understands this relationship and can use it to meet individual and group goals will be more likely to achieve success. Often individuals view the use of power negatively; however, it is through the exercise of power that the leader influences the behavior of others.

Power can emanate from several sources. French and Raven (1959) have identified five sources of power: formal or legitimate power, reward power, coercive power, expert power, and referent power. These authors suggest that each of these sources of power is interrelated. An individual may use situationally one type of power or a combination of types of

Even if you're on the right track, you'll get run over if you just sit there.

Will Rogers

power. A discussion of these five types of power, as related to recreation, parks, and leisure services leaders, follows.

Legitimate or Formal Power. We often think of legitimate or formal power as the influence that the recreation, parks, and leisure services leader has a result of his or her position within an organization. The swimming pool lifeguard, for example, holds power by occupying the position. Individuals choosing to use the swimming pool facilities have an obligation to accept the influence of the lifeguard's position. Formal or legitimate power is created through the establishment of hierarchical structures where superior–subordinate positions are established.

Reward Power. Reward power can be thought of as the leader's ability to provide positive reinforcement to individuals. As such, the leader influences others by offering rewards to those who comply with or follow the leader's direction. As will be stressed later in the chapter on motivation, the leader can provide many different types of reinforcement, both tangible and intangible. The leader can provide praise, recognition, status, money, special privileges, and other incentives that positively influence behavior. The playground leader can, for example, use reward power to influence and shape the behavior of children in the program. This can be accomplished by praising a child for returning equipment, providing ribbons and certificates for attendance, or allowing certain children to assume leadership roles for exemplary behavior, or a combination of these.

Coercive Power. When individuals do not follow the direction of the leader, the leader may use the threat of punishment to influence behavior. Coercive power is used in both direct, overt ways and indirect, covert ways. Suggesting to an individual that he or she will lose privileges as a result of inappropriate behavior, or withholding praise and recognition are common examples of the use of coercive power. We often use coercive power when individuals are threatening the safety and well-being of others. For example, if a child on a playground is throwing rocks at other children, the leader may threaten banishment from the playground. Caution should be exercised by the leader when employing coercive power. Constant threats of punishment can result in feelings of hostility, frustration, and rage on the part of participants. The authors suggest that the use of coercive power should be employed only when other forms of power have been exhausted or hazardous conditions are involved, or both.

Referent Power. Often individuals will gain power because they have the ability to attract other individuals by virtue of

A first principle of leadership is that it is a relationship between a leader and followers. Without followers there is no one to lead.

Richard Beckhard

their personalities. Certainly, this is an important source of power for recreation, parks, and leisure services leaders. We can all visualize the dynamic, enthusiastic, energetic, and personable recreation, parks, and leisure services leader. We often talk about the charismatic qualities of this type of person. Participants may become involved and stay involved in activities solely because of their attraction to a particular leader, regardless of the types of rewards and punishments provided.

Expert Power. When an individual leader has a particular skill, level of knowledge, or type of expertise, he or she is able to influence others by virtue of this special knowledge. We can all visualize the leader who is not personable, but who can captivate and influence others because of his or her thorough knowledge of and expertise in a given subject. For example, the recreation, parks, and leisure services leader interpreting nature may be able to instill an excitement and enthusiasm for this subject in spite of a lack of charismatic qualities.

Although little research has been conducted relative to the impact of various sources of power, one might speculate on the effectiveness of each of these five types of power within recreation, parks, and leisure services organizations. First, it is likely that the effectiveness of different types of power will be situationally determined. For example, in a situation in which there are rules and regulations that result in narrowly defined role expectations for participants, the use of legitimate or formal power may be the most appropriate and effective means of influence. In another situation that is more informal and is based on voluntary participation, a combination of reward and referent power may be the most effective means of influence. Second, the use of punishment may have unexpected and undesirable results. Coercive power may result in and produce greater resistance on the part of participants. Often, resistance to threats of punishment results in hostile acts by participants that are more disruptive than their original negative behavior. Third, referent and expert power are perhaps the two most influential sources of power in recreation, parks, and leisure services settings where the leader works on a face-to-face basis with a small group of individuals.

The way in which the recreation, parks, and leisure services leader uses power and the type of power he or she employs will affect the ability of participants to engage in satisfying leisure experiences. Power is the means whereby the leader assists individuals and groups in forming and achieving goals. It is not something to be avoided by the recreation, parks, and leisure services leader, but rather a tool to be used in a positive way. Leaders who become power hungry, using

Self-leadership is the essence of leadership.

Richard J. Leider

LEADERSHIP: A POINT OF VIEW FROM THE PROFESSION

Marco "Tony" A. Cisneros, CPRA

Marco "Tony" A. Cisneros is Director, Parks and Recreation Department, City of Mesquite, Texas. Responsibilities include the direct management and supervision of 113 employees and a $6.1 million annual operating budget. He started as a landscape architect earning his bachelor's degree from Rice University and his masters from Texas A&M University. He has used his landscape architecture skills and training to design parks and other recreational facilities at the many Texas cities that he has worked for over the years, including McAllen, College Station, Bryan, Corpus Christi, and Mesquite, all in Texas. He is a member of the American Academy for Park and Recreation Administration and has been involved in a variety of roles with the Texas Parks and Recreation Society, Texas Municipal Parks, Recreation, and Tourism Association, and the National Recreation and Park Association. Tony has been involved in parks and recreation his whole life. Whether it was teaching others to swim when he was a youth or building recreation programs for many to enjoy, he has always been looking for constant improvement in his delivery of diverse recreation services to his clients.

On leadership. . . . To me "leadership" means making a positive difference in one or more person's lives.

Leadership and success. . . .Leadership in and of itself is an opportunity to make a positive difference in someone's life, young or old.

The exemplary leader. . . is the person that will do the best job possible given their talents and strengths and then some. In other words, they will not just do the job; they do the job and then some. They will always strive to exceed the mark since they are not content to simply meet the mark. That is a leader!

leadership in action. . . I feel that a successful PARD leader and professional will always demonstrate integrity, commitment, and support as well as a "never say die" attitude on a day-to-day basis. They will not be content to settle for any second-rate service or product for their staff or customers. Finally, a leader will work with his/her people to succeed while a manager will typically be content to simply work with things.

their influence to increase their own self-importance or their dominance over others, are using their influence inappropriately. There is often a thin line between the leader who uses power for his or her own ends and one who uses power to help others achieve individual or group goals. Power should be understood and used in appropriate and positive ways by the recreation, parks, and leisure services leader.

Leaders and Followers

Where there are no followers, there are no leaders. Surprisingly, leaders often forget this axiom. They don't realize that their base of support is centered in their followers. The leader who does recognize the importance of followers will, in all likelihood, be a more successful leader than one who does not. Perhaps the best training for being a leader is actually being a follower. In fact, we have all been involved in the role of follower, and many of our perceptions of what it takes to make a good leader are based on our own previous experiences and observations. We have all observed individuals who were able to fulfill successfully the leadership role, and many of us have attempted to model our own leadership styles after such individuals.

Why do individuals follow others? Sessoms and Stevenson (1981) have suggested that there are three explanations for this behavior, related to the concepts of efficiency, satisfaction, and experience. These are detailed in the following discussion.

Efficiency. One possible reason that individuals follow leaders is that they don't want to become involved themselves in the leadership function. As Sessoms and Stevenson (1991, p.81) indicate, people follow because "it is easier to let someone else do it". Often individuals view the delegation of their power to a leader as being the most efficient and practical method for achieving group goals.

Satisfaction. Followers who are satisfied with the status quo or the projected plans will tend to follow willingly. In other words, if things are moving along smoothly and followers are content with the way that events are arranged, there is a tendency to follow the current leader or leaders. It is interesting to note that in unstable economic times, more people file to run for elected offices than in stable times.

Experience. One's previous experience will also influence whether or not he or she assumes the role of a follower or leader. Individuals who have not occupied leadership roles

A servant leader's results. . . will be told in the changed lives of others. There is no scarcity of feet to wash.

C. William Pollard

in the past are not as likely to occupy them in the future. Individuals who have had successful experiences as followers or as leaders often seek out those same roles. For example, it is often heard that an individual is "more comfortable as a follower."

Individuals become followers in certain situations because their needs are being met, whether because of their past experiences or the satisfaction they derive as group members. It is interesting to note that in times of crisis people tend to rally behind a leader, almost as if they acknowledge their need to be followers and to be led through the event. By recognizing the importance of the motivation of the follower, the leader will gain insight that may be useful in dealing effectively with his or her followers. This may aid in the choice of a type of leadership style and the choice of processes and methods to be used.

Leadership and Ethics

It has been suggested that leadership and ethics go hand in hand (Hitt, 1990, p. 1). Supporting this notion, Bennis and Nanus (1985) have written that "The leader is responsible for the set of ethics or norms that govern the behavior of people in the organization. Leaders set the moral tone." Effective leaders are individuals who set the moral tone for their work with individuals, groups, and organizations. There is a direct relationship between the values that leaders espouse and act on. The recreation, park, and leisure service leader greatly influences individuals by their ethical behavior and actions. Individuals look at the behavior and actions of every leader in any organization for their symbolic importance. The ethical conduct of individuals within any recreation, park, and leisure service organization may very well be reflected in their observations of the leader's actions. Simply stated, people are greatly influenced by what they see and what they believe to be appropriate, ethical ways of behaving.

The values that a recreation, park, and leisure service leader espouse help contribute greatly to their ethical conduct and behavior. One's values can be thought of as what one believes to be worthwhile or desirable. Values are principles or standards that individuals use to guide their behavior and actions. Values of any recreation, park, and leisure service leader are reflected in their every action and decision. What values are important to reflect as a recreation, park, and leisure service leader? The leader must be a visionary with integrity, and must also be caring, supportive, loyal, driven, joyful, happy, cheerful, courageous, trustworthy, creative, ambitious, and fair. These values are important elements

> Ethics and leadership go hand in hand.
>
> *William D. Hitt*

upon which one builds one's journey through life. The recreation, park, and leisure service leader that operates with a focus on these values often creates conditions that lead to ethical actions and behaviors.

People are our most important asset.

Jeffrey Pfeffer

▉ Leadership and the Leisure Experience

Leisure experiences by definition require voluntary involvement and a sense of freedom, and they are often spontaneous in nature. As a result, individuals must be attracted to the programs, activities, and services and must perceive them to be desirable, beneficial, and meaningful in order to participate in them. The recreation, parks, and leisure services leader must appeal to the needs, wants, and interests of potential participants in order to involve them in services and activities. For example, it has been determined that a participant, in order to have a leisure experience, must feel a sense of freedom and perceived competence and must also be intrinsically motivated. The role of the leader, therefore, is to create an environment in which these needs can be met. This will be discussed more fully in Chapter 6, which deals with the subject of participant motivation.

Although the leader must initially attract individuals to participate voluntarily in activities and services, once individuals do become involved, the intensity of the experience is in great part due to the voluntary commitment of participants. The leader has a special responsibility to use the power or bond that emerges within the leisure experience in ways that are beneficial to the participant. The enthusiasm, energy, sense of humor, wit, empathy, and warmth of the leader may determine whether or not participants enjoy a successful leisure experience, once attracted to it. The degree to which the face-to-face leader communicates effectively with each participant and the way that the participant perceives the leader may well determine the success of the participant's experience.

Some of the desirable relationships that can be established between the face-to-face leader and the participant that are useful in facilitating the leisure experience are:

Shared Expectations. The participant comes to the leisure setting with certain expectations, and the leader likewise has his or her own expectations. If the expectations of both parties are not congruent or complementary, the possibility that the participant will experience successful leisure will be diminished. The feeling of perceived competence, necessary for the achievement of a successful leisure experience, is related to the concept of shared expectations. The participant's expectations for his or her performance should be related to the leader's expectations, expressed in terms of the skill level that has been established.

Trust. Trust occurs between individuals when they have a mutual confidence in the capabilities and intentions of one another. Without a trust relationship, the extent to which the leader can influence the participant and vice versa in order to produce a satisfying leisure experience is limited.

Effective Communication. Two-way communication between the leader and the participant is essential. Providing opportunities for feedback, as well as use of active listening skills, is necessary to facilitate effective two-way communication. Effective communication helps the leader and the participant mold the leisure experience to meet their respective needs.

Shared Decision-Making. One of the key elements of a successful leisure experience is perceived freedom. Shared decision-making helps to create the feeling of participants that they have control and freedom within the leisure experience.

Cooperation. There must be a willingness to engage in a give-and-take exchange on the part of the participant and the leader. For example, the participant must be willing to take direction from the leader in exchange for the opportunity for a particular leisure experience.

Sense of Risk and Spontaneity. Spontaneity helps to create the illusion of freedom, which is necessary to the leisure experience. Spontaneity is often associated with a sense of risk or the unpredictability of a situation.

Positive Reinforcement. Leaders encourage others to give their best, have fun, express their feelings, and relax. We often view enthusiastic and energetic leadership as a way of positively reinforcing individuals. In turn, when participants positively reinforce the leader, they encourage the leader to do his or her best. Positive reinforcement can contribute to the climate of the leisure environment, building camaraderie and cohesiveness.

Social and Emotional Bond. The leader's interest in each participant and the way that interest is expressed in terms of warmth, humor, and empathy can create a special bond between the participant and the leader that contributes to the leisure experience.

As any leader knows, past glory does not guarantee future success.

Leonard Berry

In most cases, it is the responsibility of the leader to initiate the preceding types of relationships. The leader, for example, may ask participants to share their expectations and may offer his or her own expectations. The leader will often initiate the action that reinforces others and establishes a social and emotional bond. The responsiveness of participants or their willingness to become involved in these relationships will, in turn, support the leader and contribute to the power or potency of the leisure experience.

> To develop effective leaders is also to understand that leaders cannot act alone.
>
> *Steven Kerr*

Goal-Directed Behavior and Leadership

If the recreation, parks, and leisure services leader guides, directs, and influences the participant, a logical question that can be asked is, "Toward what end?" In other words, "What ends, values, or behaviors does the leader promote?" The reader should understand that most behavior is goal directed. This means that people participate in activities because they have a need, want, or interest that can be met by the activity. The role of the leader, therefore, becomes one of directing, guiding, or influencing individuals to take action in order to satisfy their needs, wants, and interests. Thus, recreation, parks, and leisure services leadership is goal directed.

Not only are recreation, parks, and leisure services organizations interested in meeting participants' needs, wants, and interests, but they also have their own goals and objectives that they must attempt to meet. For example, most recreation, parks, and leisure services organizations are concerned with the promotion of leisure experiences that will have a long-term effect on the participant. These types of agencies are concerned not only with the immediate benefits of the leisure experience to the participant, but in a broader sense also with the eventual impact on the community and society as a whole of the individual who was influenced and shaped by leisure experiences. Thus, the leader in any recreation, parks, and leisure services organization will have to understand both the needs of participants and the broader goals of the organization.

One of the basic questions that the leader may want to encourage participants to consider is whether or not their participation in a given activity is "worthwhile." As Godbey (2003) has written, "In choosing leisure activity, I believe that the first question is not 'What is pleasurable?' but rather, 'What is worth doing?'" Godbey indicates that the search for pleasure should not be the primary focus of participation, not because pleasure is unimportant, but rather because the individual should seek experiences that provide opportunities for learning and growth. In the light of this concept, the role of the leader to guide, direct, and influence the behavior of participants in such a way that their leisure experiences become worthwhile.

Some of the goals of recreation, parks, and leisure services organizations that relate to shaping the behavior of the participant are as follows. (This list was drawn from a study conducted in the United States and Canada to determine the goals of municipal park and recreation departments.)

Exploration. Exploration involves testing new ideas, involvement in new environments, and sampling experiences that have not been previously encountered. The leader can foster a sense of exploration by creating new and different leisure opportunities.

Self-Discovery. As the word self-discovery implies, opportunities for it center on helping the participant explore his or her own feelings, values, and ideas. There are many ways that the leader can arrange opportunities for self-discovery, from retreats to writing to photography classes. Self-discovery is a by-product of most recreation, parks, and leisure services activities.

Creativity. Creativity occurs when an individual has an opportunity to make an original or unique contribution. It is the act of being inventive and constructing something that can be appreciated from an aesthetic standpoint. We think of the creative writer, artist, dancer, and so on. All these types of activities can be fostered and promoted by the recreation, parks, and leisure services leader.

Mental Health. Many recreation, parks, and leisure services activities foster relaxation, a sense of well-being, a feeling of being refreshed mentally, and a feeling of stress reduction. These, in turn, may contribute to a positive outlook on life or, in other words, a healthy mental attitude. The leader can play an important role in contributing to the positive mental health of participants.

Social Relations. Interaction with other individuals has historically been a primary goal of recreation, parks, and leisure services organizations. Recreation parks and leisure sevice leaders can provide opportunities that allow individuals to interact with others and develop their social skills. Social relations with others can help individuals overcome feelings of social isolation, and can give individuals feelings of stability and self-worth.

As leaders we always preach teamwork, but often excuse ourselves from its practice.

Marshall Goldsmith

Intellectual Growth. Creating opportunities for the participant to learn new skills and acquire new knowledge is a major part of the work of the recreation, parks, and leisure services leader. Not only does the participant acquire cognitive knowledge during some leisure activities, but also may adopt new attitudes, values, and opinions.

Physical Fitness. Physical development is an activity that is fostered by the recreation, parks, and leisure services leader. Many physical activities and programs are led by leaders, including individual, dual, and team sports; new games; and so on.

A Sense of Self-Determination and Independence. Many recreation, parks, and leisure services activities are designed specifically to promote a sense of self-determination and independence on the part of participants. Such activities as hiking, camping, backpacking, canoeing, field trips for children, and scuba diving usually require some independence of thought and judgment, and freedom of action.

Wise Use of Leisure. By participating in activities and programs offered by recreation, parks, and leisure services organizations, participants are likely to develop an appreciation for the wise and full use of leisure. Values are promoted within the context of activities and programs that teach participants about worthy, productive, and socially accepted ways for using one's leisure.

Promoting Family Unity. Many recreation, parks, and leisure services organizations have, as their primary function, the development of family unity. The leader works to strengthen families by encouraging family participation in activities and the reinforcement of existing family ties. Even though a family may not participate in a structured activity together, often families will congregate to watch one or more family members engage in activities or sports, contributing to a feeling of support and togetherness within the family.

Enjoyment of Life. By taking part in recreation, parks, and leisure services activities, participants can enhance their enjoyment of life. Encouraging participants to value, appreciate, and become sensitized to life experiences can help them enjoy life more fully.

Concern for the Environment. Encouraging participants to understand, value, and appreciate our ecological system is an important goal that is often pursued by recreation, parks, and leisure services organizations and leaders. Two themes have emerged, one focusing on preservation and one on conservation of the environment. No matter what the focus, the participant gains an appreciation of and is more in touch with, his or her environments.

Promoting Cooperation. Recreation, parks, and leisure services organizations foster cooperation by providing opportunities for individuals to work and play together noncompetitively. New games serve as an example of the promotion of this ideal. Leaders also can encourage cooperation by sharing decision-making and teaching respect for others.

Learning About Others and Other Cultures. Leaders can help individuals understand other individuals and their cultures by offering recreation, parks, and leisure services settings and activities that are based on these other cultures. An appreciation of other cultures can broaden an individual's horizons and perspective on life.

Citizenship. The leader can help develop citizenship among participants by promoting an understanding of our country and government and our social customs, norms, and mores. Learning how to be a "good citizen" might involve learning and understanding how democracy works, how the rights and privileges of others are protected, and so on. Encouragement of citizenship was a prime goal in the development of many early playgrounds and continues to be so in many youth-serving organizations.

These, then, are the goals or ends toward which most recreation, parks, and leisure services organizations work. They provide the justification or basis for influencing the behavior of participants.

To Lead or Not to Lead?

To what extent do recreation, parks, and leisure services leaders direct individual participants? To what extent do leaders guide participants? Do leaders use their skills, knowledge, and expertise to move participants toward predetermined goals? Or do leaders use their skills to help individuals make their own decisions and come to their own conclusions? Jean Mundy (1982), a noted expert in leisure education, provided the following insight:

> There is one course that I would like to go somewhere and teach: that is how not to lead. . . . [As students] . . . you all know the right things to do. You know, for example, all the mechanical moves . . . how

The human being needs a framework of values, a philosophy of life, a religion or religion-surrogate to live by and understand by, in about the same sense that he needs sunlight, calcium, or love.

Abraham Maslow

to get people in a circle, in two lines . . . etc. [When] . . . some kid comes up to you on the playground and says . . . "Johnnie took the box hockey stick," you can walk over with the discipline that you've learned and say in your best first grade voice, "Johnnie, give him back the box hockey stick."

You have learned how to discipline, control, and to get kids to do what you want them to do by intimidation. However, those two kids do not know any more about resolving conflict. They do not know any more about other ways to share, or alternative types of decision making [because of your intervention]. We exercise our leadership abilities, but the kids are not that much better off in terms of their own skills or knowledge. I think if we are going to help people in leisure we have got to begin developing facilitators. helping people to learn how to govern, make their own decisions and be self-determining.

As one can see, the type of leadership Mundy is referring to requires that the leader focus on the development of individuals, especially their ability to think for themselves, make independent decisions, and exercise self-control and self-discipline. The type of leadership that Mundy is suggesting requires that the leader take risks: risks in allowing individuals to explore their own feelings and values, risks in establishing meaningful relationships with people, and risks in allowing the participant to interact with the environment in new and different ways. In order for significant growth to occur, some individuals may need an opportunity for self-testing and freedom independent of a control-oriented leader.

As a means of facilitating independent decision-making and self-control, an open responsive dialogue can be established. For example, leaders can enable participants to develop an internal locus of control by allowing them to draw their own conclusions about their behavior and the environment. In other words, the leader, rather than "telling" the participant what to do or what to think, can ask probing questions that allow the participant to formulate intelligent and accurate conclusions. Questions, such as, "What do you think you should do about this?," and "What do you think I should do as the leader and why?," "How can you help this to be a better experience for you and the others?," can help participants develop perceptions and conclusions that will aid them in dealing with current problems or successes, as well as with future situations that are similar.

No limits are set to the ascent of man, and to each and every one the highest stands open. Here it is only your personal choice that decides.

Martin Buber

In order to be successful, the leader must not only develop skills, knowledge, and expertise of a technical nature, but must also establish a philosophy or set of assumptions that can guide their use. Each situation that the leader will be faced with will require a unique blend of knowledge and skills. Research in the area of leadership has supported the idea of situational relevance of methods. However, although the methods employed should be varied to meet each given situation, the philosophical assumption of the leader should remain constant. For example, the leader serving as a coach may employ different coaching methods in working with various age groups or skill levels; however, the leader's underlying philosophical assumption emphasizing skill development and fun rather than "winning at all costs" should remain constant with all groups.

The Leader As a Standard Seeker

There are diverging philosophies concerning recreation, parks, and leisure services. One contemporary philosophy of leisure suggests that pleasure should be pursued as an end in itself with no thought of purpose or of whether or not it is "worthwhile." Another philosophy suggests that individuals should pursue leisure in order to fulfill their potentials, the term potential being undefined. Still another philosophy would suggest that individuals' use of leisure should be measured by the establishment of standards or norms. In terms of the first philosophy, is it not a waste of our human resources to focus only on the importance of the leisure experience for pleasure rather than considering the many outcomes in addition to pleasure that can be derived from such participation? As Paul Haun (1965) wrote over four decades ago in *Recreation: A Medical Viewpoint*, "Fun is the steadfast goal of recreation, yet not its purpose" (p. 18). The second philosophy mentioned often frustrates participants, for they have no way of determining whether or not they have achieved their potential. In addition, use of this philosophy can result in a tendency of the individual to focus inward, concentrating only on his or her own potential. The third philosophy can be challenged in terms of how and by whom standards for successful leisure experiences are set. Poor standards might result in an inaccurate perception of one's leisure experiences.

It is our opinion that recreation, parks, and leisure services leaders are, in fact, standard seekers and setters, as suggested by the third philosophy. We do establish levels of expectations and norms of behavior for individuals engaged in leisure. Therefore, it is extremely important that leaders

> The leader of the past was a person who knew how to tell. The leader of the future will be a person who knows how to ask.
>
> *Peter Drucker*

understand and appreciate their roles as standard seekers and setters. They must be cognizant of the fact that the standards that are set by leaders will have a profound effect on the leisure experience of participants and may even overlap into other areas of their lives. A coach of a youth sports team, for example, exerts tremendous influence on the lives of the children he or she supervises. The standards that are set by the coach, as well as the coach's behavior as a model, will directly influence the children's formulation of values concerning their participation in this type of activity. If the coach is very competitively oriented, de-emphasizing honesty in favor of winning ("cheat to win"), this value may be transmitted to the children and may even be carried over by them into other sports and other life activities.

The prevailing philosophy in the recreation, parks, and leisure services field is one of helping individuals develop themselves to their potential, promoting individual growth and development. We see this goal as a desirable one. Often, the terms enabling or facilitating are associated with this philosophy. We see the role of the leader using this philosophy as one of assisting individuals to identify, define, and achieve their potential. This may involve helping individuals establish goals and identify the means by which goals can be achieved. In helping individuals establish goals, the leader may also work to help them enlarge or broaden their perspectives. The leader may serve to measure their progress toward their goals. Thus, even using the prevailing philosophy, one emphasizing the development of individual potential, the leader may find himself or herself acting as a standard setter.

We feel that recreation, parks, and leisure services leaders have a special responsibility as standard setters. The leader should operate in a moral and ethical manner, establishing high ideals to guide his or her own behavior, and should serve as a model for participants. The leader should also establish high standards that challenge individuals to do their very best personally. Furthermore, the leader should establish ideals that foster an appreciation of the social, cultural, and physical environment.

SUMMARY

Leadership is found at all levels within recreation, parks, and leisure services organizations. The leader is an individual who leads others by guiding, directing, and influencing their behavior. Among the major responsibilities of leaders are building camaraderie and cohesiveness, identifying and defining goals, developing methods to achieve goals, organizing the work of others, motivating others' potential, evaluating the work of others, representing others, developing others, establishing a group atmosphere, and promoting the ideals of the profession. A leader can be appointed or elected, or can assume his or her position by emerging spontaneously to meet group needs, or because he or she possesses charismatic qualities that others find attractive.

Leadership is a process by which the leader assists individuals and groups to identify and achieve their goals. Successful leaders are often able to influence the interpretation of group goals and processes. They are usually perceived by their followers as open-minded, rational, consistent, and non-manipulative. Individuals may follow a leader because they do not want to become involved in the leadership task themselves, because they are satisfied with the leader's work, because they do not have the appropriate experience to lead or because of a combination of these factors. It is important for the leader to remember that where there are no followers, there are no leaders.

Recreation, parks, and leisure services leadership can be thought of as a process that helps individuals and groups meet their needs while at the same time meeting the goals of the recreation, parks, and leisure services organization. Leadership is found and practiced at four levels within recreation, parks, and leisure services organizations: direct or face to face, supervision, managerial, and civic or community levels. Effective leadership helps participants meet their leisure needs, wants, and interests. When working with participants to facilitate the leisure experience, the leader should attempt to share expectations, build trust, communicate effectively, share decision-making, foster a sense of cooperation, create a sense of risk or spontaneity, provide positive reinforcement, and establish a social and emotional bond with the participant.

The work of the recreation, parks, and leisure services leader is value laden, directed toward promoting a number of professional goals. Among these goals are the fostering of a sense of exploration, self-discovery, and creativity. Other goals are promotion of mental health, social interaction, intellectual growth, physical fitness, a sense of self-determination and independence, and a wise use of leisure. Still other goals are promotion of family unity, enjoyment of life, concern for the environment, citizenship, cooperation, and assisting individuals to understand others. We view leaders as standard setters, establishing levels of expectations and norms of behavior for individuals engaged in leisure.

> Trust is the lubrication that makes it possible for organizations to work.
>
> *Bert Nanus*

Discussion Questions

1. What is a leader? What is leadership?

2. Identify ten functions and responsibilities of leaders.

3. Identify and discuss four ways that leaders assume their roles.

4. Identify six specific guidelines that can be used to measure the effectiveness of a leader.

5. What is the relationship between power and leadership?

6. Identify and define five sources of power.

7. What is the relationship between leaders and followers?

8. Identify four distinct types of leadership within recreation, parks, and leisure services organizations. What is the difference between each of these types of leadership?

9. Identify eight factors that contribute to a positive relationship between the leader and the participant. What are some of the goals of recreation, parks, and leisure services organizations?

10. How can the leader's philosophy influence his or her relationship with participants? What is meant by the statement "The leader is a standard setter"?

THE CASE FOR LEADERSHIP
An Ethical Dilemma

Points of Consideration

The Cedar Center Parks and Recreation Department has for several years worked in partnership with an organization that provides opportunities for youth to participate in service learning programs throughout the world. This nonprofit organization, known as Cedar Center Youth Services (CCYS), is focused on providing educationally based service learning programs for high school-aged youth. CCYS focuses on encouraging global awareness and cultural sensitivity while at the same time promoting inclusion and diversity.

The Cedar Center Park and Recreation Department has found this to be a worthwhile and highly successful collaborative partnership. For a number of years, CCYS has worked through an intermediary in China to locate service-learning opportunities and place high school students in a variety of positions working with children. The aim of these programs is to build positive friendships between Americans and Chinese and assist children in better understanding conversational English. This method of informal education has been highly successful, creating a win-win situation for both the high school students participating and the children receiving the services.

Recently, dialogue between CCYS and the intermediary organization that locates opportunities in China has resulted in the following e-mail transactions.

Intermediary: Can you please confirm the names of the high school students coming this summer to participate in the program?
CCYS: Contained in this attachment are the names of the high school students who will be participating in our program in China this summer.
Intermediary: I have a problem with two counselors. One is James Wong and the other is Jane Hong. Are they Asian? Our programs in China are not expecting Asian faces.
CCYS: We cannot discriminate among the students that we send to you based on their race. They are Americans. James was born in the United States. Both were raised in America and have lived their entire lives in this country. They speak and write fluent English. Let me know your further concerns.
Intermediary: I have mentioned well in advance that students participating must not include Asian-look individuals as this is a selling point for the program. From the schools and organizations that I deal with, they all insist that they do not expect Asian-look counselors. I know this is not fair to the Asian-look U.S. citizens, but this is the unique feature of the program. If we cannot have a replacement, I would rather cut the two individuals from the program.
CCYS: America is a diverse country. It is made up of Anglo-Americans, African-Americans, Asian-Americans, Hispanic-Americans, and others. Our program reflects this diversity. To do otherwise would be un-American. If these two Asian-Americans are not acceptable, none are acceptable. Your choice—all or none.
Intermediary: I know that it is not fair to the students who are Asian-American. It will be the first time that a Chinese child may be approached by an American. They have high expectations to see and have contact with an Anglo-American. I have no special preference. My clients all state that the students should not be Asian-American. This will be big trouble for me. It's totally a psychological feeling for the children. They won't complain as long as they have fun, but the parents will. They will think I am a liar. I don't even think they will pay me at the end. The risk is too high for me. I have to maintain the educational exchange project and meet their expectations.
CCYS: There is no defensible position for you in this matter. We must insist that the students in question be assigned to positions in China. Your comments are offensive to me and to CCYS. We may no longer be compatible with your organization.

Questions of Consideration
- Do leadership and ethics go hand-in-hand?
- What ethical concerns must be addressed in this situation?
- How does this relate to one's leadership within the recreation, park and leisure service area?
- Is there a clash of cultural expectations?
- How does that relate to one's ethical concerns?

REFLECTING ON LEADERSHIP
Is it Traits, Skills, or Style?

Traits, Skill or Style?

It is often stated that leaders are born, not made. Is this true? Can one develop one's ability to lead others? The trait approach to leadership suggests that certain individuals possess qualities and characteristics that make them great leaders. The skills approach suggests that a person may learn and develop the required skills and abilities to be a successful leader. Still further, the style approach to leadership focuses on the behavior of the leader while interacting with others. What is important is what they do and how they interact with others. What do you think is the most appropriate way of approaching the development of your leadership potential?

What characteristics do you believe make a great leader? Which of these characteristics do you feel you possess? Please list. What skills are required for an individual to be a successful leader? What skills do you feel you have that contribute to your success as a leader? How would you describe your leadership style? Last, is it possible that different situations require different applications to leadership? Can you think of various leaders who possess different traits, skills, or styles yet have been successful in their particular situation?

References

Bannon, J. (1999). *911 Management: A comprehensive guide for leisure service managers*. Champaign, IL: Sagamore.

Bennis & Nanus. (1985). *Leaders: The strategies for taking charge*. New York: Perennial Library.

Bennis, W., & Nanus, B. (1985). *Leaders: The strategies for taking charge*. New York: Harper & Row.

Bennis, W., & Townsend, R. (1995). *Reinventing leadership*. New York: Morrow.

Blackwell Dictionary of 20th Century Social Thought (1994). Editors; William Outhwaite and Tom Bottomore. Oxford, UK; Malden, MA: Blackwell.

The Drucker Foundation. (1996). About the Drucker Foundation. *Leader to Leader*, p. 48.

Edginton, C. R., Hudson, S. D., Dieser, R. D., & Edginton, S. R. (2004). *Leisure programming: A service-centered and benefits approach*. (4th edition). Boston, MA: McGraw-Hill.

Edginton, C.R. (1998, April). The Art and Science of Managing Leisure Services: Reflecting, Rethinking & Repositioning for the 21st Century. J.B. Nash Scholar Award. Invited keynote paper presented at the American Association for Leisure and Recreation, American Alliance for Health, Physical Education, Recreation and Dance National Convention, Reno, NV.

Edginton, Hudson, Ford. (1999).

French, J. R. P., Jr., & Raven, B. (1959) The basis of social power. In D. Cartwright (Ed.), *Studies in social power*. p. 150-167. Ann Arbor, MI: Institute for Social Research.

Godbey, Geoffrey. (2003). *Leisure in your life: An exploration*. (6th edition). State College, PA: Venture Publishing.

Haun, P. (1965). *Recreation: A medical viewpoint*. In E. M. Avedon and F. B. Arje (Eds.). New York: Bureau of Publications, Teachers College, Columbia University.

Henderson, K. A., Bialeschki, M. D., Hemingway, J. L., Hodges, J. S., Kivel, B. D., & Sessoms, H. D. (2001). *Introduction to leisure services*. (8th ed.). State College, PA: Venture.

Hesselbein, F. (2002). *Hesselbein on Leadership*. San Francisco, CA: Jossey-Bass

Hesselbein, F. (1996). A star to steer by. *Leader to Leader*. Premier Issue.

Hesselbein, F., Goldsmith, M., & Beckhard, R. (1996). *The leader of the future*. San Francisco: Jossey Bass.

Hitt, W. D. (1990). *Ethics and leadership*. Columbus, OH: Battelle Press.

Jones, L. Y. (1980). *Great expectations: America and the baby boom generation*. New York: Ballantine Books.

Jordan, D. 1996. *Leadership in leisure services: Making a difference*. State College, PA: Venture.

Kouzes, J. M., & Posner, B. Z. (2004) *Christian reflections on the leadership the challenge*. San Francisco, CA: Jossey Bass

Kouzes, J., & Posner, B. (1995). *The leadership challenge: How to keep getting extraordinary things done in organi zations*. San Francisco: Jossey Bass.

McCarthy, P. D., & Spector, R. (1995). *The Nordstrom way*. New York: John Wiley & Sons.

Mundy, J. (1982, February 25). Leisure manifestations of human problems [Speech]. Department of Recreation and Park Management, New York.

Northouse, P. G. (2004). *Leadership theory and practice* (3rd ed). Thousand Oaks, CA: Sage Publications.

Resser, C. (1973). *Management: Functions and modern concepts*. Glenview, IL: Scott, Foresman.

Rost, J. C. (1993). *Leadership for the twenty-first century*. Westport, CT: Praeger.

Russell R. (2001). *Leadership in Recreation. 2nd ed*. Dubuque: IA McGraw-Hill.

Sessoms, H. D., & Stevenson, J. L. (1981). *Leadership and group dynamics in recreation services*. Boston: Allyn & Bacon.

Shivers, J. S. (1980). *Recreational leadership: Group dynamics and interpersonal behavior*. Princeton, NJ: Princeton Books.

U.S. Bureau of the Census. (2004). *Statistical Abstracts of the United States: 2004* (124th edition). Washington, DC: Author.

Webster's New World Dictionary. (1988). Victoria Neufeldt, editor in Chief. New York: Prentice-Hall.

http://www.eisenhowerseries.com/events/bios%20for%20E NSC/hesselbein.html

CHAPTER

2

Leadership: Basic Concepts and Theories

LEARNING OBJECTIVES

1. To gain an understanding of theories of leadership.
2. To attain an awareness of theoretical and conceptual orientations of leadership.
3. To obtain knowledge of the progression of leadership studies, styles and models.
4. To gain an awareness of the elements that contribute to one's leadership style and, with this knowledge, to analyze one's personal approach to leadership.

KEY TERMS

- Leadership Theories
- Leadership Styles
- Democratic Leadership
- Autocratic Leadership
- Laissez Faire Leadership
- Initiating Structure (Task)
- Consideration (People)
- Transformation/Transactional Leadership
- Collaborative Leadership
- Leader Presence
- Servant Leadership
- Authentic Leadership

INTRODUCTION

While we can think of leadership as an art, an underlying foundation or science to the process of leadership also exists. Over the past 75 years, numerous leadership models have been proposed, and many research studies have been undertaken to help us better understand the process of leadership. A brief review of some of the major ideas regarding leadership can be helpful in understanding the various dimensions that may impact one's effort as a leader.

In this chapter, we will explore leadership in terms of two major areas of concern. The first of these explores the theoretical or conceptual orientations from which our ideas of leadership have emerged. Second, we will explore various leadership studies, styles, and models.

THEORIES OF LEADERSHIP

A number of approaches to explaining leadership have been developed in the past century. Prominent among these theories is the idea that leaders are a product of their times or, in fact, born with certain leadership characteristics inherent in their personality. Still other approaches suggest that individuals possess traits of leadership, which they can develop. Yet another approach suggests that leaders emerge from the conditions of the setting that individuals working in groups seek as goals. These approaches to leadership are described below.

The "Great Man" Theory. This approach to leadership is built on the idea that certain historical events provide a platform for one's emergence as a leader. It is built on the idea that the capacity for leadership is inherent within these individual's and that they were born to be leaders.

The Trait Theory. Traits or individual characteristics become the foundation of this approach to leadership. The idea is that traits such as honesty, vision, ability to inspire others, competence, fair-mindedness, ability to be supportive, open-mindedness, intelligence, maturity, ambition, and others are linked to effectiveness.

The Group Theory. The group theory is built on the idea that leadership is an exchange process that occurs between leaders and group members. Group members are willing to subordinate themselves to the leader because the rewards are greater than the costs. Likewise, the leader provides direction and receives support from the group and rewards in terms of recognition, psychic rewards, or monetary compensation.

The Situation Theory. This idea suggests that situational variables dictate the type of leadership style that is needed in a given setting. The idea here is that no one best leadership style exists and that the leadership qualities one needs may vary depending on where a group or organization finds itself in its life cycle. More mature groups may need individuals who are able to schedule, delegate, and evaluate, whereas groups just starting out may require risk-takers, visionaries, and/or leaders who operate with great independence.

Excellence Theory. This approach first appears in the literature in the 1970s. Leadership is seen as the ability to promote or create excellence within organizations, as reflected in services or products that are of greater quality or value. The concept of leadership and excellence comes from the writings of Peters and Waterman (1982). These individuals basically "have spawned a movement in leadership studies that equates leadership with the process of transforming to achieve excellence" (Rost, 1993, p. 83).

LEADERSHIP STUDIES, STYLES, AND MODELS

Since the 1930s, a number of efforts at identifying leadership patterns have been undertaken. Perhaps the benchmark study on leadership was reported in the *Journal of Social Psychology* by Lewin, Lippitt, and White in 1939. In the 1940s, '50s, and '60s several leadership models were proposed. Perhaps the most interesting concepts emerging from these models were the ideas that two types of leadership elements— task orientation and people orientation—may constitute one style.

In the 1970s and 1980s great emphasis was placed on the effectiveness of one's leadership style. Such ideas as one's task-relevant maturity was introduced as a factor to be considered when adopting a particular style of leadership. The essential idea forwarded is that no one best leadership style exists. In the 1990s and beyond, new theories have expounded the importance of collaborative leadership. Table 2.1 provides an analysis of these studies and models.

People are unreasonable, illogical and self-centered. Love them anyway. If you do good, people will accuse you of selfish ulterior motives. Do good anyway. If you are successful, you will win false friends and true enemies. Succeed anyway. Honesty and frankness make you vulnerable. Be honest and frank anyway.

Robert Schuller

A LEGACY OF LEADERSHIP
Frances Hesselbein

 Frances Hesselbein has been noted as the "best nonprofit manager in America." Formerly Hesselbein served as the Chief Executive Officer of the Girl Scouts of the USA and currently is the Chairman of the Board of Governors of the Leader to Leader Institute (formerly the Peter F. Drucker Foundation for Nonprofit Management). She has brought great focus and attention to the management of nonprofit organizations through her work as a practicing professional and through her literary contributions. Hesselbein's civic engagement and work in nonprofit organizations can be traced to her initial volunteer activities leading Girl Scout Troop 17 in Johnstown, Pennsylvania.

In 1998 Hesselbein was awarded the Presidential Medal of Freedom, the United States of America's highest civilian honor. In addition, she has been the recipient of 16 honorary doctorates and has received many other significant awards in recognition of her leadership and community service including the Girl Scouts of the USA National Woman of Distinction Award, Henry A. Rosso Medal for Lifetime Achievement in Ethical Fund Raising from the Center on Philanthropy at Indiana University, the International ATHENA Award, the Dwight D. Eisenhower National Security Series Award; the Legion of Honor Gold Medallion from the Chapel of the Four Chaplains, and the Distinguished Alumni Fellow Award from the University of Pittsburgh. She has presented commencement addresses and lectures at a host of colleges and universities including Boston College, University of Pittsburgh, University of Richmond, Fordham University, Harvard University, Stanford University, University of Michigan, Arizona State University, Princeton Theological Seminary, and Yale University.

She serves as a member of many boards of directors including Josephson Institute for the Advance of Ethics, Mutual of America Life Insurance Company, Veterans Corporation, Center for Social Initiative and Hauser Center for Nonprofit Management at Harvard University. In addition, she serves as the chairman of the national board of directors for Volunteers of America. Hesselbein has been featured in/and or on the cover of Fortune, Business Week, Savvy, and Chief Executive.

Her writings in the area of leadership have provided great clarity and focus for the nonprofit sector. Author or co-editor of numerous books including *The Leader of the Future*, *The Community of the Future*, *Leader to Leader*, *Leading Beyond the Walls*, *Leading for Innovation*, *Organizing for Results*, *On High-Performance Organizations*, *On Creativity: Innovation and Renewal*, *On Mission and Leadership*, and *Hesselbein on Leadership*, she has brought practical information to inspire leaders. Currently, she serves as the Editor-in-Chief of the quarterly journal *Leader to Leader*.

Hesselbein has been described as a "beacon of leadership excellence." She has been described as a living leadership role model. Her insights have provided "clear, thought-provoking leadership experiences and principles." As Hesselbein states "leadership is a matter of how to be, not how to do it." In this respect, others have suggested that she is unpretentious, warm and friendly. She treats every individual as if they are important and is accessible and ready to assist others.

The Lewin, Lippitt, and White Studies

The Lewin, Lippitt, and White studies are especially important and interesting to the recreation, parks, and leisure services profession because they deal with leaders who worked with boys' hobby clubs (1939, pp. 271–276). Basically, Lewin, Lippitt, and White engaged in a number of experiments to determine the impact of various leadership styles on the behavior of ten-year-old children. Their first experiment viewed various leadership styles over a three-month period of time with a group involved in the activity of theatrical mask making. Their second set of experiments, which were considerably more extensive than their first, also viewed various leadership styles in clubs organized on a voluntary basis with a broader selection of activities, including mask making, mural painting, soap carving, and model airplane construction.

A key element in the Lewin, Lippitt, and White studies was the designation of different classifications of leader behavior. In the first study, two leadership styles, democratic and authoritarian, were identified and studied. In the second set of studies, a third leadership style, laissez faire, was added. These leadership styles can be defined as follows.

> **Democratic Leadership Style.** A democratic leadership style implies that individual group members are consulted in the decision-making process by the leader.

> **Authoritarian Leadership Style.** Activities of the group are tightly controlled by the leader using an authoritarian leadership style. All policies and interpretation of policies are spelled out by the leader.

> **Laissez Faire Leadership Style.** The laissez faire leadership style is characterized by a lack of control or structure. In other words, the leader gives the group complete freedom in decision making.

The major contribution of the Lewin, Lippitt, and White studies was the description of leadership styles. These have served as a basis for the teaching and training of recreation, parks, and leisure services leaders and, as well, have served as a basis for other research projects and studies.

The Ohio State Studies

The next important set of studies on leadership was initiated in 1945 by the Bureau of Business Research at Ohio State

I pay less attention to what men say; I just watch what they do.

Andrew Carnegie

Table 2.1					
Leadership Studies and Models					
Study/Model	**Period**	**Major Contributors**	**Key Elements**	**Major Contributions**	**Other Remarks**
Lewin, Lippitt & White Studies	1930s	Kurt Lewin Ronald Lippitt Ralph K. White	Democratic leader-shop style, Authoritarian leadership style, and Laissez-faire leadership style	Description of leadership styles	Beginning of the study social psychology
Ohio State Studies	1940s	Ralph M. Stogdill Alvin E. Coons	Initiating Structure (task orientation) Consideration (relationship orientation)	Discovery of integrating elements of leadership behavior—task (T) and human relations (HR) orientation	Mixing of elements results in 4 styles. Low HR, Low T; High T, Low HR; High HR, Low T; High T, High HR.
University of Michigan Studies	1940s	Daniel Katz Nathanial Naccoby Nancy C. Morris	Postulated that leadership is on the continuum	Continuum finds participant centered leadership at one end and production-oriented at the other end	Participant centered leadership promotes satisfaction
Management Grid	1950s	Robert R. Blake Jane S. Mouton	Concern for production Concern for people	5 leadership styles, framed on x & y axis. 1.1 Impoverished, 1.9 Country Club, 9.1 Authority-Obedience; 5.5 Organization Man, 9.9 Team Management	Helps understand what constitutes effective leadership
Systems of Management	1960s	Rensis Likert	Leadership on a continuum, autocratic to participative	4 basic styles. Exploitive autocratic, benevolent autocratic, consultative, and participative	Suggests that participative is the most appropriate
Contingency Model of Leadership Effectiveness	1960s	Fred Fiedler	Leadership style must be situationally determined	Style is determined by degree of favorableness to the leader by 3 factors, leader-member relations, task structure and position-power	Provides empirical evidence that there is need to match one's leadership style with situational elements
Tannebaum & Schmidt's Leadership Continuum	1970s	Robert Tannebaum Warren H. Schmidt	Leadership on a continuum	Authoritarian, task-oriented leadership involves the leader making most of the decisions at one end of the continuum, at the other democratic relationship leader provides great freedom	Promotes the idea that there is no one best style of leadership
Path-Goal Theory of Leadership	1970s	Robert J. House Terence R. Mitchell	Directive leadership, Supportive leadership Participative leadership Achievement-oriented leadership	Role of the leader is to "clear the path" to help achieve goals	Promotes the idea that there is no one best style of leadership
3-D Theory of Management Effectiveness	1970s	William J. Reddin	8 basic styles. Executive, compromiser, benevolent autocrat, autocrat, developer, missionary, bureaucrat, and deserter	Major determinant of style should be the results that are achieved.	Leader must have the ability to "flex" style to be effective
Tri-Demensional Leaders Effectiveness Model	1970s	Paul Hersey Keith H. Blanchard	4 basic styles. Telling, Selling, Participating, Delegating	Mixes task relevant maturity into leadership discussion	Combines human relations orientation and task orientation with effectiveness

Table 2.1 Continued

Study/Model	Period	Major Contributors	Key Elements	Major Contributions	Other Remarks
Transactional & Transformational Leadership	1970s	James MacGregor Burns	Transactional leadership Transformational leadership	Transactional leaders exchange one thing for another. Transformational leaders lift people to focus on higher goal and needs	Help individuals transcend self-interest
Servant Leadership	1970s	Robert Greenleaf	Characteristics include: Listening, empathy, healing, awareness, persuasion, conceptualization, foresight, stewardship, commitment to the growth of people, and building community	A theological perspective supporting the idea that to lead is to first serve others	Promotes teamwork, ethical caring behavior, sense of
Hitt's Dreamer and Doer Model	1980s	William D. Hitt	4 basic styles. Victim, Dreamer, Doer, Leader-Manager	Effective leader is both a dreamer and a doer, combining vision with implementation	The essence of leadership found in the ability to transform no action

Source: Carroll V. Kroeger, "Managerial Development in the Small Firm." ©1974 by the Regents of the University of California. Reprinted from *California Management Review*, Vol. XVII, No. 1, p. 43, by permission.

University (Stogdill & Coons, 1957). These individuals established a number of in depth research studies focusing on leader behavior. A group of researchers from such disciplines as psychology, sociology, and economics created and developed an instrument that could be used to analyze leadership behavior in a variety of situations and settings. Two key facets of leadership behavior identified by the Ohio State studies were initiating structure and consideration. These two important dimensions of leadership behavior can be defined as follows.

> Successful people keep moving. They make mistakes, but they don't quit.
>
> *Conrad Hilton*

Initiating Structure. Initiating structure refers to the way in which the leader establishes and defines group goals as well as to the resulting group structure and role expectations. We often think of initiating structure as the task or production orientation of the leader.

Consideration. Consideration can be thought of as the relationship that develops between the leader and his or her subordinates, with regard to the ideas and feelings of the latter. We often think of the consideration factor as the "people orientation" of the leader.

The value of the Ohio State studies was the discovery that the two elements of leadership behavior—consideration and initiating structure—could be combined. Prior to these studies, an individual's leadership style was viewed in only one dimension or direction. These studies demonstrated that the combination of these two variables was important in certain leadership situations. The findings of the Ohio State studies have influenced the development of leadership and management style theories and models. Figure 2.1 presents a leadership style model that portrays the two dimensions identified in the Ohio State studies.

> If I could, I would always work in silence and obscurity, and let my efforts be known by their results.
>
> *Emily Bronte*

	(Low) Task Orientation (High)
(High) Human relations orientation	High human relations orientation and low task orientation	High task orientation and high human relations orientation
(Low)	Low human relations orientation and low task orientation	High task orientation and low human relations orientation

Figure 2.1
**A leadership style model portraying
the Ohio State studies' dimensions**

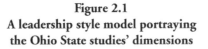 The New Managerial Grid

A widely recognized leadership style model was developed and perfected in the 1950s by Robert R. Blake and Jane S. Mouton (Blake & Mouton, 1978, p. 11). Their model, called "The New Managerial Grid," includes two dimensions: concern for production and concern for people (see Figure 2.2). Concern for production, according to these individuals, involves an orientation toward the production of products or services and focuses on quantitative measures such as the volume of sales, and so on. Concern for people involves the establishment of trust relationships, friendship, and concern for the well-being and worth of other individuals.

As indicated in Figure 2.2, The New Managerial Grid places the two variables concern for people and concern for production along two axes. A concern for production is represented by the horizontal axis, and a concern for people is represented by the vertical axis. A nine-point scale is used to characterize the level of intensity of commitment on either of the two variables. The number 9 would represent a high concern, whereas the number 1 would represent a low con-

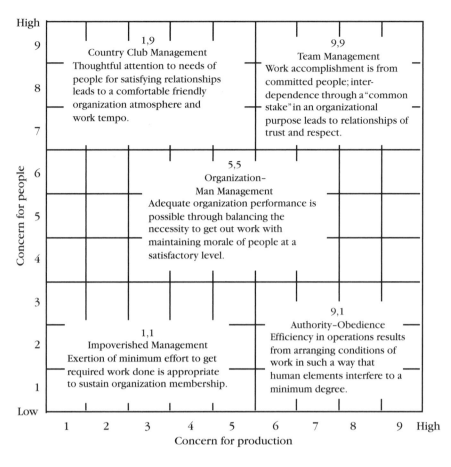

Figure 2.2
Blake and Mouton's management grid

Source: The Managerial Grid Figure from *The New Managerial Grid*, by Robert R. Blake and Jan Srygley Mouton(Houston: Gulf Publishing Company, copyright ©1978), p. 11. Reproduced by permission.

cern. Using this method, Blake and Mouton have identified five different managerial leadership styles.

1,1 Impoverished Management. The impoverished managerial leadership style is characterized by low concern for production and a low concern for people.

1,9 Country Club Management. A high concern for people and a low concern for production is the general orientation of the 1,9 managerial leadership style.

9,1 Authority-Obedience. The 9,1 orientation to managerial leadership style finds the leader with a high concern for production and a low concern for people.

5,5 Organization-Man Management. This is a middle-of-the-road style of managerial leadership.

9,9 Team Management. Team management is accomplished by creating relationships of trust, openness, and respect for one another through a mutual commitment to the goals of the organization and to one another.

Blake and Mouton suggest that the first four managerial leadership styles do not represent effective approaches. They feel that effective managerial leadership occurs when an individual is using the 9,9 team management style. They argue that a leader should have high standards and should seek a high level of performance from subordinates. They feel that when subordinates have an opportunity to be involved in the planning and decision-making activities within a group or organization, or have developed a high level of trust and confidence between each other, they are most productive. Thus, the effective leader is one who is equally concerned with the needs of people and the work of the organization or group.

The University of Michigan Studies

In 1947, the University of Michigan Survey Research Center also began to investigate leadership behavior (Katz, Maccoby, & Morse, 1950). Funded by the Office of Naval Research, this research group was interested in determining the factors that contribute to the productivity of the group and to the satisfaction that is derived by group members participating in group activities.

The Michigan study team postulated that leadership behavior could be plotted on a continuum. At one end of the continuum would be the leader whose behavior is participant centered. This leader would be interested in the feelings, ideas, opinions, and values of individual group members. At the other end of the continuum would be the leader whose behavior is production oriented. The individual possessing this style would be task oriented and concerned primarily with achieving the goals of the group as a whole. This type of leader would be more concerned with arranging conditions, methods, and procedures used by the group in order to accomplish group goals.

Two findings emerged from the Michigan studies. First, it was found that individual satisfaction in a work situation was contingent on the presence of a participant or employee-

Leadership is a potent combination of strategy and character, but if you must be without one, be without strategy.

Norman Schwarzkopf

centered leader. The study also suggested that satisfaction was not related to productivity.

Rensis Likert's System of Management. The Michigan studies provided the basis for the development of Rensis Likert's four basic styles of leadership behavior in his "systems of management" (Likert, 1967). Likert has suggested that leadership styles exist on a continuum ranging from autocratic to participative. Four basic styles are as follows:

Exploitive Autocratic. The recreation, parks, and leisure services leader using this style of leadership makes all the decisions for the group. There is a low degree of trust and mutual confidence between the leader and the members of the group when this system is employed.

Benevolent Autocratic. The leader using the benevolent autocratic approach to leadership behavior still makes all the decisions for the group, but allows some variances in the performance of group tasks, as long as individuals abide by established policies and procedures. This is a paternalistic approach to leadership and results in a relatively low level of trust and confidence between leaders and group members.

Consultative. The consultative approach to leadership finds the leader seeking input from group members and allowing them to assist in the decision-making process. In situations where this type of leadership style is employed, individuals feel free to offer their ideas, suggestions, and opinions concerning both the goals of the group and the methods used to achieve them.

Participative Team. This is a democratic approach to leading groups. It suggests that there is a need for the full involvement of group members in the planning and decision-making process. Individuals feel free to offer their ideas and suggestions, and there is a high degree of confidence and trust between the leader and group members.

Likert suggests that the participative team approach to leadership is the most effective. The system's concept can be criticized from the standpoint that not all leadership situations may require a high degree of confidence, trust, and shared decision making in order to achieve intended goals.

Tannenbaum and Schmidt's Leadership Continuum. Another leadership model that dichotomizes leadership style along a continuum in terms of its orientation is the

> A man can succeed at almost anything for which he has unlimited enthusiasm.
>
> *Charles Schwab*

Tannenbaum and Schmidt leadership continuum (1973, p. 166). As indicated in Figure 2.3, the leader has a number of options regarding decision-making and the way in which individuals are allowed to work within a group situation. At one end of the continuum, the leader is authoritarian and task oriented. At the other end of the continuum, the leader is democratic and human relations oriented.

These authors do not suggest that the leadership style at one end of the continuum is more appropriate than the leadership style at the opposite end. They stress the importance of situational leadership, basing the choice of a style of leadership at the various points along the continuum on the needs of each situation. There is no "one best" style of leadership, according to Tannenbaum and Schmidt. They recommend that the leader remain flexible and open to the use of different styles in different situations.

> A good leader inspires others to have confidence in him or her. A great leader inspires others to have confidence in themselves.
>
> *Anonymous*

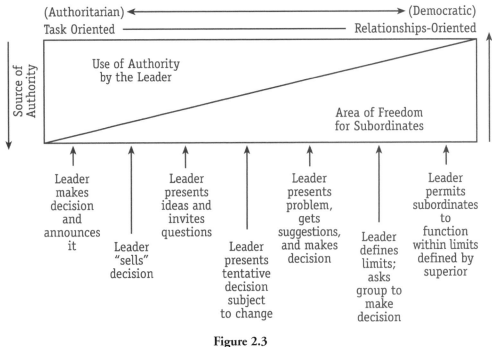

Figure 2.3
Tannenbaum and Schmidt's continuum of leadership behavior

The Attribution Theory of Leadership. The attribution theory of leadership was advanced by Pfeffer (1977). This concept of leadership suggests that leadership is a social construction or label that is given to individuals who attribute meaning in the lives of others. Attribution theory suggests that individuals attribute the cause of certain of events to the actions of leaders. Calder (1977) has written that "leadership is a label which can be applied to behavior . . .

[and] . . . exists only as a perception." Thus, the attribution theory of leadership maybe best viewed as a "construct of leadership defined as the degree to which the behavior of a group member is perceived as a acceptable attempt to influence the perceiver regarding his or her activity as a member of a particular group or the activity of other group members" (Stogdill, 1974, p. 345).

Discussing the application of the attribution theory to leisure service organizations, Jordan (1996, p. 36) suggests that this theory "explains leadership through the belief that leadership is attributed to one who looks and acts like a leader." She suggests that it is valuable to understand attribution theory because these types of beliefs can impact the success of the individual leading recreational and service programs. In group settings, judgments are made of the capabilities of this individual. As Jordan writes, "attribution theory can be utilized to help explain why people attribute leadership to certain individuals based on overall perceptions, whether or not that person is actually designated the leader" (1996, p. 37)

Transformational/ Transactional Leadership

The idea of transformational/transactional leadership was advanced by Burns (1978) in the late 1970s. Burns suggests that there are two distinct approaches to leadership: transactional and transformational. Burns used the social exchange theory of leadership developed by Hollander (1978) to frame his ideas. Using exchange theory, Burns wrote that "leadership occurs when one person takes the initiative in making contact with others for the purpose of an exchange of valued things. The exchange could be economic or political or psychological in nature." Burns saw leadership as "a mutual influence process grounded in shared perceptions of followers" (p. 156).

Transactional Leadership. Transactional leadership involves an exchange between the leader and those who could be defined as followers. In a work-related environment, an employee would exchange labor or effort for a wage. In a leisure setting, a participant would exchange something of value, perhaps time, money, or some other tangible, for an experience, or for the acquisition of a skill or some knowledge base that would lead to experiencing leisure. The transactional leadership process leads to a carrot or stick approach to dealing with individuals. On one hand, the opportunity for rewards or punishment is placed in front of the individual as an incentive. Fear of loss of the reward is the motivating factor for the individual. In the transactional

Whenever you see a successful business, someone once made a courageous decision.

Peter Drucker

leadership model, the implied threat of withdrawal of the incentive is an overarching concern.

Transformational Leadership. Transformational leadership is built on a different set of assumptions than transactional leadership. As Burns has written, leadership as a transformational process occurs "when one or more persons engage with others in such a way that leaders and followers raise one another to higher levels of motivation and morality" (1978, p. 20) In other words, Burns was suggesting that individuals working together could transform individuals in ways that would lead to higher levels of satisfaction and performance. Writers such as Peters and Waterman (1982) have suggested that leadership is a process of transforming individuals and organizations to pursue excellence.

Transformational leadership is built on the concept that individuals can be empowered to do greater works. They can be encouraged by appealing to more altruistic ends, which promotes a greater sense of commitment that leads to greater productivity, more intense involvement, and higher levels of satisfaction. In a sense, transformational leaders appeal to the spiritual or emotional side of individuals by encouraging them to pursue ends that are worthwhile; present a greater sense of value to individuals; and contribute in some meaningful way to more global, visionary ends. By empowering people to pursue a more visionary-enhanced pathway, transformational leaders unlock the reservoir of potential within individuals.

> Transforming leadership, while more complex than transactional leadership, is more potent.
>
> *James MacGregor Burns*

Transformational leadership activates people. The process of leadership is one of influencing people toward worthwhile ends that are mutually beneficial. Transformational leadership creates the opportunity for extraordinary human performance. It is a process that results in creating real change within individuals that leads to enhanced performance. As Burns notes, "transformational leadership is elevating" (1978, p. 455) The transformations that individuals experience "can take place in many aspects of our personal, professional, and moral lives. These transformations can be physical, intellectual, aesthetic, psychological, social, civic, ecological, transcendental, moral, spiritual, and holistic (Rost, 1993, p. 126). Essentially, this proposition of leadership suggests that leadership is fundamentally about transforming the lives of individuals in many different ways.

Situational Models of Leadership

Although previous investigations have provided insight into the leadership of individuals, many of the theories have not provided an adequate explanation for the situational factors influencing leadership. Such variables as the expectations of those being led, the external factors influencing the work of a group, the opportunities for interaction between the leader and group members, and the type of task undertaken by a group, focus attention on the need for a situational model to explain leadership behavior.

Fiedler's Contingency Model of Leadership Effectiveness. Fiedler's (1967) model purports that there is no "one best" leadership style. Like the Tannenbaum and Schmidt continuum, this model suggests that a particular individual's leadership style must be situationally determined. This means that, in order to be effective, a leader must use a leadership style that complements the needs of a given situation. The heart of the contingency model has to do with the degree of favorableness of the situation to the leader. Favorableness is determined by three basic factors.

Leader-Member Relations. This factor influencing favorableness toward the leader can be thought of as the extent to which the leader feels that he or she is accepted by group members.

Task Structure. Task structure can be thought of as the extent to which role expectations are clearly defined within the group. In certain situations, the roles that individuals occupy are highly structured and defined with clarity and precision.

Position Power. Position power refers to the degree of influence of a leader.

According to Fiedler, the concept of favorableness can be viewed as existing on a continuum. At one end of the continuum are situations highly favorable to the leader. At the other end of the continuum are situations highly unfavorable to the leader. Situations at one end—that are characterized by good leader-member relations and a well-defined structure and task and where the position of power of the leader is well established or high—are characterized by Fiedler as being highly favorable to the leader. On the other hand, situations at the other end of the continuum that are characterized by poor leader-member relations and lack of a well-defined structured task and where the position power of the leader was not established—are characterized by Fiedler as being highly unfavorable to the leader. Along the continuum, there could be varying degrees of favorableness, including an intermediate degree of favorableness of a given situation to the leader. This concept is illustrated in Figure 2.4.

Fiedler was interested in determining which leadership styles would be most effective at various points on his continuum. In order to measure leadership style, he developed an operational procedure to calculate how individuals were perceived in the group environment by their leader. The first part of this procedure attempted to determine the leader's perception of his or her least preferred co-worker (LPC) and most preferred co-worker (MPC). Measurement of how leaders perceive co-workers was based on the assumption that this perception would affect their relationship with others and, hence, their effectiveness. The second procedure was a measurement Fiedler called "the assumed similarity between

Pay less attention to what men say; I just watch what they do.

Andrew Carnegie

Task-oriented style	Relationship-oriented, considerate style	Task-oriented style
High assumed similarity or least preferred co-worker scores	Low assumed similarity or least preferred co-worker scores	Low assumed or least preferred co-worker scores

← ———————————— ———————————— ————————————→

Favorable leadership situation	Situation intermediate in favorableness for leader	Unfavorable leadership situation

Figure 2.4
Fielder's Contingency Model of Leadership
Source: From Fred E. Dielder, A Theory of Leadership Effectiveness (New York: McGraw-Hill Co., 1967, p. 14

> By believing passionately in something that still does not exist, we create it. The nonexistent is whatever we have not sufficiently desired.
>
> *Nikos Kazantzakis*

opposites (ASO) score." This was determined by calculating the difference between LPC and MPC scores. These two procedures were related to two leadership styles identified by Fiedler. They are:

Human Relations or "Lenient" Style. The leader using the human relations leadership style tends to be permissive. Leaders who do not perceive a large degree of difference between the most preferred co-worker and the least preferred co-worker are likely to fall within this category of leadership style.

Task-Directed or "Hard-Nosed" Style. The leader using the task-directed style of leadership is task oriented and controlling. Leaders who perceive a large degree of difference between the most preferred co-worker and the least preferred co-worker are likely to fall within the task-directed category of leadership style.

Empirically based research evidence that was collected by Fiedler indicates that the task-directed or "hard-nosed" style of leadership is more successful in situations that are very favorable and very unfavorable to the leader.

Interestingly, Fiedler maintains that it may be better to structure a situation to fit a leader's style than to use the traditional approach of training the leader to adapt to his or her environment. This idea has implications for recreation, parks, and leisure services leadership in that certain individuals may be better suited to lead in certain situations than others.

It is apparent that not every recreation, parks and leisure leader may be good at instructing, lecturing, coaching, counseling, and leading games and activities. Therefore, it may be more appropriate to match the leader with the situation for which he or she is best qualified.

Path-Goal Theory of Leadership. The path-goal approach to leadership attempts to combine various elements of motivation with leadership. The path-goal theory of leadership is concerned with the assessment of the satisfaction, motivation, and performance of group members and the relationship of these elements to leadership style (House & Mitchell, 1974). This theory suggests that a leader's behavior may be tied to group members' immediate or long-term satisfaction. In turn, group members are motivated when their satisfaction triggers performance.

The path-goal theory of leadership suggests that different leadership styles should be used in different situations. The role of the leader is to be aware of and use the various styles appropriately to affect employee motivation, satisfaction, and productivity. A leader may use one or more of the styles presented in this theory, depending upon the situation. These styles can be summarized as follows.

> **Directive Leadership.** This approach to leadership is very authoritarian and task oriented. No attempt is made to involve individuals in the decision-making process.

> **Supportive Leadership.** Supportive leadership relates to the needs, interests, and desires of group members. The leader using this style of leadership is concerned with establishing a positive, supportive relationship with group members and is open and responsive to suggestions.

> **Participative Leadership.** This style of leadership is open, wherein the leader is responsive to opinions, ideas, and suggestions of group members. The leader, however, retains the final authority to make decisions.

> **Achievement-Oriented Leadership.** In this style of leadership, the role of the leader is to challenge group members. This might involve the establishment of high standards or the expectation of high output.

The role of the leader using the path-goal theory of leadership can be thought of simply as employing the appropriate style to "clear the path" for group members to achieve their own goals as well as the goals of the group or organization. Thus, this leadership style is used to remove barriers, result-

You do not lead by hitting people over the head—that's assault, not leadership.

Dwight Eisenhower

ing in improvement of satisfaction, in turn resulting in greater motivation and performance.

Tri-Dimensional Leader Effectiveness Model. Hersey and Blanchard (1977) have developed a situational leadership theory called the tri-dimensional leader effectiveness model. This model is represented in Figure 2.5. It uses the elements of the Ohio State studies (human relations orientation and task orientation) as well as the "effectiveness" dimension delineated by Hersey and Blanchard which suggests that one's leadership style will vary according to two variables. The first variable is the level of maturity of group members. The second variable is the demands of the situation. They argue that the leader should diagnose both the demands of the situation and the level of maturity of group members in order to determine what leadership style would be most appropriate.

> The world hates change, yet it is the only thing that has brought progress.
>
> *Charles F. Kettering*

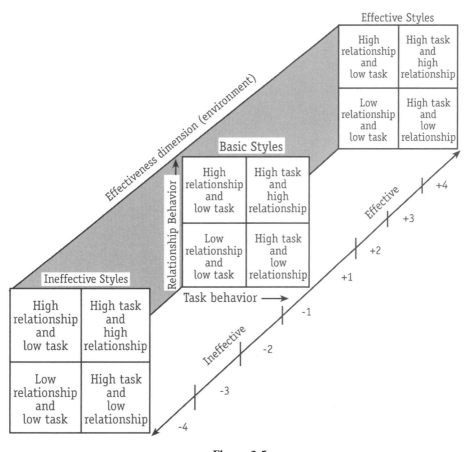

Figure 2.5
Tri-dimensional leader effectiveness model
Source: P. Hersey & K. H. Blanchard, *Management of Organizational Behavior: Utilizing Human Resources*, 3rd ed., ©1977, p. 106. Reprinted by permission of Prentice-Hall, Inc., Englewood Cliffs, N.J.

Hersey and Blanchard also suggest that maturity can be viewed as existing on a continuum. Specifically, they suggest that a mature individual has "the capacity to set high but attainable goals, willingness and ability to take responsibility, and education and/or experience" relevant to a given task to be performed (Hersey & Blanchard, 1977, p. 101). They point out that the concept of maturity should not be viewed in a total sense but rather, should be considered only in relation to the undertaking of a specific activity. Thus, it follows that in certain cases some groups will have a higher degree of maturity than others. The leader's style, according to this model, should then complement the level of maturity of the

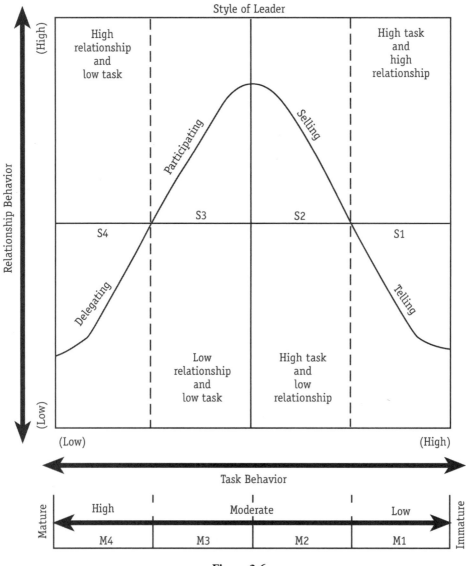

Figure 2.6
Situational leadership

Source: P. Hersey & K. H. Blanchard, *Management of Organizational Behavior: Utilizing Human Resources*, 3rd ed., ©1977, p. 170. Reprinted by permission of Prentice-Hall, Inc., Englewood Cliffs, N.J.

group. Figure 2.6 details the way in which leadership styles vary, depending on the maturity level of an individual or group. Four classifications of styles emerge: telling (S1), selling (S2), participating (S3), and delegating (S4).

Hitt's Model of Leadership

Hitt (1988) has proposed a leadership model that translates vision into action. He writes that: "Leadership is what gives an organization its vision and its ability to translate the vision into reality" (1985). We can think of this approach to leadership as being one of pragmatic idealism. In other words, it is a leadership style that seeks higher ends yet at the same time recognizes real-life conditions that influence the behavior of others. Leadership becomes a process of establishing a realistic, attractive vision for the future and then creating a plan of action to achieve desired ends.

Although one might surmise that simply creating a credible, attractive future might be enough to motive others to spring into action, Hitt suggests that the effective leader is not only good at visioning but also must be able to make things happen. He refers to these two qualities as dreaming and doing. Figure 2.7 illustrates Hitt's two-dimensional model combining dreaming and doing. There are four types of potential behaviors or leadership styles in this model. They are:

> Any man or woman can achieve what I have if he or she would put forth the same effort and cultivate the same hope and faith.
>
> *Mahatma Mohandas*
> *Gandhi*

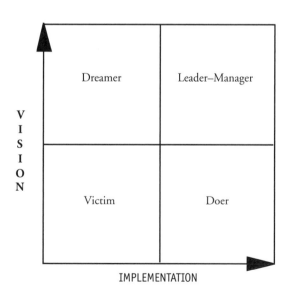

Figure 2.7
The nature of leadership

Source: Hitt, Williams D. (1998). *The Leader-Manager: Guidlines for Action*.
Columbus: Battelle Press.

- Victim: Low on both vision and implementation. Complains that the organization is unfair.
- Dreamer: High on vision, but low on implementation.
- Doer: High on implementation, low on vision.
- Leader-Manager: High on both vision and implementation.

One can see the four basic styles in viewing the different quadrants in the model. The victim is an individual who lacks vision or the ability to turn ideas into action. The dreamer is an individual who can articulate a vision but does not necessarily move the organization to that end. We have all met individuals who have great ideas but lack the ability to turn them into reality. The doer is an individual who can make things happen but lacks a vision. Often, such individuals are excellent followers within a group or organization and can contribute to its work. The same could be said about dreamers or idea people; however, the commensurate leader is one who combines the vision with action, dreaming with doing.

Collaborative Leadership

Building collaborative relationships between individuals is a key element in contemporary concepts regarding leadership. Collaboration means to work together or to cooperate with others. The hallmark of collaborative effort is found in the process of "teaming" with other individuals. Those who collaborate do not work independently but rather work to produce synergistic opportunities between individuals or group members. The idea of synergistic, collaborative behavior is that the work of the team will out perform the combined outputs of individuals working alone.

Collaborative leaders understand the importance of creating a dialogue with others. In fact, Kouzes and Posner (1995, p. 11) suggest that "leadership is a dialogue not a monologue." Leaders "breathe life into the hopes and dreams of others and enable them to see exciting possibilities that the future holds." Collaborative leaders are concerned with building trust, listening, and finding ways to draw others into decision-making and action.

Partnership Models. Eisler (1995) offers an interesting perspective that can be applied to leadership in comparing and contrasting dominator and partnership models. In the partnership model, males and females are equally valued in governing ideology. As a result, feminine traits, such as providing nurture and acting in nonviolent ways, can become a part of a leadership model. In this model, conflict resolution becomes the norm, as does a more egalitarian approach to others. In the dominator (authoritarian) model of leadership, command and control of others based on a hierarchical

A leader has the vision and conviction that a dream can be achieved. He or she inspires power and energy to get it done.

Ralph Lauren

If you can dream it, you can do it.

Walt Disney

order is the prevailing norm. As a result, most directives or efforts at encouraging action are coercive in nature. On the other hand, in the partnership model, mutual respect is the norm, with an emphasis on freedom of choice. This is further extended in the relationship that develops between individuals, wherein providing life-giving support and nourishment is the norm, as contrasted with punitive type behaviors and a more authoritarian structure. Empathy, caring behaviors, equity, and unconditional support are the hallmarks of the partner leadership model.

Leading the Journey. An interesting model of collaborative leadership is advanced by Belasco and Stayer (1993) in The Flight of the Buffalo. They suggest that collaborative leadership is important today because of changing relationships between leaders and followers. Using the behavior of buffalo herds, they suggest that in past times loyalty was highly valued in groups, and followers waited for leaders to whom they were loyal to provide direction to guide their actions.

The new model of leadership, a collaborative model, suggests that a shared process of leadership is desirable. Using the analogy of the V formation used by flying geese, Belasco and Stayer (1993) see the process of leadership as changing, depending on the type of roles necessary. Leaders alternate within the group depending upon the type of function or task that is required. In this model, geese flying in a V formation change roles frequently, with different geese taking the leadership role when one becomes tired or the task changes.

In this model, collaborative leadership is encouraged. The hallmark of this collaborative model involves creating open communication and trust among individuals. It is exemplified by the sharing of leadership as well as the encouragement of those individuals who step forward to take leadership roles. This collaborative model is rich in that it provides opportunities for multiple resources and leadership talents to be brought into play to solve problems. It also provides for individuals to share responsibilities within a group or organization. The sharing of responsibility creates a stronger commitment to the ends pursued. In this way there is a stronger and more personal involvement by each individual in the work of the organization. The total endeavor is strengthened dramatically when individuals share in both the completion of assigned tasks and the taking of leadership roles.

Eagles don't flock— you have to find them one at a time.

H. Ross Perot

Leader Presence

The idea of leader presence is drawn from the works of de Oliveira, Edginton and Edginton (1996, p. 38). Using a foundation of Christian theology, they constructed and coined the term "leader presence." Presence as understood and applied in Christian theology suggests that "an individual may convey a greater, spiritual essence through an individual and his or her work." Thus, it is possible for an individual through their efforts to transform another. As they note, intangible qualities held by one individual and shared by another may literally be transformed into tangible outcomes.

Discussing leadership in the recreation, parks, and leisure servicess, as well as allied areas, they write:

> Leaders use their "presence" to influence values, attitudes and behavior. Great teachers and coaches exude energy, warmth, sincerity, and a genuine love of others. These qualities have the potential to transform people. Simply by living one's life in contact with others where such characteristics are present conveys meaning. Expanding the idea of role modeling, the concept of leader presence promotes more encompassing relationships. Those involved in such relationships not only incorporate desirable characteristics, as in the process of role modeling, but achieve the merging of intellectual, experiential, and spiritual essence that make for significant encounters with others. Such encounters produce societal and cultural values that contribute to the advancement of civilized behavior.

de Oliveira, Edginton, and Edginton suggest that an individual is influenced through a mingling of one's essences. We have all known individuals who reflect the inner qualities that we seek to emulate or influence our lives in some way. Their presence is a force in and of itself. Their leadership qualities influence others simply by the fact that they are with others, often interacting with them in a nonjudgmental way. They provide leadership to others by serving as role models or reference points upon which others can build qualities to incorporate into their lives.

Servant Leadership

Robert K. Greenleaf brought into focus the idea of servant leadership. In 1970 he coined the term "servant-leader" in an essay entitled "The Servant as Leader" (1970, p. 7; 1991). In this essay, Greenleaf wrote:

> The servant-leader is servant first. . . . it begins with the natural feeling that one wants to serve, to serve first. Then conscious choice brings one to aspire to lead. . . . The difference manifests itself in the care

We cannot live only for ourselves. A thousand fibers connect us with our fellow men, and along those fibers, as sympathetic threads, our actions run as causes, and they come back to us as effects.

Herman Melville

taken by the servant—first to make sure that other people's highest-priority needs are being served. The best test, and the most difficult to administer, is: Do those served grow as persons? Do they, while being served, become healthier, wiser, freer, more autonomous, more likely themselves to become servants? And, what is the effect on the least privileged in society; will they benefit or, at least, not be further deprived?

Greenleaf suggested that the leader as a servant is a nurturer of the human spirit. Recreation, parks, and leisure services leaders likewise work to nurture the human spirit. As a profession recreation, parks, and leisure services leaders create hope in the lives of individuals. When people come to a leisure experience, they come to it with the expectation—with the hope—that good things will happen to them. People seek through leisure joy, happiness, and fulfillment. Through leisure, many positive benefits are possible and are sought by individuals.

Servant leadership involves building a positive, mutual relationship between the leader and those he or she is serving. Again, as Greenleaf (1996, p.13) writes:

> The test of any of any kind of leadership is if leaders enjoy a mutual relationship with followers. Are these followers numerous enough and constant enough to make an effective force of their effort? The leader is always attached to an effective force of people. Among those who are normally followers are those who from time to time will also lead. The titular leader gives continuity and coherence to an endeavor in which many may lead.

A servant leadership approach requires varied skills and attributes. Spears (1995) has suggested that servant leaders have a need to possess a number of different characteristics. Characteristics of servant leaders cited by Spears include 1) listening; 2) empathy; 3) healing; 4) awareness; 5) persuasion; 6) conceptualization; 7) foresight; 8) stewardship; 9) commitment to the growth of people; and 10) building community. All of these characteristics are elements that are important in the leadership roles played out by recreation, parks, and leisure services professionals in all settings and at all levels, including face-to-face, supervisory, and administrative. Edginton, Hudson, Dieser, and Edginton (2004, p. 83) confirm this by noting that "the servant leadership approach . . .should be the basis for programming and leadership in all types of recreation, parks, and leisure organizations – commercial, private, nonprofit, and public organizations."

Any leader worth following gives credit easily where credit is due. He does not take someone's idea, dress it up and offer it as his own. He offers it as theirs... He plays fair with everyone and recognizes the strong points in people as well as the weak ones

Franklin J. Lundling

The application of servant leadership principles to the recreation, parks, and leisure services field have been advanced by DeGraaf, Jordan, and DeGraaf (1999, p.13). They note that there is a need for a new type of leadership model in the recreation, parks, and leisure services field; one that places serving others at the focal point of their efforts. They note that "a servant leadership approach to delivering services encourages partnerships between constituents and professionals". Affirming Spears characteristics of servant leaders, they suggest that ". . . leisure professionals must learn to be good leaders by learning to good followers, by listening to participants and by helping them lead so we as leisure professionals can follow (DeGraaf, et al., p. 15).

Example is always more efficacious than precept.

Samuel Johnson

Authentic Leadership

George (2003, p.5) also makes the case that there is need for a new approach to leadership. This call has emerged as a result of the crisis that has unfolded from the lack of ethical leadership in all sectors of our society—business, government, and nongovernment organizations. The lack of integrity and honesty and the duplicity demonstrated by leaders in all of these types of settings has promoted his call for greater authenticity in the process of leadership. He suggests that it is paramount that we seek "authentic, moral, and character-based leaders." George offers the following:

> We need authentic leaders, people of the highest integrity, committed to building enduring organizations. We need leaders who have a deep sense of purpose and are true to their core values. We need leaders who have the courage to build their . . .[organizations] . . . to meet the needs of all their stakeholders, and who recognize the importance of their service to society.

What does it mean to be an authentic leader? As George suggests, leadership is a matter of authenticity, not style. He believes "leadership begins and ends with authenticity. It's being yourself; being the person you were created to be (George, p.11). Leadership is not a search for a popular style or approach, or even the desire to attain celebrity status. Rather, George suggests, similarly to Greenleaf's concepts, that "authentic leaders genuinely desire to serve others through their leadership. They are more interested in empowering the people they lead to make a difference than they are in power, money, or prestige for themselves. They are as guided by qualities of the heart, by passion and compassion, as they are by qualities of the mind" (12).

George suggests there are five essential dimensions of authentic leaders. They are:

1. Understanding Their Purpose. Authentic leaders have a real sense of their purpose, role, and function in encouraging the best efforts of others.

2. Practicing Solid Values. A leader's values can be thought of as the guiding principles, standard, or quality, which serves to underpin their leadership and behavior as an individual.

3. Leading With Heart. Belief in oneself and others as well as belief in the vision or mission of an organization, often requires a commitment of the heart, the ability to operate with a great deal of passion, and the ability to energize, inspire, and motivate others.

4. Establishing Connected Relationships. The ability to develop relationships with others, to build community, and to connect with others in a meaningful and relevant fashion is essential in developing authentic leadership.

5. Demonstrating Self-Discipline. As indicated in Hitt's (1988) model of leadership, there are dreamers and there are doers. Doing is the action part of leadership. It requires great self-discipline to convert one's dreams into tangible outcomes.

> The most important key to success in life, even financial success, is to develop a servant's heart, to become engaged in the human race and desire to benefit others.
>
> *Thomas Kinkade*

There are many compelling examples of authentic leaders in recreation, parks, and leisure services. In each chapter we have featured one individual. who because they understood their role as a leader and promoted a great vision with passion, were successful. They were individuals who had the ability to connect in meaningful ways with others and had the self-discipline to produce viable social inventions.

SUMMARY

Leadership has been aggressively studied for nearly a century. Leadership in this text is seen as an art or a craft that involves influencing individuals or groups to work together with enthusiasm, dedication, and skill toward some common end. It is a transformational process, whereby both leaders and participants exchange meaning in a powerful interplay of ideas, concepts, and, ultimately, action. No one best leadership style or method exists; rather, the literature on the subject teaches us that a variety of strategies need to be employed depending on the situation, especially the task-relevant maturity and conditions faced by the leader when working with others.

In this chapter we have presented and discussed a number of leadership theories, studies, styles, and models. From a theoretical standpoint, leadership has been studied from four perspectives. First, the "great man" theory is built on the notion that leaders are born and not made, and have emerged throughout history to occupy positions of leadership. Second, the trait theory is based on the idea that certain personality characteristics or traits are possessed by successful leaders. The next approach, the group theory, suggests that leaders emerge within groups when a reciprocal relationship of rewards exist between the leader and the group. Finally, situational theories suggest that there is no "one best" leadership style, but that the leader must be flexible in his or her leadership style to meet the demands of a given situation. We presented several different leadership studies, styles, and models as contributing significantly to our understanding of leadership. The Lewin, Lippitt, and White studies investigate three different leadership styles: democratic, authoritarian, and laissez faire. Two dimensions of leader behavior—initiating structure and consideration—are identified in the Ohio State research study concerning leadership. The managerial grid by Blake and Mouton is a model that identifies five different managerial leadership styles aligning concern for production and concern for people along two axes. The University of Michigan studies views the two variables, concern for people and concern for production, as existing on a continuum. Rensis Likert perfected this concept and offers a number of styles that could exist on such a continuum, including exploitative, autocratic, benevolent autocratic, consultative, and participative groups. Tannenbaum and Schmidt also use the continuum concept to present different combinations of freedom and use of authority.

Recently, situational models of leadership have come to the forefront of discussion in the leadership area. Fiedler's contingency model of leadership effectiveness suggests that the favorableness of the situation can influence the type of leadership style used by the leader. Such factors as leader-member relations, task structure, and the position power of the leader influence the favorableness of the situation. The path-goal theory of leadership suggests that different styles should be used by the leader to remove barriers that affect employee motivation, satisfaction, and productivity. The tri-dimensional leader effectiveness model, developed by Hersey and Blanchard, suggests that the task-relevant maturity level of group members is a critical variable influencing the adoption of a leadership style. In addition to the aforementioned styles of leadership, we also included discussion of new models such as leader presence, servant leadership, and authentic leadership. Each of these models calls for the leader to operate with integrity and to build their efforts around service to others on a greater moral premise or set of values.

▩▩▩▩ Discussion Questions

1. What is the "great man" theory of leadership? Trait theory? Group theory? Situational theory? Excellence theory?

2. Identify traits that are related to effective leadership from your own experience.

3. What are the characteristics of democratic, authoritarian, and laissez faire leadership styles?

4. What are the characteristics of a task-oriented leader? A relationship-oriented leader?

5. Some leadership studies and style models present task-relationship orientations on a continuum; others present them on a grid. What are the implications of these ways of viewing the dimensions of leadership behavior?

6. What does it mean to say that there is no "one best" leadership style?

7. How can one's leadership style assist group members in removing barriers?

8. What does the term task-relevant maturity mean? What implications does this have for one's leadership style?

9. What is the difference between transactional and transformational leadership? What does the idea of the leader being a servant imply?

10. Compare and contrast leader presence, servant leadership, and authentic leadership. What are the main points about these three approaches to leadership? What are the differences? What are the similarities?

A leader is a dealer in hope.

Napoleon Bonaparte

THE CASE FOR LEADERSHIP
A New Supervisor for Cedar Center

Points of Consideration

Cedar Center Parks and Recreation Department seeks a new supervisor for its community center's program. Currently the city operates three community centers. Each center includes three meeting rooms, a gymnasium, fitness center, racquetball courts, and indoor/outdoor swimming pool. The community centers are directed by full-time center directors and include a receptionist as well as part-time and seasonal staff providing general and specific leadership to programs and activities under their responsibility.

The three community centers are located geographically throughout Cedar Center. Addams Community Center is located at the south end of town. This area is economically well to do and participation at the center is high with an emphasis on fitness activities. Bannon Community Center is located in the northern part of the city and serves a middle-class population. Programs and services are varied, but there is a greater emphasis on activities for children and youth, especially before and after-school care and youth sport programs. Peterson Community Center is located in the heart of the community. Individuals attending this center tend to be upwardly mobile, often two-income families with no children. In recent years, attendance at this center has declined, although the facility is often used by outside community groups on a fee basis.

Each of these community centers faces different challenges. Addams Community Center has been able to generate on a fee base a very positive cash flow in support of its operations. Its programs and services, although limited, are well received by the community. The center director of this program has had difficulty in the past relating effectively to the community and to the staff. Bannon Community Center is struggling financially. However, its center director is well received by the community and perceived to be an asset in the neighborhood. Known as people-oriented person, this center director is at times difficult to work with because of the belief that he should operate on an independent basis with little supervision. Peterson Community Center has great potential, but does not seem to connect effectively with the community. Its center director at times appears to be unfocused, lacking vision and an awareness of how to organize programs to meet the needs of the community. This person has been with the Cedar Center Parks and Recreation Department for 15 years and has seniority in the civil service system.

Questions of Consideration

Two finalists have emerged for the position. Carol, a graduate of Cedar College with a Bachelor's Degree in Recreation and Parks, is known as a people-oriented person. She has had three years of previous work experience as a recreation supervisor in a nearby community. She is best known as a person who is creates a comfortable work environment for her employees, handles problems in a way that attempts to satisfy all concerns, and has good public relation skills. Carol's references note that she is a positive person who works well with others. The other finalist, Terri, holds a Bachelor's Degree in Business and a Master's Degree in Park and Recreation Management from the state university. She is known as a driven and task-oriented supervisor who has great ability at moving programs and services forward in an effective fashion. Terri's references indicate that she is very performance-oriented and capable of bringing about change within organizations.

- Who would you hire for this position?
- What kind of managerial leadership skills are most needed to move the program forward?
- Should a person with greater people skills be selected or would you hire an individual who is more task oriented?
- What types of questions would you ask in an interview that would help reveal one's managerial leadership style?
- What factors should you take into consideration when selecting an individual for this position as it relates to their managerial leadership styles?
- How important is one's managerial leadership style in the overall equation for selecting an individual for a position?

REFLECTING ON LEADERSHIP

Finding Your Leadership Style

Directions: Circle the response number in each section that best describes your typical leadership tendencies. When you have finished, determine your total score by adding all the numbers together. Select only one response for each section. To determine your leadership style, refer to the following scale: 10 – 25 points = task-oriented leadership; 26 – 40 points = relationally-oriented leadership.

	1	2	3	4
As a leader I am:	1 analytical	2 productive	3 creative	4 supportive
I believe a recreation, parks and leisure services leader should concentrate most on:	1 planning	2 producing results	3 team building	4 listening to others
The first characteristic I look for when hiring a new youth work staff is:	1 skill level	2 ability to make informed decisions	3 innovativeness	4 ability to work collaboratively with others
As a communicator I am most skilled at:	1 being direct and clear	2 presenting the big picture	3 clearly stating my own thoughts and ideas	4 listening to others' feelings and ideas
I typically handle problems by:	1 taking control	2 clarifying the role of each individual	3 seeking to establish harmony	4 collaboratively working with all involved
My success as a leader in a recreation, parks, and leisure services organization or program depends on:	1 the effectiveness of the plan I create	2 my ability to achieve the goal I seek to accomplish	3 the professional social climate with in my organization	4 the people I work with
I typically find out about problems in my program or organization through:	1 evaluation procedures	2 determining how much progress has been made toward achieving goals	3 intuitively sensing that plans beginning to not	4 interactions with others
When presented with poor quality work, I:	1 insist that project guidelines are followed	2 clarify expectations and provide a set a new project deadline	3 provide an example of quality work and a plan for improvement	4 talk to those involved and create a plan for improvement
I motivate others in my organization or program by:	1 modeling high professional standards	2 praising a job well done	3 promoting enthusiasm and creativity	4 providing the freedom for others to express their professional talent
When others question my leadership, I:	1 demand immediate compliance	2 provide justification for the decisions that have been made	3 meet with individuals and seek to build consensus	4 seek input from others and establish a new plan of action

Source: Adapted from Randall, S. (2004). *Youth Worker Leadership Inventory.* University of Northern Iowa.

References

Belasco, J. A., & Stayer, R. C. (1993). *Flight of the buffalo*. New York: Warner.

Blake, R. R., & Mouton, J. S. (1978). *The new managerial grid*. Houston: Gulf.

Burns, J. M. (1978). *Leadership*. New York: Harper & Row.

Calder, B. J. (1977). An Attribution Theory of Leadership. In B. Shaw, & G. Salanick (Eds.), *New directions in organizational behavior*. Chicago: St. Clair Press.

DeGraaf, D. G., Jordan, D., & DeGraaf, K. H. (1999). *Programming for parks, recreation, and leisure services: A servant leadership approach*. State College, PA: Venture.

de Oliveira, W., Edginton, S. R., & Edginton, C. R. (1996). Leader Presence. *Journal of Physical Education, Recreation, and Dance* 67(1), 38-39.

Eisler, R. (1995). *Sacred pleasure*. New York: Harper Collins.

Fiedler, F. (1967). *A theory of leadership effectiveness*. New York: McGraw-Hill.

George, B. (2003). *Authentic leadership*. San Francisco, CA: Jossey-Bass.

Greenleaf, R. K. (1996). *Seeker and servant: Reflections on religious leadership*. San Francisco, CA: Jossey-Bass.

Greenleaf, R. K. (1970, 1991). *The servant as leader*. Indianapolis, IN: Robert K. Greenleaf Center for Servant-Leadership.

Hersey, P., & Blanchard, K. (1977). *Management of organizational behavior-utilizing human resources* (3rd ed.). Englewood Cliffs, NJ: Prentice-Hall.

Hitt, W. D. (1988). *The leader manager: Guidelines for action*. Columbus, OH: Battelle Press.

House, R. J., & Mitchell, T. R. (1974, Autumn). Path–goal theory of leadership. *Journal of Contemporary Business*. (p. 81-97)

Jordan, D. J. (1996). *Leadership in leisure services: Making a difference*. State College, PA: Venture.

Katz, D., Maccoby, N., & Morse, N. C. (1950). *Productivity, supervision, and morale in an office situation*. Ann Arbor: Survey Research Center, University of Michigan.

Kouzes, J., & Posner, B. (1995). *The leadership challenge: How to keep getting extraordinary things done in organizations*. San Francisco: Jossey Bass.

Lewin, K., Lippitt, R., & White, R. K. (1939, May). Patterns of aggressive behavior in experimentally created social climates. *Journal of Social Psychology.* (p. 271-299)

Likert, R. (1967). *The human organization.* New York: McGraw-Hill.

Peters, T. J., & Waterman, R. H. (1982). *In search of excellence.* New York: Harper & Row.

Pfeffer, J. (1977). The ambiguity of leadership. *Academy of Management Review, 2*(1), 104–112.

Rost, J. C. (1993). *Leadership for the twenty-first century.* Westport, CT: Praeger.

Stogdill, R.M. (1974). Handbook of leadership: A Survey of Theory and Research. New York: The Free Press

Stogdill, R. M., & Coons, A. E. (1957). *Leader behavior's description and measurement.* Columbus: Bureau of Business Research, Ohio State University.

Tannenbaum, R., & Schmidt, W. H. (1973, May-June). How to choose a leadership pattern. *Harvard Business Review.* (p. 162)

CHAPTER

3

Leadership
Roles

LEARNING OBJECTIVES

1. To distinguish four types of leadership found in recreation, parks, and leisure services organizations.
2. To identify three general roles in face-to-face leadership.
3. To explain the various supervisor responsibilities.
4. To define the primary function of an administrator or executive.
5. To identify the various roles of civic leaders.

KEY TERMS

- Face-to-face leadership
- Leader as Instructor
- Leader as Counselor
- Leisure Counselor
- Youth Worker
- Leader as Coach
- Supervisor Leadership
- Managerial Leadership
- Community Leadership
- In Loco Parentis

INTRODUCTION

Leadership is found at all levels within recreation, parks, and leisure services organizations. Not only is it essential in the actual delivery of services where the trained professional interacts with participants on a face-to-face basis, but it also exists in a broader context where the recreation, parks, and leisure services professional provides leadership to the community as a whole. It exists within organizations as professionals lead their subordinates and peers, assisting them in the planning, organizing, and implementation of their assigned tasks. Professionals do not exclusively practice leadership in recreation, parks, and leisure services organizations; volunteers, laypersons, and other individuals interested in supporting and encouraging the development of the activities, programs, and services of an agency also exercise leadership. Generally speaking, we can identify four distinct types of leadership found in recreation, parks, and leisure services organizations. They are direct or face-to-face leadership, supervisory leadership, managerial leadership, and civic or community leadership. This chapter relates to the role of the leader in various recreation, parks, and leisure services settings and the skill associated with each level of leadership.

As one advances from face-to-face leader to that of supervisor, and then is promoted to an administrator, the relationship between technical skills, human skills, and conceptual skills change (See Figure 3.1). The skills that all recreation, park, and leisure services leaders need include: technical skills, human skills, and conceptual skills. Technical ability is necessary for leaders to be competent at performing the task for which they are responsible. For example, when teaching an aerobics class the leader must be physically fit, able to sequence a fitness session, knowledgeable about the signs of overexertion, and prepared to deal with any challenges that arise during the activity. Human skills focus on how a leader relates to others and therefore must have effective communication, problem solving, and decision-making abilities. Finally, leaders need conceptual skills of understanding the overall goals of the organization and the role one plays in order to meet these goals. Although the leadership skills needed at each level will vary, all leaders need proficient human relation skills in order to motivate the individuals they are working with to achieve the goals of the activity, program, or organization.

TYPES OF DIRECT, FACE-TO-FACE LEADERSHIP

The face-to-face leader works directly with people. There are many situations that demand an obvious, direct, and influential leader. Examples include leaders of games, songs, initiative tasks, dance, drama, special events, tours, tournaments, conferences, social events, arts and crafts, community centers, and countless other activities. The material in this section relates to situations where the leader faces the group and leads, directs, explains, teaches, or, in some manner, influences the behavior of the group as a whole. While there are many types of face-to-face leaders, examples of three general, yet diverse, direct face-to-face leadership roles are presented here. They include the leader as instructor, counselor, and coach.

Leader as Instructor

Whenever the success of an activity depends upon the ability of the participant to execute specific skills, the leader of that activity should be an instructor. Instructional leadership is a first type of face-to-face or direct leadership. Programs in which participants learn to play musical instru-

Leadership Levels

The administrator

The supervisor

The face-to-face leader

Skill Needs

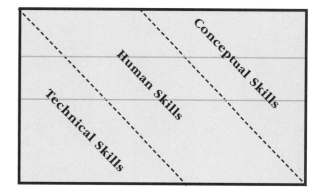

Figure 3.1: Levels of Leadership.

Adapted from Hersey, P., Blanchard, K. H., & Johnson, D. (1996). *Management of organizational behavior: Utilizing human resources.* Englewood Cliffs, N.J.: Prentice Hall.

ments, learn new songs, execute sports skills, perform dances, play new games, follow directions, learn to dive or climb, or perform myriad other skills should have instructors. The instructional leader may, in some circumstances, be more effective if an authoritarian leadership style is used. Certainly, activities involving risk or danger need tighter control and more precise skills development than activities that entail creative arts. This does not mean that the leader should be a dictator or use harsh commands. It does mean that the leader, as an authority on the topic, will set up certain prerequisites (safety policies and order of action) in order to ensure safety and the optimal development of the skill.

It is assumed that the instructional leader will attempt to teach the participants to perform in an exemplary manner. Whether it is serving a tennis ball, singing a duet, writing invitations by calligraphy, square dancing, or cooking over charcoal, the leader should have the expectation that the learner will acquire well-developed skills that will enable successful execution of the activity. It is incumbent on the instructional leader to teach the skills correctly and safely and still maintain interest and enthusiasm. A good instructor knows how to balance the work of learning with the play of performing and is able to help learners persist through the arduousness of practice sessions for the reward of successful performance to come.

There are times when precise skill instruction may be modified. If a participant cannot perform as the skill is described because of a physical or cognitive limitation, the leader must be able to modify it. A tennis player with the limited use of one arm may not be able to toss the ball for the service as described in the books on teaching tennis. The ball may be played, however, on the racquet face and tossed into the air by the serving arm, which can then executive the serve. This is not the regulation serve, but one necessary for the player's success. It is in these types of situations that instructors must be innovative and flexible.

In addition to teaching there are times when the leader of a program activity may need to serve in other roles and perform other functions. It may appear as if all that is expected is to coach a sport, teach crafts, lead dances, or relate to one specific skill. One is likely to find out that, even in such an assignment, there are problems involving interpersonal relationships, scheduling, special events, programs or exhibitions, irregular attendance, and morale. Thus, even in an activity-centered group, group dynamics represent an important concern.

There are times when the leader is working with a group in which the dynamics of interpersonal relationships are more important than the particular activity the group happens to be carrying on. When this occurs, a number of different leadership roles are assumed. Therefore, in addition to leading the specific activity, the leader may also need to assume any of the following roles.

Policymaker. Helping the group make decisions relating to goals, membership, meeting time and place, dues, and similar matters.

Planner. Helping the group develop specific plans for activities, programs, trips, special events, and other projects.

Organizer. Helping the group evolve ways of structuring themselves, of making concrete plans for action.

Resource Person. Acting as a source of information, knowledge, skills, and contacts.

Stimulator. Inspiring the group and helping to get things going; acting as a source of ideas, suggestions, and motivation.

Referee. Helping the group resolve conflicts and disagreements.

Disciplinarian. In a constructive sense, helping the group members develop rules and other forms of control and impose them of their own volition; exerting controls when necessary.

Group Symbol. Acting as an adult image or model, whom group members admire and respect and whose values and behavior they emulate.

Spokesperson. Acting as a spokesperson for the members of the group, either in the sponsoring agency or in the community at large.

When these functions of the face-to-face leader are examined, it is apparent that the leader is in a position to make a major contribution to the successful operation of the group. In many situations there are choices that must be made, and leadership behavior must be based on sound judgment and an assessment of the probable results of several courses of action. The leadership roles just described are carried out to meet the needs of participants while at the same time meeting the goals of the sponsoring organization. Figure 3.2 is an example of an internship description for a direct program leadership position.

> Don't tell people how to do things, tell them what to do and let them surprise you with their results.
>
> *George S. Patton*

A LEGACY OF LEADERSHIP

Aldo Leopold (1887-1948)

Known as the father of wildlife conservation in America, Leopold was the first naturalist to introduce the concepts of philosophy and ethics into conservation. He espoused that humans were a part of nature, not its adversary and suggested that humans needed to develop a "land ethic," a basic respect for plants, animals, and resources in order to live in harmony with our natural world. Although the term biodiversity was not used in his time, Leopold understood and promoted the concept that all organisms have a role in an ecosystem. The principles at the time primarily viewed land for its economic potential. It was Leopold that questioned a need for an ethical treatment of the land. Leopold felt that land and wildlife also held an ethical and aesthetic value that was necessary for sustainability. One of Leopold's famous quotes is that "a thing is right when it tends to preserve the integrity, stability, and beauty of the biotic community. It is wrong when it tends otherwise."

Best known for *A Sand County Almanac* (1949), Leopold also authored the cornerstone text *Game Management* (1933), from which the fundamental principles for managing and restoring wildlife populations are still in use today. In addition, Leopold wrote over 350 articles, most on scientific and policy matters, and was an advisor on conservation to the United Nations.

Aldo Leopold's professional career began in 1909 with the U.S. Forest Service. His primary areas of specialization were forestry and wildlife management. After 19 years with the Forest Service, Leopold left to do independent contract work conducting wildlife game surveys. In 1933, Leopold was appointed as a professor of wildlife management at the University of Wisconsin in Madison and in 1935 was one of the founding members of The Wilderness Society, an organization whose sole mission is the protection of America's Wilderness.

Aldo Leopold is remembered world-wide as a leader for his ground-breaking work on an ethical treatment of the land. Leopold is internationally respected as a scientist and conservationist, a scholar, an outstanding teacher, and a philosopher. He is the individual who combined concepts from biology, ecology, and forestry for the first time. Leopold's leadership was fundamentally through the distillation and promotion of an ecological attitude between people and the land expressed in his essays, speeches, editorials, and letters. His work has been instrumental in the formulation of policy that set a precedent for the designating of wilderness areas.

Leader as Counselor

The counselor is a second type of face-to-face or direct leader. The term counselor is used in several diverse recreation, parks, and leisure settings to designate one who advises an individual or group concerning behaviors, activities, values, decisions, and the like. For example, a camp counselor who is assigned care of approximately eight children is tantamount to in loco parentis for day-to-day living situations (rest, bathing, eating, cleanliness, deportment, and so on) plus the teaching of one or more skills related to the program of a camp program. It might be said that, of all face-to-face leaders, the camp counselor is expected to be the most versatile of all leaders (acting as parent, teacher, friend, and confidant). Interestingly, this leader usually is the youngest and least experienced of all face-to-face or activity leaders. The camp counselor is on duty many hours of the day, on call at night, probably has only 24 hours off each week, and holds a temporary job that lasts from two to ten weeks. The sample job description in Figure 3.2 illustrates the diversity of the camp counselor's responsibilities.

The leisure counselor, on the other hand, may be one of the most educated and experienced of leaders. Leisure counselors focus on helping clients understand their leisure potential and on finding ways to add some meaning to their lives through the leisure experience. Leisure counselors generally work with one client at a time and must be trained and knowledgeable in counseling methods, leisure opportunities, the scope of leisure, leisure activities, and leisure values.

In communities where a need is found for someone to help the residents of economically deprived neighborhoods achieve successful recreation, leisure, and social experiences, youth workers are employed. These leaders, often called detailed youth workers, roving leaders or sometimes youth counselors, street club workers, or street gang leaders, have been employed in cities such as New York, Philadelphia, Los Angeles, Washington, D.C., and Richmond, Virginia, since the 1950s. The inhabitants of inner city areas, the impoverished, and the hard-to-reach rarely seek out or know of organized forms of recreation, such as sports leagues, tournaments, talent shows, arts and crafts, and other special interest programs. Their recreation usually involves random movements from one place to another, with long stretches of boredom and frequent acts against society.

A youth worker can provide face-to-face leadership different from that normally given by a recreation worker. The recreation programs designed to reach and serve low-income, hard-to-reach youth and young adults must be concerned

Life is like a dogsled team. If you ain't the lead dog, the scenery never changes.

Lewis Grizzard

Marin County Outdoor School at Walker Creek Ranch

1700 Marshall-Petaluma Road

Petaluma, CA 95952

Residential Outdoor Science School for 5th and 6th grade students located at Walker Creek Ranch, one hour north of San Francisco. Pristine setting, 1,740 acres, abundant wildlife, 27 miles of hiking trails, creeks, pond, bay woodlands, grassland, close to tide pools, redwood forests. School program operates September through June. Camp Soulejule (Soo-la-whoo-lay), arts and ecology summer camp program operates during summer months.

Job Title:	Garden Intern
Job Description:	Facilitation of organic garden-based activities and curriculum and supervision of 5th/6th grade students. Active care and up keep of the garden. Intern will assist with the design and implementation of garden components and care procedures. Provide additional support to the Ranch programs as a substitute Naturalist. Internship runs for 12 months from approximately July 15, 2004 to June 15, 2005. (Possible start in May 2004).
Qualifications:	Completion of college level course work in Agriculture, Horticulture, Natural Sciences and Environmental Education. The ideal candidate would have strong interpersonal skills, a basic understanding of organic gardening techniques, and experience working with children.
Salary and Benefits:	Room and Board, plus $54/day stipend ($270/week). Minimal Camp Health Insurance also provided.

Figure 3.2: Internship job description for face-to-face leadership position.

with the "how" of reaching them, as well as the "what" of serving them. The youth leader usually spends weeks, sometimes months, establishing rapport with individuals and groups. This leader starts at the level of the group. This is not a short-term undertaking. The leader works with the youth for a longtime, sometimes several years. The final test of the youth leader's success is when he or she is no longer needed.

> Management is doing things right; leadership is doing the right things.
>
> *Peter F. Drucker*

Youth workers are sometimes assigned to a specific area of the inner city. They are there to strengthen, extend, and stimulate the participation of hard-to-reach youth in wholesome recreation programs. They do so by assisting them in utilizing, to the fullest, community resources in the educational, health, employment, and related social service areas. The leader may be a resident of the neighborhood, often a member of a minority group. The leader is often a peer of the participant who shares a common background, language, ethnic

American Camping Association New York Section	
The American Camping Association - NY Section is seeking staff for its 300 accredited member camps throughout the Northeast. If you have a love for the great outdoors, enjoy working with children, and want to experience a rewarding and memorable summer, then a camp job is for you. Camp staff get to live, work and play in the outdoors, while making a difference in the lives of children. The Staff Placement Service at ACA-NY can assist you in finding the perfect summer job. Just fill out an online application at www.acampjob4u.org and camps that have openings in what you are looking for will contact you directly. It's that easy. Apply now and secure a great summer camp job for 2004!	
Job Title:	Summer Camp Counselor / Activity Specialist
Qualifications:	Experience working with children is a plus, though not required. Some college courses preferred. Those applying for medical, waterfront, or outdoor adventure positions should have the appropriate certifications. When applying for specialist positions, please have some experience in the area you would like to teach (ex: art, sports, drama, etc). Please apply online at www.acampjob4u.org!

Figure 3.3: Camp Counselor job description

origin, style, and interests. Because of his or her ability to work comfortably with the community, the worker is viewed as a community advocate, interpreting its needs, interests, and concerns. A sample job description for a youth leader is shown in Figure 3.4.

Leader as Coach

A third type of face-to-face leadership is the coach who facilitates team leadership. The word team usually brings to mind a competition of two groups vying against each other for higher scores. Certainly football, basketball, baseball, volleyball, soccer, and all other team sports need leaders, either as coaches, instructors, or captains, to guide the members toward a cooperative effort that can ultimately lead to winning. A team leader may also direct a group involved in fund raising or lead any other group with a common predetermined goal that can be reached only through successful, cooperative group efforts. The coach should perpetuate a group spirit, which means that individual success can be accomplished only through the cooperative efforts of everyone working together and each contributing according to such diverse, specific assigned roles as catcher, neighborhood coordinator, and so on.

> I'd like to be a bigger and more knowledgeable person 10 years from now than I am today. I think that, for all of us, as we grow older, we must discipline ourselves to continue expanding, broadening, learning, keeping our minds active and open.
>
> *Clint Eastwood*

It is usually expected that a coach can arouse enthusiasm, direct specific actions, demand discipline, arouse positive

Clemson University/Youth Learning Institute

246 Poole Agricultural Center
Clemson, SC 29634-0133

The Youth Learning Institute Centers are located in Summerton and Aiken. We provide a variety of programs including outdoor education, at-risk, adventure, leadership and summer camping to a variety of audiences from kids to adults of all walks of life. These are year round facilities that operate through Clemson University. Our goal is to positively impact the lives of the people we contact and to better prepare them for the lives ahead of them.

Job Title:	House Mother for New Horizons (At-Risk/Un-Wed Mothers Program)
Job Description:	Purpose and Scope: The Residential House Mother will work directly with the mother and child, providing 24-hour care and assistance. This position will function in a mentoring role in the development of life and parenting skills. The primary responsibilities will be to provide childcare during the mothers' absences and assist mothers in preparation of group meals. The House Mother will be a reliable resource for the mother and child, providing daily support and guidance and helping prepare mothers for life on her own. Responsibilities: • Provide 24-hour care for the child and mother. • Promote wellness through activities directed toward prevention and reduction of risk factors affecting the life of the mother and child. • Provide child care during the mothers' absence. • Assist the mothers in the preparation of meals for the group and their children. • Plan and participate in recreational and cultural activities for the mothers' children. • Participate in the development, implementation and documentation of the treatment plan for each mother and child. • Attend, as necessary, to the personal, health, and behavioral needs of the mothers.
Qualifications:	Be at least 21 years of age and possess a four-year college degree or combination of education and experience, experience in youth care and counseling preferred. • Possess a strong desire to help mother and child grow to overcome adversity. • Possess a valid driver's license with a good driving record, and obtain University certification for driving in SC. • Have the physical stamina and flexibility necessary to perform assigned duties. • Must have strong communication skills, an ability to set limits, and model appropriate behavior. • Successfully complete background and drug screening. • An outdoor adventure experience or aptitude is recommended.
Salary and Benefits:	$400-$440 a week plus room, board, and insurance. EOE

Figure 3.4: Youth worker job description

goal-oriented emotions, resolve personality differences, and teach skills. In recreation and leisure services, the coach should possess the philosophy that what happens to the individual and to the group may be much more important than winning. In some municipalities exist regulations that each sports competition team is limited to X number of members, each of whom (regardless of skill) must play a designated minimum number of minutes each game—the leader of such a team is true team leader. In fund raising events, the final amount raised is the goal but it is not achieved at the expense of any individual on the team. A sample job description for a sports camp coach is seen in Figure 3.5.

Perseverance is the hard work you do after you get tired of doing the hard work you already did.

Newt Gingrich

The coach may be autocratic at times (obeying rules, accounting for money raised, delegating assignments), democratic at times (consensus on new projects or uniforms, brainstorming for new ideas, discussion of alternative recruiting strategies), but cannot display an attitude of laissez faire without weakening the function of the position. Functions of the coach will often include:
• Responsibility for liability;
• Responsibility for the medical fitness of the players;
• Responsibility for safe facilities;
• Knowledge of the need for plenty of liquids and how to administer them;
• Decisions on the number of games and practice sessions to hold;
• Knowledge of the rules;
• Ability to discipline players firmly and fairly;
• Maintaining personal emotional control;
• Encouraging and practicing cooperation;
• Demonstrating loyalty;
• Exemplifying perseverance; and,
• Responsibility for care of injuries.

SUPERVISORY LEADERSHIP

Supervisors or middle managers within recreation, parks, and leisure services organizations are also leaders. Supervisors provide direction to individuals, helping them to carry out their tasks and to resolve both personal and job-related problems. Supervisory leadership involves overseeing the work of others in such a way that they are helped to accomplish the goals of the recreation and leisure service organization. Supervisors are employed for their technical knowledge as well as for their human relations skills. They must have the ability to encourage, stimulate, motivate, and evaluate their subordinates. They often lead by example and are the individuals primarily responsible for assisting the direct, face-to-face leader in the accomplishment of his or her assigned tasks. Neipoth (1983) listed a number of activities that super-

Challenger Sports Corporation

757 Whitneys Landing Drive
Crownsville, MD 21032

Challenger Sports is the fastest growing camp company in the country with a mission to ignite a passion for sports in all children through fun, educational, and age appropriate camp programs. This year Challenger aims to coach 55,000 children throughout the USA in both Single and Multi Sports Camp Programs. In order to deliver our program Challenger is seeking to employ individuals who are great role models, who desire to work with children in a sports context, and who have the following qualities: reliability, enthusiasm, good communication skills, empathy, patience, and energy, along with an ability to coach one or more sport.

Job Title:	Summer Sports Camp Coach
Job Description:	As a camp coach you will be required to teach, lead, and be a friend to a group of young children aged anywhere from 4 – 12 years of age, both girls and boys. As a coach the primary responsibility is to ensure the child's safety and well-being and to help make the children's camp experience fun and rewarding. Responsibilities under the leadership of the Camp Director:

Responsibilities under the leadership of the Camp Director:
- Overall supervision of all children enrolled in the program.
- Utilizing the Challenger Curriculum plan in advance all daily coaching sessions including activity breaks.
- Organize and maintain all camp equipment, supplies and work areas.
- Document all accidents, injuries, incidents, complaints, and problems.
- Ensure Health and Safety precautions are met according to both Challenger's and the host organization guidelines.
- Contact camper's prior to start of camp.
- Meet, greet and communicate with parents.

Camp Director Responsibilities. As above but in addition, under the supervision of your Regional Director:
- Organize coaching groups, rotation of groups and daily plan to include before and after camp staff meetings.
- Supervision, monitoring, support and evaluation of coaches.
- Preparation and maintenance of coaches and children's records and files.
- Storage and administering of medication.
- Ensure documentation of all accidents, injuries, incidents, complaints and problems.
- Act as liaison between coaches and Regional Director, coaches and organizations site staff, camp and parents. Report daily to regional Director.
- Communicate details of camp activity to parents on day one of camp- calendar, first day letter. Ensure pre-camp calls are made.

(continued on next page)

Figure 3.5: Summer Sports Camp Coach job description

(continued from previous page)

	• Plan and direct Opening/Closing ceremonies and oversee writing of camper certificates and distribution of T-shirts.
Qualifications:	• Must be 18 years of age. • Experience playing at least one sport at High School level. • Experience working with children. • Provide own reliable transportation. • Successfully completed Criminal Background Check. • First Aid/CPR certification. • Able to relate to children, set an example as a role model, and show enthusiasm and professionalism at all times. • Director positions-Junior, Senior, or graduate status pursuing a degree in Physical Education, Recreation, Coaching, or Education preferred. • Physical demands of the job may include light lifting, sports demonstration and participation, and working in the outdoors. • Attendance at mandatory staff training.
Salary:	• Three-hour camp programs are typically Monday through Friday, 8:45 a.m. to 12:15 p.m. Coaches receive $140-$160 per week, directors receive $180-$200 per week. • Six-hour camp programs are typically Monday through Friday, 8:45 a.m.-3:15 p.m. Coaches receive $260-$280 per week, directors receive $310-$330 per week.

visors are responsible for when directing other staff members.

Teaching and Leading. Teaching is the communication of skills, knowledge, or values. It is the leadership process that helps the staff learn and understand what is necessary to achieve certain goals of the organization.

Selection of Staff. This process is sometimes the direct responsibility of the supervisor. If so the supervisor may also have the responsibility of developing a written job description, which gives the title of the position, the education and experience requirements, and the duties.

In-service Training. There are four types of training a supervisor may need to provide: (1) orientation to the job; (2) training related specifically to the position for which the employee was hired; (3) training to keep the worker up-to-date, and, (4) general career development.

Scheduling Staff. Besides providing the work assignments and hours that staff will work, other scheduling responsibilities may include outlining: (1) the various hours the facility will be open, (2) the general program responsibilities for at each site, (3) dates when staff meetings will be held, (4) when reports are due, and (5) when budgets are available for each department or site.

Evaluation. To enhance the effectiveness of staff members, the supervisor must evaluate staff performance. This may be accomplished with rating forms, observations, and review of the work produced by staff. These evaluation not only help the staff improve their performance but are also reviewed when employees are being considered for promotion.

Providing Resources. In most cases, it is the responsibility of the supervisor to make sure that the staff have the material, equipment, and help to carry out their duties.

Linking Administrative and Functional Levels. Supervisors are the link between administrators and face-to-face leaders. The supervisor is responsible for interpreting agency policies and other relevant information from administration to the workers at the service level.

Directing, Controlling, and Taking Corrective Action. There are times when a supervisor must be autocratic in their leadership approach and give staff members clear direction of the requirements of specific tasks that must be accomplished to meet the objectives of the organization. In addition, it may also be necessary for the supervisor to take discipline and corrective action when the performance of an individual staff member is inappropriate, such a coming to work late, taking supplies from work to home, or not following organizational policies.

Supervisors typically are concerned with carrying out professional or organizational responsibilities, and frequently there are times when a supervisor must share the process of exploring problems, making decisions, formulating plans, or agreeing on recommendations with co-workers. At these times, the supervisor is instrumental in helping members of the group define their objectives, maintain a strong group structure, develop plans for attaining their goals, carry out a course of action, and maintain a high level of cohesion and group satisfaction. In order to accomplish these purposes, the leader may need to carry out the following functions or may share them with the members of the group.

Initiating. Getting the action under way and keeping it going (examples are suggesting steps to be taken, pointing out goals).

A life spent in making mistakes is not only more honorable but more useful than a life spent doing nothing.

George Bernard Shaw

Setting the pace. Regulating the speed, influencing the direction and tempo of the group's work (examples are summarizing, pointing out time limits, restating goals).

Informing. Bringing information, both facts and opinions, to the group.

Supporting. Holding the group together and compromising on differences.

Evaluating. Helping the group evaluate its decisions, goals, or procedures (examples are testing for consensus, noting group processes).

Throughout the process, the role of the supervisor can include the following: (1) helping group members define the limits of the problem or challenge they face and decide which aspect(s) they intend to address; (2) encouraging all group members to express their ideas and implement ways to have all participate; (3) maintaining a cooperative atmosphere that eliminates stress and tension; and (4) keeping the deliberations of the group focused on the work to be accomplished, moving steadily from theoretical considerations to practical results and steps.

MANAGERIAL LEADERSHIP

Managerial leadership is that leadership which is provided by the organization's top administrators or executives. These individuals provide overall direction to the organization, establishing broad goals, providing motivation, engaging in long-range planning, establishing and administering reward systems, and overseeing those individuals who are directly accountable to them. Most organizations have a vertical organization structure that identifies the various departments and functional units of the recreation agencies (See Figure 3.6). In an organization that has vertical organizational structure, the authority, information, and decision-making moves from the top, then downward, through a number of supervisors and departments. Managerial leadership is also evidenced in the efforts of administrators or executives to interpret the organization's services, programs, and activities to its target population. In this sense, the manager guides a community's efforts in establishing and providing recreation, parks, and leisure services. Managerial leadership tends to be broader, more expansive, and more conceptual in nature than face-to-face or supervisory leadership.

When leading an organization, effective managerial leadership requires that the leader be attuned to the life cycle of

The essence of knowledge is, having it, to apply it; not having it, to confess your ignorance.

Confucius

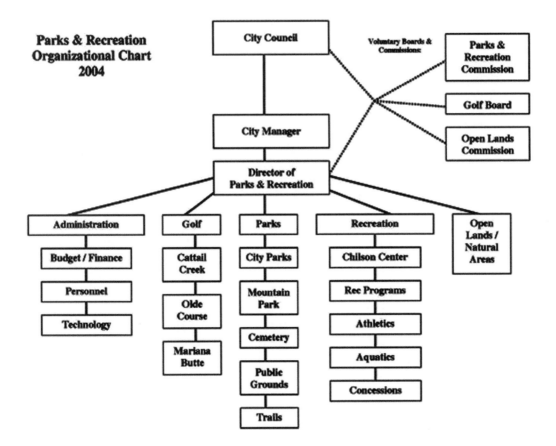

Figure 3.6: Organizational Chart of Loveland, Colorado Parks and Recreation

the organization or the development stage of the organization (Hesselbein, Goldsmith, & Beckhard, 1996). An organization may be in its initial development stage and just getting off the ground. A different organization may be a well-established institution. The manager's vision, guidance and planning must be in concert with the organization's life cycle; otherwise problems may result due to mismatched leadership action for the actual needs of the organization's culture and stage of development. Hesselbein, Goldsmith, and Beckhard (1996) list four different managerial leadership considerations in leading an organization.

Creating: The leader as animator. Energy is needed to get the organization off the ground. The leader must be the energy behind making the vision happen and transmit this energy into their subordinates. This energy is born out of the

LEADERSHIP: A POINT OF VIEW
FROM THE PROFESSION
Jody L. Stowers

Jody L. Stowers is Director, Parks & Recreation Department, City of Westerville, Ohio, which has a population of 36,000. The Park & Recreation Department is a National Gold Medal award winning agency consisting of 55 full-time and over 400 part-time dedicated staff. The Department's annual operating budget is over $7.5 million dollars and the Department generates over $3 million dollars in revenue. In 1998, citizens of Westerville rallied around the PROS (Parks, Recreation, Open Space) 2000 strategic plan initiatives and passed a 1/2 of 1 percent income tax that has generated over $27 million dollars for capital improvement projects. The citizen-driven initiative has lead to the completion of a 96,600 sq. ft. Community Center, the development of a sports complex, a BMX/Skateboard park, an outdoor amphitheater, a community-wide bikeway/leisure path system, a new six acre neighborhood park, improvements to an existing baseball complex and neighborhood park, the development and renovation of a historical barn and homestead park, and the acquisition of over 50 acres of land for future parks. The Department now manages over 500 acres of open space in 39 sites, 18 miles of bikeways, a community center, a senior center, a program center, and an outdoor pool complex, and offers over 1900 programs for all ages and abilities.

On leadership. . . .a person who has passion toward a vision and has the ability to motivate others to take the steps necessary to turn that vision into reality.

Leadership and success. . . . our success is largely due to leaders at all levels creating an environment in which there is a contagious reaction in which everyone wants to get involved and participate in planning and achieving the task at hand. Frontline leaders often are the only contact our citizens . . .If the participant doesn't have a quality experience it directly effects their impression. . . Supervisory and management levels need strong leadership skills to develop and implement quality leisure programs.

The exemplary leader. . . . competent, always looking for ways to improve, good organizational and administrative skills; passionate, speaks from the heart; visionary, knows how to achieve, innovate, and change; good communicator, listens well, can clearly express oneself, and can gain group consensus; motivator, a people person, enthusiastic, a sense of humor; accountable, trustworthy, takes responsibility and follows through; has consistently high standards set for themselves and sets obtainable high standards for their staff and organization.

Leadership in action. . . . dedicated, full of energy and passion . . . strength is people skills; clear communication of expectations, patience and encouragement of others, sets an excellent example and is a role model, always positive, well organized, willing to try new things and take on more responsibility.

leader's strong personal convictions, which motivates the leader and builds excitement in others. These leaders breathe life into the organization.

Building: The leader as a creator of culture. To build the organization culture, the leader must be able to transfer the beliefs, values, and basic assumptions into the beliefs and values of the subordinates. The leader will model the behavior that he or she would like the subordinates to copy in order for employees to identify with and thereby internalize and support the beliefs, values, and assumptions of the organization.

Maintaining: The leader as the sustainer of culture. As an organization grows there must also be individuals in the organization who are good at the finance, planning, marketing, and human resources functions. There may come a time when it is necessary to consolidate the elements needed to function and grow. To maintain the organizational culture, it may be necessary to "institutionalize" the successful elements of the organization and give them permanence and stability. Leaders need to look at what worked on a small scale with a young organization and work on a more global scale with maturing employees.

Changing: The leader as the change agent. Leaders need to think like change agents: not only acquire new concepts and skills, but also unlearn things that are no longer serving the organization. To do this, a leader must look at how to evolve the organization by continually building on its strengths and letting the weaknesses atrophy over time.

CIVIC OR COMMUNITY LEADERSHIP

Public recreation, parks, and leisure services agencies promote and encourage involvement of citizens and laypersons in the governance and operation of their programs, services, and activities. This is evidenced by the large number of community leaders serving as board members, commissioners, advisory group members, and individuals serving as volunteers in programs dealing with youth sports, older persons, cultural arts, and so on. Individuals engaged in this type of leadership may act as policymakers, who represent citizens' interests. They may provide leadership by interpreting needs, providing input regarding the distribution of organizational resources, and actively promoting the work of the agency to the community as a whole. The degree of support and leadership provided by individuals assisting recreation and leisure service agencies as volunteers in the capacities mentioned earlier can often determine the success or failure of the organization's efforts.

SUMMARY

Leadership is found at all levels within recreation, parks, and leisure service organizations. The leader is an individual who leads others by guiding, directing, and influencing their behavior. Among the major responsibilities of leaders are building camaraderie and cohesiveness, identifying and defining goals, developing other methods to achieve goals, organizing the work of others, motivating others' potential, evaluating the work of others, representing others, developing others, establishing a group atmosphere, and promoting the ideals of the profession. A leader can be appointed or elected, or can assume his or her position by emerging spontaneously to meet group needs, or because he or she possesses charismatic qualities that others find attractive.

Leadership is a process by which the leader assists individuals and groups to identify and achieve their goals. Successful leaders are often able to influence the interpretation of group goals and processes. Their followers usually perceive them as open-minded, rational, consistent, and non-manipulative. Individuals may follow a leader because they do not want to become involved in the leadership task themselves, because they are satisfied with the leader's work, or because they do not have the appropriate experience to lead or because of a combination of these factors. It is important for the leader to remember that where there are no followers, there are no leaders.

Recreation, parks, and leisure services leadership can be thought of as a process that helps individuals and groups meet their needs while at the same time meeting the goals of the recreation, parks, and leisure services organization. Leadership is found and practiced at four levels within recreation, parks, and leisure services organizations: direct or face-to-face, supervision, managerial, and civic or community levels. Effective leadership helps participants meet their leisure needs, wants, and interests. When working with participants to facilitate the leisure experience, the leader should attempt to share expectations, build trust, communicate effectively, share decision making, foster a sense of cooperation, create a sense of risk or spontaneity, provide positive reinforcement, and establish a social and emotional bond with the participant.

▆▆▆▆ Discussion Questions

1. What is the role of a instructor? Identify five (5) settings in which recreation and leisure services are delivered where these types of roles exist. Name ten (10) specific job titles reflecting this type of leadership.

2. What is the role of a coach? Identify five (5) settings in which recreation and leisure services are delivered where these types of roles exist. Name ten (10) specific job titles reflecting this type of leadership.

3. What is the role of a counselor? Identify five (5) settings in which recreation and leisure services are delivered where these types of roles exist. Name two (2) specific job titles reflecting this type of leadership.

4. Define the term in loco-parentis. How are camp counselors affected by this role?

5. What are the basic purposes of supervision? Pretend that you have access to one gym that has a storage area for equipment and the restrooms. Prepare the rules and regulations needed for the operation of an after-school playground program.

6. In what ways are leading, instructing, and supervision related?

7. What are the characteristics of effective supervision? In what ways do effective supervisors differ from ineffective supervisors? Outline the steps to be taken to dismiss a recreation aid in your after-school program.

8. What is the role of a managerial administrator? Create a job description of a professional recreation position (sports specialist, outdoor leader, etc.). Prepare the administrative rules and guidelines for overtime work and pay.

9. Organizations have a life cycle. What roles must the leader be able to accomplish to match with the organization's culture and stage of development?

10. Create an organization chart for a recreation agency. List common job titles for each position in your recreation agency from executive through recreation trainee and interns. Include job responsibilities for each position.

THE CASE FOR LEADERSHIP

When lightning strikes: What would you do?

Points of Consideration

The City of Cedar Center has just built a new indoor aquatic facility. The community is excited about this new facility, for it replaced the outdoor pool that was built in 1959 and was literally falling apart. This new aquatic center has both a 50-meter lap pool and a leisure pool with a family slide, an inverted slide, a drop slide, a wave pool, rock architecture, and diving boards. The Cedar Center Aquatic Center is also expanding the number of programs to include aqua-aerobics, aqua-jogging, water-walking, lap swimming, training and competitive events for swimming and water polo, learn-to-swim programs for all ages and abilities, adequate water space for unstructured play, and various water therapy programs for rehabilitative purposes.

During the process of updating the risk management policies for the new pools, there was a heated debate whether the pools should be closed during an electrical storm. The director of the aquatic facility is opposed to closing the indoor pools. The city manager is in disagreement and he feels that the policy should be that everyone should get out of the pool. Listed below is each person's point of view.

Director of Aquatic Facilities: The pools at this facility are totally enclosed in structural steel. These pools are not under a fabricated dome or mostly glass enclosure. The steel of the building shunts the electrical current in the same way that people in cars are protected during a lightning storm. In addition, there has never been a lightning fatality at an indoor pool, compared to the thousands of people who drown each year and the hundreds of neck injuries that occur each year when people are swimming and diving. Pulling people out of the pools creates more chaos and increases the potential for accidents when people are scared and emotional. A decision to close the indoor pools during a lightning storm should be driven by facts, not fear.

City Manager: It is better to err on the side of caution and get everyone out of the indoor pools during an electrical storm. There have been incidents inside pool buildings of lightning destroying the circulation pumps, injury to employees who were touching the electrical panels, and concrete footings of a pool slide being blown apart. We do know that there have been lightning accidents in houses, apartments, and offices where people have been in contact with water in places such as sinks, tubs, or showers

Questions of Consideration

- Who do you agree with: the director of the aquatic facilities or the city manager? Why?
- If you were to follow the city manager's advice and get people out of the pool, what procedures would you recommend, from who makes the decision when to get everyone out to when it would be safe to resume swimming again?
- Identify safe and unsafe locations within the aquatics facility that you would want identified for your patrons when there is an electrical storm.

As a recreation, parks, and leisure services professional, there are many career opportunities available in working for the City of Cedar Center in the recreation division, the parks division, the cultural division, or the visitor and tourism division. The recreation division has four departments with career opportunities recreation programs, athletics, aquatics, or concessions. The parks division, has three departments, which include city parks, the cemetery, or the hiking and biking trails. The cultural division has an art center as well as the public library. The visitor and tourism division has two offices which include conventions and visitors or chamber of commerce.

Identify an organization chart for a recreation agency that includes different levels of leadership. At what level of leadership do you envision yourself initially working? At what level of leadership do you envision yourself working in five years? What is your ultimate level of leadership? What do you need to do to prepare for each level of leadership?

▰▰▰References

Hesselbein, F., Goldsmith, M., & Beckhard, R. (Eds.). (1996). *The leader of the future*. San Francisco, CA: Jossey-Bass.

Niepoth, E. W. (1983). *Leisure Leadership: Working with people in recreation and park settings.* Englewood Cliffs, NJ: Prentice-Hall.

Part Two—The Group

CHAPTER

4

Leadership
Across the
Lifespan

LEARNING OBJECTIVES

1. To classify the stages of human development and its relation to the leisure experience.
2. To explain the factors that can affect the social health of youth.
3. To describe goals and principles of youth development programs and types of services.
4. To identify demographic characteristics of adults and the benefits of participation in a variety of recreation, parks, and leisure services programs in their lives.

KEY TERMS

- Face-to-face leadership
- Youth Worker
- Children
- Adolescence
- Adults
- Youth Development
- Youth Potential
- Competence
- Older Adult
- Attitudes and Stereotypes
- Community-Based Programs
- Adult Daycare Facilities
- Long-Term Care Facilities

INTRODUCTION

Generally speaking, recreation, parks, and leisure services programs and activities are designed to enhance the quality of life of all children, youth and adult participants. There is some similarity as to the recreation, parks, and leisure services needs among the different age groups. All individuals have a desire to grow and develop, to have friends, to engage in constructive and worthwhile activities, to test themselves, and to engage in physical, social, intellectual, and other types of activity. However, a leader needs to be aware of an individual's particular stage of development and should attempt to gain an understanding of the capabilities of each participant and adjust their program to reflect these variations. This will enable the leader to provide a program that will be interesting and challenging to each participant. In addition, the leader should have a firm understanding of the goals that participants should accomplish. In other words, the leader should have a plan of action for the activity and should have in mind the outcomes that should result from participation in the activity.

This chapter presents a general overview of the developmental stages across the lifespan, specifically addressing leadership variations when working with children and youth. We will also discuss common stereotypes applied to older persons, settings in which programs for older persons may occur, and the benefits of participation in leisure programs and activities.

LEADERSHIP AND THE LEISURE LIFE CYCLE

As individuals progress through their lives, they go through different stages. This progression through the lifecycle affects the form and function of leisure, which in turn impacts leisure activity and interest (see Table 4.1). These changes in recreation, parks, and leisure activities and interests take place for a number of reasons such as the physical changes that occur in the body as one ages; the social changes as one builds a variety of relationships with others through friendship, marriage, and raising a family; and the cognitive changes one might experience in respect to education, career and work. Two of the earliest researchers to investigate the importance of the life cycle in relation to leisure activities were Rapaport and Rapaport (1975). They concluded that the changes that occur in what and why individuals participate in activities are related to their developmental stage. Kleiber and Kelly (1980) examined the leisure activities of individuals and the fluctuation and constraints on leisure over the life cycle and concluded that engagement in leisure activities is an important part of the socialization process. This socialization process continues to develop over the life cycle.

Build a dream and the dream will build you.

Robert Schuller

Table 4.1: Stages of Human Development

Life Stage	Age	Developmental Characteristics and Activities
Early Childhood	2-5	This age is marked by the development of free expression of skills in movement and thought, such as crawling, pushing, pulling, tumbling, climbing, running, pretend games, rhythm activities.
Middle Childhood	6-11	There is more concern over how well a task is done (task mastery) at this stage. These children are goal oriented and activities become less spontaneous and more carefully planned. Self-testing is important: Hunt and chase games, catch and throw games, guessing games, noisy games.
Adolescence	12-19	Strong loyalties to peers and a preoccupation with physical appearances mark this age group. Goal-oriented fun prepares the individual in this group for independence. Coeducational social activities, socials with same sex, team games and partner sports, performance activities, outdoor activity, whatever is "cool", "no parents allowed."
Young Adulthood	20-40	This group is self-directed and interested in group recreation. Socials, fitness, mini-education courses and workshops.
Middle Adulthood	40-65	Family members are active partners in leisure pursuits: Family parties with eating/picnics/games/movies are popular, outdoor activities, all age activities, mini-education courses and workshops.
Late Adulthood	65+	This stage has marked decrease in strength, reflex, speed, and coordination, yet this group experiences an increase in leisure time for fun, socializing, and learning. Less strenuous physical activity is enjoyable: Socials, mini courses and workshops, travel.

A LEGACY OF LEADERSHIP
Fran P. Mainella

Fran P. Mainella currently serves as the Director of the National Park Service. The 16th director in the history of the National Park Service, she is the first woman to ever be appointed to this position. Mainella has over 30 years of experience working in the park and recreation field. She has served as Director of the Division of Recreation and Parks for the Florida Department of Environmental Protection. Prior to that position, she served as Executive of the Florida Parks and Recreation Association. In addition, she has served as the Director of Recreation for Lake Park, Florida, and as an Assistant Center Director for the Tallahassee (Florida) Parks and Recreation Department.

In her current role as Director of the National Park Service, Mainella is responsible for overseeing 20,000 full-time and seasonal employees with a budget of $2.7 billion. The National Park Service administers 388 park areas covering over 83 million acres in 49 states, the District of Columbia, American Samoa, Guam, Puerto Rico, Saipan, and the Virgin Islands. These areas have been established as symbols of evidence of our history; they include battlefields/military parks, cemeteries, heritage areas, historical parks/sites, monuments/ memorials, parks (e.g. National), parkways, rivers/recreation areas, seashores/lakeshores, and trails. The National Park system was started with the establishment of Yellowstone National Park in 1872. The National Park Service was established in 1916 ". . . to promote and regulate the use of the . . . national parks . . . which purpose is to conserve the scenery and the natural and historic objects and the wild life therein and to provide for the enjoyment of the same in such manner and by such means as will leave them unimpaired for the enjoyment of future generations" (National Park Service Organic Act, 16 U.S.C.1.).

Mainella is the recipient of the 2002 Walter T. Cox Award for her sustained achievement in public service; the 2001 Senator Bob Williams Award for her work for historic preservation; the 2002 Harold D. Meyer Professional Award from the National Recreation and Park Association Southern Regional Council; the 1999 Distinguished Service Award from the National Association of State Park Directors; the 1998 Pugsley Medal from the American Academy of Park and Recreation Administration; and the 1998 William Penn Mott, Jr. Award for excellence presented by, the National Society for Park Resources. In addition, while she served as Director of Florida state's park system, it was awarded the "State Park's Gold Medal" from the National Sporting Goods Association. She has served as the past president of the National Recreation and Park Association and the National Association of State Park Directors. Mainella is a member of the Florida Tourism Commission, the statewide Eco-Tourism/Heritage Tourism Committee, National Recreation and Park Association, National Association of State Park Directors, Florida Recreation and Park Association, National Society of Park Resources, National Association of State Recreation Liaison Officers, American Academy of Park and Recreation Administration, Tallahassee Society of Association Executives, and Zonta International.

When appointed as the Director of the National Park Service, Secretary of the U.S. Department of Interior Gale Norton praised Mainella as "an extraordinarily talented public servant with a unique blend of skills and experience, that will serve her and the Administration well as Director of the National Park Service."

LEADING EARLY AND MIDDLE-AGED CHILDREN

Perhaps the most important factor that the leader should keep in mind when working with early and middle aged children is to make the experience enjoyable and fun for all. For children in the early childhood stage, the leader should create an environment that is warm and friendly, attempt to involve the parents, and both parents and leader should be patient and relaxed. Often simple games can be used with young children to teach and have fun at the same time. When giving instruction to very young children, the leader must bear in mind that children at this age have a short attention span and cannot be given lengthy instructions. Rather, a young child will respond best to short directions supported by demonstrations and then by repetition of the directions again. Children in early childhood are often not well coordinated; the leader should keep this factor in mind.

For children in a middle childhood stage, the leader may have to make a special effort to work effectively with group members that progress more quickly or more slowly than the majority of the group. The leader may want to have fast learners engage in extra practice of more difficult skills, for example, so that more time can be spent with slow learners to help them overcome some of their challenges. Generally speaking, children between the ages of six and eight will progress more slowly and more unevenly than children who are nine and older. As with all children, the leader will want to attempt to make the activities a fun, enjoyable, and rewarding process. The leader should exhibit assured confidence. If children at this age feel that their leader is competent and assured, the children themselves will gain confidence. It is also important that the leader keep children at this age busy and active. They are generally a very responsive age group to work with if the activities are presented in an enjoyable way, are demonstrated well, and are presented in a supportive atmosphere, free of ridicule.

A NEED FOR YOUTH LEADERS

Working with youth is a challenging task. In many ways leading youth programs and services is one of the most rewarding professional experiences, yet at the same time it can be very demanding. Recently, great concern has been expressed regarding the social health and well-being of today's youth. As a result, many recreation, parks, and leisure services

> Do not confuse motion and progress. A rocking horse keeps moving but does not make any progress.
>
> *Alfred A. Montapert*

organizations are devoting more energy and organizational resources to this age grouping. The Carnegie Corporation (1992) has written:

> America's interest in youth waxes and wanes. Periods of intense social reform lasting one or sometimes several decades occur after longer periods of indifference and neglect. One such surge came around the turn of the century, when the reformers of the Progressive Era worked to protect and support youth through improved services, laws, and other policies. In recent times, however, America has been in a period of indifference and neglect, especially regarding low income rural and urban areas, and the violence is everywhere: public schools in many parts of the country have deteriorated and the quality of public education has fallen, city parks and recreation centers are dilapidated, financial support for facilities and programs for young people is decreasing. It is the view of the report that the time for a new era of reform, requiring leadership and collective effort, has arrived.

Interestingly, the Carnegie Corporation reports that the greatest challenges to youth come during non-school, discretionary time hours. Citing a study conducted by Timmer, Eccles, and O'Brien (1985), funded by the Carnegie Corporation, "about 40 percent of adolescents' waking hours are discretionary, not committed to other activities (such as eating, school, homework, chores, or working for pay) [and] many young adolescents spend virtually all of this discretionary time without companionship or supervision from responsible adults" (p. 28). Obviously, the challenges are great; however, opportunities are also great. When youth are alone or with peers, they are often at significant risk. They may engage in inappropriate or illegal activities. Pressure from peers and others is great. "Many adolescents have not been taught to take care of themselves, how to handle emergencies, and how to cope with negative pressures from peers or adults" (Carnegie Corporation, 1992 p. 33). Those individuals working with youth have a great opportunity to influence their behaviors in constructive and positive ways. Positive interactions between youth and leaders create opportunities for resourcefulness, responsibility, and reliability.

Who Are Our Youth?

Youth is a term used to define a period of life between childhood and maturity. It is also referred to as adolescence. The

You must have long-term goals to keep you from being frustrated by short-term failures.

Charles C. Noble

term adolescence was promoted around the turn of the century by G. Stanley Hall (1904). Adolescence can be thought of as a stage of human development. It is a time of great physical, social, intellectual, and moral development. The French sociologist Newman suggests that we are who we have become by the age of seventeen. In other words, he believes that our primary self-concept is established during our adolescence. Feelings of competence, social well-being, and other important life skills are formed during this life period and are carried with individuals throughout their adult lives.

In America today there are over 40 million adolescents. In other words, "nearly one in seven Americans is between the ages of ten and nineteen" (U.S. Bureau of Census, 2000). This figure will grow to over 42 million by the year 2020. When viewed by race and ethnicity, white Caucasian youth make up about 68 percent of the total youth population, 15 percent are African American, 17 percent are Hispanic, 3.5 percent are Asian/Pacific Islanders, and one percent Native Americans. From 1990 to 2000, the number of individuals under the age of 18 increased by 13 percent; currently such individuals make up 26 percent of the total United States population.

Numerous studies have been conducted to determine the social health of youth in America today. Such factors as physical well being, drug and substance abuse, educational achievement, teenage suicide rates, and others suggest that the social health of youth has declined over the past several decades. Edginton and Edginton (1994) have written concerning current social trends that may influence youth today. They relate the following:

Physical Health. A 1990 national commission reported, "For the first time in the history of this country, young people are less healthy and less prepared to take their places in society than were their parents" (National Commission on the Role of the School and the Community in Improving Adolescent Health, 1990).

Social Health. Social health includes such factors as success in school, being substance-free, and other behaviors in accordance with social mores, or what is considered "normal" in society. According to a study by the Fordham Institute, the social health of youth in the United States dropped almost 50 percent within the last 20 years (Jennings, 1989). Research for the Carnegie Commission states that approximately one half of youth between 10 and 17 are at risk of failing at school, drug abuse, becoming an adolescent parent, or delinquent behavior (Ooms & Herendeen, 1989).

Being tolerant does not mean that I share another's belief. But it does mean that I acknowledge another one's right to believe, and obey, his own conscience.

Viktor Frankl

Physical/Emotional Abuse. Depending on the definition of abuse used in reporting incidents, the following are reported. Mistreatment of children increased between 60 percent and 150 percent during the 1990s. Youth ages 12 to 14 were found to be abused at a higher rate than any other age group, according to the U.S. Department of Health and Human Service (http://www.hhs.gov).

Family Structure/Patterns. Family structure and family patterns have changed greatly in the last two decades. It is predicted that nearly all children in the six- to twelve-year-old age group will need out-of-school care by 1995 (Scales, 1991).

As one can see, youth today are challenged. Recreation, parks, and leisure services and leisure service programs and services can play a key role in helping to support the positive development of youth. Recreation, parks, and leisure services programs and services provide numerous opportunities and avenues for positive development. Constructive use of the leisure of youths can help promote and foster greater self-awareness, social skills, physical development, and emotional maturity, among other factors.

Pro-Social Youth Development

There are a number of prevailing philosophies of working with youth. One is to view youth as being at risk. The work of the recreation, parks, and leisure services leader, viewing youth from this orientation, is to provide treatment and prevention programs that enable youth to cope with negative situations such as alcohol and drug abuse, misuse of free time, and so on. Another way of viewing youth is to see them as individuals who have potential. The work of the recreation, parks, and leisure services professional using this orientation is one of helping youth become better. The goal is to help build youth into self-reliant, independent, and wise adult decision makers. This approach to working with youth is a pro-social approach and focuses on helping youth to develop life skills and assets that will carry into adult life. It is often referred to as pro-social youth development. Numerous ways exist to think of and define youth development. Edginton and Oliveira (1995) have suggested that the concept of youth development is multidimensional. They write that it can be viewed from a human growth, philosophical, and/or programming perspective. Although there is no universal definition of youth development, one that seems to have gained favor among professionals is to view the idea of youth development in terms of the competencies that youth need to demonstrate or can gain from participation in a recreation, parks, or leisure services program.

Coleman (1974) has suggested that competence should be developed in three basic areas: personal competence, a sense of social maturity, and a sense of identity and self-esteem. Perhaps these could be stated as general objectives for youth. Table 4.2 presents information defining each one of these areas. Another perspective is offered by Pittman and Wright (1991). These authors have suggested a set of competencies that are desirable ends for programs emphasizing youth development. As adapted by Edginton and Edginton (1994, p. 85), the competencies are as follows.

> We make a living by what we get, we make a life by what we give.
>
> *Winston Churchill*

Health/physical competence. Youth need to have good current health status and appropriate knowledge, attitudes, and behaviors exercise good diet, nutrition to ensure future health.

Personal/social competence. It is important that youth gain: intrapersonal skills (ability to understand personal emotions, have self-discipline); interpersonal skills (ability to work with others, develop friendships and relationships through communication, cooperation, empathizing, negotiating); coping/system skills (ability to adapt, assume responsibility); and judgment skills (plan, make decisions, solve problems).

Cognitive/creative competence. Youth need to develop: a broad base of knowledge; ability to appreciate/participate in areas of creative expression; good oral and

Table 4.2
Competencies for Youth

Personal Competence	Social Maturity	Sense of Identity & Self-Esteem
• the cognitive skills and non-cognitive skills necessary for economic independence and for occupational competence	• enlarged horizons through experiences with persons differing in social class, subculture, and age	• personal competence and social maturity
• the capability to effectively manage one's own affairs	• a sense of responsibility, gained by having the experience of having others dependent on one's actions	
• the capability to be a consumer, not only of goods, but of the cultural riches of the civilization	• leadership and membership skills, gained through involvement in interdependent activities directed toward collective goals	
• the capability for engaging in intense, concentrated involvement in an activity		

written language skills; problem-solving and analytical skills; and ability to learn or an interest in learning and achieving.

Vocational competence. It is important for youth to develop: a broad understanding or awareness of vocational (and avocational) options and steps to act on choices; and adequate preparation for a career, understanding the value and function of work and/or leisure.

Citizenship competencies (ethics and preparation). Youth need to understand their nation's and community's history and values, and form a desire to contribute the nation and community.

The focus on competencies suggests that as youth master each of the above areas, their self-concept is enhanced.

Johnson (1992) has written that the process of youth development involves transforming the lives of youth. Recreation, parks, and leisure services leaders using youth development strategies are involved in empowering youth to transform their lives. Johnson has provided a set of guidelines that can be useful in planning, organizing, and implementing recreation, parks, and leisure services programs for youth built on the principles of youth development. These are as follows:

> All young people have a right to equal access to resources and opportunities. Youth development necessitates shared power and responsibility. Leadership is collaborative and communicative.

> Youth development connects self, parents, family, culture, and community. Youth development should be taught in a multicultural context.

> Program staff and youth planning boards reflect the youth development thrust. Youth and families are involved in planning, decision-making, and implementation.

> Youth are viewed as a productive resource, rather than a problem. Community-based organizations provide support.

> Youth development supports youth to become active in issues important to their lives.

> Youth are involved in the planning process in terms of conducting surveys, setting agendas, shaping programs, and leading programs.

You are a very special person – become what you are.

Desmond M. Tutu

Programs can be approached from the needs of youth or the needs of adults (e.g., getting kids off the street, alleviating social problems). It is important that programs are based on helping youth meet their needs.

A youth development program is not based on the deficiencies of youth. A youth development approach invests in programs for the whole young person, rather than as a young person with specific problems.

Youth development occurs in programs where leaders are trained in terms of principles of youth development and working with youth. It will not occur in programs that are led by paid workers who don't care if kids play basketball for eight hours.

No single organization, program, or institution can ensure the healthy development of children. Schools are a part of this web, as are many other organizations.

Youth need to be our number one priority in terms of effort and funding, not a distant priority behind roads, stadiums, and other factors.

Too much emphasis is placed on academic competency and classroom learning and not enough emphasis is placed on experiential learning.

Youth leaders and organizations often put the cart before the horse and focus on fixing problems related to youth before they look at underlying principles of youth development. Youth development is often "defined" in terms of what we wish youth to be, or not to be. Leaders focus on fixing youth, as opposed to preparing them for the future.

> The best measures of a person's character are (a) how he treats people who can't do him any good, and (b) how he treats people who can't fight back.
>
> *Abigail Van Buren*

What does a competent youth look like? If you as a recreation, parks, and leisure services leader were successful in developing an individual into a mature, capable, and positive individual, what specific behaviors would you be looking for? The Carnegie Council on Adolescent Development suggests that a competent individual would be best defined as: (1) an intellectually reflective person, one with good problem-solving skills, good oral and written expression, and an appreciation of other cultures and languages; (2) a person en route to a lifetime of meaningful works, one who is aware of career options, understands the importance of formal education, has the ability to learn, and has pursued a course of study that keeps occupational options open; (3) a good citizen, one who accepts responsibility for and connection to the world community; (4) a caring and ethical individual, one who recognizes the distinction between good and bad, understands the importance of developing and maintaining close relationships, embraces virtues such as courage, honesty, tolerance, and caring and demonstrates these through sustained service to others; and (5) a healthy person, one who is physically and mentally fit, has a self-image of competence and strength based on being good at something, has developed self-understanding and appropriate coping skills.

Edginton and Oliveira (1995a) have identified the following orientations to working with youth: (1) leisure, (2) sports/fitness, (3) social services, (4) character building, (5) religious, (6) vocational/career, (7) advocacy/social policy, and (8) social pedagogy. These authors write that the goals, assumptions of working with youth, basic values, program formats, and professional roles may change according to the type of orientation selected by a youth service organization. The larger point to be made is that multiple and diverse strategies can be used to provide services for youth. Also, strategies may be combined under one agency. For example, the leisure orientation and the sport/fitness orientation may be compatible with the character building orientation and found operating in the park and recreation departments, Boy Scouts, Girl Scouts, Camp Fire, and various other organizations. The religious orientation may be combined with the leisure orientation in a church setting.

Working With Youth Groups

Many activities for youth are organized in ways that require leaders to work with groups. Teams, clubs, councils, and other forms of organizing youth all require effective group leadership. Heath and McLaughin (1993) suggests that youth programs must have the following features based on voluntary participation of participants to be successful: (1) the maintenance of strong identity structures that tie the individual to the group, (2) the presence of strong models in youth or adult leaders, and (3) a strong peer culture. Interestingly, gangs have all of the aforementioned common elements, making them very attractive to youth. These factors promote a sense of commitment and dedication to the work of the group.

How does one create a vibrant youth group? Research conducted by Astroth (1996) suggests that a number of essential elements have an impact on youth groups. According to this

The world is a great mirror. It reflects back to you what you are. If you are loving, if you are friendly, if you are helpful, the world will prove loving and friendly and helpful to you. The world is what you are.

Thomas Dreier

author, vibrant youth groups are ones that ". . .pulsate with vigor, fostering a personal sense of influence in each young person that they have impact over life's events rather than passively submitting to the will and whim of others" (Astroth, 1996. p. 9). Eleven key factors make a vibrant youth group. They are:

1. **More concern with weaning than winning.** Effective youth groups are more concerned with developing independent youths that have a sense of ownership or control over their lives. The emphasis is on promoting learning and growth as opposed to winning.

2. **Firm yet flexible.** Vibrant youth groups are ones that have a set of core values but change on the margins. In other words, there is consistency while at the same time opportunities for flexibility.

3. **Work hard and play hard.** Youth like to participate in activities in which they have fun, but on the other hand, they want to be involved in meaningful programs. Today, youth want to engage in activities that are fun but also challenging and that encourage their best efforts.

4. **Empower rather than embalm young people.** Youth ownership is very important. Youth want to be encouraged; they want to feel as if they are in charge and have ownership. Effective youth leaders guide rather than try to control behaviors. It is a process of guiding, coaching, and encouraging rather than dictating.

5. **Communicate and listen.** Youth, like all human beings, want to feel as if their ideas and input count. Vibrant groups are groups that have a dialogue among members and between the youth and their leaders. Listening to people actively is a challenging task. It often requires a great deal of patience, empathy, and tuning into another person's feelings.

6. **Achieve a balance between chaos and rigidity.** The leader needs a balance between very rigid and letting the actions of the group become too chaotic. Edginton, DeGraaf, Jordan, and Edginton (1995) uses the term "creative chaos." It describes environments that are creative, fluid, and flexible, yet at the same time appear to be lacking in structure or rules.

7. **Affirm and support one another.** Giving support to others is important, and affirming their essence is essential in building a healthy self-concept among youth. Support often is a two-way street. As the leader affirms youth they, in

The future belongs to those who prepare for it.

Ralph Waldo Emerson

turn, often affirm the leader's influence within the group. Positive affirmations lead to an improved sense of self-esteem and self-worth amongst individuals.

8. **Use mentors to socialize newcomers into the group.** Peer mentors or a buddy system is an effective way of involving members in a youth group. Such mentoring provides an opportunity for an individual to gain knowledge of the norms, customs, and rituals of the group in a supportive manner.

9. **Value and practice service to others.** Service learning is an important component to youth programs. Giving to the community is an important way of building value within a youth group. By contributing to others, one's sense of self-worth and value are enhanced. Individuals are made to feel as though their contributions are worthwhile and important.

10. **Take time for training.** Vibrant youth groups train their members in the roles that they are to assume. You cannot assume that individuals will have the appropriate skills and knowledge to effectively participate in group tasks without proper training and development. Interestingly, preparation for such roles often builds life skills that transfer effectively into one's adulthood.

11. **The whole is greater than the sum of these elements.** The concept of synergy applies here, meaning that the value created by the entire group will exceed the sum of individual contributions. For youth this is an important lesson that can be learned by participating in groups. This demonstrates the importance of group work and the potential of such activity (ibid., 1996, pp. 8–10).

Youth Development Programs

What types of youth development programs can be provided by recreational and leisure service organizations? The list of potential programs is nearly inexhaustible. There are as many youth development programs as there are ideas. Edginton and Oliveira (1995b) proposed a youth development program framework in which they suggest the following program areas:

Academic Enrichment. Scholastic, educational, or learning activities can be thought of as academic enrichment programs. Such programs can be remedial in nature or can provide greater depth to one's knowledge base.

Praise works with only three types of people; men, women, and children.

Anonymous

LEADERSHIP: A POINT OF VIEW FROM THE PROFESSION

Gordon Mack

Gordon Mack has had a distinguished career in the youth and human service field. He graduated from Southern University with a Bachelor's Degree in Education. He attended New York University, graduating with a Master's Degree in Guidance and Personnel Administration. Between these two degrees, he found time to serve as a 1st Lieutenant in the U.S. Army Transportation Corps. Immediately concluding his graduate study, Gordon took a position with the Hyde Park YMCA in Chicago. He later became the Assistant Director of the Central Atlantic Area Council of YMCAs in Princeton, New Jersey, and was later named the Director of Recruitment and Manpower Planning for the National Board of YMCAs. In 1970, he was named the Dean of the Division of Field Services and Leadership Development for the world famous Bank Street College located in New York City. Following a decade of university teaching, he became the Associate Director of Human Resource Planning for the YMCA of the USA in Chicago, Illinois. He progressed to become the Director of Personnel Services and his final position was the Director of Cultural Diversity for the same organization. In 1994, he became the Director of the American Humanics, Inc. program at the University of Northern Iowa and retired in 2004.

On leadership. . .Leadership is a process of developing people to their fullest potential, inspiring them to do the best they can do, living up to their fullest potential.

Leadership and success. . . If you have good leadership, you have success. Success is a completion of one's goals. Setting and accomplishing goals through the work of the team and the leader. It is a cooperative venture, sharing leadership, sharing activities with people you're working with so that they are part of the enterprise. The leader needs to create synergy with others.

The exemplary leader. . .One with a lot of physical and intellectual energy, ability to work in high-risk situations and succeed, ability to deal with ambiguity, being well thought of by his or her peers, being able to develop a team and form a successful conclusion to a project.

Leadership in action. . .One who has an engaging personality, able to communicate their aspirtations and intentions clearly, in a way that was not dictatorial, but supportive of the people that work with them.

The greatest discovery of my generation is that human beings can alter their lives by altering their attitudes of mind.

William James

Leisure Activities. Leisure programs for youth cut across a wide variety of interest areas including: arts and crafts; sports, games, and athletics; social recreation; hobbies; self-improvement; and touring and travel. Such programs emphasize fun as well as other benefits such as social, physical, cultural, intellectual, or spiritual development.

Leadership Development. This type of program is directed toward assisting youth in exploring and developing the capacity within themselves to lead. Such programs often provide experiential opportunities for leadership.

Service Learning. Service learning is experiential learning usually focused on helping to gain an understanding of community service. It involves some attempt to combine a meaningful volunteer learning opportunity with reflection.

Outreach Service. As previously noted by Edginton and Edginton (1996), outreach "may involve a complex web of activities, programs, services, and personal interactions which respond to situation specific, site specific, and individual specific needs." Orientations to outreach include viewing it as: (1) an activity or program, (2) an intervention, (3) a state-of-mind or attitude, (4) a presence, (5) a time and/or location, and (6) holistic.

Life Skill Building. This type of program involves the teaching of skills for surviving, living with others, and succeeding in society. It may involve teaching youth problem solving, conflict resolution, decision-making, or other skills necessary for practical, daily living.

Health Promotion Programs. Health promotion or wellness focuses on conditions that affect one's health or well-being and the development of healthy lifestyles. Programs dealing with fitness, nutrition, sexuality, stress, safety, leisure, and time use are all activities that could be developed in this category.

Peer Mentoring. This youth program is one of "youth leading youth." It involves youth providing some type of assistance, support, guidance, advice, or instruction to others.

Vocational/Career/Employment. Vocation can refer to how people define their place in the social world. Helping youth to define their "vocation in life" and assisting them with skills necessary to pursue their life's calling is a part of this program area.

Club/Social Interests Groups. Clubs in the form of packs, dens, groups, teams, troops, and others provide youth with a way to develop self-identity. They often promote a sense of loyalty, morality, and sacrifice for others as well as enjoyment.

The Carnegie Corporation of New York (1992, p. 12—13) has identified a number of best practices for programming for youth. In general, these best practices focus on ensuring that youth are involved in the planning and implementation of programs. Program content and processes need to be tailor-made to the needs and interests of youth. Recognition of the fact that youth bring diverse backgrounds and experiences should be considered when planning activities. Further, it is important to specify and evaluate program outcomes and also make sure that youth are viewed as resources in the process of program development.

LEADING YOUNG AND MIDDLE ADULTS

When a person moves into a period of young and middle adulthood, the emphasis tends to be on leisure activities that are "intrinsically satisfying" (Kleiber & Kelly, 1980, p. 114). Often recreation, parks, and leisure services leaders make the error of instructing adults in the same manner as they instruct children. Adult learners expect to be treated with respect despite any inexperience and lack of skill. Adults attend class, workshops, and activities because they want to; consequently, the leader initially has a motivated group of participants. Whether or not the group continues to be enthusiastic and involved in the activity depends on the leader's ability to instill confidence, provide meaningful recognition, create an enjoyable social atmosphere, and provide good, solid information. The adult is very discriminating and will respond poorly to a leader who is not well informed and who is uncomfortable or uninteresting. It is important for the leader to recognize that adults may become involved in recreation, parks, and leisure services activities for a variety of reasons. They may want to learn or improve a specific skill, and they may also want to socialize and make new friends. Often the social aspect of an activity will be primary over the instructive value of the experience.

During the young and middle adulthood stage, relationships with other adults are developed and enjoyed and strong bonds form (such as courtship and the early phase of marriage) and are reinforced through leisure experiences. The

Success is a journey, not a destination. It requires constant effort, vigilance, and reevaluation.

Mark Twain

arrival of children has an enormous influence on leisure activities and patterns. Parents are less likely to have time to pursue their own leisure interests, recreation activities will become strongly family-oriented, and parents are likely to withdraw from many outside activities that take away from spending time with their family.

LEADING OLDER ADULTS

It is important that the leader have knowledge of the demographic characteristics of late adulthood in order to have a greater understanding of this age group. We have chosen to use the term older people or older persons, as opposed to terms such as senior citizens or golden agers. This term is used because it is our belief that this segment of the population differs little from any other age group except that they are older and at a different point in the life cycle.

Although older people are similar to other age groups, they have unique demographic characteristics. Perhaps the most important demographic factor that relates to older people is that they are living longer than they ever have before. In 1900 the average life expectancy for an individual was 47.3 years. Now it is 78 years for women and 75 years for men. In addition, individuals living beyond the age of 65 are expected to live an average of an additional 15.5 years. It is projected that in the year 2028 more than one-fourth of the American population will be over 65. Although today older persons make up 19 percent of the population, this figure will continue to grow as the "baby boom" generation (those born between 1945 and 1960) reaches age 65.

Most older people live in urban areas (approximately 75 percent). Forty-one percent live alone and 38 percent live in family units usually composed of a husband and wife. Many older persons have a lower median income than that of the general population, although the new generation of older people is beginning to retire with a higher income rate than their predecessors. This obviously affects their leisure behavior patterns. In fact, in the future, older people will be at their most educated, healthy, and financially independent than at any other time in history.

Benefits of Participation in Recreation, Parks, and Leisure Services Programs and Activities

For many older persons, work has lent structure to their lives and provided them with a sense of identity and status. Upon retirement, they often face a difficult transition. Participation in recreation, parks, and leisure services programs and activities can provide older persons with opportunities that can assist them in this transition. Many activities provide structure by encouraging individuals to become involved on a regular basis and to take on organizational and leadership roles. Other recreation, parks, and leisure services activities offer older people opportunities for recognition, status, creativity, a sense of accomplishment, and opportunities to make a contribution to others.

Recreation, parks, and leisure services programs and activities can also offer older persons opportunities for social interaction with others. The opportunity to form close personal friendships with others can be important to individuals within this age group who may face diminishing contact with family. Such activities can also provide a setting in which friendship between the sexes can be developed for participants who are divorced or widowed.

Finally, leisure activities and programs can offer older persons opportunities to develop themselves physically and mentally. Physical activities can improve circulation and muscle tone, assist in weight loss, assist in tension release, and generally contribute to a feeling of physical well-being. Activities and programs that offer opportunities for participants to expand their knowledge and skills lead to feelings of achievement, interest in further development, and excitement about acquiring new knowledge. Individuals of all ages enjoy and seek out opportunities to learn and grow.

> No one person can accomplish much if they don't work with others.
>
> Daniel Levinson

The Role of Attitudes and Stereotypes

Perhaps the greatest problems with which older people must deal are related to the negative attitudes and stereotypes that are held about them. For example, when one hears the term "nice little old lady," an immediate image comes to mind: one who is pleasant, caring, talkative, dwells in the past a little too much, lonely, confused at times, and involved in mostly sedentary activities. Are these perceptions accurate? Consider the following: Ronald Reagan became president of the United States at age 69; Picasso continued to paint productively into his nineties; Cervantes wrote Don Quixote after age 60; John Glenn flew in space for the second time well into his 70s; and Herman Smith-Johanneson was name Dubonnet "Skier of the Year" at 99 years of age and was named to the Cross-Country Skiing Hall of Fame at age 108! All these examples suggest that older people have the potential to be active and involved and continue to seek challenges throughout their life spans.

Although, indeed, older persons are often faced with health problems, many stereotypes and myths are far more limiting. Stereotypes and myths concerning older persons often affect the ability of a leader to work with this age group effectively. In fact, if the leader's perceptions and attitudes are inaccurate, the activities that he or she offers may be inappropriate and may be limiting to participants. Therefore, it is essential that the leader first examine his or her attitudes, perceptions, values, and stereotypes concerning older persons prior to assuming the leadership of this population. A list of 14 questions to help leaders clarify their perceptions regarding older people follows:

- Do you "automatically" include games and activities that older people are "supposed to like," such as bingo, card games, and sing-alongs?
- Do you tend to encourage discussion of topics that relate to the past rather than current issues and events?
- Do you avoid activities that require physical exertion?
- Do you plan activities that are basically passive and sedentary in nature?
- Do you find yourself "talking down" to older participants?
- Do you recognize the needs and interests of older people in typical male-female relationships?
- Do you approach older people from the perspective of what they can't do rather than what they can do?
- Do you assume that older people do not have the capacity or interest to learn new things?
- Do you assume that older people no longer want to be involved in the important activities of the community?
- Do you assume that all people over the age of 65 are the same rather than representative of several age groups?
- Do you assume that all older persons are set in their ways and are uninterested and unwilling to change?
- Do you assume that individuals in their retirement years limit their activities rather than expand them?
- Do you assume that all older people are just a little confused and like to be directed (as opposed to wanting to be self-directed)?
- Do you assume that aging is a process that is uniform for all individuals? That there is a "typical" aging process?

If you have responded affirmatively to any of these questions, you should reevaluate your prejudices, stereotypes, preconceptions, and values regarding older people. Recreation, parks, and leisure services experiences are probably more limited by the attitudes of society and the leader than by older persons themselves. Obviously, it is an error to generalize about a group of 22 million people (in the United States) or 2.5 million (in Canada), who cover a 30-year span. The range of differences between older persons in matters of health, leisure interests, and personality characteristics is very broad. In fact, a case could be made for the notion that older people are more different from one another than most other segments of the general population owing to their greater variety, depth, and breadth of experience.

It is important that the leader be able to view older persons objectively in order to be able to interact with them appropriately and to "play to their strengths" rather than their weaknesses. Some characteristics of older people include the following:

- Aging is a normal developmental process and is universal.
- While the aging process is normal, aging per se is very individual and variable.
- Illness and handicapping conditions are not universally related to the aging process.
- Older people represent more than one generation, ranging from around 60 to at least 100 years of age.
- Older people can and do change and are capable of adjusting to new circumstances.
- Older people can and do learn new things.
- Older people desire to, and can, remain self-directing.
- Older people want to use their capabilities to contribute to others.
- Older people are not very different from people in other age groups; they just happen to be older in years.

These observations provide a more realistic picture of older persons. Based on knowledge and understanding of such information, the leader should be able to interact with older persons in a positive way without the problems associated with our typical stereotypic values, attitudes, and prejudices.

Leadership Goals When Working With Older Adults

Recreation, parks, and leisure services organizations that provide services and programs to older persons are concerned with enhancing their quality of life and life satisfaction. Halberg (1985) has suggested that the work of the recreation, parks, and leisure services leader should be focused on two basic areas. First, leaders should work with older persons to help them develop positive attitudes toward themselves and their leisure experiences. Second, the leader should assist older persons to become involved in the

I'd rather attempt to do something great and fail than to attempt to do nothing and succeed.

Robert Schuller

community and in self-help programs. If older persons are encouraged to become involved in their community and to give of themselves to others, feelings of self-worth, dignity, and self-esteem are fostered. Hallberg (1985) further suggests the following goals for the leader working with older people:

- To serve as a leisure and social resource for older people.
- To encourage and support the pursuit of former, current, and potential interests, abilities and skills.
- To provide opportunities for physical, intellectual, emotional, and social challenges.
- To provide opportunities for enjoyment and satisfaction.
- To stimulate social interaction and satisfaction.
- To encourage self-expression and creativity.
- To facilitate and provide experiences that support the development of feelings of self-worth and usefulness.
- To facilitate independence through the development of personal leisure and social skills, positive attitudes, and resources.
- To encourage the development of leadership skills and assumption of leadership roles.

SETTINGS IN WHICH THE LEADER WORKS WITH OLDER PERSONS

The recreation leader may work in a variety of settings with older persons. However, it is important to remember that 95 percent of people over the age of 65 are found in the community. Only five percent live in residential institutions of one kind or another at any one time. Consequently, this chapter will focus primarily on community-based programs for older people.

Community-Based Programs

Historically, many public recreation, parks, and leisure services organizations have operated senior citizens clubs. In the past several decades, these senior citizen clubs have expanded their nature and function. Concerning the transformation of the community senior center from primarily a social club to a multiservice agency, Hallberg (1985) has written:

> The traditional senior center has been concerned with providing leisure and social opportunities for participants. In more recent years this concept has broadened considerably to a more inclusive focus of the multipurpose senior center, which has been defined by the National Council on the Aging as "a community focal point on aging where older persons

The desire of knowledge, like the thirst of riches, increases ever with the acquisition of it.

Laurence Sterne

as individuals or in groups come together for services and activities which enhance their dignity, support their independence, and encourage their involvement in and with the community.

The multipurpose senior center may offer a variety of social, leisure, and health-related programs and services focused on music, sports, games, outdoor adventure, social activities, service activities, arts and crafts, drama, dance, literature, and educational programs. Table 4.3 lists a number of specific activities in each of these categories that are often found within the recreation component of multipurpose senior citizen centers.

Although specific activities are listed in this table, it is important to recognize that possible leisure activities are as varied as are people. This listing is presented to provide the leader with possible activities initially and should in no way be viewed as all-inclusive.

In addition to recreation and education programs, centers frequently offer the following services: information, counseling, and referral; health education and services; meals and nutrition education; housing arrangements referral; legal and income counseling; protective services and education; employment referral and training; transportation; outreach programs; and volunteer opportunities.

Are the leadership techniques that an individual would employ when dealing with older persons any different from those employed with any other age grouping? Generally speaking, the answer to this question is no. Leadership techniques and methods used in other settings are applicable to work with older people. However, it may be that the recreation, parks, and leisure services leader would emphasize certain leadership techniques when working with older persons. As indicated previously, it is important for the leader to keep in mind that older persons span a 30-year range in age. Therefore, although leadership techniques for older people are generally the same as for other age groupings, the leader should use common sense in leading programs and activities for individuals in the upper portion of this 30-year age span, or for the relatively small number of older persons who experience health problems of some kind. Some of the techniques and methods that might be used by the leader working with older people in a community-based setting include the following:

- The leader working with older people often acts as a facilitator, encouraging participants to plan, organize, and implement their own activities.

Sometimes things can go right only by first going very wrong.

Edward Tenner

Table 4.3
Some Programs and Services of Senior Citizen Centers

Music
Music lessons	Music appreciation classes	Playing in ensembles
Barbershop quartet contests	Choral singing	Attending concerts

Active sports
Billiards	Table tennis	Yoga
Tennis	Walking	Bowling
Badminton	Canoeing	Horseshoes
Shuffleboard	Swimming	Golf

Table games
Bridge	Bingo	Poker
Canasta	Chess	Euchre
Cribbage	Checkers	Whist

Outdoor
Hiking	Boating	Camping
Hunting	Collecting	Photography
Fishing	Nature study	Tours

Social
Dances	Picnics	Roasts
Potlucks	Special events	Other
Teas	Theme parties	

Service
Gray Ladies	Grandparents	
Red Cross	Political party volunteers	

Arts and Crafts
Painting lessons	Cooking classes	Ceramics
Woodworking	Pottery	Sketching
Quilting	Photography	Candlemaking
Embroidery	Stained glass	Sewing
Macrame	Art shows	

Drama
Attending plays	Costuming	Producing plays
Critiquing dramatic events	Acting	Movie parties

Literature
Book review groups	Book discussions	Creative writing groups
Reading	Library programs	Poetry clinics

Educational
Tours	University and college courses	Workshops
Slide shows and films	Conferences	Personal development courses

Dance
Attending the ballet	Folk dancing	Ballroom dancing
Square dance calling	Square dancing	Aerobic dancing

- The leader is often more assistive, providing information, helping the group identify resources, and suggesting alternative courses of action.
- The leader should attempt to maintain positive, productive communication, interacting on an equal level with participants. For some reason, neophyte leaders (and even some experienced leaders) tend to project their voices, slow down, and articulate carefully when talking to groups of older persons and individuals. The leader should avoid this because it may appear that he or she is "talking down" to them.
- Older persons often like to share their experience and knowledge. The leader may encourage opportunities for participants to be able to engage in this type of contribution. Some organizations are designed to facilitate this, such as SCORE (Senior Core of Retired Executives), Foster Grandparents, RSVP (Retired Senior Volunteer Program), and others.
- Refreshments or meals served in conjunction with recreation, parks, and leisure services activities should complement any dietary restrictions of participants, such as low sugar or no salt diets.
- Older persons often view themselves, as society views them, incapable of more than sedentary activity, unable to grow and learn. The leader working with these types of participants should attempt to promote individual confidence in ability to perform and participate.
- Because some older people experience hearing loss, it is important to be sensitive to this factor in verbal communication, especially in the group setting, where such losses are magnified by the level of noise. In addition, the leader may want to have large print reading materials available because some older persons may have visual problems.
- It is important to be cognizant and respectful of the differences in values between generations. The values of an older person are based on his or her experiences, and although they may be different, they are not "wrong." Nor are the leader's values, based on different experiences, "right."
- The leader should avoid viewing older persons in terms of the stereotypes of society. We find what we look for. If the leader looks for confirmation of these stereotypes, he or she will find them. If the leader, on the other hand, attempts to view older persons objectively, he or she will find that most participants contradict these stereotypes.
- The leader should be sensitive to any financial limitations that may be experienced by participants. For example, prior to suggesting an expensive excursion for the entire group, the leader might want to evaluate whether anyone might be left out as a result of the cost.

The difficult we do immediately. The impossible takes a little longer.

U.S. Army Corps
of Engineers

I know this now. Every man gives his life for what he believes. Every woman gives her life for what she believes. Sometimes people believe in little or nothing, and so they give their lives to little or nothing. One life is all we have, and we live it as we believe in living it and then it's gone. But to surrender who you are and to live without belief is more terrible than dying—even more terrible than dying young.

Joan of Lorraine

- Leaders should avoid suggesting activities and programs that are below the level of sophistication of participants. Older persons are sometimes encouraged to participate in activities and programs that are almost childlike. This can adversely affect their feelings of dignity, self-worth, and self-respect.
- The leader should encourage involvement of participants in programs and activities that include a variety of age groups, and not just participation in age-segregated activities. For example, friends and relatives can be invited to attend social functions and trips offered by the sponsoring agency.

Adult Day-Care Centers

Another community-based setting in which older persons are found is the adult day-care center. The purpose of such a center is to provide additional health-related services not available in the senior citizens center, thus helping older persons to maintain residence in the community. These health-related services might include provision of medication; specific care from a physician, nurse, or other health care professional; or provision of programs that enable family members to work during the day. Although the older participants in such programs are more limited by health-related problems than older persons found at senior citizens centers, they remain, for the most part, independent with the assistance of the programs available at the adult day-care center. The leadership techniques discussed in relationship to senior centers typically apply to participants in adult day-care programs, although greater assistance and adaptation may be necessary. Because this population may be somewhat more physically limited, it is especially important that the leader not assume stereotyped perceptions of the participants; they are essentially healthy older people who find particular benefit in being dealt with as such.

Long-Term Care Facility

Five percent of those over the age of 65 are found in institutions, especially long-term care facilities such as, nursing homes and assisted living. The long-term care facility is a residential institution for those older persons and others who are in need of more complex and sophisticated health care, but not at the more costly level available in hospitals. The leader should recognize that some older people do indeed benefit from the programs available in long-term care facilities and return to the community.

In the long-term care facility, the leader will find himself or herself in the position of activities coordinator. In this role, the leader assists residents to maintain their lifestyle through motivation and development of opportunities in which they can use their abilities and continue the daily and more periodic activities that were previously taken for granted. These opportunities may include not only the kinds of recreational activities typically conducted by the leader, but also the less formal spontaneous activities which may be taken for granted. For example, a resident can continue to read a particular newspaper or magazine that he or she has read throughout his or her life, can watch particular television programs, can discuss current events or sporting events, or care for plants. In other words, the leader encourages the maintenance of lifestyle and life routine. Although the residents of long-term care facilities are obviously more limited than the older persons discussed earlier, and more specialized leadership techniques and methods are frequently necessary, the role of the activities coordinator in providing and facilitating the more typical aspects of living is essential to the well-being and positive self-concept of the resident. The leader who views the resident as a total person with strengths as well as areas of lesser strength and then focuses on a familiar and typical part of life can positively impact the quality of life of the resident of the long-term care facility.

> Some people waste too much time on a lot of unimportant things, don't you think?
>
> *Georgia O'Keefe*

SUMMARY

Today youth present one of the most challenging populations for recreation, parks, and leisure services professionals. Youth or adolescence can be thought of as the stage of life between childhood and maturity. Recreation, parks, and leisure services professionals work to build assets within youth that will assist them in becoming self-reliant, independent, and wise adults. Pro-social youth development programs view youth as being incomplete yet worthy, and then work to make them better. The types of programs that can be offered by recreation, parks, and leisure services organizations are broad. These include academic enrichment, leisure activities, leadership development, service learning, outreach service, peer mentoring, vocational/career/employment preparation, and club/special interests groups. A key factor in working with youth groups is creating a sense of ownership among participants.

We also discussed the role of the recreation leader working with older persons. Although leadership skills and techniques that apply to other populations also work with this age group, the leader should ensure that he or she does not limit his or her perceptions of older people by believing the stereotypes commonly used to describe them. The leader should attempt to remain objective. We have offered a number of suggestions for leaders who work with older persons in order to help them interact effectively with this age group.

Discussion Questions

1. Define the term youth. Define the term adolescence. Are they the same?

2. What is pro-social youth development?

3. What competencies do we seek to build in youth through youth programs? What does a competent youth look like?

4. List five (5) programs that can be found in your community in the areas of (1) academic enrichment, (2) leisure, (3) leadership development, (4) service learning, (5) outreach, (6) life skill building, (7) health promotion, (8) peer mentoring, (9) vocational career employment, and (10) clubs or special interest groups.

5. Identify and discuss eight (8) orientations to youth work.

6. What are some of the major demographic characteristics of the older population?

7. List some of the major stereotypes held about older people.

8. Describe the role of the leader in working with older people.

9. Describe the purpose and program of an adult day-care center.

10. Describe the role of the activities coordinator in a long-term care facility.

THE CASE FOR LEADERSHIP
A Need for Resolution

Points of Consideration

In Cedar Center, the senior population congregates at the Peterson Community Center. For years, the Peterson Community Center has been the focal point of activities and services for older persons as a part of the Cedar Center Parks and Recreation Department basic program offerings. Currently, the program is offered in a club format. The senior population takes an active role in organizing the center's various programs. The club is organized with a president, secretary, and treasurer and has several standing committees to oversee its operations, including program, finances, and outreach services. There are 100 active members. There is a weekly activity that draws nearly all members to a luncheon, which often features a speaker from the community. The center operates a daily drop-in program that provides opportunities for informal activities, enabling participants to socialize with one another and engage in service projects.

Recently, there has been some discontentment amongst the senior population regarding the depth and scope of program offerings. Many seniors have indicated that while they enjoy the daily drop-in opportunity that provides opportunities to meet friends, play bingo and cards, read, and in general interact with one another, is too limited. Further, there appears to be the emergence of several competing groups or cliques of seniors that have been excluding some individuals from their daily activities. As a result, the day-to-day program activities have witnessed a reduction in the number of individuals participating in the program. Furthermore, letters to the editor have raised concerns in the community that a few seniors are verbally abusing some members of the older population.

The director of parks and recreation has asked the staff to review this situation and make recommendations regarding a new structure for the senior citizen's program. She has suggested that there is a need to find a more appropriate mechanism for members of the group to interact with one another. She further suggested that there is a need for a more vibrant program design with greater options and choices. In addition, she recommended that there should be a greater influence on intergenerational programming. However, the president of the senior citizen group has taken great offense to the intrusion of the director of parks and recreation into the affairs of the group. In fact, there is now great resistance to change and the leadership of the senior citizen group is organizing itself to present its case to the city council.

Questions of Consideration

The above situation has the potential to be a public relations challenge for the Cedar Center Parks and Recreation Department. In addition, there is a group of individuals at the Peterson Community Center who have become exclusive rather than inclusive to their fellow seniors. This is contrary to the mission of the Cedar Center Parks and Recreation Department, which calls for serving the entire community.

- What leadership principles would you apply in working with groups of senior citizens that would enable them to maintain control of their activities, but at the same time enable them to bring about meaningful change?
- How would you go about bringing different age groups together to develop strategies for intergenerational programming?
- How do you overcome the influence of potentially destructive cliques within senior citizen groups?
- How should the director of parks and recreation and the professional staff approach the senior citizens?

REFLECTING ON LEADERSHIP
Listening to Youth

Working with youth requires that the leader is able to listen to what young people have to say. The ability to listen in a helpful manner is not an easy task. What can youth workers do to become better listeners? Think back to when you were a teen. Rank the following items from 1 to 10 as what was easier and what was harder to discuss with your parents.

_____ School grades	_____ Use of the phone
_____ Drugs and alcohol use	_____ Money
_____ Sexual issues	_____ Something that makes you feel proud or happy
_____ Choice of friends	
_____ Family time vs. time spent with friends	_____ Family or personal goals
	_____ A personal problem that causes you to feel anxiety or depression

Add your own:

What is it that makes it easier to talk about a problem with a friend or at times a stranger, than with a parent? When you are talking with someone, what responses make you feel that the other person is really listening? What responses make you feel that the other person is not listening or only pretending to listen? Who is the best listener you have known? Why? Rate yourself as a listener, with 10 being the best. What stops you from listening? What makes you a good listener?

Source: Gaetano, R., Grout, J., & Klassen-Landis M. (1991). *Please talk to me: A guide to teen-adult dialogue.* Dubuque, IA: Kendall/Hunt Publishing

References

Astroth, K. (1996, Fall). The Leading Edge: Eleven essential elements of vibrant youth groups. Humanics: *The Journal of Leadership for Youth and Human Service, 6*(1). p. 8-10

Carnegie Council on Adolescent Development, Task Force on Youth Development and Community Programs. (1992). *A matter of time: Risk and opportunity in the nonschool hours.* New York: Carnegie Council on Adolescent Development.

Edginton, C. R. DeGraaf, D., Jordan, D., & Edginton, S. (1995). *Leisure and life satisfaction.* Dubuque, IA: Brown & Benchmark.

Edginton, S. R., & Edginton, C. R. (1994). *Youth programs: Promoting quality service.* Champaign, IL: Sagamore.

Edginton, S. R., & Edginton, C. R. (1996). *Youth outreach and service excellence.* U.S. Army Youth Services.

Edginton, C. R., Hanson, C. J., Edginton, S. R., & Hudson, S. D. (1997). *Leisure programming: Service centered and benefits approach.* Dubuque, IA: WCB/McGraw-Hill.

Edginton, C. R., & Oliveira, W. (1995a). A model of youth work orientations. Humanics: *The Journal of Leadership for Youth and Human Service, 4*(2).

Edginton, C. R., & Oliveira, W. (1995b). Youth development: A program framework. *PERS Review, 1*(2).

Hall, G. S. (1904). *Adolescence: Its psychology and its relations to physiology, anthropology, sociology, sex, crime, religion, and education* (Vol. 1). New York: Appleton Century-Crofts.

Hallberg, K. J. (1985). The Role of the Leisure Services Professional. In G.H. Maguire (Ed.), Care of the elderly: A health team approach. Boston, MA: Little, Brown and Company.

Heath, S. B., & McLaughlin, M. W. (Eds.). (1993). *Identity and inner city youth.* New York: Teachers College, National Center for Service Learning in Early Adolescence.

Jennings. L. (1989). Fordham Institute's Index documents steep decline in children's and youth's social health since 1970. *Education Week, 9*(9).

Kleiber, D., & Kelly, J. (1980). Leisure, socialization, and the life-cycle. In S.E. Iso-Ahola and C.C. Thomas (Eds.), *Social psychological perspective on leisure and recreation*, (pp. 91-137). Springfield:

National Commission on the Role of School and the Community in Improving Adolescent Health. (1990). *Uniting for healthier youth.* Alexandria, VA: National Association of State Boards of Education.

Ooms, T., & Herendeen, L. (1989). Adolescent substance abuse treatment: Evolving policy at federal, state, and city levels. Washington, D.C.: Family Impact Seminar American Association for Marriage and Family Therapy.

Pittman, K. J., & Wright, M. (1991). *A rational enhancing the role of the nonschool voluntary sector in youth development.* New York: Center for Youth Development and Policy Research.

Scales, P. (1991). *A portrait of youth adolescents in the 1990s.* Carrboro, NC: Center for Early Adolescents.

Rapoport, R., & Rapoport, R. N. (1975). *Leisure and the family life-cycle.* Routlege and Kegan: London.

Timmer, S., Eccles, J., & O'Brien, I. (1985). How children use time. In F.T. Juster & F.B. Stafford (Eds.), *Time, goods and well-being.* Ann Arbor: University of Michigan, Institute for Social Research.

U.S. Bureau of the Census. (2000). *Statistical Abstract of the United States: 2000.* Washington, DC. http://www.census.gov/

CHAPTER

5

The Dynamics
of Leadership
in Groups

LEARNING OBJECTIVES

1. To understand the importance of group dynamics for the recreation, parks, and leisure services leader.
2. To understand the difference between primary and secondary groups and their effects on the recreation, parks, and leisure services experience.
3. To identify the different functions of groups and the roles played by individuals in a group.
4. To identify various techniques that can be used by the leader as he/she works with groups.

KEY TERMS

- Group Dynamics
- Primary Groups
- Group Properties
- Group Functioning
- Group
- Secondary Groups
- Sociometry
- Group Roles

INTRODUCTION

Sarah was confused about her two beginning swimming classes at the Cedar Center swimming pool. She was sure that the classes were identical in number, gender, and ability. In addition, she used the same instructional method in both classes. However, her 10:00 a.m. class was not making as much progress as her 1:00 p.m. class. Class members were grumbling and she felt discouraged over the situation. She knew that something needed to be done but couldn't figure out where to start. Maybe she wasn't a good leader after all.

What makes a leader an excellent teacher in one situation and not the other? Why do some groups respond to leaders and others reject them? How can you analyze group behavior when things go wrong?

As mentioned in the prologue, leadership is an interactive process that involves not just the talent of the leader but also the behavior of the group and the setting. In the above scenario, since the leader and the setting were the same, something must be going on with the third component—the group.

Groups are a fundamental element within any recreation, parks, and leisure services agency. The majority of program delivery systems in public, private, commercial, and non-profit sectors have group-oriented activities and services at their core.

Individuals belong to groups for varied reasons. Some individuals establish membership in a group for the purpose of socialization and camaraderie, whereas others join groups in an effort to contribute their skills to enhance or better the community in which they live. Membership in some groups is short term in nature, whereas membership in other groups is long term, or perhaps life-long.

The study of groups and group dynamics is especially important in the recreation, parks, and leisure services profession. This chapter will look at the interaction of individuals in groups and how these interactions contribute either positively or negatively to the recreation experience. Further, the chapter will examine group leadership and roles and discuss how a recreation, parks, and leisure services leader can work with groups to enhance their enjoyment of recreation, parks, and leisure services activities.

DEFINING GROUP DYNAMICS

When individuals interact in groups, patterns of action occur that influence their behavior. We can think of group dynamics as the study of the interaction that takes place between individuals within a group setting. The term group dynamics not only is concerned with the factors that influence communication and interaction between individuals, but is also concerned with other forces in the physical, social, and cultural environment that influence these patterns of interaction. We study group dynamics in order to understand group behavior, with the goal of improving the kind and quality of interaction that take place within the group process.

Our concern with group dynamics is not only with the way that people interact and behave in a group situation, but also with the techniques that can be used to improve group effectiveness. The techniques employed by recreation, parks, and leisure services leaders can vary from goal setting to organization of small-group discussions. The more familiar the leader is with available techniques and their successful group performance, the more effective the leader will be. The ability to use the appropriate technique at the appropriate time to facilitate positive group interaction distinguishes a good leader from a poor one.

Thus we can define group dynamics as the study of groups, including patterns of interaction within the group, external forces that influence the group, and techniques and processes that can affect group behavior. An analysis of these variables allows us to understand why groups behave as they do. Patterns of interaction within the group can also be referred to as internal group dynamics.

The term internal group dynamics involves group communication as well as other factors that influence interaction such as group goals, size, atmosphere, leadership patterns, and participation. External forces that affect group activities include such factors as organizational and institutional values and expectations, physical structures, community values and expectations, and other group affiliations. Techniques and processes used to influence group behavior can be thought of as the tools that the leader can use to assist the group in achieving its goals. For example, the leader can serve as a facilitator, resource person, enabler, or a combination of these, when acting on his or her knowledge of such techniques as leadership style, communications styles, role playing, brainstorming, small-group discussion, and problem solving.

> The path to greatness is along with others.
>
> *Baltasar Gracion*

Group Dynamics and the Recreation, Parks, and Leisure Services Leader

You don't get the breaks unless you play with the team instead of against it.

Lou Gehrig

There is a variety of situations in which the recreation, parks, and leisure services leader can benefit from a knowledge of group dynamics. Consider the leader who works with classes, clubs, teams, activity groups (i.e., camp groups), and neighborhood groups. All these formats for recreation, parks, and leisure services activities require knowledge of group dynamics. In addition, the leader also works with professional peers and lay persons interested in the provision of recreation, parks, and leisure services. Thus, knowledge of group dynamics is useful in conducting professional relationships, including working with staff members (in a formal organizational structure), advisory and policy-making boards, volunteer associations, and with colleagues in professional societies and associations. The use of group dynamics within some of these types of groups is as follows.

Instructional Groups. An important component of many recreation, parks, and leisure services organizations is the provision of opportunities for development of skills, knowledge, and attitudes through instructional groups. Most instructional programs are operated as classes in a group setting or situation. The leader in this setting should have knowledge of such variables as group atmosphere, group learning principles, communication styles, and group interaction. It is interesting to note that recreation, parks, and leisure services organizations operate these types of programs for individuals who choose to participate rather than for individuals who are required to participate. Therefore, the motivation of participants is strong. Leisure counseling and education groups fall within the category of instructional groups because they focus on attitude and skill development.

Social Groups. Often individuals attend recreation, parks, and leisure services programs in order to interact with others. In fact, individuals often enroll in instructional groups with the purposes of not only learning something, but also socializing with others. The leader of social groups should be familiar with ways that he or she can assist individuals to meet, mix, and interact with others within a positive and supportive environment. The leader in this setting should have knowledge regarding how to establish and work with clubs, manipulate large and small groups, and implement counseling techniques.

Volunteer Groups. Many recreation, parks, and leisure services organizations use volunteers. The development, organization, and operation of a volunteer network may involve the establishment of standards for behavior and the creation of a sense of membership within the organization. Volunteers become involved in organizations for many reasons. One reason may be the need for a sense of group affiliation. Another may be a need for social interaction, and still another may be a need to serve others. In any case, the leader should be aware of those forces that influence the volunteers who work in the group environment.

Competitive Groups. Competitive groups are comprised of those individuals who are members of teams and who play in leagues, tournaments, and contests provided by recreation, parks, and leisure services organizations. Knowledge of group dynamics can be essential in dealing successfully with these types of groups. Knowledge of recognition mechanisms, reward structures, and methods for the establishment of group norms should be possessed by the leader working with competitive groups. It is also important that the leader have the ability to build group morale or a sense of esprit de corps. Considerable status is associated with winning and being a part of a winning team in our society. A knowledge of group dynamics may also be used to transfer the focus of competitive groups away from the competitive aspect of the recreation experience and toward the value of participation as an end in itself.

Boards, Citizen Advisory Groups, and Neighborhood Associations. The involvement of citizens or laypersons in the policy and decision-making processes of the recreation, parks, and leisure services organization is a well-established tradition within our field. These individuals are paid or volunteer their services to assist the organization in developing its programs and services. Specific knowledge related to the conducting of formal meetings and the formulation of goals can assist the leader in working effectively with boards, citizen advisory groups, and neighborhood associations. The leader should be able to help such groups establish meeting agendas; seek out, acquire, and process information; make decisions; and interact with other groups.

Professional Colleagues. The recreation, parks, and leisure services leader often works within a formal organization. This is the case within public park and recreation departments, voluntary youth-serving agencies, or commercial recreation enterprises. In all these formal organizations, the most common work unit is the group. The ability of the leader to have an impact on a large organization may very

> We don't accomplish anything in this world alone.
>
> *Sandra Day O'Connor*

well be a direct result of his or her ability to work successfully in small groups. The leader's knowledge of group dynamics can be useful in establishing rapport with others, building group morale, solving problems, identifying goals, and communicating effectively with others.

Professional Societies and Associations. Most leaders in the recreation, parks, and leisure services field belong to one or more professional societies or organizations. They engage in these types of activities in order to promote the work of the profession as well as their own professional interests. Most work in these types of organizations occurs in smaller groups that are task oriented. The individual's knowledge of group dynamics can be useful in this type of setting in terms of committee organization, management of conferences, workshops and training institutes, and communication and interaction. Professional organizations also confer status on individuals through the process of certification or registration. Knowledge of why and how groups confer status could be useful to the leader in establishing a successful program of this type.

WHAT IS A GROUP?

There are a number of definitions for the term group. Some individuals have suggested that a group can be thought of as a highly unified collection of individuals. Others have suggested that groups work toward goals. Still others have maintained that individuals within a group must be dependent on one another. To categorize "a collection of individuals" as a group is not sufficient. In order to be termed a group, a collection of individuals must have ties to one another that result in a sense of interdependence or interrelatedness or both. Interdependence or interrelatedness refers to the extent to which individuals are tied together in their actions and behavior. Therefore, we can define a group as "a collection of individuals who interact with one another in such a way that they are interdependent to some degree" (Cartwright & Zander, 1968, p. 46). Interdependence or interrelatedness is the variable common to all groups.

The use of a gymnasium by individuals is one example of the concept of "the group" suggested in the preceding definition. On any given night, a number of individuals may be present at a gym shooting baskets, exercising, running, and so on. This collection of individuals does not constitute a "group." Why? Because each of the individuals has his or her own goals and is not tied to the others present in the gym.

By working together, pooling our resources, and building on our strengths, we can accomplish great things.

Ronald Reagan

A LEGACY OF LEADERSHIP
Joseph Lee (1862-1937)

Joseph Lee is known as the "father of the recreation movement" in the United States. Born in Brookline, Massachusetts in 1862 to a wealthy family whose origins in America were traced to the Puritans, Lee grew up in a privileged household. He attended Harvard University where he was an avid sportsman, participating in various recreational activities including boxing, sailing, riding, club sports, music, drama and dance. He also became a skilled painter.

Upon graduation, he toured Europe and began, with the help of his Scottish tutor, to develop his liberal thinking towards the values of life. Returning from Europe, he attended Harvard Law School, receiving his law degree in 1888. Although his father hoped he would join him in the family business, Lee became a nonconformist, more interested in public service projects than Wall Street. He returned to Europe in 1889, to think, converse with friends, and formulate his philosophy about social reform.

In 1889, he returned to Boston and began a famous ten-year study of child delinquency in that city. By 1900, he had become a nationally known social worker, devoting his life and personal fortune to the solution of social problems. He was not only a donor to philanthropic causes but a doer. He was an active social reformer in many venues: medical inspections and health laws in public schools, establishment of Boston Juvenile Court, care of the homeless, and immigration. However, it was in the field of recreation that his leadership had the most lasting impact.

Lee's work in the recreation movement began in 1892, when he did considerable research on play in Boston playgrounds, sand gardens, and in the streets. This interest was further fueled during his trips to Europe, in consultations with play leaders in the United States, and in conversations with his wife, Margaret, who was a student of the principles of Froebel, the father of the kindergarten. Through all of these sources, Lee developed his philosophy that play was not a meaningless pasttime but a means of human expression and education.

His study of the play areas in Boston led him to realize that the playground needed to be organized and supervised in order for children to experience the value of play. As such, he proposed and developed a model playground program in 1900. This playground soon became a model for other cities.

The extent of Lee's contributions to the field of leisure, recreation and parks are too numerous to detail. Dr. Allen Sapora, a biographer of Lee, probably best summed up these contributions when he wrote: Joseph Lee's "major work may be explained through his activities in three general phases: (1) His leadership in recreation in New England after 1907 and his early work with the Playground Association of America (PAA); (2) His outstanding leadership as president of the National Recreation Association (NRA) and his promotion and broad development of its program for 27 years; (3) The effect of his financial contributions to promote the movement; and his accomplishments as the leading philosopher of the early movement." Joseph Lee was not only the "father of the recreation movement in America," but was the inspirational leader whose influence and impact cannot be fully measured.

On the other hand, the same collection of individuals could come to a gym to participate with others as a basketball team, and they would be categorized as a "group." because they would possess the same or similar goals and would engage in interaction and cooperation and, as such, would be interrelated and interdependent.

Primary and Secondary Groups

Individuals join different groups for different reasons. We affiliate with different professional societies and associations to enhance our careers. We join religious groups to affirm our spiritual values. Social and fraternal groups provide us with an opportunity to interact with others, develop friendships, and use our leisure. We join community-oriented associations and groups in order to contribute to the development and well-being of our cities and towns. We are involved in numerous informal groups based on a variety of factors, including the interests of our neighborhood's children, recreation interests, and so on. Membership in one's family constitutes a group affiliation as well. All these different types of groups can be categorized according to their presence in two major categories: primary groups and secondary groups.

Primary Groups. The term primary group refers to a setting in which intimate, face-to-face interaction and cooperation occurs. This type of group offers opportunities for individual interaction and self-expression. In situations where individuals live, work, or play together, intimate, face-to-face interaction occurs; hence, primary groups are formed. Perhaps the most easily identified example of a primary group is the family. Although the size of a group can affect its degree of intimacy, large groups as well as small groups can be primary.

Secondary Groups. Secondary groups involve human interaction that is transferable, readily redirected to other individuals, and defined in specific standardized terms. Whereas a relationship within a primary group assumes holistic acceptance of the individual and deep and extensive communication, secondary groups' transactions are narrow and limited to the transaction itself. For example, when an individual purchases a ticket to the theater, the interaction between the ticket seller and the participant is stereotyped to conform to the "normal" and routine behavior that occurs between other clerks and clients. Were the ticket seller to be replaced, the individual could readily redirect the process of interaction to the new ticket seller.

Alone we can do so little, together we can do so much.

Helen Keller

The activities, programs, and services provided by recreation, parks, and leisure services organizations can be viewed as involving secondary groups; that is, the interaction that takes place between the leader and the participant is transferable from one person to another. Interestingly, however the leisure experience occurs as a result of primary group interactions. It is a highly personal, individually defined experience and requires satisfaction on the part of the participant. Although the relationship that develops between the leader and the participant is often formal, emphasizing the characteristics of secondary group interaction, the result for the individual may be more consistent with primary group interaction. Murphy and others have suggested that there is a need to view individuals in a more holistic sense in order to facilitate deeper and more extensive communication as a desirable aid to the leisure experience.

If he works for you, than you work for him.

Japanese Proverb

On the other hand, this is not to suggest that the establishment of a primary relationship between the leader and the participant is necessary or even desirable. Individuals may be engaged in recreation, parks, and leisure services pursuits for a host of reasons, including recognition, achievement, and self-worth, as well as other motives that have social value. In certain situations, it may be desirable to maintain a more formal relationship, especially where there is a need to maintain objectivity. An individual may, for example, value the recognition provided by the leader. A leader who is biased by his or her personal relationship with a participant may not have the ability to make objective judgments about the participant's performance.

Why Do People Join Groups?

There are numerous reasons why individuals join a group. Obviously, individuals have a great desire to affiliate with a cause, worthwhile activity, or area of interest. Further, membership in such groups brings a certain amount of recognition and, in fact, often provides status and/or mutual support for group members. Jordan (1996, p. 120) has provided a list of some of the reasons why individuals join groups. Some of the reasons are: social reasons (e.g., to meet new people); to learn a new skill, or to increase personal knowledge; self-enhancement or advancement (e.g., resume builder); to share a common activity with a significant other (e.g., achieve intimacy); coercion (e.g., parents "force" children to join after-school groups); to make a statement (e.g., rebel against the "establishment"); and for self-identity. As one can see, there are many reasons why individuals are drawn to participate in groups. They form the basis of many of our life's activities and provide great meaning to one's journey through life.

People who work together will win.

Vince Lombardi

The Influence of Groups in Our Lives

Membership in groups can directly influence our lives, can shape and mold our behavior, and can influence our perceptions. Groups provide individuals with information and role models and may influence individuals through peer pressure. Zimbardo and Ruch (1976) have suggested that there are at least four sources of group influence. These are shared participation, public commitment, social support, and normative standards. A description follows each of these sources of group influence.

Shared Participation. Shared participation refers to the involvement of individuals in the decision-making process. When an individual becomes personally involved in decision-making processes, he or she becomes an active part of the change process. When this occurs, the individual is more likely to undergo changes in his or her behavior as it is related to group activities.

Public Commitment. When an individual makes a commitment in a group publicly, the individual is more likely to follow through on the commitment than if the commitment were made in private. Because individual behavior is influenced by the approval of others, the behavior of an individual is shaped by the expectations formed when that individual makes the commitment public. In order to receive group approval, the individual must follow through on his or her commitment.

Social Support. Involvement in a group reinforces individual decisions to act. When an individual has the support of a group, his or her confidence is increased as decisions made are appropriate. Group support, in other words, reinforces individual decision making and increases the individual's confidence in the viability of his or her decisions.

Normative Standards. Groups also provide expectations for the way that group members are supposed to behave. We can think of these expectations or standards as social norms. Social norms are the stated or implied rules that govern the way that individuals are to respond in a given situation. They provide a benchmark against which individuals can compare their behavior with the established standards for the group.

The influence of group participation on individuals in recreation, parks, and leisure services settings is evident within many activities and programs. Basketball team members, for example, will be influenced as a result of association with their group. Individual team members are provided with social support through teammates' encouragement of their decisions made while playing, which leads to increased confidence. Individuals often become involved in group decision making in the form of game strategy (formally or informally), which leads to a commitment to the decisions made and to a greater commitment to the group as a whole. Individual team members may also begin to assume behavior indicative of group norms. For example, we have all seen the "athletic strut" that is practiced by many. Team members may also wear certain clothing to practice, or adopt distinctive clothing into their street wear (jackets, shoes, wristbands). In addition, they may adopt roles for themselves. One member may formally adopt the leadership role; another, the mediator role; and still another, the role of hard worker. These roles may or may not be carried over into other areas of life. Status may also be conferred on team members, depending upon the situation. There would be a great deal of status, for example, attached to membership on the senior high first-string team because there are relatively few individuals who can attain such a position. Less status would be attached to membership on the seventh-grade third-string team because membership is not as exclusive and does not involve the acquisition of unusual skills. Within the group itself, status may be accorded to various members of the team, for example, the high scorer, the best defensive player, the player getting the most rebounds, and so on.

Groups Promote Psychological Stability. Having groups in our lives also plays an important role in maintaining individual psychological stability. Groups provide opportunities for direct, face-to-face interaction with other individuals. Without this opportunity, relationships become less intimate and fragile, leading to a state called anomie. This term, coined by the sociologist Durkheim, suggests that the more highly specialized and complex society becomes, the more likely it is that some individuals within society will find themselves without adequately defined roles or rules regulating behavior. Groups formed as a result of programs and services offered by recreation, parks, and leisure services organizations and led by the recreation, parks, and leisure services leader, do provide opportunities to counter the adverse effects of anomie. Participation in group recreation activities can provide opportunities for intimate social relationships and norms or rules to regulate behavior and can

> The impossible is possible when people align with you.
>
> *Gita Bellin*

confer status on group members. All these benefits can contribute to the psychological well-being of the individuals participating.

Group Properties

As the reader will recall, a group can be thought of as a collection of individuals who interact with one another and, as a result, develop a degree of interdependence. Group interdependence can also be thought of as the cohesiveness or unity that exists between group members. Some groups show a higher degree of interdependence than others. Thus, it can be suggested that the degree of interdependence of a group can be viewed as existing on a continuum. At one end of the continuum a high degree of unity exists among group members, and at the other end of the continuum a lack of cohesiveness or unity exists among group members. Groups at the latter end of the continuum are often characterized by feelings of anomie.

Wilson (1978) has suggested that there are six properties that influence the degree of interdependence necessary to solidify a collection of individuals. They are interaction, norms, status structure, goals, cohesiveness, and a common perception of membership. The extent to which group interdependence exists will be affected by each of these six properties. The more highly developed a group is in terms of one or more of the properties, the greater the degree of interdependence within the group. The following is a description of these six properties.

Interaction. Interaction refers to the communication that takes place between individuals within a group. A high degree of interrelatedness within a group exists when there is high frequency of communication and an equal distribution of communication between individual group members. Furthermore, the tone or nature of the interaction will influence the degree of interrelatedness. Friendly interaction characterizes highly interrelated groups, whereas antagonistic interaction produces the reverse effect.

Norms. Norms can be thought of as the behaviors expected of group members. Norms represent the view of the majority of group members regarding what individuals "should do, ought to do, and are expected to do" (Wilson, 1978, p. 29). Groups that have a high degree of interrelatedness usually develop a large number of norms to guide behavior, and, more important, a high degree of consensus exists among group members concerning these norms. Conversely, groups with a low degree of interrelatedness have few norms and a low degree of consensus. In groups that have a high degree

Individual commitment to a group effort – that is what makes a team work, a company work, a society work, a civilization work.

Vince Lombardi

of interrelatedness, individuals who deviate from norms are negatively sanctioned (e.g., scolded, embarrassed, or censured).

Status Structure. Status structure can be thought of as the roles of individual group members. Whereas norms involve similar behavior for members of the group, the status structure within the group results in diverse roles for individual members. Roles are expectations that are defined or developed for each group member. When group members have a high degree of consensus regarding their roles, there is correspondingly a high degree of interrelatedness within the group. Furthermore, a high degree of interrelatedness can also be said to exist when there are few challenges to the status or role structure within the group. As is the case with group norms, in highly interrelated groups an individual who deviates from the role expected of him or her (the status structure) is negatively sanctioned.

Goals. Group goals differentiate from personal goals in that group goals require group members to cooperate with one another to achieve them. Group goals, in fact, are characterized by their cooperative nature. Regardless of the individual or individuals who contribute the most toward achievement of the goal or goals, it is the entire group that attains them. Groups that have a high degree of interrelatedness have many defined goals and a high degree of consensus among members as to which goal to pursue. Moreover, groups with a high degree of interrelatedness cooperatively pursue goals for group-oriented motives rather than personally oriented motives. Conversely, groups that have a low degree of interrelatedness have few defined goals and a high degree of disagreement as to which goals to pursue.

Cohesiveness. Cohesiveness refers to the degree to which individuals are attracted to their group. The satisfaction or pleasure that group members derive from group participation is a major determinant of cohesiveness, as is the interpersonal attraction between individuals. The stronger the attraction between individuals and the stronger the satisfaction derived, the higher the degree of interrelatedness. Cohesiveness is often determined by using sociometric techniques, which will be discussed later in this chapter. When individuals are not isolated and an absence of cliques exists within groups, cohesiveness is increased. On the other hand, when a low degree of interpersonal attraction, a high degree of isolation, and a large number of cliques exist, the degree of interrelatedness declines significantly.

It's amazing how much you can accomplish when it doesn't matter who gets the credit.

Harry S. Truman

Awareness of Membership. Awareness of membership refers to the extent to which individuals perceive themselves as a part of the group. Often this is measured by simply asking individuals whether or not they feel they are part of the group. Awareness of membership can also be thought of as the individual's sense of belonging to a group. Another factor contributing to awareness of membership is the morale or, esprit de corps, of the group. Groups that have a high degree of awareness and high morale are said to have a greater degree of interrelatedness.

Knowledge of these six properties can be useful to the recreation, parks, and leisure services leader in establishing groups that contribute to the psychological well being of its members. If the leader understands that factors such as positive interaction, role consensus, an even distribution of communication, or the lack of cliques within a group can influence its degree of interrelatedness, he or she can work to create a group environment in which desirable elements are present. In working with existing groups, the leader can attempt to strengthen those weak areas that will adversely affect group functioning. For example, the leader could clarify the status structure in such a way that roles would be more explicit, providing group members with a clearer understanding of what to expect from one another. It is interesting to note that recreation, parks, and leisure services activities are often used within groups to build morale or esprit de corps.

Analyzing Interpersonal Relationships

A technique that can be used to view interpersonal attraction in groups has been developed by J. L. Moreno (1934). Moreno terms this procedure sociometry. Sociometry can be thought of as a procedure for identifying patterns of interaction among group members. Within a group, the patterns of interaction that emerge will vary from group to group. Within groups, some individuals will be sought out by others whereas other individuals will be isolated, even from within the group. By understanding these patterns of interaction, the leader can reshape the group patterns to increase opportunities for interaction and, hence, for satisfaction between and among group members.

In order to interpret and analyze the patterns of interaction that take place within a group, Moreno set forth a method for visually interpreting this information. He termed this visual interpretation a "sociogram." A sociogram portrays the structure of the group, including subgroup patterns, friendship patterns, and patterns of interaction between individu-

A group becomes a team when all members are sure enough of themselves and their contributions to praise the skills of others.

Anonymous

als within the group. Figure 5.1 represents the patterns of interaction for a group of Cub Scouts and serves as an example of a sociogram.

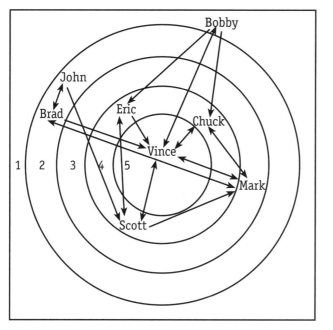

Figure 5.1
Sociogram of a Cub Scout den

In the preceding example, a leader was asked to have each of the Cubs "name their three best friends within the group." Characteristics other than friendship could have been explored, such as intelligence, athletic ability, citizenship, and so on; however, this particular exercise investigated friendship for the purpose of dividing boys into two dens according to this variable. In the investigation of a basic area, it is important to avoid ambiguity and ensure that group members understand clearly what information is being sought. In the diagram presented, the boys' choices of best friends within the group are represented by arrows. The arrows that are directed only one way represent the choice of one boy by another. Arrows that are directed both ways represent choices by two boys of one another. The concentric circles represent the number of times the boys were chosen by the other boys. Boys were thus chosen five or more times—or as few as once—and placed accordingly within the circle. In the sociogram, Bobby can be identified as being relatively isolated. He was chosen only once by the seven other boys. On the other hand, Vince is viewed positively by the boys as he was a choice of six of the eight other boys. There seems to be an interactive relationship between

Eric, Chuck, Vince, Scott, and Mark. All these boys are choosing one another as friends. The relationship between Bobby and Vince keeps Bobby involved in the group. The relationship between John and Scott and Brad and Mark keeps them involved in the group.

In this case, the sociogram was used to identify friendships in order to place the boys in two dens. However, it also pointed out the importance of finding ways to integrate boys who are isolated into the main group. For example, we did not want to separate Bobby and Vince because of their relationship and Bobby's isolation. We also wanted to maintain the relationship with John and Brad and ultimately place them in a group with Mark and Scott. Use of the sociogram in this case offers a satisfactory way of dividing the boys and helping them maintain their friendships. Without this tool, the leaders of the group would have made the separation based on their "best guess," possibly resulting in unhappiness on the part of some of the boys.

The sociogram should be looked at as a tool that can be used by the recreation, parks, and leisure services leader to provide an indication of the cohesiveness of a group. It allows the leader to determine personal attraction of individuals to one another based on some criteria. This technique could be especially useful in a therapeutic recreation setting, where the leader is attempting to promote interaction and friendship. By using various techniques, the leader might promote new relationships that result in increased contact and interaction between individuals.

Group Size

The size of a group will influence its operation. Small groups may offer, for example, more opportunities for communication with others within the group. Small groups also offer group members more opportunity for the development of social relationships. Although small groups may have less "talent" to be used in problem solving, they are also characterized by a greater willingness of group members to participate in problem-solving and decision-making processes, for small groups are perceived as being less threatening than large groups. In addition, the small-group member has greater access to the leader than the large-group member. The role of the leader is more difficult when in charge of a large group because he or she may not have the time to interact meaningfully with each group member.

Group size may play an important role in the selection of leadership techniques. For example, the leader will want to use communication techniques that are suited to the size of the group. A lecture type format may be appropriate for a large group, but a group discussion might be more appropriate for a small group. However, the leader can create a small-group atmosphere within a larger group by clustering individuals into smaller groups for discussion or problem solving. By doing this, the leader can take advantage of the larger number of individuals in terms of their expertise, knowledge, and information and still make them feel more comfortable and willing to share by placing them within the small group atmosphere.

Many of us are more capable than some of us ...but none of us is as capable as all of us.

Tom Wilson

Group Leadership

As the status structure of a group emerges, certain individuals occupy roles that we call leadership roles. The status structure allows for the identification of role expectations for group members. The higher the status conferred on an individual, the more likely he or she is to be referred to as a leader. Conversely, the lower the status of an individual within the group, the lower the probability that he or she will occupy a leadership role. One's status within a group may change, however, depending upon the tasks to be accomplished or the processes to be employed. Thus, depending upon the circumstances, leadership roles can change hands.

Generally speaking, three variables influence whether or not an individual occupies a role of leadership within a group. The first of these is the amount of influence that an individual has within the group. The amount of influence that one possesses is based on the authority associated with one's role within the group. Authority may be conferred as a result of a formal position that one holds, or by virtue of one's knowledge or ability to persuade others. A second variable that can be indicative of leadership has to do with the process of communication or interaction within a group. Individuals who hold leadership roles are often at the center or focal point of group interaction. The individual may serve to generate, organize, or distribute information to group members or effect a combination of these actions. The person occupying this role is often viewed as a leader. The third variable associated with leadership is sociometric popularity. Sociometric popularity is based on one's ability to solve instrumental and socioemotional problems associated with group functioning. Sociometric popularity, more specifically, is based on the perception of a group that an individual has the ability to lead them to their goals successfully.

Leaders in groups perform various functions. As one function, they enforce the norms of the group, thereby increasing group interrelatedness. This is done via a system of rewards and punishments that the leader is able to use by virtue of his or her status within the group. Furthermore, the leader serves as a role model. Group members usually place higher expectations on the leader than other group members. They expect the leader to exemplify the highest ideals and exhibit the highest level of performance.

With regard to recreation, parks, and leisure services organizations, Sessoms and Stevenson (1981) have suggested several responsibilities that a group leader can assume. These include:

1. **To develop a sense of "we-ness."** It is the leader's responsibility to develop the group's capacity to work together toward a common goal.

2. **To develop a positive group climate.** It is the responsibility of the leader to develop a pleasant group climate or to see that one is established.

3. **To identify goals.** The key to successful group functioning is the group's ability to identify its goals and objectives.

4. **To organize for goal achievement.** Organizing the group for action implies a sense of priorities, the recognition and utilization of individual group members' skills, and the ability to motivate the group to act.

5. **To initiate action.** Leaders initiate action. Action is fundamental to the group achieving its goals.

6. **To develop patterns of communication.** The leader is key in providing the communication pattern for other members—what is communicated and in what form.

7. **To facilitate group structures.** One of a leader's major responsibilities is to establish and maintain the group's structure.

8. **To develop and implement group philosophy.** Philosophy is the glue that holds the group's purpose together. Groups reflect the philosophy of the leader, but they also respond to the leader's public statement of their purpose and underlying principles.

It is important to recognize that leadership can emerge as a function of the group process, or it may be assigned. For example, within a recreation, parks, and leisure services activity, there may be a person who emerges from within the group to assume an informal leadership role. At the same time, there may be a leader formally assigned by the recreation, parks, and leisure services organization to instruct,

Behind an able man there are always other able men.

Chinese Proverb

lead, coach, or otherwise supervise the activity of the group. In the latter case, the individual's influence as a leader comes primarily through the formal authority assigned by the agency. In the former case, the leader's authority may be a result of knowledge, personality, and so on. In other words, the recreation, parks, and leisure services leader is characterized by a formal sanction of leadership, some formal training, and stability as a leader. The informal leader is characterized by group support due to some form of inherent leadership ability.

In either case, it is important to remember that the leader is a vital member of the group. The leader serves to stimulate others and facilitate achievement of group goals. The leader is often an individual who can provide insight into group problems and initiate action to solve them. The wise formal leader should try to identify the informal leader or leaders within the group and seek their assistance. The informal leader or leaders can provide support for the formal leader or, conversely, can undermine the effort of the formal leader, depending upon the working relationship that is developed between them.

Communication in Groups

Groups, especially small ones, provide the basis for intimate interpersonal interaction. Therefore, it is extremely important that the recreation, parks, and leisure services leader have an understanding of the communication process as it applies to small groups. Skill in communication is tied to the quality of behavior within small groups. Although we will discuss the process of communication more thoroughly in Chapter 7, it may be useful to identify the types of interaction that potentially can occur in small groups. Success in recognizing and encouraging appropriate forms of communicative interaction within small groups can directly affect the achievement of group goals. The use of inappropriate or ill-conceived patterns of interactions can be detrimental not only to the achievement of group goals, but also to personal success of the individuals within the group.

Small-group communication demands a more intimate, direct process of interaction than that employed with large groups. Individuals involved in small groups do not, for example, expect to be addressed as if they were a part of a formal audience. Individuals expect to be able to interact with the leader and others within the group freely and to participate in an exchange of information rather than receive only one-way communication from the leader. The small-group communication process should be one of give-and-take. Individuals within small groups are only willing to listen if their responses are also heard and acknowledged. Individuals

What we have here is a failure to communicate.

Cool Hand Luke (film)

involved in the process of communication within small groups often communicate their personal needs and goals while at the same time contributing to the group problem-solving process in order to achieve group goals. The more sensible and coherent the process of communication is within a small group, the more likely it is that the group will achieve its goals.

Avedon has identified five types of communication that can occur within a small group. These include interindividual, unilateral, multilateral, intragroup, and intergroup communication (1974, pp. 166–170). The communication process within the small group implies an exchange of information between parties. In other words, there are expectations within the small group that the group members will be responsive to one another, and that they will take into account the feedback received from others in formulating further responses. A description of each of the five types of communication Avedon cites as being used within small groups follows.

Interindividual. Communication of this type involves interaction of one individual with another. This type of group is referred to as a dyad, meaning that it involves two people. The direct interpersonal transaction that takes place within a dyad can result in several outcomes. It can create greater commitment on the part of both individuals to achieve goals that have been mutually agreed to, or it can result in hostility, competition, aggressiveness, or other behavior that prevents goal attainment.

Unilateral. Unilateral communication involves interaction between an individual and two or more persons. In other words, a number of interindividual interactions take place simultaneously. The unilateral relationship is usually a competitive one, where the focus of the group's attention is toward one individual who tends to be an antagonist.

Multilateral. Multilateral interaction or communication involves three or more individuals. Multilateral communication is often competitive with individuals interacting with one another laterally. However, no one individual is an antagonist as in the unilateral communication described earlier.

Intragroup. Intragroup communication focuses on the achievement of a goal that is mutually subscribed to by all members of the group. Requiring two or more individuals, this form of communication is cooperative rather than competitive. Groups that have achieved positive intragroup communication have a higher degree of interrelatedness than those that do not. Interaction tends to be give-and-take in nature with individuals willing to compromise their posi-

Relationships are the key to effectiveness.

Jan Perkins

tions and take into account the ideas, feelings, and values of others.

Intergroup. Intergroup communication occurs between groups and is focused on the achievement of a goal that is sought by both groups. This form of communication often operates with the mutual understanding of rules and regulations, as well as standards of behavior.

The recreation, parks, and leisure services leader, depending on the goals of the group or the expectations of participants, will want to encourage different types of communication. For example, in competitive game situations, unilateral or multilateral communication that contributes to the group structure may be appropriate. However, if the purpose of the group is to solve problems or to encourage cooperative group behavior, intragroup and intergroup communication may be more effective.

Group Conflict

Within all groups there is potential for conflict. Group conflict is not necessarily something that one should fear or attempt to avoid. In fact, many individuals would suggest that conflict, which is inevitable in many group situations, is necessary to facilitate positive group change. Therefore, the recreation, parks, and leisure services leader should be aware of the causes of conflict, as well as the ways in which it can be used to assist group behavior in a positive fashion. Conflict within groups can be due to three factors: incompatible goals, status incongruities, and differences in perceptions.

Incompatible Goals. Often individuals come together in a group situation with divergent opinions and values concerning the goals of the group. This incompatibility of goals can lead to conflict. An example of this in the recreation field can be found when differences in coaching goals exist on sports teams. One coach on a team may see his or her role as one of winning games, whereas another coach on the same team may view his or her role as helping to develop skills. Team members or parents of team members or both may also have goals of their own, or may have goals aligned with one of the two coaches.

Status Incongruities. Status incongruities are frequently a source of conflict within groups, especially where there is no formal authority structure established and accepted by the group members. Status incongruity refers to the differences in opinion that arise regarding of the status accorded to roles within the group. Conflict can occur when an indi-

Coming together is a beginning, staying together is progress, and working together is success.

Henry Ford

vidual perceives his or her status in a different light from other group members.

Differences in Perceptions. The differences in perceptions that group members have of goals, processes, roles, and so on can all be sources of conflict. Each person receives information and screens it according to such variables as their past experience, beliefs, values, interests, and knowledge. Differences in perceptions due to the influence of these variables can lead to conflict. The process of perception will be discussed fully in Chapter 7, which deals with perception and the communication process.

There are a number of strategies that can be used to overcome conflict within groups. First, the leader can attempt to create a buffer between group members involved in conflict. The leader using this approach would try to have each of the parties avoid each other in order to minimize the friction that would ordinarily occur. Another strategy that can be employed by the leader is to help group members to understand how they influence one another. The leader using this strategy does not attempt to help group members avoid conflict, but rather attempts to help them understand their own behavior and its influence on others. Often an individual will not be aware of the effect of personality quirks, methods of giving direction, attentiveness, and responsiveness. The leader can attempt to provide group members with insight and strategies for changing their behavior in order to facilitate positive group interaction. Lastly, the leader can rearrange the group structure in order to reduce conflict. This might involve changing the roles and expectations of individuals.

The leader's and group members' perceptions of conflict can have a great deal of influence on whether such conflict has a negative or positive impact on individual or group behavior, or both. If the leader and group members view conflict as a way to bring about change and encourage innovation, the conflict will be seen as natural and useful to the group. If, on the other hand, conflict is viewed as something to be ignored or as being unnecessarily disruptive to the group, a negative attitude toward conflict will develop. The leader should work toward developing a positive orientation toward conflict, one that can be of assistance in achieving group goals.

GROUP FUNCTIONING

All primary and secondary groups share a similar pattern of functioning regarding their reason for being. They progress

> Conflict is essential for growth, change, and the evolution of living things.
>
> *Brent Ruben*

LEADERSHIP: A POINT OF VIEW
FROM THE PROFESSION

Michelle Park

 Michelle Park is Executive Director, Ohio Parks and Recreation Association OPRA. She has over 25 years experience in the parks and recreation profession after receiving her Bachelor's and Master's degree in the field from the University of Florida and the University of Southern Mississippi. She spent 11 years, 1978–1989, working with the Palm Beach County Parks and Recreation Department, eight years as Director of Recreation. In 1990, she was hired by the National Recreation and Park Association as director of Professional Services, providing education and training opportunities on a national level to professionals and citizens in the field. In 1996, Michelle became the executive director of OPRA, a non-profit corporation dedicated to the promotion of parks and recreation services for all Ohioans and the sound stewardship of Ohio's natural resources. OPRA represents over 1,800 park and recreation professionals and citizen board members. A major function of her job is sharing the important benefits that public park and recreation agencies bring to the citizens and businesses of Ohio. Michelle also manages the OPRA Foundation, the fundraising ally of the Ohio Parks and Recreation Association.

On leadership. . .I think in very visual terms so when the word leadership is mentioned I visualize someone physically standing out in front of a group of people guiding them to action and the group is following their leader with determined faces and enthusiastic cheers for the bond they share.

Leadership and success. . .Face-to-face leadership creates strong ties directly between individuals and is necessary to advance individual objectives. Supervisory leadership is shared between a supervisor and his/her subordinates, allowing for a team approach to accomplishing goals once everyone understands the goals. Managerial leadership provides the support and resources to the entire team, meaning all levels, so the mission of the agency can be accomplished. Community leadership provides our citizens the opportunity to participate in the development of 'their' park and recreation programs and facilities and is absolutely necessary for acquiring the resources and support to carry out 'their' vision. Working backwards you can see the pattern: community leadership provides the vision, managerial leadership provides the vision, supervisory leadership addresses goals and individual leadership addresses objectives. Almost like a pyramid.

The exemplary leader. . .I'll describe our lobbyist and why I think he is an exemplary leader. He relies on a base of knowledge and expertise that guides him on a daily basis and when he is faced with a situation that is new to him, he seeks expert advice and information from those he trusts and respects. He thinks from both sides of an issue by always asking the question "Who will oppose us and why?" This gives him the ability to share both sides of an issue and explain why our position is the best position. He does this in a very constructive manner with a positive approach, complimenting those who offer ideas and aren't afraid to ask questions, making

continued on next page

everyone feel like they are contributing to the cause thus allowing everyone to buy-in-to the cause. When he has consensus, we move forward with specific duties that will lead us to the common goal. He does this with the confidence and humility of a good leader. I've learned allot from watching how he works!

Leadership in action. . . . I think there are some core characteristics that make a good leader. Vision, trust, self-confidence, loyalty, balance, humility, respect for others, consensus-building, flexibility, humor and passion are just a few.

People have been known to achieve more as a result of working with others than against them.

Dr. Allan Fromme

through various stages of action and share common elements of structure. Because all stages are important to the overall health and cohesion of group activities, recreation, parks, and leisure services leaders need to be aware of them. These stages of functioning include:

Stroking. When people get together, the first thing they do in a group situation is exchange social amenities. This may be no more than one person asking another if they are having a good day, or talking about the weather. It may take the form of shaking hands, smiling, or doing anything that sends the message, "I am glad you are here." Stroking is imperative to setting the tone of the group. The more familiar members are with each other, the more time they will devote to stroking. New groups often spend little time in stroking because they have not developed enough commitment to each other to stroke. The stroking period of this group is usually very formal and minimal time is spent, whereas well-established groups need lots of stroking time. The leader must allow time for stroking to occur, as lack of stroking can cause members to undermine other actions of the group. For instance, a person who has not been able to fully communicate to others during an abbreviated stroking period may whisper, pass notes, or otherwise disrupt the orderly proceedings of the group in order to fulfill this function.

Organizing. Every group has some form of structure and a way of doing business. The rules of behavior may be conscious or unconscious, but its members are aware of them. For instance, a group that meets on a regular basis will have an informal seating chart; the same person will sit in the same seat for every gathering. If the person is missing, many times no one will sit in that particular seat. Groups may also be formally organized with bylaws and officers who carry out its procedures, or they may function on some loosely structured, informal process. Groups must be organized in order to act. Without organization, chaos occurs and the group cannot move on to the next stage of functioning: producing.

Producing. Producing is action. That moves the group towards its goals and objectives. When a team scores points, it is producing. When an aerobic class starts exercise routines, it is producing. When members are talking and debating points on an agenda, they are producing. Production can take many forms, but it is all directed at achieving some end. For groups to stay together for a period of time, members of the group must have a sense of movement toward common goals. That is producing.

Creating. Although not a prerequisite for group maintenance, creativity helps to keep a group vital and fulfilled. Some groups are very creative, having little trouble in moving toward this level of performance. Other groups never achieve this level of production. When groups are creative, they are usually unaware of time and space. They are in a state of "flow," where members are caught up in the experience and are totally involved in it.

Even eagles need a push.

David McNally

Groups do not necessarily go through these stages in a lock-step manner. Rather, groups usually move from one level to another, back and forth, as time together progresses. For instance, if in the producing stage process begins to get very tense, the group may drop back to stroking (joking) in order to clear the atmosphere so that more productive activities can take place. The group members may then reorganize themselves to move on to positive production.

Occasionally, a group may get stuck in one stage and have extreme difficulty in move to another stage. This may mean that the group has lost its focus and reason for being. At this point, the leader needs to intervene and ask the members some important questions such as: (a) Does the group have meaning?, (b) Has it organized itself sufficiently to move to the next stage?, and (c) Is it productive to all members? By analyzing where the group is and what it is doing, the leader and members of the group can take appropriate action to allow the group to become a dynamic entity again.

Recreation, parks, and leisure services leaders must understand group functioning and be able to step in to help the groups successfully produce. The key is for the leader to recognize which level the group is in, as well as the importance of all four functions for the total group experience.

GROUP ROLES

There are various roles that individuals can assume within a group situation. Some roles contribute to the effective functioning of the group as an interpersonal unit whereas other roles contribute to the effective functioning of the group as it relates to the tasks at hand. Still other roles played out within groups have nothing to do with the solving of problems or the maintenance of group activities, but rather focus on the individual needs of one or more group members at the expense of others within the group.

These types of roles are often viewed as being detrimental to overall group behavior. Individuals can play more than one role within a group. For example, an individual may volunteer information in one situation within the group whereas in another situation within the same group he or she may seek to clarify the opinions of others. Basically, we can think of group roles as existing in three categories: general task roles, group building and maintenance roles, and individual antigroup roles (Beal, 1967).

General Task Roles

Individuals engage in general task roles in order to contribute to the work of the group. Often they will become involved in identifying, defining, and suggesting solutions to problems affecting the group. Some of the specific ways that an individual can act out general task roles include the following.

Initiator-Contributor. The individual who contributes his or her ideas is characteristic of the initiator-contributor. Often this role involves making suggestions or proposing solutions to problems.

Information Seeker. The individual this role attempts to clarify information presented by others. This individual seeks additional relevant facts or seeks to validate the accuracy of information presented, or both.

Opinion Seeker. The opinion seeker attempts to clarify values rather than facts. This individual would ask for assessment of the moral implications of actions proposed.

Information Giver. The individual in this role offers information to others that is based on facts and experience. The information given is "authoritative" in nature and can help to enhance understanding of the task at hand.

Opinion Giver. The opinion giver offers his or her values or beliefs regarding the task at hand. This individual does not offer factual information, but rather offers personal values, beliefs, and opinions.

Elaborator. The elaborator attempts to give depth to the discussion by giving examples and rationales, and by attempting to discover what would happen if a certain

The key elements in the art of working together are how to deal with change, how to deal with conflict, and how to reach our potential.

Max DePree

course of action was adopted. The elaborator expands the discussion to enable the group to develop a more comprehensive understanding of a particular concern.

Summarizer. The individual who pulls facts, opinions, and values together is the summarizer. The person in this role tries to assist the group in determining where it was, where it is, and where it wants to go.

Coordinator-Integrator. The role of coordinator-integrator involves selection of various ideas, opinions, values, beliefs, and facts and organizing them into an integrated concept. The coordinator-integrator tends to work with ideas and concepts and attempts to determine the relationships that exist between them.

Orienter. The orienter keeps the group on task. This is often done by reminding the group of the task to be accomplished or the goals to be achieved.

Disagreer. The person who disagrees looks at the other side of the issue. This may involve taking an opposite point of view and arguing accordingly. This person questions the facts, opinions, and values of others.

Evaluator-Critic. The evaluator-critic uses standards to elevate the progress of the group. The individual in this role measures the group's procedures, facts, and other factors relevant to the group's progress against standards of excellence.

Energizer. The energizer can be thought of as a motivator. The individual in this role attempts to rouse the group toward action or increase the productivity of the group in terms of quality or quantity.

Procedural Technician. The procedural technician assists group procedure by handling the distribution of materials and objects, as well as by dealing with seating arrangements and notifying group members of meetings.

Recorder. The recorder is involved in the writing down of concepts or ideas. Often a recorder will work at a blackboard or with an overhead projector, setting down information presented by group members. The recorder is important to the group process, as many ideas can be lost in a verbal exchange.

Teams share the burden and divide the grief.

Doug Smith

Group Building and Maintenance Roles

Group building and maintenance roles focus on encouraging and building cooperation among group members. These roles are extremely important to successful group functioning. There is often a need to assist individuals positively by suggesting ideas, clarifying positions, and presenting facts. Group building and maintenance roles can be thought of as the social-emotional support activities that group members provide one another in the group setting. Often the leader who is using a democratic leadership style will focus on these types of roles. Some of the group building and maintenance roles in which individuals can engage include:

Encourager. The encourager is the cheerleader. He or she provides praise, encouragement, and support to others. This is done by actively supporting other individuals without necessarily agreeing with their points of view.

Harmonizer. Often within groups there are disagreements and conflicts. The harmonizer works to help individuals overcome their disagreements and attempts to help relieve tension within the group. Timing is important in the harmonizer role, for the right comment or intervention at the right time can serve to head off conflict or break tension.

Compromiser. The compromiser role also deals with the mediation of conflict. The compromiser provides alternatives to points of view or yields in his or her point of view, or both, in order to maintain group harmony.

Gatekeeper. Often channels of communication will become clogged in group interaction. The role of the gatekeeper is to keep communication channels open and ideas and facts flowing.

Standard Setter. The individual in this role attempts to establish standards for the group in terms of its output and internal processes. The group can use these standards to engage in evaluation of its progress or effectiveness.

Group Observer-Commentator. The individual involved in this role provides information in the form of "feedback" to group members concerning the processes used by the group. This might involve informing the group of the extent to which communication is open and appropriate procedures are being employed, and so on.

Follower. There are certain situations in which the follower role is extremely important. By listening and being attentive to the ideas of others, one can facilitate the group process.

This is especially true when others in the group are extremely excited or have a strong commitment to their ideas and values.

■■■■■Individual Antigroup Roles

We term individual behaviors that adversely affect group performance as "individual antigroup roles." The incidence of such roles can provide an enormous problem for the leader as well as for other group members. In a recreation, parks, and leisure services setting, one must be careful to balance the desires of individuals with the needs of the group. When individual behavior is clearly detrimental to group functioning, the leader must act to resolve the problem in order to protect the quality and integrity of the group experience. Some of the individual antigroup roles are:

Aggressor. As the term aggressor implies, the individual in the aggressor role attacks others within the group by challenging their ideas, values, or feelings. The aggressor will often attack the personality of the other individual rather than the issue at hand. Attacks by the aggressor may involve personal disapproval, questioning the status or value of another, and so on.

Blocker. The blocker disagrees with everything presented. This role involves an extremely negative orientation, wherein the individual opposes others without a rational justification. Such behavior is a serious problem in group and interpersonal communication.

Recognition Seeker. Often an individual will try to be the focus of group attention. As a result, the recognition seeker will engage in such behavior as clowning, boisterous behavior, bragging, and so on.

Self-Confessor. The individual who is a self-confessor uses the opportunity presented by the group setting to present personal ideas, feelings, and values that he or she feels are important. The self-confessor, for example, may attempt to increase the "cosmic awareness" of the group at the expense of the tasks at hand.

Clown. Often an individual will come into a group with a nonchalant or cynical attitude. As a result, he or she will make a mockery of the group process by horsing around, making loud asides, having restless behavior, and so on.

Dominator. An individual within the dominator role will try to dominate the work of the group. The dominator monopolizes conversation or uses threats of his or her position of authority or superior knowledge to limit discussion and

If I could solve all the problems by myself, I would.

Thomas Edison

interaction. This is usually reflected in an authoritarian leadership style of behavior.

Help Seeker. The individual engaged in the role of help seeker pleads for the assistance of others because he or she feels unqualified, confused, or not able to grasp the ideas and concepts being presented. The expectation is that the other group members will shoulder the work and responsibilities of this "weaker" group member.

Special Interest Pleader. The special interest pleader is the cause-oriented individual who uses the group forum to promote personal interests by using such catch phrases as "the environment," "grass roots," "the poor," and "the participant" to justify his or her ideas, values, or beliefs.

The role or roles that are assumed within a group can have a direct influence on its success or failure because some roles (group task roles or group building-maintenance roles) are conducive to effective group performance, whereas others (individual antigroup roles) are characteristic of groups that perform poorly. The leader, with a knowledge of group roles, may be able to change his or her own role or the roles of others within the group to facilitate a more positive group atmosphere or to facilitate completion of a task. Consider the youngster in a Little League program who is not satisfied with anything. This type of child may not like the rules, the position played, the coach, the field, and so on. In other words, the child's enactment of this role (the blocker) is interfering with the group process; the needs of one individual are interfering with the needs of the group for cohesiveness and cooperativeness. The leader with a knowledge of group roles may be able to transform the blocker role into a positive one so that the child is able to achieve recognition in a positive way. For example, the leader may allow the child to lead the exercise program, serve as a base coach, or serve as the scorekeeper.

TECHNIQUES USEFUL TO THE LEADER

There are a number of specific techniques that can be useful to the recreation, parks, and leisure services leader working with large and small groups. For example, there are specific techniques that can be used in the organization of such large groups as clinics, workshops, conferences, and retreats. There are also specific techniques that can be used for the organization of pageants, festivals, and other special events. Techniques for these groups will be discussed in Chapter 11.

None of us is as smart as all of us.

Ken Blanchard

Small-group Techniques. Most work in organizations is done in small groups. Therefore, it is appropriate to have knowledge of some of the techniques that can be useful in assisting small groups achieve their goals. In this section, a brief overview of some of the general techniques that can be useful to the small-group leader will be presented. In later chapters of the book, we will focus more specifically on detailed techniques that can be used by the leader in a number of different settings.

The most important variable influencing the choice of techniques to be employed by the leader is group size. As the term small group implies, it is being assumed that the number of individuals with whom the leader is working is between three (3) and twenty (20) individuals. It is not appropriate to identify a specific number of people as constituting an optimal group size, for other variables, such as the task to be performed, the willingness of the participants to contribute, and the need for a large or small input of information, may affect this factor. However, whatever small-group techniques are employed, they should provide an opportunity for all group members to give and receive information. In larger groups, because of sheer size, there is a possibility that exchange will be limited or that it will be confined to a one-way interaction. Small-group techniques, on the other hand, are characterized by the opportunity for individuals to exchange ideas, opinions, and values in an open and free manner. Two small group techniques to be discussed are the small group discussion and committee meetings.

Small-Group Discussion. When individuals meet within a group structure to present and discuss ideas, opinions, and beliefs, we call it a small-group discussion. Small-group discussions can be thought of as informal meetings of group members directed toward the establishment of the goals of the group, and the process or processes to be used to accomplish these goals. Small-group discussion is used when group members are willing to engage in open communication, are relatively skilled in terms of human relations, and are willing to contribute to the solving of problems and the creation of new ideas. The small-group discussion method might be chosen for one or more of the following reasons.

- To identify and explore mutual concerns, issues, or problems.
- To increase awareness, appreciation, and understanding of mutual concerns, issues, or problems.
- To generate interest in ideas, issues, and problems.
- To supply and diffuse information and knowledge.

A committee is a group that keeps minutes and loses hours.

Milton Berle

- To motivate a group to action.
- To involve members in the problem-solving process.
- To get members to crystallize their own thinking.
- To form group opinions or consensus.
- To assist members to express their ideas in a group.
- To create an awareness of issues and problems.
- To encourage and stimulate members to learn more about problems and ideas.
- To develop a core group of people for leadership purposes.
- To develop an informal and permissive group atmosphere. (Beal, Bohlen, & Randabaugh, 1967, p. 182)

In leading small-group discussion, the leader should have a clear understanding of the goals of the group as well as the problem or issue to be reviewed. The leader should work to ensure that each group member has an equal and adequate opportunity to present his or her ideas in a supportive environment. The leader should help clarify viewpoints while at the same time stimulating group members to offer alternative viewpoints. Often the leader will want to insert humor or other comments to break the tension that may develop in this type of discussion.

Some of the specific techniques that can be used to aid small-group discussions are the following:

Circular Discussion Method. The leader using the circular discussion method arranges group members in a circle and allows them to present their viewpoints, in order, around the circle. This is done after a brief initial presentation of the topic. This method is designed primarily for discussion of controversial issues.

Brainstorming. Brainstorming is a problem-solving process. It focuses on obtaining input from group members about a problem at hand. The critical step in the brainstorming process is the generation of ideas, and it is the quantity of ideas, not the quality, that is important. No critical judgment is made of ideas, and all are welcome.

Buzz Group. The buzz group technique involves the subdivision of a group into smaller units so that they are encouraged to interact. This method is often used with larger groups, although it can be useful in smaller groups when there is a need for more intimate, face-to-face interaction. It encourages group members to express their ideas and opinions, more so than any other form of small-group discussion.

The Huddle Method. The leader using the huddle method breaks a large group into small groups and limits discussion to a very short period of time (usually under 10 minutes).

This method has the same advantages as the buzz group, although the timed discussion encourages the quick presentation of ideas.

Case Study. A case study is a written portrayal of a real life or lifelike situation. With this technique, individuals are asked to read a case study prior to discussion and offer solutions to the problem in the "case." Group members also try to identify factors that would affect various solutions. The case study may have implications for a similar situation that has been, is, or will be confronted by the group. The case study method may be seen as a way for group members to hone their problem-solving and decision-making abilities.

Role Playing. Role playing is another technique that can be used to aid small-group discussion. The idea behind role playing is to have individuals within the group act out various scenarios. The role-playing dialogue is allowed to unfold spontaneously to a predetermined situation. This exercise allows group members to assume roles they normally wouldn't assume and react to situations within those roles. Thus, group members can gain insight that they might not otherwise attain. Once the role has been played, group members engage in a discussion of the responses that have taken place.

Experiential Exercises. Experiential exercises are structured learning exercises that focus on the group members' feelings or values toward a particular topic or subject. Group members are given a written hypothetical situation and asked to imagine themselves within that situation and solve the problem involved. Usually, progression through these types of exercises teaches group members a larger lesson or "truth." These types of exercises allow group members to personalize concepts to be used as a basis for discussion. Structured experiential exercises are often useful ways of channeling or shaping a group's thinking so that it is focused on the topic at hand.

Although many small-group discussions are spontaneous, a large number of small-group discussions require some pre-planning. For example, the leader should determine the most appropriate time for the meeting and should also consider the location, materials, supplies needed, and so on. Will the group need an overhead projector? A blackboard? Is one day better for most of the members than another? The seating formation of group members may also be planned ahead to facilitate the type of discussion desired. For example, the leader should attempt to ensure that group members are able to have eye contact with one another. Figure 5.2 presents different types of seating arrangements that can be used in small-group discussions.

Many meetings are like panda matings. The expectations are always high, but the results are disappointing.

Anonymous

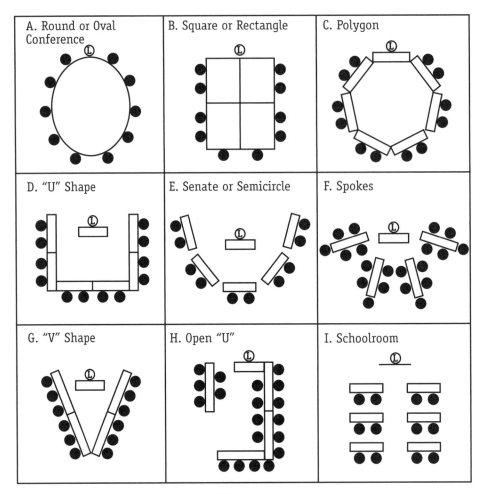

Figure 5.2
Possible seating arrangements for meeting

Committee Meeting. Committees are found in all organizations, including recreation, parks, and leisure services organizations. In most cases they operate on a more formal, structured basis than the small-group discussion. Committees usually specify roles and tasks to individuals, hence conferring their status. Some committees are appointed on a permanent basis, whereas others are ad hoc in nature. Ad hoc committees are usually organized for a short period of time in order to investigate or solve a specific problem or issue or both. A committee can be thought of as a group of individuals who have been designated, as a group, to accomplish a specific set of goals and objectives.

A committee may perform a number of different functions (see Figure 5.3). Some committees are advisory in nature, whereas others have final decision-making authority. In addition, some committees have the coordination of various activities within an organization as their primary function or

A camel is a horse designed by a committee.

Fred Luthans

task. Two other functions that may be assumed by committees include provision of information and implementation of services. In the recreation, parks, and leisure services field, there are committees, such as the municipal park and recreation board, that can be either a decision-making body or an advisory body, depending on the type of enabling legislation of the state. Committees can be elected or appointed. Again, in the case of the municipal park and recreation board, members may be elected or appointed to various committees, such as finance, planning, and personnel.

Committees are not always viewed in a positive light. Many individuals disdain committee work. They feel that it is laborious, time-consuming, and tedious.

Many times there are problems with committees. One of the largest disadvantages of a committee is that it is time-consuming and can be costly. Furthermore, individuals often question consensus or group decision making. The criticism is that individuals water down their positions in order to accommodate the needs of others. Some individuals would also suggest that committee members can stand behind group decisions, thereby avoiding the responsibility for errors. It is difficult to hold a committee member responsible for the actions of the entire group.

On the other hand, committees can help promote cooperation and collaboration among individuals. The pooling of ideas, knowledge, and other resources often enables the for-

> When he took time to help the man up the mountain, lo, he scaled it himself.
>
> *Tibetan Proverb*

---

1. To make decisions on matters of policy, program, or action.
2. To make recommendations regarding policy, program, or action.
3. To give advice to an executive or to some policy-determining body.
4. To direct or supervise an executive, sub-executive, or staff member.
5. To effect coordination among the members and departments, groups, or other units which they represent.
6. To study, make inquiries, or carry on fact finding.
7. To visit or inspect.
8. To educate the committee members.
9. To promote sound public relations.
10. To carry on administrative or service activities
11. To select, appoint, or approve personnel.
12. To render judgment or to arbitrate in cases of conflicting claims or interests.
13. To sponsor or endorse an agency, program, or undertaking.
14. To assist in a ceremonial function.

Figure 5.3
Major functions of committees

Source: *Leadership and Group Dynamics in Recreation Services*, Sessoms and Stevenson, 1981. Boston: Allyn & Bacon.

mulation of creative and expansive solutions to problems.
Committees also provide an opportunity for individuals to
receive recognition and status as a result of their committee
membership. This often serves to motivate individuals to
become involved when ordinarily they would not.
Committees can also serve as training grounds for individuals. As new members are circulated into the committee, older
members can serve as role models and offer information.
Thus, a committee can offer an excellent opportunity for
individuals to learn and grow.

Committees usually follow a formal agenda format; that is,
they plan, in advance, the items or topics to be discussed at
a meeting. A typical agenda format follows:

1. Call to order
2. Roll call
3. Reading of the minutes
4. Committee reports
5. Old business
6. New business
7. Announcements

Agendas are useful because they provide information to committee members, as well as present the order events are to
occur at the meeting. They tell the committee members what
topics will be covered in the meeting and when. If there are
special reports for committee members to make or hear, they
will know at what point these are to occur.

An important role in a committee is that of the chairperson.
The chairperson can be thought of as the official leader of
the committee. He or she is responsible for leading the meeting, including moderating and controlling the discussion. The
chairperson will want to be conscious of the time involved
in the meeting itself. Ensuring that the committee meeting
follows an appropriate tempo and pace is an important function of the chairperson. The committee chairperson must not
only be a good listener, but also must be supportive of other
individuals. He or she should have the ability to cut to the
heart of issues and concerns. The chairperson is also responsible for establishing and following the rules of procedure
that the committee is to follow. The most common format
used in committees is that found in *Robert's Rules of Order*.
These rules aid in processing information in the committee
meeting. They are often referred to as parliamentary procedures.

Another important task undertaken in committees is the
recording of transactions. We refer to this as keeping the
minutes of the committee. Minutes of meetings usually
record who attended the meeting, when and where it was

held, and what decisions were made. Minutes often include summaries of discussions, debates, or other items that were useful in formulating committee strategy. Taking minutes can be a demanding task. The individual who acts as the recorder must be able to understand the issue at hand and record with accuracy the substance of the committee's discussions and decisions.

The interaction of committee members with one another and the chairperson is essential to group effectiveness. The cohesion or tension that develops between committee members may directly influence the success or failure of the group. Committee members should be willing to share their ideas and should be open to the suggestions and comments of others. They must be willing to compromise their opinions in order to work toward broader group goals. Committee members, like the chairperson, must be sensitive to group dynamics. The timing of their statements and their ability to listen actively to other committee members are vital.

A truly effective meeting ends conclusively. Progress has been made on some issues; other issues have been completely resolved.

Paul Sandworth

SUMMARY

In this chapter we focused on the topic of group dynamics. Group dynamics can be thought of as the study of groups that deals with patterns of interaction within groups, external forces that influence groups, and the techniques and procedures that can be used to affect group behavior. There are a number of situations in which the recreation, parks, and leisure services leader can apply his or her knowledge of groups, such as in instructional groups, social groups, volunteer groups, competitive groups, citizen groups, and professional societies and associations.

A group can be thought of as a collection of individuals who are interrelated and interdependent. There are two types of groups: primary and secondary. Primary groups involve face-to-face, intimate interaction and cooperation among individuals. Secondary groups involve human transactions in which communication is transferable from one person to another. There are a number of factors, or properties, that determine the degree of interrelatedness or interdependence within given groups. Six of these properties are interaction, norms, status structure, goals, cohesiveness, and awareness of membership. A tool that can be used to measure one or more of these properties is known as sociometry. Sociometry can be thought of as a procedure for identifying patterns of interaction among group members.

As the status structure of a group emerges, so do leadership roles. The extent to which an individual occupies a leadership role is dependent on three variables: influence, communication, and sociometric popularity. Influence is related to power and can be conferred as a result of formal position or by virtue of one's knowledge or ability to persuade others. Individuals who are the center or focal point of group interaction assume leadership roles because of their integral involvement in the communication process. Knowledge of sociometric popularity can help the leader to guide the group toward the achievement of group goals.

All groups share a similar pattern of functioning regarding their reason for being. They progress through various stages of action and share common elements of structure. Because all stages are important to the overall health and cohesion of group activities, recreation, parks, and leisure services leaders need to be aware of them. These stages of functioning include stroking, organizing, producing, and creating.

There are a number of roles within the group that group members can assume. These roles can be divided into three categories: general task roles, group building and maintenance roles, and individual antigroup roles. Some of the behaviors that are associated with general task roles include serving as an initiator-contributor, information seeker, opinion seeker, information giver, opinion giver, elaborator, summarizer, coordinator-integrator, orienter, disagreer, evaluator-critic, energizer, procedural technician, or recorder. Behavior associated with group-building and maintenance roles include acting as an encourager, harmonizer, compromiser, gatekeeper, standard setter, observer-commentator, or follower. Individual antigroup roles that have an adverse or negative effect on the group include acting as an aggressor, blocker, recognition seeker, self-confessor, clown, dominator, help seeker, or special interest pleader.

Knowledge of techniques involved in working with small groups and committees can be useful to the recreation, parks, and leisure services leader because most work in organizations is handled by small groups. A key to working with small groups is understanding the processes that are involved in small-group discussion. These types of discussions allow group members to present their ideas, opinions, and beliefs. Some of the techniques that can facilitate small-group discussions are the circular discussion method, brainstorming, buzz groups, the huddle method, case study, role playing, and experiential exercises. Finally, committees are found in all organizations. They usually operate on a more formal, structured basis than small-group discussion, and engage in a number of functions, including providing advice, coordinating, providing information, implementing services, and serving as a final decision-making body.

▰▰▰Discussion Questions

1. Define group dynamics. What three components are involved in group dynamics?

2. Identify and discuss various groups with which the recreation, parks, and leisure services leader may work.

3. Define the term group. What does it mean to say that individuals must be interrelated and interdependent on one another in order to be a group?

4. What is the difference between the primary and secondary group? In terms of the leisure experience, what is the role of primary and secondary group? Explain.

5. Identify and define six properties of groups.

6. What is sociometry? How can this be used in the recreation and service field?

7. What variables affect the ability of an individual to assume a leadership role?

8. What are four causes of group conflict? What can the leader do to overcome conflict within groups?

9. List behaviors that can be exhibited in general task roles, group building and maintenance roles, and individual roles.

10. Identify techniques that can be used by the leader to facilitate a small-group discussion. What are some problems in working with committees?

THE CASE FOR LEADERSHIP
The Girls Demand their Football Helmets!

Points of Consideration

Recently, your sports program coordinator informed you of a petition circulating the community. It seems that two girls, Lisa Todd and Linda Ronee, both excellent young athletes, and their parents started the petition. The petition was initiated because, according to the bylaws of the sports association affiliated with the department, girls are not allowed to participate in the same sports as boys. The programs have always been gender specific. The only exception to this rule is tennis. The girls and their parents feel that this rule is unfair and discriminatory. Furthermore, both girls tried to enter the boy's youth football program last fall and were turned down because of the bylaws. They expressed disappointment, but the issue ended there. Now they are back with much more community support, and an agent from the state's department on discrimination is investigating.

To add to the problem, fifteen of the parents whose sons participate in the sports program are attempting to counter the petition by having representatives meet with the Cedar Parks and Recreation Advisory Board to keep the current bylaws intact.

You also have been in contact with the board. You have been studying the problem and feel that a separate girls' sports program is the solution. However, the board has informed you that there is not enough money in the budget to run a girls' sports program without the boys' program suffering some cutbacks. This would not satisfy the boys' parents' interest group. There is a definite problem.

Questions of Consideration

There is a meeting scheduled in one week. The states agent has an appointment with you before the meeting.
- Should you merely have the agent inform both groups of the discrimination policy and leave it at that?
- Would this alienate one of the groups and leave the problem unsolved?
- Ultimately, the decision will be yours. Would you call another meeting of both groups?
- Together or separate?
- Should you release a statement to inform the entire community since it is so deeply involved?
- What principles of group dynamics will you employ to help resolve this conflict?

Adapted from: Bannon, J. (1981). *Problem Solving in Recreation and Parks* (2nd ed.). New Jersey: Prentice Hall.

REFLECTING ON LEADERSHIP
Lessons from the Geese

Most of us have seen the beautiful migration flight of geese and the interdependence seen on the way they function. There are lessons for us who want to work effectively as teams.

Fact: As each bird flaps its wings it creates an uplift for the bird following. By flying in a V formation the whole flock adds 71 percent greater flying range than if each bird flew alone.

Lesson: People who share a common direction and sense of community can get where they're going quicker and easier because they are traveling on the thrust of one another.

Fact: Whenever a goose falls out of formation it suddenly feels the drag and resistance of trying to fly alone. It quickly gets back into formation to take advantage of the lifting power of the bird immediately in front.

Lesson: If we have as much sense as a goose, we will stay in formation with those who are headed where we want to go.

Fact: When the lead goose gets tired it rotates back into the formation and another goose flies at the point position.

Lesson: It pays to take turns doing the hard tasks and sharing leadership. People as with geese, are interdependent on each other.

Fact: The geese in formation hunt from behind to encourage those up front to keep up their speed.

Lesson: We need to make sure our honking from behind is encouraging and not something less helpful.

Fact: When a goose gets sick, wounded, or shot down, two geese drop out of formation to follow him down, to help and protect him. They stay with him until he can fly again or dies. Then, they launch out on their own in another formation or catch up with their own flock and continue on their journey.

Lesson: If we have as much sense as the geese, we will stand by each other. There is a strong message here, in terms of quality, looking at the connection between teamwork, the quality of life and relationships, and the quality of learning. Relate the lessons from the geese to different situations you have encountered in working with groups.

References

Avedon, E. H. (1974). *Therapeutic recreation service: An applied behavioral science approach*. Englewood Cliffs, NJ: Prentice-Hall.

Beal, G. M., Bohlen, J. M., & Raudabaugh, N. (1967). *Leadership and dynamic group action*. Ames, IA: Iowa State University Press.

Cartwright, D., & Zander, A. (1968). *Group dynamics*. New York, NY: Harper & Row.

Jordan, D. J. (1996). *Leadership in leisure services: Making a difference*. State College, PA: Venture.

Luthans, F. (1977). *Organizational behavior* (2nd ed.). New York, NY: McGraw-Hill.

Moreno, J. L. (1934). *Who shall survive?* Washington, D.C.: Nervous and Mental Disease Publishing.

Sessoms, H. D., & Stevenson, J. L. (1981). *Leadership and group dynamics in recreation services*. Boston, MA: Allyn & Bacon.
Wilson 1978

Zimbardo, P. G., & Ruch, F. L. (1976). *Psychology and life* (2nd ed.). Glenview, IL: Scott, Foresman.

Leadership and Motivation

LEARNING OBJECTIVES

1. To gain an understanding of leadership and motivation.
2. To understand the motivation process.
3. To gain an awareness of the role of the recreation, parks, and leisure services leader in the process of motivating participants.
4. To obtain an awareness of participation benefits and their relationship to motivation.

KEY TERMS

- The Motivation Process
- Needs
- Drives
- Goals
- Goal-Directed Activity
- Participant Motivation
- Cues in the Physical Environment
- Cues in the Social Environment
- Cues in the Psychological Environment
- Leader/Participant Interaction
- Barriers
- Participation Benefits

INTRODUCTION

What moves people to participate in leisure? How can the recreation, parks, and leisure services leader influence individuals in such a way as to encourage participation in meaningful and relevant leisure experiences? How can the leader create attractive opportunities for individuals that help them move forward in ways that "make something happen . . . change the way things are . . . or . . . create something that no one else has ever created before (Kouzes & Posner, 1995, p. 11)? This is the challenge of leadership and motivation. As Kouzes and Posner note:

> Leaders cannot command commitment, only inspire it. People must believe that leaders understand their needs and have their interests at heart. Only through an intimate knowledge of their dreams, hopes, aspirations, visions, and values is the leader able to enlist support. Leadership is a dialogue, not a monologue. Leaders breathe life into the hopes and dreams of others and enable them to see exciting possibilities that the future holds. (ibid.)

Individual behavior is based on principles of motivation. Therefore, it is important for the recreation, parks, and leisure services leader to have a basic knowledge of these principles. Understanding the process of motivation helps us understand causes of human behavior, including leisure behavior. Motivation is not something we can "see," but rather involves assumptions about physiological and psychological operations (internal variables) that are inferred from observations.

The recreation, parks, and leisure services leader who understands the motivation process is able to influence the behavior of participants. The leader can use a knowledge of motivation to predict its influence on behavior and perhaps, ultimately, to help participants shape their behavior in such a way that their leisure needs are met. An understanding of motivation also allows the leader to account for differences in behavior among participants. In short, a leader with such knowledge is able to gain insight into the causes of certain participant behaviors and to predict and assess the influence of leader behavior on participants.

THE MOTIVATION PROCESS

Figure 6.1 illustrates the motivation process. The motivation process is characterized by six steps. These are: (1) the existence of needs; (2) the initiation of drives; (3) selective attention to relevant stimuli; (4) initiation of goal-directed activi-

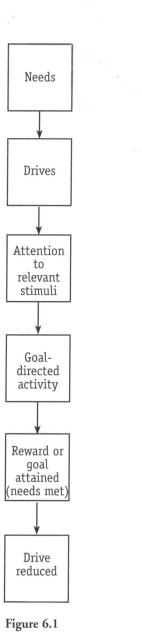

Figure 6.1
The motivation process

You have to find something that you love enough to be able to take risks, jump over the hurdles, and break through the brick walls that are always going to be placed in front of you. If you don't have that kind of feeling for what it is you're doing, you'll stop at the first giant hurdle.

George Lucas

ty; (5) attainment of a reward or goal; and (6) the reduction of the drive. A discussion of each of these variables follows.

Needs

The term often associated with need is that of deficiency. When an individual has an imbalance—physiologically, psychologically, or socially, he or she has a need. Physiological needs are those deficiencies associated with biological drives, such as the need for food, water, sex, and sleep. Physiological needs reflect the desire of individuals to maintain an internal equilibrium, or homeostasis. Psychological and social needs are more difficult to assess, but equally important. The need for companionship, social interaction, safety, love, self-esteem, self-worth, self-actualization, recognition, power, and achievement are all examples of psychological and social needs.

How does the recreation, parks, and leisure services leader gauge needs? What sources of information are available to measure this factor? Mercer (1973, p. 39) has suggested that a leisure need can be conceptualized from four different perspectives; Godbey (1981, p. 275) has added a fifth component to this model. These conceptualizations are the following:

Expressed Needs. Expressed needs can be thought of as those activities, programs, and services in which an individual currently participates.

Felt Needs. Felt needs are those needs that an individual feels he or she would like to experience in the future.

Normative Needs. Normative needs are established by expert groups who suggest minimum standards for services.

Comparative Needs. When an individual compares himself or herself with another in terms of needs, interests, and wants, he or she may identify comparative needs.

Created Needs. Created needs are developed when individuals are taught to value a particular leisure experience and, as a result, are inclined to want to continue to participate in it.

A classic conceptualization of needs is offered by Abraham Maslow. Maslow suggests that needs can be hierarchically arranged from lower order needs to higher order needs. His arrangement of needs is predicated on the assumption that needs are arranged according to priority and that lower order needs must be satisfied before the next higher order of needs can be met, and so on up the hierarchy. At the bottom of Maslow's hierarchy are physiological needs. These include the need of the individual for food, drink, and sex. These needs are followed by the need for safety, the need to belong, the need for love, the need for self-esteem, and the need for self-actualization. According to Maslow, the lower order needs are of top priority as long as they are unsatisfied. Once they are satisfied, however, the individual is free to pursue the higher needs. Maslow notes, however, that it is

There can be no progress if people have no faith in tomorrow.

John F. Kennedy

possible for one to achieve higher level needs without lower level needs being met—consider the starving artist, for example.

The recreation, parks, and leisure services leader attempting to help participants meet their needs should also be aware of Erikson's stages of psychosocial development. These stages of development have a profound effect on the types of needs that individuals must attempt to meet. Erikson specifically postulates eight stages from infancy to old age, which are described in the following list. Each stage is characterized by a conflict that must be resolved for the individual to be able to cope with conflict at later stages. These conflicts and their resolutions are related to the motivation process and the needs that the individual experiences at each stage.

> It's amazing what ordinary people can do if they set out without preconceived notions.
>
> *George F. Kettering*

Trust versus Mistrust. (First year of life.) Depending on the quality of the care received, the infant learns to trust the environment and perceive it as orderly and predictable; or to be suspicious, fearful, and mistrusting of its chaos and unpredictability.

Autonomy versus Doubt. (Second and third years of life.) From the development of motor and mental abilities and the opportunity to explore and manipulate emerges a sense of autonomy, adequacy, and self-control.

Initiative versus Guilt. (Fourth to fifth year of life.) The way parents respond to the child's self-initiated activities, intellectual as well as motor, creates either a sense of freedom and initiative at one extreme or, at the other, a sense of guilt and a feeling of being an inept intruder in an adult world.

Industry versus Inferiority. (Sixth to eleventh year.) The child's concern for how things work and how they ought to operate leads to a sense of industry in formulating rules, organizing, ordering, and being industrious.

Identity versus Role Confusion. (Adolescence from 12 to 18 years of age.) During this period, the adolescent begins to develop multiple ways of perceiving things, can see things from another person's point of view, and behaves differently in different situations according to what is deemed appropriate.

Intimacy versus Isolation. (Young adulthood.) The consequences of the adult's attempts at reaching out to make contact with others may result in intimacy (a commitment to other people), or else in isolation from close personal relationships.

A LEGACY OF LEADERSHIP
Rachel Carson (1907-1964)

Long before words such as ecology and ecosystem found their way into the public dialogue, Rachel Carson wrote of a philosophy of environmentalism. Through her writings and biological research, Rachel Carson helped millions of people develop an environmental consciousness. As a trained marine biologist, she devoted her life to exploring, understanding, and sharing the wonders of ocean life. Her first books include *Under the Sea-Wind* (1941), *The Sea Around Us* (1951), and *The Edge of the Sea* (1955), in which she exquisitely inscribed that all the life of the planet is inter-related, that each species has its own ties to others, and that all are related to earth.

Her fourth book, *Silent Spring* (1962), warned of the hazards of pesticide misuse and abuse. This book might not have been written had it not been for a letter Carson received from Olga Owens Huckins. Huckins owned a private bird sanctuary in Duxbury, Massachusetts. One day in 1958, Owens became horrified to find birds dead and dying on her property. Just days earlier, local agencies had conducted a massive, unannounced spraying of the pesticide DDT. Huckins asked Carson to look into governmental regulations regarding chemical spraying.

With more than a quarter million copies sold in the first three months it was officially published, *Silent Spring* sparked a blaze of public outrage. The favorable reviews described this book as a "devastating, heavily documented, relentless attack upon human carelessness, greed and irresponsibility...." On the other side, the chemical and pesticide industry tried to have the book suppressed and challenged its findings. These corporations labeled Carson as a food-faddist, nature nut, and fish-lover. After many governmental investigations and reports on pesticide use confirming Carson's findings, DDT was eventually band in the U.S. in 1972.

Before her death in 1964 due to cancer, Carson received many honors for her work, among them the Schweitzer Medal of the Animal Welfare Institute; the National Wildlife Federation's "Conservationist of the Year;" and the first medal awarded to a woman by the National Audubon Society. In 1980, she was posthumously awarded the highest civilian decoration in the nation, the Presidential Medal of Freedom. Rachel Carson's contributions to the recreation, parks, and leisure services field is the awareness that she brought about increased awareness and interest in our natural and wild places, spawning the growth of outdoor recreation and environmental education.

Generativity versus Self-Absorbtion. (Middle age.) Here one's life experiences may extend the focus of concern beyond one's self for family, society, or future generations.

Integrity versus Despair. (Old age.) As a consequence of the solutions developed at each of the preceding stages, one can enjoy the fulfillment of life with a sense of integrity. Despair is what faces the person who believes that their life has been unsatisfying and misdirected.

These stages offer the leader profound insight into the human being at various stages in his or her life. This insight should help the recreation, parks, and leisure services leader plan more effectively for individuals at each of these stages.

Drives

The step in the motivation process that follows the existence of needs is the initiation of drives. We use the term drive to mean an activator and director of behavior. A drive is the energizing process that results in movement toward the fulfillment of a need. Different needs will result in the activation of different drives. Also, the stronger the drive (e.g., a great thirst), the more the activity. Specifically, a drive is a result of internal conditions within the individual that direct that person toward a specific goal. For example, a drive to socialize might result from a need for companionship.

Drives cannot be "seen," only inferred. By considering available information regarding stimulus conditions and behavior that is observable, one can make assumptions regarding the internal variable "affecting" behavior. Drives are often linked with the concept of energy arousal. This concept implies that the individual becomes active in order to meet a need. Drives are directed by needs. Drives enable individuals to focus or channel their energies in such a way that their behavior results in the fulfillment of a need or alleviation of a deficiency.

It is important to recognize that drives can vary from culture to culture. Moreover, drives can vary among individuals within a given culture. In certain cultures, the motivation to engage in leisure behavior may be stronger than it is in the United States or Canada. In other cultures, the motivation to work may be stronger due to a greater likelihood that individuals will experience deficiencies of food, shelter, and

> No man's knowledge here can go beyond his experience.
>
> *John Locke*

security if they don't considerable work effort. Although there is no clear-cut agreement on how drives should be classified, most psychologists suggest that primary and secondary drives exist. Primary drives are related to such factors as hunger, thirst, sex, sleep, and avoidance of pain. Although primary drives are important to a comprehensive understanding of the motivation process, secondary drives are more relevant to our discussion. An important distinction to be made between secondary and other drives is that secondary drives must be learned. They are not biologically innate, but rather are initiated and satisfied by social and psychological factors. Although the inability to attain social and psychological goals may not be life threatening, as are biological deficiencies, it can result in emotional deprivation and limitation of life satisfaction. The following motives or drives (Luthans, 2002) have been categorized as secondary:

Competence. Competence refers to the ability of individuals to interact successfully with their environment.

Novelty or Curiosity. Individuals desire to explore or manipulate their environment, or both. Psychologists have suggested that individuals, when placed in novel situations, have a natural curiosity to search or explore them.

Activity. Individuals have a desire for activity. Activity allows individuals to interact with their environment.

Affection. Human love or affection, as a drive, is focused on the individual's desire for nurturing, emotional support, and comfort.

Achievement. The desire to achieve or excel is a strong motivator in today's society. The need for achievement is characterized by goal-seeking behavior.

Power. The desire for power can be thought of as the desire to control or influence others.

Affiliation. The drive to interact, create associations, and create and maintain friendships are all factors associated with the desire for affiliation.

Freedom of Choice. Individuals desire to retain their freedom of choice. This is related to the concept of reactance. Reactance can be thought of as the actions of individuals to resist decisions that are "made for them."

Social Approval. As individuals, we are involved in many activities so that others will "notice, appreciate, honor, help, or love and cherish us" (Zimbardo & Ruch, 1976, p. 385). The desire to gain approval from others is extremely strong, and individuals will go to considerable lengths to accomplish this.

Altruism. Altruism can be thought of as helping others without expectation of external rewards. Altruism is thought to be related to feelings of empathy by some theorists.

Consistency. Individuals have a desire for balance and consistency in their lives. Leisure is often viewed as a counterbalance to work.

Security. Individuals have a desire to be secure. They will avoid situations that are dangerous or that threaten their security.

Status. Many individuals have a desire to possess and maintain material symbols of status in our society, such as expensive homes, expensive clothes, and so on.

> Absolute identity with one's cause is the first and greatest condition of successful leadership.
>
> *Woodrow Wilson*

Attention to Relevant Stimuli

Once an individual's needs have resulted in drives, the next step in the motivation process occurs. The individual, at this point, becomes engaged in attention to relevant stimuli. Relevant stimuli can be defined as information that relates to the individual's current state of need. This information may be in the form of words and phrases or may involve other information processed through the five senses. For example, an individual motivated by a desire for safety will attend to such relevant stimuli as stoplights, traffic signs, or sirens. With the knowledge gained from such cues or information, the individual may accomplish one or more of the following: to predict the likelihood of future events, to actually control events, to alter his or her behavior to make it more appropriate and effective in terms of the events being forecast, or a combination of these. In short, the individual receives information (or cues) that are psychological, social, or physical in nature that signal the imminent occurrence of such varied events as danger, pleasure, or relief.

How does the concept of attention to relevant stimuli relate to participant–leader interaction? The participant attending a recreation, parks, and leisure services activity is immediately subjected to many cues and bits of information. The participant will look around and perhaps see smiles, friendly faces, special equipment, brightly colored posters, and individuals in casual clothing suggesting activity, and will listen to verbal cues such as "fun," "good time," or "glad you are here." From these cues, the participant will be able to predict the likely occurrence of a pleasurable and possibly exciting and creative experience. In other words, the participant is able to form expectations based on the verbal and visual cues that are received. As the participant begins actually to engage in the activity, he or she will continue to receive cues, possibly ones such as laughter, movement, and jumping up and down, and will receive verbal cues such as "great catch," "this team played great," or "boy, are you fast." As the participant receives initial cues and these later cues, he or she is able to shape his or her behavior to correspond to the opportunities that are currently being offered. In this way, the participant's behavior is more effective in terms of the opportunities offered, and it is more likely that his or her needs will be met.

How does the participant know that certain cues, such as smiling, positive verbal phrases, and play equipment, signal the likelihood of certain outcomes? In order for the participant to predict an outcome, he or she must have had prior experience with the stimulus. Specifically, the stimulus must have been paired, sometime in the past, with a certain type of outcome. Smiling, for example, has been paired many times with positive outcomes. Consequently, the participant would have learned that smiling is a very reliable predictor of "fun." In the same vein, play equipment would likely have been paired many times with fun. However, had it not been paired with "fun" but with misfortune instead, it might signal "danger" to the participant and act as a predictor of the likelihood of a fear-laden experience. The signals that cues impart, then, vary with the individual participant. A positive signal to one individual may be a negative signal to another. The topic of "cues" will be covered in more depth later in this chapter.

Goal-Directed Activity

The step in the motivation process that follows attention to relevant stimuli is an actual behavior or goal-directed activity. Goal-directed behavior is the detectable manifestation of drives, such as desire for power, affection, approval, and so on. It can be defined as behavior that results in the reduction of a need or drive. In simple terms, this means that goal-directed activity should be viewed as an indication of the individual's inner state. It should not, however, be viewed as a total picture of the individual's needs. Observing behavior

The soul that has no established aim loses itself.

Montaigne

provides us with an opportunity to learn about the individual by associating stimulus conditions and observable behavioral outcomes with the motives that are likely to cause that type of behavior.

When motivation acts as a catalyst for behavior, that behavior is said to be "goal directed" or "purposeful." Goal-directed activity is engaged in to meet the needs of the individual. For example, the need for companionship may result in a drive for affiliation with others. Recall that the drive for affiliation involves the desire to interact with others and to produce friendships. The goal-directed activity associated with this drive might find the individual joining a club, attending group social activities, or becoming a member of an athletic team. In other words, goal-directed behavior works to alleviate the needs and drives of the individual. When an individual is hungry, the goal-directed activity becomes the search for food. Obviously, more complex secondary motives, such as the desire for power, altruism, status, and achievement, often result in complex patterns of goal-directed behavior.

Goal-directed activity can be "assisted" by attention to relevant stimuli. Input from the leader can nudge participants toward the type of goal-directed activity that will best meet their goals. For example, the participant engaged in a creative activity might assimilate such information as "praise is given for extensive use of color," "praise is given for individuality," and "praise is given for using several types of mediums," and then use these cues to give direction to his or her behavior in order to fulfill needs related to recognition, achievement, competence, status, and social approval.

Leisure behavior can be a result of many and varied drives. All the drives listed in prior pages serve as motivators for leisure. Some drives may be stronger for one person than for another. Certain drives seem to be more evident today than in past years. For example, more individuals today are involved in high adventure, risk-oriented programs, which suggests an increased need for novelty, risk, and adventure. The great interest in travel provides another example of the increased need for novelty, adventure, and change. Leisure is also often used as a vehicle for social approval and status, as evidenced by participating in cultural activities, engaging in "in" sports such as tennis, sailing, and racquetball, and installing of expensive home entertainment centers.

▰▰▰ Attainment of Reward or Goal

The next component of the motivation process, goal attainment, is dependent on the previous component, goal-direct-

> Always do what is right. This will surprise some people and astonish the rest.
>
> *Mark Twain*

ed activity. Goal-directed activity often results in the individual's goal attainment. The point at which this occurs and the individual's needs are met is a subjective measure that can only be determined by the individual himself or herself. One individual involved in a sport may have to hit only one base run to meet needs for recognition, achievement, and social approval. Another individual involved in the same sport may have to hit several home runs to meet the same need. In a social situation, one individual may need to make only one friend to achieve goals related to affiliation, whereas another individual may need to be "the center of attention" in order to meet this same need.

When the individual's goal is met, a reinforcement process occurs. Because the behavior that the individual has engaged in has, indeed, brought about the realization of the intended goal, the individual forms an expectancy that similar behavior in the future will again bring about similar results. For example, the individual who has participated in a summer day camp program may, as a result of the activity and effort expended in this program, have fulfilled such needs as recognition, novelty, achievement, pleasure, and social approval. This individual will expect, as a result of this experience and the consequent fulfillment of needs and meeting of goals, that similar future experiences will meet these same needs. In other words, he or she will be more likely to participate in next year's summer program and may even generalize his or her experience to include an expectancy that all recreation, parks, and leisure services organization activities are likely to provide opportunities for goal fulfillment.

As mentioned, goal attainment and goal-directed activity are interrelated. Not only does goal-directed activity have an influence on goal attainment, but goal attainment and the way that the goal is attained will have an influence on future behavior related to the same goal. How strongly or how quickly the goal is achieved will affect the likelihood that the individual will engage in behavior to reproduce the experience. On the other hand, if the goal is delayed, the individual may not pursue it as strongly in the future. We don't like to "wait" for things.

██████ Need and Drive Reduction

The final step in the motivation process is the reduction of needs and drives. When needs and drives are reduced, the individual, as an obvious consequence, will not actively attempt to engage in behavior associated with meeting the need, even though the habit may be a strong one. For example, an individual who loves to play tennis, but who has not been able to play all winter, will be strongly motivated to take action that will enable him or her to play tennis in the spring and early summer. However, by late fall the same individual may have had enough tennis playing and, as a result, may decline an invitation to play even if it is offered. Therefore, the degree to which an individual's need has been met influences behavior usually associated with meeting the need. It is important that the recreation, parks, and leisure services leader be aware of this phase of the motivation process, because it can have a considerable effect on the motivation of participants. For example, it may be relatively easy to interest children in a summer playground program at the beginning of the summer, but by midsummer or the end of the summer when the children have been involved in the program for some time, their drive to participate actively may not be as strong. The leader may have to put forth some extra effort in order to maintain interest in the program.

The Role of the Environment in the Motivation Process. The motivation process just presented is based on the stimulus-response theory of motivation. This motivation model suggests that individual behavior occurs in response to primary biological needs and learned secondary needs. Further, it has been suggested that using this need reduction model to explain motivation, especially as it relates to leisure, fails to take into account the influence of the individual on the environment. Discussing the influence of the individual on the environment, Kusyszyn (1979, p. 167) writes:

1. There is a strong basic human motive: to have an effect on our environment. . . .
2. We need to have an effect on our environment in order to confirm our existence . . . We confirm our existence when we have an effect on our environment by becoming aroused. . . .
3. Having an effect on our environment can . . . give us a sense of self-worth. . . . When we consciously and purposefully set out to have a specific effect on our environment and we succeed in producing that effect, we feel good about the whole event. . . .
4. By having an effect on our environment and by becoming aroused through feedback we get from producing the effect, we put ourselves into an altered state of consciousness.

The altered state of consciousness produced by an individual's arousal, as a result of being able to affect the environment, is often associated with a leisure or play experience. Various terms have been used to describe this state, including peak, arousal, and flow. The term peak experience was coined by Maslow (1968); arousal, as it relates to leisure, by Ellis (1973, p. 118); and flow by Csikszentmihalyi (1975). Each of these individuals has developed models to explain his respective concepts.

Courage and perseverance have a magical talisman, before which difficulties disappear and obstacles vanish into air.

John Quincy Adams

Ellis's "arousal-seeking" theory of play suggests that play occurs when individuals seek arousal by interacting with the environment in ways that are above and beyond those needed for survival (Ellis, 1973). While engaged in an arousal-seeking activity, the individual "learns." As a result of this learning, future play behavior is shaped and, with the continuance of arousal, play behavior becomes more complex. Developmental stages reflect his progression to more and more complex levels of play. In short, this model suggests that the environment and the individual interact, resulting in learning, which, in turn, influences future behavior.

Csikszentmihalyi's concept of flow is a compelling construct for explaining the interaction of the individual with the environment (Ellis, 1973). It provides a basis for understanding boredom and anxiety. He suggests that the leisure experience is influenced by the individual's skill level as it relates to the challenge present in the environment. When the challenge presented in the environment is greater than the individual's skill level or knowledge, the individual experiences anxiety. Conversely, when the challenge presented in the environment is less than the individual's skill level or knowledge, boredom results. When the two factors—challenge of the environment and skill level of the individual—are matched, the individual enters into a state of flow or, as Csikszentmihalyi indicates, the "autotelic" experience. The environment (challenge) and individual (with skills) interaction described in this model provides a basis for explaining outcomes of the leisure experience. This may account for the fact that some individuals are motivated to participate in certain activities whereas others are not.

PARTICIPANT MOTIVATION: THE ROLE OF THE LEADER

What is the role of the recreation, parks, and leisure services leader in motivating participants? What does a leader do that motivates participants to engage in activities and derive expected as well as unanticipated benefits from their involvement? These are complex questions, primarily because of the individual nature of the leisure experience, variables in individual dispositions and perceptions, and the unpredictability of the interaction between the leader and participants.

In reviewing the process of motivation, it is important to establish some assumptions. First it can be assumed that individuals seek out experiences, not products, activities, services, facilities, and so on. In other words, the individual who buys ski equipment is really purchasing a "ski experience." A second assumption is that individuals participate in activities because of the expectation of some gain or benefit. More specifically, individuals participate in activities in order to meet needs. The third assumption is that the leader will play a key role in shaping, molding, or providing experiences that meet leisure needs. In the case of the face-to-face recreation, parks, and leisure services leader, this key role is one of structuring the environment in order to motivate individuals in such a way that they experience leisure successfully. The leader's knowledge of appropriate communication, group dynamics, and leadership techniques enables this to occur.

Structuring of the environment primarily involves the creation of cues that signal to the participant that a certain type of experience is available. For example, participants often seek out experiences that are exciting. By shaping the environment, the leader can produce conditions that indicate the likelihood of an exciting experience. The leader, for example, might use a communication style and pattern that have a high degree of energy and enthusiasm and that reflect a keen interest and excitement about the impending experience. This type of cue provides a signal to the participant that his or her need for excitement can be met. Even though it is trite, we often say that enthusiasm is contagious. This is an example of that maxim.

The idea of cueing an individual to an experience has its basis in social occasions theory. This theory suggests that the leisure experience is produced as a result of the interactions of individuals in social occasions (Rossman, 1995). In social occasions, we find a generic structure made up of six elements including: interacting people, physical place, social objects, interaction rules, relational history, and the animation of the event. The role of the recreation, parks, and leisure services leader is to cue individuals to physical, social, and/or abstract objects that exist in the environment that can produce a meaningful leisure experience. The leader does this by directing individuals toward a course of action that will result in a meaningful leisure experience.

The leader can mold the environment in such a way that participants are unaware that their expectations are being shaped. Consider, for example, the leader who wants to plan and implement a dance for teenagers. The experience that the teenagers desire is one full of excitement, social interaction, euphoria, and fun. What can the leader do to set the stage for this type of experience? In advance, through various promotional mechanisms, the leader may advertise the activity in such a way that its potential for excitement and fun is emphasized. This advertisement of the dance will present cues that create expectations. Expectations, in turn, will motivate participants to go to the dance. Once the leader has

> When one door closes, another door opens; but we often look so long and so regretfully on the closed door that we don't see the ones which open for us.
>
> *Alexander Graham Bell*

advertised the dance, he or she might engage in preparations that will provide further cues that meet participants' anticipation of excitement. These preparations might include dramatic lighting, festive decorations, or the selection of exciting and loud music. All these preparations by the leader may not be consciously acknowledged by participants; however, the environment will be shaped in such a way that their expectations for excitement will be met, and they will have a good time.

At the dance itself, the leader may interact one on one with participants in such a way that further cues are given as to the nature of the experience that enable participants to be self-motivated and meet their needs for excitement and fun. For example, the leader might interact with participants in an effusive, enthusiastic manner, might attempt to insert some element of unpredictability into the evening's activities to heighten the excitement further, and might dance with some of the participants that are not yet dancing. This type of interaction with participants, one on one or leader of a group, is the crux of face-to-face activity leadership. The dynamics of interaction between the leader and the participant or participants is at the heart of recreation, parks, and leisure services leadership. The success or failure of this interaction is often directly tied to the extent to which a participant achieves the desired ends of a leisure experience.

Figure 6.2 presents a model demonstrating the process of participant-leader interaction. In this process of interaction, the leader usually is aware of the participant's needs either from the participant himself or herself or via the leader's perceptions. In order to create an environment in which these needs can be met and individuals can become self-motivated, the leader must become aware of the participants' expectations. For some participants, fantasy might be the major reason for pursuing leisure. For another participant, escape might be the desired outcome of the leisure experience. The leader can structure the environment by providing cues to either influence expectations or reinforce behavior. In the former case, cues attempt to shape the preliminary attitudes, interests, and emotions of the participant to "fit" the experience at hand. In the latter case, cues reinforce or reward the participant for behavior that occurs during the leisure experience in order to help the participant meet needs.

There are three basic types of cues that the recreation, parks, and leisure services leader can provide to the participant by structuring or arranging the physical, social, or psychological environments or a combination of them. By structuring or arranging the environment, we mean that the

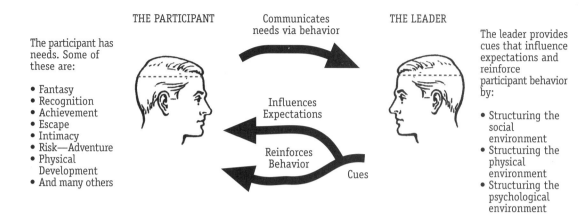

The participant has needs. Some of these are:

- Fantasy
- Recognition
- Achievement
- Escape
- Intimacy
- Risk—Adventure
- Physical Development
- And many others

THE PARTICIPANT

Communicates needs via behavior

Influences Expectations

Reinforces Behavior

Cues

THE LEADER

The leader provides cues that influence expectations and reinforce participant behavior by:

- Structuring the social environment
- Structuring the physical environment
- Structuring the psychological environment

Figure 6.2
A model demonstrating the process of participant-leader interaction

leader organizes it, consciously or unconsciously, in such a way that it evokes or reinforces desired leisure behavior.

Cues in the Physical Environment

The way in which the physical environment is arranged has a great deal of influence on participant behavior. In simplistic terms, the recreation, parks, and leisure services leader can manipulate the physical environment by changing such things as lighting, spatial arrangements, color, decorations, and other factors. For example, the seating arrangement of individuals for a group discussion can be set up in such a way that all individuals are facing each other in a circle. This arrangement of the physical environment may promote group interaction and discussion. In another situation, the leader may want to arrange the chairs so that the participants focus toward the individual at the front of the room. Leaders often try to create a mood with lighting, for example, by lowering the lighting in a dance situation in order to allow participants to feel less inhibited and thus create a more dramatic effect. Decorations may also be put up to give a festive, light, colorful, and cheery feeling. Again, this is a manipulation of the physical environment.

Spatial arrangements can be manipulated to create feelings of intimacy, or perhaps freedom from restrictions. For example, it would be inappropriate to hold a knitting class in a gymnasium. The leader would want to conduct this type of class in a more intimate, smaller area. Individuals also feel more intimate in environments with more objects (e.g., couches, chairs, tables) than they do in rooms that are relatively bare. If a leader wanted to create a mood of intimacy and belonging in a teenage center, for example, he or she might want to manipulate the environment so that it would be "comfortably cluttered."

In terms of larger spatial arrangements, theme parks serve as a good example of how the manipulation of the physical environment is used to evoke certain participant responses. The location of the soda pop stand will be placed directly after a popcorn stand, thus manipulating the environment to serve the participant best.

The color of the environment can also have an influence on the participant's behavior and feelings. Green and blue, for example, are soothing, restful colors that might be incorporated into areas designated for discussion and introspection. Red and orange are exciting, stimulating colors that might be used effectively in areas designated for high-energy leisure experiences. The manipulation of color, like the other manipulations of the physical environment (light, spatial effects, etc.), provides cues to the participant as to the type of experience that is available. It contributes to the anticipation and expectations of the participant in a channeled or focused manner.

▬▬▬Cues in the Social Environment

Organization or manipulation of the social environment can also influence participant behavior. When we speak of the manipulation of the social environment, we are referring to the leader's ability to create opportunities for friendship, interaction, love, companionship, membership, recognition, and so on. Because of the nature of face-to-face leadership, social manipulation is often directly dependent on (and related to) the individual leader's personality, demeanor, and behavior. When the recreation, parks, and leisure services leader is open, effusive, energetic, enthusiastic, and interested in others, this behavior affects the social environment. This type of behavior is natural with many leaders and occurs without conscious awareness of its impact on the behavior of participants. This type of behavior evokes responses from participants; it motivates people. In the right situation and circumstance, it is a very powerful factor, directly related to the success or failure of participants to anticipate and achieve experiences.

In addition to the effective behavior of the leader, there are actual structural manipulations of the social environment that the leader can initiate to influence participant behavior. As discussed in Chapter 5, the types of groups and group sizes can affect the likelihood that friendships, companionship, interaction, and so on will occur. If a group is divided into threes for discussion or activities, these triads may be

Success is the satisfaction of feeling that one is realizing one's ideal.

Anna Pavlova

subject to dissension, argument, and hostility. By dividing the group by twos for activities, one can minimize these problems and achieve greater harmony among and between participants.

There are also very direct ways that the leader can intervene or provide cues that will result in the participant's feeling of recognition, hence being motivated. Leaders can use tangible rewards (such as ribbons, trophies, medals, certificates), and intangible rewards (such as verbal recognition, praise and special privileges) to manipulate the social environment and provide cues that stimulate participant involvement and interest. These two types of cues can be used by the leader in conjunction with one another; intangible recognition can be reinforced with tangible rewards, and vice versa. The leader can motivate participants without the use of tangible cues or forms of recognition; however, it is difficult, if not impossible, to motivate participants without intangible forms of recognition, such as verbal praise.

Cues in the Psychological Environment

The manipulation of the psychological environment can also influence participant behavior. When we speak of the psychological environment, we are referring to the participant's need for self-knowledge, novelty, aesthetic satisfactions, self-worth, self-identification, achievement, power, mastery, and transcendence (Heywood, 1979). The manipulation of the psychological environment may be more difficult than manipulation of the social or physical environments. There are many things that the leader can do, however, to influence the perceptions of the participant, which may, in turn, influence whether he or she is motivated. For example, it has been suggested that individuals must have an illusion of competence and freedom in order to enter into the leisure experience successfully. It is possible for the leader to create freedom within the environment by allowing the participant to choose among alternatives. Although those alternatives may be carefully structured, the individual can be led to feel a sense of freedom. The leader can give the illusion of competence by creating challenges equal to individual skill levels, or the leader may group participants according to level of skill (e.g., slow-break versus fast-break basketball). Participants may develop feelings of self-worth and identification by being part of a team and perhaps by being delegated a leadership role. A leadership role may also provide the participant with a sense of power and prestige. In fact, the leader may want to provide opportunities for all group members to become involved in a leadership role in some way.

The most useful person in the world is the man or woman who knows how to get along with other people. Human relations is the most important science in the broad curriculum of living.

Stanley C. Allyn

It is important for the leader to allow the participant to evaluate his or her own performance and benefits from leisure participation. The leader can help participants develop self-knowledge and a sense of self-worth by offering appropriate dialogue or cues that allow participants to formulate their own opinions regarding their leisure experiences. For example, the leader should mirror the participant's feelings and observations rather than offering his or her own observations, allowing the participant to develop the conclusions. Rather than telling a child, "You did a good job," the leader should say, "You look as if you feel pretty good about your performance today," prompting the child's internal response, "I am pretty pleased!" This type of psychological cue allows the participant to assess himself or herself and develop conclusions that are more conducive to feelings of self-worth. When we are told that we "did a good job," often our response is to think, "I could have done better," or "I really didn't." If we draw our own conclusions, this is avoided.

Leader-Participant Interaction

Figure 6.3 depicts a model that links the process of leader-participant interaction with the more comprehensive model of motivation. Recall the model of motivation presented earlier in the chapter. Our discussion will now focus on the role of cues used by the recreation, parks, and leisure services leader to facilitate in the motivation process. As individual needs are perceived by the leader, the leader can begin to form cues that will respond to these needs. Cues can also be presented as the participant moves to the second stage of the motivation process, that of attention to relevant stimuli.

It is at this stage that the participant is likely to interpret the leader's cues and form his or her expectations, anticipating events. Following the formation of participant expectations, the participant will exhibit behavior; the leader can use cues to direct this behavior toward more goal-directed ends. The leader at this time also receives information from the participant that is useful in determining the effectiveness of the cues being given and is useful in determining whether or not cues should be changed or modified. These efforts by the leader and the participant are continued until the need or needs of the participant are fulfilled.

In discussing the motivation process, Edginton, Hudson and Lankford have suggested that the recreation, parks, and leisure services professional can directly influence four important variables (2001). They indicate that a leader can assist an individual to meet his or her leisure needs through the processes of expectancy, availability, ability, and satisfaction. Following is a description of each of these processes

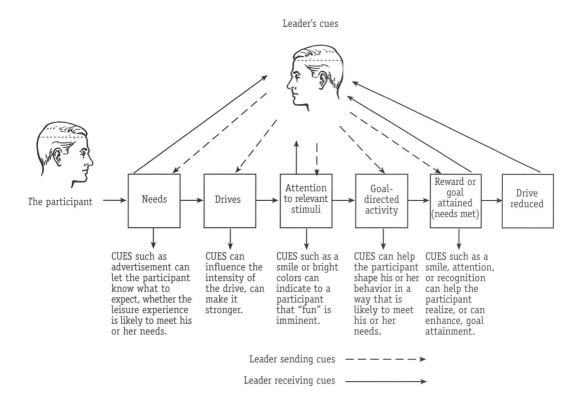

Figure 6.3
A model relating the effects of participant-leader interaction on motivation

that can be used by the leader in relation to the motivation process.

Expectancy. According to the theory of expectancy, whether an individual will participate in a given activity is dependent on past experience. Those individuals who have had their needs satisfied in the past through participation in an activity are more likely to participate in similar types of activities to meet similar needs in the future. The leader's knowledge of those activities that have previously resulted in meeting an individual's expectations of receiving benefits can aid the individual in planning future activities and services that will meet these same needs. Often cues that are related to the individual's past experiences will motivate him or her to participate in current or future experiences or both. Very simply, the leader can remind the participant of the "great time" he or she had before to motivate him or her to participate in a future activity.

Availability. Availability is related to the individual's perception of his or her environment. Individuals may or may not perceive that a situation can meet their needs. One individual may perceive a situation to be a great opportunity to meet a need, whereas another individual may view the same situation as being devoid of such an opportunity. In the case of the first individual, motivation to become involved will occur because he or she perceives that goals can be achieved and needs satisfied. In the case of the second individual, involvement is not likely to occur because benefits and rewards are not perceived as being available. The leader can influence participants' perceptions by making the goals appear more accessible. For example, the leader can structure an activity so that a lower skill level is needed to be successful.

Ability. The recreation, parks, and leisure services leader can work with individuals to help them to improve their ability, which, in turn, will influence their perceived competence. The participant must have a perception of ability in an area of activity in order to seek out an opportunity for participation in it. A focus of recreation, parks, and leisure services organizations is the development of leisure skills and abilities. Instructional programs provided by organizations are directed toward helping individuals attain not only exposure to activities, but also minimum competence in them. Individuals who become frustrated and lose their motivation because of a lack of ability will not only be more likely to drop out of the activity, but may avoid it in the future because of expectancy.

Satisfaction. The leader can greatly influence the amount of satisfaction an individual derives from an activity. Satisfaction is influenced by the willingness of the leader to provide praise or recognition. In Chapter 1 we stressed the importance of providing positive encouragement to individuals and cited it as a key to successful leadership. The ability to provide praise in such a way that participants are positively reinforced is an important leadership skill, as it has major influence on the motivation process and is appropriate with any age group and at any skill level. Meaningful feedback is crucial to the participant's development of feelings of self-worth, self-esteem, and satisfaction (ibid.).

Removing Barriers

Perhaps another way of viewing the role of the recreation, parks, and leisure services leader in the motivation process is as an individual responsible for assisting in barrier removal. Many barriers can occur that prevent individuals from achieving desired goals. These barriers sometimes are within the influence of the participant, whereas at other times they are within the leader's sphere of influence. The inability to overcome barriers to the leisure experience often results in frustration, anxiety, and aggression, and neg-

LEADERSHIP: A POINT OF VIEW
FROM THE PROFESSION
James R. Hall

James R. Hall is Director, Boise (Idaho) Parks and Recreation Department. He has had a 34-year career in parks and recreation, and currently is Co-Chair of NRPS's Park, Recreation, Open Space, and Greenway Guidelines. The Boise Parks and Recreation Department is a multifaceted organization (adult and youth recreation programs, Idaho Ice World, three cemeteries, AZA accredited Zoo Boise, urban forestry with 36,000 trees, Foothills open space management, Ridge to Rivers Trail program, Park Resources, Design & Planning, Administration) with an operating budget of $15.9 million and 154 full time employees with an additional 600 recreational temp and seasonal employees. Over 3,000 acres of park space in 93 parks, a beautiful 21-mile Greenbelt along the Boise River, 39,000 acres of public land that contains over 90 miles of trails in the Boise Foothills, and one of the top rated indoor ice facilities in the country (*American Hockey Magazine*). Hall is a member of the American Academy of Park and Recreation Administration.

On leadership. . . .is about passion for your job, your community, your mission, and your long term vision of how you want your surroundings to look. Being the true believer in what you do. . . .focus your career . . . on the richness you create for your community. That is the most pleasing thing you will ever do!

Leadership and success. . . . all leadership levels in an organization are equally as important when focusing your goal on being a highly effective, innovation, productive, and respected department in the eyes of political leaders, citizens and customers.

The exemplary leader. . . .A highly effective leader in our organization is one who has great enthusiasm, knows how to tell the story of our department, lives integrity, learns from mistakes, puts themselves at risk every day and questions process.

Leadership in action. . . . There are not too many role models left in our society for young people to look up to except in our profession. Our work touches the lives of countless people every day, to some we are their true family. Always live your life full of respect, compassion, hope and opportunity, so that your time serves as a positive example to those around you. The goal is to have them watch, question and learn how to become the best human being possible.

atively influences the psychological and social development of individuals.

Some of the barriers that can prevent individuals from achieving a satisfying leisure experience have been identified by Edginton, Hudson, Dieser and Edginton (2004, p. 477-478). They are the following:

> Attitudinal. A person's attitude toward leisure may influence his or her ability to participate successfully in a leisure activity, program, or service. Since attitudes are learned, the leader can help the individual develop new and more positive attitudes.

> Consumptive. The consumptive type of barrier relates to the influence of commercial organizations on leisure behavior. Commercial organizations exert considerable effort and expense to encourage consumption of products that may not meet individual needs.

> Temporal. Not all leisure experiences are linked to mechanical, linear clock time. The bondage of the clock often affects leisure fulfillment. Too much time, as well as a lack of time, can create barriers.

> Communicative. The way in which information is transmitted to individuals can contribute to the formation of barriers, especially if it is transmitted at the wrongtime, using the wrong channel of communication, and without sufficient opportunity for feed back.

> Social-Cultural and Economic. Often an individual's social, cultural, and economic status will determine his or her leisure preferences. Lack of money obviously can be a barrier. The leader can attempt to equalize opportunity that might be affected by these variables.

> Health. An individual may have physical or emotional factors that act as barriers. The leader can attempt to structure activities in such ways that circumvent these barriers to participation.

> Experiential. Previous adverse experiences or the simple lack of previous involvement can act as barriers. The leader can attempt to help the individual overcome adverse feelings regarding participation or develop skills and knowledge that will facilitate a successful leisure experience, or both.

These barriers can adversely affect leisure motivation and participation. Recreation, parks, and leisure services leaders should work with individuals to help them identify and for-

People are not remembered by how few times they fail, but by how often they succeed. Every wrong step is another step forward.

Thomas Alva Edison

mulate solutions to overcome such barriers. There are some recreation, parks and leisure services leaders who create more barriers than they remove. The leader should establish a positive atmosphere in which his or her primary consideration is the removal of barriers. By doing so, the leader can contribute positively to the motivation process.

PARTICIPATION BENEFITS

A chapter on motivation is incomplete without addressing the benefits that are derived by the participant. It is the anticipation of benefits (the fulfillment of psychological, social, and physical needs rather than activities or products, that motivates the individual to become involved in leisure experiences. Individuals look for experiences that will meet their needs in a way that is beneficial to them. The recreation, parks, and leisure services leader should view activities, programs, and other services as vehicles that enable individuals to satisfy their expectations and achieve desired benefits. In this sense, programs are not the ends but the means to an end. They are a way of organizing and distributing agency resources to meet participant needs.

Murphy, Williams, Niepoth, and Brown (1973) suggest that recreation, parks, and leisure services agencies provide opportunities for a variety of behaviors. They also suggest that "the basic method used by agencies to structure opportunities that encourage different kinds of leisure behavior is the creation and/or manipulation of physical and human environments (p. 73–76.) Murphy et al. add that the human environment may be manipulated or influenced through communication techniques, leadership styles, and other instructional activities as well as by the creation of a positive interpersonal climate. These authors suggest that recreation, parks, and leisure services agencies can provide opportunities for some of the following behaviors:

> **Socializing Behavior.** Often individuals seek opportunities to interact with one another. This is characteristic of socializing behavior.

> **Associative Behavior.** Often individuals seek opportunities to gather together around a common interest. This is indicative of associative behavior.

> **Acquisitive Behavior.** Acquisitive behavior involves the desire of individuals to collect and gather together items of interest. Often individuals will then form clubs or groups to display and discuss their collections.

Your goals are the road maps that guide you and show you what is possible for your life.

Les Brown

Competitive Behavior. The desire to test one's skills, strategies, and endurance against others is indicative of in competitive behavior.

Testing Behavior. Testing oneself against a standard is characteristic of testing behavior.

Risk-Taking Behavior. Often individuals seek out experiences that are novel, unpredictable, and dangerous. This is an example of risk-taking behavior.

Vicarious Experiencing. Individuals may derive satisfaction from viewing or reading about the experiences of others. This is an example of vicarious experiencing.

Explorative Behavior. Seeking out environments new to the individual through travel, reading, or even scientific investigation is characteristic of explorative behavior.

Sensory Stimulation. The stimulation of the individual's senses can provide pleasure and is sought by individuals as a benefit of the leisure experience.

Physical Expression. The opportunity to experience physical expression through both fine and gross m o t o r movement, is an experience often chosen by individuals.

Creative Behavior. The ability to express oneself in new and meaningful ways is an experience that individuals often pursue. There are many avenues for this type of behavior.

Appreciative Behavior. The appreciation of the efforts of others can be a satisfying experience sought by individuals.

Variety-Seeking Behavior. Individuals seek opportunities that will enable them to have experiences that are not in their daily routine. Leisure is often an alternative to the routine of work, for example.

Anticipatory and Recollective Behavior. The anticipation that occurs before involvement in an activity often produces a sense of excitement and euphoria. Furthermore, the recollection of previous leisure involvement produces similar feelings. (ibid.)

A number of conceptualizations have been proposed regarding leisure benefits. Driver, Brown and Peterson (1991) have presented information regarding the state of knowledge of leisure benefits in relation to a number of measures. They group these measures into four general areas: 1) physiological and psychophysiological measures, 2) psychological measures, 3) sociological measures, and 4) economic and environmental measures. When referring to physiological and psychophysiological measures, such terms as health benefits, cardiovascular benefits, and psychophysiological benefits are mentioned. Psychological measures include self-actualization benefits, self-identity benefits, personal and social benefits, skill benefits, spiritual benefits, learning and developmental benefits, and one's emotional disposition or mood as a benefit of leisure. Psychological measures include family bonding benefits, organizational wellness benefits, community satisfaction benefits, and in general, quality of life benefits associated with leisure. Economic measures are focused on several elements, including improving wage-earning capacity of individuals as a result of improving one's well being by participating in leisure. Environmental elements as leisure benefits refer to necessary life support benefits, aesthetic benefits, historical benefits, and others which are derived through leisure experiences.

Edginton, Jordan, DeGraaf and Edginton (2002, p.19-20), building on the works of Driver and Brown (1986) and Ibrahim and Cordes (1993), have identified a number of factors that serve as motivators for individuals pursuing leisure. They suggest that these motivators for leisure may apply to experiences in both outdoor and indoor settings. They are:

Personal Development. The nature of the leisure experience is such that much of what motivates individuals to pursue leisure is personal. Leisure experiences can contribute to building self-concept, self-actualization, self-reliance, humility, and spiritual growth. They can also provide opportunities for values clarification and introspection, leadership opportunities, aesthetic enhancement, and learning. These all may be strong motivators influencing a person to participate in a given leisure activity or program.

Social Bonding. Leisure provides opportunities for individuals to meet interactional needs. As Driver and Brown (1986) indicate, social bonding increases the social cohesiveness of personal relationships and can take place in various forms, occurring in primary groups such as the family, or in group that have been constructed to facilitate leisure experiences, such as teams, clubs, or instructional classes.

Therapeutic Healing. We live in a world of great stress, complexity, and demands. Many individuals need to escape or recover from the pressures or problems that arise in day-to-day living. Leisure provides opportunities for temporary escape from the stress of work, family, and interpersonal relationships, among other things. Participation in positive, con-

Place the team above yourself always.

John Wooden

structive forms of leisure provides an excellent alternative to negative forms of escape, such as substance abuse.

Physical Well-Being. Human beings have a basic need for physical activity—to engage in fine and gross motor movement—so they often seek such activity during leisure participation. In fact, most scales of leisure pursuits show that among the highest rated activities are those associated with fitness or physical movement. For many people, active leisure pursuits provide the only alternative to the sedentary, work-oriented behaviors of a technological information-based society.

Stimulation. Human beings are curious by nature. We constantly seek stimulation to satisfy our desire for newness or novelty, desire for exploration, and our need to relieve boredom and anxiety. Leisure pursuits provide an excellent medium within which new forms of stimulation can be introduced and experienced—observe the variety of stimulation provided by electronic home entertainment equipment, computers, and other technological developments that are available to people to use during their leisure.

Freedom and Independence. Some philosophers have argued that freedom and independence are necessary to nurture the human spirit. Because most leisure activities are noncompulsory, pursued on a voluntary basis, or freely chosen, a strong element of independence and freedom exists in such pursuits. Thus, the need to be free and independent can be nurtured, encouraged, and pursued through leisure. Leisure and freedom are often thought of in synonymous terms. There are few definitions that do not include "freedom" as a component of leisure.

Nostalgia. The need for reflection or for reflecting upon one's heritage or roots appears to be basic among all humans. Leisure often provides opportunities to learn about one's historical, cultural, and family heritage. As the philosopher Eric Hoffer once noted, when humankind was first freed from toiling in the soil and had the opportunity to think and explore, the first questions asked were "Where did we come from?" and "Why are we here?"

In an attempt to understand the benefits of the leisure experience, it appears that these benefits can be either subjective or objective. It is often difficult to measure the leisure experience, for it may consist of feelings, experiences, and thoughts that are not easily observable. Often the leisure experience must be inferred by observing the relationship between behavior prior to and after actual participation. Thus, the anticipation and recollection stages of the leisure experience become valuable cues that the leader can use to determine the nature of the leisure experience and the motives that may have been involved. If it is not possible to measure objectively the benefits of leisure participation as they relate to the fulfillment of leisure needs (and hence motivate individuals to participate in them), some subjective appraisal must occur. The leader might want to be sensitive to expressions that correspond to the likelihood of a leisure experience having occurred.

The benefits that participants expect to derive should shape the leader's choice of activities, methods of promotion, and the format or way in which the program is packaged and presented to the individual. These factors will influence individuals' perceptions of whether they think the program will provide them with the benefits they expect and will meet their expectations. The manipulation of these variables in business organizations and private organizations is characterized by the tendency to sell "an idea" rather than a product or service.

> If you don't know where you are going, you might wind up someplace else.
>
> *Yogi Berra*

SUMMARY

The behavior of individuals is largely a result of motivation. The motivation process consists of six steps, including (1) the existence of needs; (2) the initiation of drives; (3) attention to relevant stimuli; (4) initiation of goal-directed activity; (5) reward or goal attainment; and (6) reduction of needs and drives.

Needs are often viewed as deficiencies. Drives or motives are activators of behavior. Primary drives can be thought of as involving such factors as hunger, thirst, sleep, avoidance of pain, and maternal care. Secondary drives, which are of concern to the recreation, parks, and leisure services leader, can be related to such factors as novelty, affection, achievement, power, affiliation, freedom of choice, social approval, altruism, consistency, security, and status. Individuals attend to relevant stimuli in order to pick up cues that will help them shape their behavior to suit the current situation. Behavior, which is goal directed, enables individuals to fulfill their needs. The environment Influences the motivation process. The interaction between the individual and the environment affects the process of motivation and results in learning. This learning, in turn, influences future behavior.

The role of the recreation leader in motivating participants is one of providing cues to assist the individual to experience leisure. There are three environments that the leader can affect: social, physical, and psychological. Cues in the physical environment involve manipulations of such things as lighting, spatial arrangements, color, and decorations. Cues in the social environment relate to facilitating interaction between two or more people. Grouping of individuals, provision of extrinsic and intrinsic rewards, providing forms of recognition, and knowing one's leadership style are the major tools of the leader in this area. Psychological cues assist the individual in developing a sense of self-worth, self-identity, power, and so on. Another important role in the motivation process is removing barriers that affect the leisure experience. Some of the barriers to leisure fulfillment are attitudinal, communicative, consumptive, temporal, social, cultural and economic, health, and experiential.

One of the major factors in the motivation process is the realization that individuals seek benefits or expectations of benefits rather than the activity or service itself. There are many, many benefits that can be achieved through leisure participation including happiness, relaxation, fantasy, fun, illusion, social interaction, and excitement.

Discussion Questions

1. Why is understanding the motivation process important to the recreation, parks, and leisure services leader?

2. What is the process of motivation?

3. Identify and discuss at least five (5) different methods used in the recreation, parks, and leisure services field to identify needs.

4. What is the difference between a need and a drive?

5. What is the role of the environment in the process of motivation?

6. What do the terms "peak experience", "arousal", and "flow" have in common? What influence does the environment play regarding these terms?

7. List ten (10) cues that the leader can give an individual in each of the social, psychological, and physical areas.

8. What barriers can the leader remove in order to assist the individual in achieving leisure?

9. Explain the statement "individuals seek benefits or the expectation of benefits rather than activities or products."

10. Identify twenty (20) possible benefits of the leisure experience.

THE CASE FOR LEADERSHIP
Benefit-Based Programming

Points of Consideration

The Cedar Center Parks and Recreation director has asked each of the supervisors for its three community centers to develop a benefits-based strategy for offering its programs. She has directed the center staff to justify their program offerings based upon the benefits that will be realized by individuals and groups participating in their basic program offerings. The National Recreation and Park Association's (NRPA) Benefits-Based Programming (BBP) concept has been adopted by the department as its major strategy for addressing this problem.

The BBP concept is based on the following principles: 1) there must be articulation of outcome-oriented goals that address social issues and concerns that socity views as significant; 2) recreation opportunities need to be structured to directly address the stated goals; 3) a comprehensive monitoring and evaluation procedure that documents goal achievements and the ensuing benefits to the individual must be established; and 4) a comprehensive information system that effectively communicates the significance of the programs and services offered by park and recreation service providers (Allen, Harwell, Stevens, & Paisley, 1998). The BBP model has for steps: 1) identifying target issues and target goals; 2) designing programs to address goals; 3) measuring benefit outcomes; and 4) realizing impacts and communicating successes (1998).

You have been asked to apply the four-step model in applying the BBP concept in creating a program linked to benefits within your organization. The scenario found in the case study in Chapter 2 provides background information that can be useful in understanding the social and economic status of each of the centers within the community. However, no information has been collected regarding the psycho-graphic background of the participants in each of the centers.

Questions of Consideration

As a new community center director, you do not have a great deal of experience in applying the BBP model. In fact, this concept is a new one that has not been applied previously by the Cedar Center Parks and Recreation Department. You are very concerned that you will not be able to adequately provide the information that has been requested of you.

- How would you go about determining what motivates individuals to seek participation at the various Cedar Center Recreation Community Centers?
- Why and how would such information be useful in applying the BBP model to programming in each of the community centers?
- How would you go about determining the "needs" of the participants in each of the areas served by the community centers?
- How would you go about determining the target issues/goals?
- How would you go about identifying and measuring benefits?
- Also, the application of the BBP model has created challenges which have resulted in a great deal of anxiety within the department. Selected individuals, including yourself, are frustrated with the lack of information presented and the demand to modify your current approach to programming. How does this fact influence the motivation of you and other staff members?
- Are the variables that impact participant motivation and staff motivation similar?

REFLECTING ON LEADERSHIP
Providing Program Cues: Leader-Participant Interactions

A situation that serves to illustrate the importance of leader-participant interaction in the motivation process is the relationship that develops between a coach and team members, collectively and individually. Team members come to this leisure experience with different desires, interests, expectations, and needs. One team member, for example, may have a desire for increased capability in the sport to be played. Another member may have a desire to achieve greater recognition through participation in the sport. Still another team member may have a need for social interaction that can be fulfilled by a team experience. Or team members may have several needs that can be met by participation in the sport. The coach, as the leader of the group, can interact with team members to provide encouragement, instruction, and direction. The coach may praise an individual team member for an outstanding play, thereby providing the team member with a sense of achievement and increased capability. The coach may also attempt to develop a sense of comradeship and cooperation that will facilitate social interaction within the group and thereby fulfill the need of some team members for this type of reinforcement. The coach might use cues in order to shape the situation so that it meets individual needs for a leisure experience. For example, the coach may give a team member a slap on the behind to signal approval for achievement or may talk in a conspiratorial, intimate manner to promote a "team" esprit de corps. These cues set the stage for self-motivation to occur on the part of team members. For example, the team member who receives the slap on the behind will continue to feel "reinforced" when engaging in the rewarded behavior.

Think back to when you were a part of a team situation. What physical, social, and psychological cues were provided to you as a team member by the coach? List the positive and negative cues in each of these categories that you can recall from such an experience. How did the interaction between you and your coach influence your continued participation in any given sport? What did you carry over from the interaction between you and your coach that may have influenced your attitudes and behaviors, both short and long term?

References

Csikszentmihalyi, M. (1975). *Beyond boredom and anxiety*. Washington DC: Jossey Bass.

Edginton, C. R., Hudson, S. D., Dieser, R. B., & Edginton, S. R. (2004). *Leisure programming: A service-centered and benefits approach*. Boston, MA: McGraw-Hill.

Edginton, C. R., Hudson, S. D. & Lankford, S. V. (2001). *Managing recreation, parks, and leisure services: An introduction* (2nd edition). Champaign, IL: Sagamore.

Ellis, M. G. (1973). *Why people play*. Englewood Cliffs, NJ: Prentice-Hall.

Godbey, G. (1981). *Leisure in your life: An exploration*. Philadelphia: Philadelphia Saunders College.

Heywood, L. A. (1979). *Recreation for older adults: A program manual*. Toronto: Ministry of Culture and Recreation.

Kusyszyn, I. (1979). A theory of new motivation. In J. Levy (Ed.), *Motivation for leisure: An interactionist approach*. Los Alamitos, CA: Hwong Publishing Co.

Kouzes, J., & Posner, B. (1995). *The leadership challenge: How to keep getting extraordinary things done in organizations*. San Francisco: Jossey Bass.

Luthans, F. (2002). *Organizational behavior* (2nd ed.). New York: McGraw-Hill.

Maslow, A. H. (1968). *Toward a psychology of being*. New York: Van Nostrand Reinhold.

Mercer, D. (1973). The concept of recreation need. Journal of Leisure Research (Winter) 39. Vol. 5(1) p. 37-50.

Murphy, J. E., Williams, J. G., Niepoth, E. W., & Brown, P. D. (1973). *Leisure service delivery system: A modern perspective*. Philadelphia: Lea and Febiger.

CHAPTER

7

Leadership and Communication

LEARNING OBJECTIVES

1. To understand the differences and similarities between interpersonal and organizational communication.
2. To understand the process of transactional communication and the important elements in the process.
3. To understand the role that individual perception has on the communication process
4. To understand the importance of active listening.
5. To identify barriers that are present that prevent positive communication between the leader and individuals.

KEY TERMS

- Interpersonal Communication
- Transactional Communication
- Conflict Resolution
- Decoder-Receiver
- Organizational Communication
- Persuasion
- Sender-Encoder
- Perception Selectivity

INTRODUCTION

Three Englishmen were riding on a bus. At the first stop, one man says, "Is this Wembley?" "No" says the second man, "this is Thursday." "So am I," says the third man, "Let's have a drink."

Denhardt, Denhardt

and Aristigueta

We live in a society in which our ability to communicate with one another determines, to a large extent, whether we will succeed in our work and leisure. Communication is a process that binds together human activity. In the recreation, parks, and leisure services setting, communication is essential in understanding and interpreting the rules of games, providing instruction, giving directions, and conveying feelings and emotions. The recreation, parks, and leisure services leader who communicates effectively can better meet the needs of those served.

This chapter will explore the various dimensions of the communication process. Specifically, we will define communication, describe the various components of communication, and present a model of the communication process. This chapter will also present information concerning types of communication, functions of communication, perception and communication, styles of communication, and barriers to effective communication. In addition, the importance of active listening will be discussed.

DEFINING COMMUNICATION

The term communication is widely used in contemporary society, although it may have different meanings to different people. Most definitions of communication suggest that concepts, ideas, and thoughts must be transformed into a set of symbols and then transmitted to another party for communication to occur. However, other theorists have also suggested that human communication is a process that is interpersonal in nature and can be said to have occurred only if changes in the behavior of the receiver take place. In other words, for communication to exist between individuals, all those involved in the communication system must attach some value or meaning to the symbols and process of exchange, and act on the information received.

We can think of communication, then, as a process of exchange that is directed toward conveying meaning and achieving understanding between individuals that leads to changes in the behavior of the receiver or receivers. It is an exchange that occurs between two or more persons through words, tone of voice, gestures, facial expressions, posture, and other means. This exchange can also be facilitated via visual representation and electronic-technological processes. Communication may be defined as a dynamic human transaction that results in the transmission of feelings and thoughts to another.

For communication to be effective, the ideas, concepts, and thoughts being transmitted must not only be clearly sent, but they also must be understood by the receiver. As just mentioned, many believe that successful communication occurs when the receiver understands and accepts the message being transmitted in such a way that it affects his or her behavior. As you will recall, an important goal of the recreation, parks, and leisure services leader is to facilitate human happiness. For this to occur, the leader must encourage behavioral change. This is done almost exclusively through the process of communication.

Interpersonal and Organizational Communication

The recreation, parks, and leisure services leader is concerned with two types of communication: interpersonal and organizational.

Interpersonal communication is the process of transferring information and influencing the behavior of people on a one-to-one basis. It is essential for effective interaction between the leader and the participant and, thus, is central to achieving the recreation, parks, and leisure services experience. The ability of the leader to establish effective communication with individual participants will directly influence the participants acquisition of skills and knowledge and their formulation of attitudes. It is also via the communication process that the leader generates enthusiasm, builds interest, conveys excitement, provides recognition and a sense of achievement, and creates a relationship of trust. Any or all of these variables may contribute directly to the building of a successful and rewarding leisure experience.

Organizational communication can be thought of as the way by which an agency transmits information to its staff and participants concerning its goals. Organizational communication involves the establishment of channels of communication with an organizational structure in order to transmit reports, complaints, requests, orders, inquiries, and information, both within and outside of the organization. Within the organization, a formal program of organizational communication establishes the methods of exchange that should occur between and among various levels within an organization, both horizontally and vertically. It provides a method for orderly transmission of financial, program, and human resource information. For example, many recreation, parks, and leisure services organizations establish formal, internal procedures for communicating information. These procedures can range from the way in which incoming telephone messages are recorded and distributed to the way in which

> The length of the meeting rises with the square of the number of people present.
>
> *Anonymous*

parties are informed of the status of financial accounts under their direction.

Organizational communication is also concerned with the information that is transmitted to an agency's constituents. This is often thought of as the official communication that the recreation, parks, and leisure services organization provides to its public or publics. This type of external communication is usually closely monitored or managed by the organization, since external communication greatly impacts the organization's image. Not only should the organization monitor such obvious techniques of communication as news releases, but also—and perhaps more importantly—it should monitor or manage the contact that takes place between the public and members of the recreation, parks, and leisure services organization. The status, well being, and success of an organization may hinge on its ability to cultivate positive feelings of goodwill toward itself. This is done primarily by understanding that patterns of exchange, whether they are via the written media or simply between individuals, should be managed and controlled. For example, many municipal park and recreation departments operating summer playground programs conduct orientation and training programs for their summer seasonal staff prior to the start of the program. Often an important part of such orientation and training programs is imparting to the new staff an understanding of the organization's goals and policies related to communication with the public.

Transactional Communication

Communication is a dynamic process that involves a transaction between one individual and another, or between one individual and a group of individuals. The term transaction suggests that communication, to be effective, must involve more than telling or talking at another individual. Transactional communication implies that communication is two-way interaction rather than one-way and, therefore, can affect the sender as well as the receiver. An individual sending a message will receive feedback that may affect his or her initial perceptions, values, or ideas. Transactional communication is interaction with people rather than communication to people. In recreation, parks, and leisure services, it is essential that the leader understands transactional communication, as it serves as the basis for meeting individual needs and interests. A two-way exchange facilitates this goal.

A transactional relationship suggests that people are both sending and receiving messages. When we discuss communication, we often think only of sending messages and not of the other responsibilities inherent in a two-way exchange. We often forget that need to get and give feedback is as

Speak clearly, if you speak at all; carve every word before you let it fall.

Oliver Wendell Holmes

important as sending information. The leader who develops listening and observing skills will be able to engage more successfully in transactional communication. Most communication in organizations is decidedly directive and one-way. Therefore, it is essential for the leader to encourage two-way transactional communication.

TYPES OF COMMUNICATION

There are numerous types of communication that the recreation, parks, and leisure services leader will use or be exposed to. Of primary concern are verbal and nonverbal types of communication, for they are involved in the leader's face-to-face interaction with participants.

Other types of communication include that which is written (visual symbols) and that which is transmitted via technological or electronic processes, or both. A brief discussion of these various types of communication follows.

> **Verbal.** Verbal communication is the form of communication most often used by the recreation, parks, and leisure services leader. It can either be a one-way or two-way form of interaction; however, one-way interaction is seldom effective. The ability of the leader to give direction, listen, provide empathy, and generate enthusiasm is accomplished primarily through verbal interaction with others. The ability to communicate effectively with individuals and groups often will spell the difference between success or failure in the implementation of activities. In the structured recreation, parks, and leisure services activity, face-to-face interaction with the participant is used to assist the participant in achieving leisure experiences. Often this interaction is the essence of the experience, especially in activities that emphasize social interaction. Through verbal interaction the leader can create a sense of excitement, euphoria, adventure, and heightened expectation.

> **Nonverbal.** Nonverbal communication refers to communication that takes place via physical cues such as an individual's apparel, facial expression, posture, body rhythms, and body movement. We often refer to nonverbal communication as "body language."

> By "observing" body language, the leader can gain clues about the intentions, level of interest, and motivation of participants. There may be inconsistencies between what is communicated verbally by individuals and what they communicate nonverbally. The use of sarcasm is an exam-

I have never been hurt by what I have not said.

Calvin Coolidge

ple of how nonverbal communication might vary from verbal communication. An individual might say, for example, "Nice day," accompanied by a grimace or a frown, meaning that it really is not.

Nonverbal communication is becoming an especially important topic as people from different cultures interact more frequently but have different culturally approved ways of expressing themselves nonverbally (Denhardt et al., 2002, p. 275) For example, facial expressions, eye contact, and body language vary widely from culture to culture. People from North America and Europe tend to maintain eye contact when speaking with others whereas people from Asia avoid eye contact (especially if they are speaking with people of higher status) (Nahavandi & Malekzadeh, 1999). People in the West consider eye contact a sign of honesty and openness, whereas people in the East consider it a lack of respect.

The leader not only should attempt to read the body language of others, but should be mindful of his or her own body language and the effect that it may have on the communication process when relating to people of different cultures.

Written. Written communication involves the use of printed or handwritten language for the purpose of transmitting information or knowledge. This could include reports, brochures, fliers, advertisements, books, pamphlets, magazines, letters, memoranda, phone messages, and so on. The rapid growth and expansion of knowledge can probably be attributed, within the last century, to the growth of written communications. The number of books published each year increases, as does the volume of correspondence that is carried out between individuals and organizations. It is important for the leader to recognize that written communication represents not only the individual writing the communication, but the organization the individual belongs to as well. Thus, it is important to carefully word and review outgoing written communication to ensure that it is accurate, complete, grammatically correct, and carries the meaning intended.

Electronic-Technological. Electronic-technological communication is involved with all forms of tech nological-electronic processing, including the computer, television, radio, telephone, and motion pictures. Although electronic-technological communication may overlap with some of the categories mentioned earlier in that it can be a vehicle for verbal, nonverbal, and written communication, we feel that it is also a unique entity. With

The ear is the only true writer and the only true reader.

Robert Frost

A LEGACY OF LEADERSHIP
George Hjelte (1893-1978)

George Hjelte was a leader in the nation's recreation movement for more than 60 years. Known as Mr. Recreation throughout his career, George Hjelte grew up in Oakland, California and lived through the San Francisco earthquake of 1906. In 1913, he entered the University of California, where he majored in education and economics. While at the University, he excelled in athletics, especially basketball, and was named the first All American west of the Rockies at the end of his senior year at Berkeley. After serving with distinction during World War I, he began his career in 1919 as the Assistant State Supervisor of Physical Education for the State of California. In 1921, he resigned this post to become Director of Physical Education and Superintendent of Recreation, City of Berkeley, California. He held both positions until 1926, when he was selected over J.B. Nash, to succeed Charles Raitt as Superintendent of Recreation, City of Los Angeles. In 1947, the parks department merged with the recreation department and Mr. Hjelte was appointed general manager of the consolidated department. He remained in his position until retirement in 1962.

As head of the Los Angeles department, he saw it grow from 46 recreation sites and seven swimming pools to 300 recreation centers, playgrounds, parks, beaches, cultural facilities, pools, and mountain camps. In addition to his work creating a model department, Mr. Hjelete worked considerably with volunteer organizations such as the YMCA, PTA, and Boy Scouts.

George Hjelte was active in professional organizations including: The American Institute of Park Executives, American Recreation Society, California Park and Recreation Society, National Recreation Association, American Association for Health, Physical Education and Recreation, and the American Academy of Physical Education. He was a frequent speaker at conferences and conventions and was called upon to chair many committees of the professional organizations.

A noted author, he wrote various articles for publications and textbooks to use in the classroom. His consistent theme was how human life could be enriched. It was through his writing that he became known as the "philosopher of the recreation movement," and through his writings that he influenced the formation of the theoretical concepts and values that helped to systematize and establish the recreation discipline.

A strong advocate for recreation on the national level, Mr. Hjelte called for the establishment of an agency on the federal level to provide for national planning for leisure. In 1962, a federal agency was established, the Bureau of Outdoor Recreation, but it failed to live up to expectations and disappeared in the 1970s. However, Mr. Hjelte held out hope that a Federal Department of Recreation functioning effectively in the same manner as the Department of Education functions and related to recreation in the broad sense, including all of the arts of leisure, would be established. It was a dream left unfilled in his lifetime.

continued on next page

continued from previous page

Working in the field of recreation as a consultant with the Los Angeles Youth Bureau until his death, Mr. Hjelte rejected the notion of retirement. He wrote, "If one has the capacity to continue his work under other auspices, he should do so, thus contributing further to longevity and to personal fulfillment.

George Hjelte contributed to the recreation movement in America by action and example. Through his leadership, his community, state, and the nation's welfare was greatly enriched and enhanced.

Never express yourself more clearly than you are able to think.

Neils Bohr

the advent of Internet and Web sites, electronic communication has become an important source of communication in society. Electronic mail is fast becoming the primary means of communicating, not only within the organization but on a worldwide basis. Recreation, parks, and leisure services organizations must aggressively become part of this new electronic communication medium if they hope to survive in the new information society.

Visual Symbols. Visual symbols are used extensively in contemporary society. They are representations of a more complex idea that provides the individual with a quick visual clue or reference point. Logos are perhaps the most obvious example of this type of communication. When we see the "golden arches" of McDonald's, we see it as a representation of hamburgers. Other uses of visual symbols include the use of signs to control routine behavior (e.g., stop signs) or the use of symbols to advocate a political ideology (e.g., the use of the donkey to represent the Democratic party). The leader can use visual symbols to enhance communication with others.

The recreation, parks, and leisure services leader should carefully consider the various types of communication in order to select the communication process that will be most effective in various situations. Although the leader is primarily concerned with verbal and nonverbal face-to-face interaction, he or she should recognize the importance of other types of communication in instruction, activity leadership, and other areas of leadership. Computer-based instruction, for example, may effectively assist lecture-type presentations made by the leader. Visual symbols can be used to create a mood or to elicit a certain type of response from participants. It should also be noted that some individuals are more visually oriented, whereas other individuals are more verbally oriented. Communication that can respond to both of these orientations will be the most successful.

FUNCTIONS OF COMMUNICATION

Communication serves a number of functions. It provides a vehicle for individuals to interact with others in four primary ways: (1) persuasion and influence, (2) information, (3) social and expressive relations, and (4) conflict resolution. A discussion of each of these functions of communication follows.

Persuasion and Influence. One of the primary functions of communication is the persuasion of others. Persuasion suggests that one will change or modify the behavior of another individual via the communication process. We persuade others by appealing to their emotions, reason, intelligence, logic, and vanity. Generally speaking, persuasion is a process of gradually securing the cooperation of others. Closely related to the notion of persuasion is that of influence.

Influence is the power of one individual to affect the behavior of another. Persuasion and influence are key into the communication process. Communication intended to influence carries values and is intended to (1) impress and stimulate, (2) change beliefs or convince, and (3) move an individual to action.

Information. Another function of communication is to pass on information that informs, reminds, or teaches. The individual involved in this type of communication provides or receives information that is useful, interesting, or necessary. The information that is communicated may be facts, figures, processes, and so on. Generally speaking, information is transmitted by using a didactic format; that is, the sender relays the information via lectures, films, tape recordings, books, periodicals, and so on. The purpose of the didactic method is to explain and expound on a particular subject. The recreation, parks, and leisure services leader is often involved in the transmission of information, especially as it is related to the teaching of skills and informing the public of leisure opportunities.

Social and Expressive Relation. A third function of communication is that of encouraging social interaction and expressive behavior. Social communication is essential to human well-being. Social communication enables individuals to develop self-image, maintain contact with others, develop sensual acuity, and develop intellectually. Our common everyday communication such as hugs, handshakes, small talk, banter, and other expressions of interest provide a vehicle for social interactions with others. Expressive communications convey our emotional reactions to situations. They are based on feelings that are associated with both verbal and nonverbal communication. A prime function of commu-

> A superior man is modest in speech, but exceeds in his actions.
>
> *Confucius*

nication is to provide us with the tools to express love, joy, pleasure, enthusiasm, interest, frustration, anger, happiness, and grief.

Conflict Resolution. Conflict resolution is another primary function of communication. Through communication, individuals are able to resolve conflicts resulting from differences in values, beliefs, and attitudes. Conflict is pervasive in our North American society. It exists between individuals, groups, organizations, and nations. It ranges from deviant thought to overt physical force and occurs almost wherever individuals interact with one another. Conflict need not necessarily be viewed in negative terms, as it may serve a productive function in some cases if it promotes effective communication. The individual communicating can be engaged in more than one communicative function. For example, an individual may give a speech that presents information and, at the same time, attempts to persuade and influence the listener. Although knowledge of all these functions of communication is important to the leader, the area of social and expressive communication may be the most important to those in the recreation, parks, and leisure services profession. As a profession, we attempt to enable participants to express their emotions and feelings and interact with other individuals. More specifically, we attempt to provide opportunities that enable individuals to express their excitement, enthusiasm, pleasure, and joy, as well as vent their frustrations, anger, and disappointment, in a socially acceptable positive manner.

THE PROCESS OF COMMUNICATION

A model of the process of communication is presented in Figure 7.1. This model, initially developed by Berlo in 1960, is still the most widely accepted depiction of the communication process found in the literature. The model suggests that communication is a process consisting of a number of interrelated components. Although these components are seen as separate and distinct elements, in reality the communication process operates in a simultaneous fashion (Berlo, 1960). Furthermore, it is important to recognize that an individual will be a sender and receiver of information at the same time. For example, in face-to-face communication with another, an individual sends a message while at the same time receiving verbal and/or nonverbal clues from the receiver.

The components that make up the communication process are the sender-encoder, message, channel, decoder-receiver and feedback. The following paragraphs explain each of these components.

Occasionally words must serve to veil facts. But this must happen in such a way that no one becomes aware of it; or, if it should be noticed, excuses must be at hand, to be produced immediately.

Nicolo Machiavelli

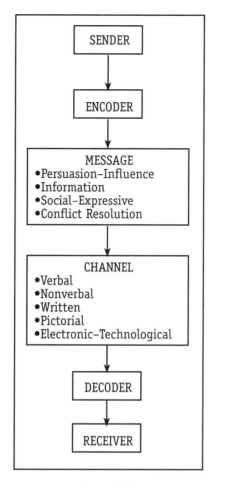

Figure 7.1
The process of communication: The Berlo model

Sender-Encoder. The sender-encoder can be thought of as the individual or electronic technological device that originates the communication. For communication to occur, one must first prepare the message for transmission. We usually think of the encoding process as a way of preparing ideas, thoughts, and concepts for transmission to another individual or other individuals. Basically, it involves the conversion of complex intellectual information into a set of symbols. Language is the most common set of symbols used for transmission of ideas. Language can be thought of as a type of code in which a set of symbols represents an idea, thought, or concept. When technological channels of communication, such as the computer, are used, the same process occurs. Ideas are coded in the language of the computer. For effective communication to occur, symbols used in the communication process must be mutually understood and accepted by both parties. Thus, it is important to avoid jargon which can confuse the message. When individuals inappropriately encode or decode information transmitted, inaccurate communication may result that leads to misunderstanding. For

It is better to keep your mouth closed and let people think you are a fool than open it and remove all doubt.

Mark Twain

example, words often have different meanings for different people. Consequently, the message may be encoded; however, the receiver may not decode the message accurately. Nonverbal messages may also be encoded or decoded inappropriately. The recreation, parks, and leisure services leader should be aware of the need for accurate encoding of information for transmission. He or she should not, for example, use an adult vocabulary when attempting to communicate with children.

> A man only curses because he doesn't know the words to express what is on his mind.
>
> *Malcolm X*

The Message. We can think of the message that is being communicated as the cognitive or affective information that is transmitted, or both; that is, it is the idea, thought, or concept that the sender is attempting to communicate to another individual. As previously indicated, communication has four functions: persuasion, information, social-expressive relations, and conflict resolution. The message being communicated to another individual will usually fall into one of these four categories.

Often a message transmitted from one individual to another may carry more than one meaning. Multiple meanings in messages create uncertainty as to whether or not the message will be transmitted accurately or as intended. Thus, the way in which messages are communicated, or the channel of communication selected, can be a critical element in effective communication, adding needed meaning. The sender, then, should not only be aware of the need for accurate encoding, but also should be aware of the importance of choosing an appropriate channel for the transmission of the message. For example, some messages are most effectively transmitted by picture rather than by the written word. It should also be remembered that every message is viewed from two different perspectives. The same message may be seen differently by the sender-encoder and the receiver-decoder. Later in this chapter, the authors will discuss the effects of perception on communication. Knowledge of differences in perception can help an individual avoid or correct encoding that might be misinterpreted owing to differences in perception.

The Channel. The channel of communication is the medium that couples the sender to the receiver. Previously we defined five channels of communication: verbal, nonverbal, written, electronic-technological, and visual symbols. These channels, in turn, can be broken into a number of sub-categories. The selection of an appropriate channel of communication is essential to the communication process, although it may not be a conscious choice on the part of the sender.

Numerous problems are associated with the selection of an inappropriate channel for communication. For example, a recreation, parks, and leisure services leader who attempts to orient his or her summer staff verbally, without written instruction in support, may find that prescribed procedures are not followed. Individuals are not likely to remember extensive organizational policy, dress codes, rules of conduct, schedules, and so on without use of a written channel of communication.

Receiver-Decoder. Decoding can be thought of as the translation of a message by a receiver. The decoding process is concerned with the acquisition of the intended meaning of the message transmitted by the sender, leading to behavioral change. In other words, decoding, like encoding, attempts to ensure that messages received are an accurate reflection of the message sent. In order for communication to be effective, the receiver should not only understand the message but should also exhibit the change in behavior that the message was intended to cause. Usually, the decoder has two primary resources with which to decode messages: his or her senses, and the mental processes. Individuals receive information through their senses: hearing, seeing, tasting, touching, and smelling. Mental processes—that is, complex intellectual thought processes—also assist in the decoding process. These mental processes, however, are value-laden and, therefore, may interfere in the decoding process. The recreation, parks, and leisure services leader should be aware that the message he or she sends may not be accurately decoded, owing to differences in perceptions or the use of inappropriate symbols (e.g., the use of professional jargon). In order to communicate effectively, therefore, the recreation, parks, and leisure services leader may want to check with the participant or participants to make sure that the intended message has indeed been received accurately.

Feedback. Feedback is an element of communication that rounds out or lends a wholeness to the communication process (Jordan, 1999, p. 167). Feedback gives the sender-encoder an understanding of how the message was received, comprehended, and acted upon. It can also indicate to the sender-encoder if any further clarification is needed or if the message needs to be modified and resent. Since feedback is a message, it uses the same channels as previously mentioned: verbal, nonverbal, written, electronic-technological, and visual symbols.

It should be noted that feedback can be as simple as a smile, a laugh, or a nodding of the head. It can also be as complex as a lengthy e-mail or a verbose answer. Whether simple or complex, it is important for the recreation, parks, and leisure services leader to recognize clues in the feedback process that point to how the message was received and understood.

> What you do speaks so loudly that I cannot hear what you say.
>
> *Ralph Waldo Emerson*

PERCEPTION AND COMMUNICATION

Perception is a major factor influencing the process of communication. The way that one selects, organizes, and interprets information will affect directly how effectively he or she communicates with others. Perception can be thought of as a psychological process. It is dependent on the use of one's physical senses (the ability to see, hear, touch, smell and taste); however, it is a complicated cognitive process that involves the processing and categorization of information received through the senses. Our senses provide us with raw data (information) from which decisions can be made that will ultimately influence how we react to, or interact with, our environment (see Figure 7.2).

Why is it important that the recreation, parks, and leisure services leader understand perception? In a general sense, the role of the recreation, parks, and leisure services leader is to create conditions that allow the participant to perceive that he or she is at leisure.

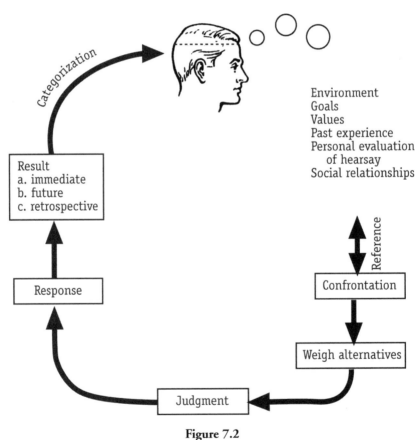

Figure 7.2
A model for processing information utilizing apperceptive mass.
Edward C. Cannon, Humbolt State University, 1981. ©Edward C. Cannon. Used by permission

Social psychologists often suggest that a number of conditions must precede the leisure experience. Among these are the need for an individual to experience perceived freedom and perceived competence.

Perceived freedom is characterized by a feeling on the part of the participant that he or she has control. Therefore, the leader, in order to be effective, must understand the conditions needed for the participant to feel that he or she is in control. Such conditions can be produced by involving the participant in the decision-making process, by not forcing participation, by allowing the participant to pace himself or herself through an activity, and so on.

Perceived competence is characterized by a feeling on the part of the participant that he or she has achieved a degree of mastery over an activity. The issue is not the actual skill level of the individual as it relates to an external standard but rather the individual's own perception of his or her ability (i.e., subjective appraisal rather than objective appraisal based on standards). The University of Chicago sociologist Csikszentmihalyi (1975) has suggested that the individual's perception of his or her skill level as it relates to the challenge offered by a given activity will influence the success with which participation is likely to take place. An individual who perceives that his or her skill level is higher than the challenge of the activity, according to Csikszentmihalyi, will experience boredom. Conversely, an individual who perceives that his or her skill level is lower than the challenge of the activity will experience anxiety. The role of the leader, in dealing with these perceptions, is to structure the environment so that it is likely that perceived skill level will correspond to the challenges offered by the activity. The leader can accomplish this in three ways.

1. The leader can attempt to change the individual's perception of his or her skill level through encouragement, support, positive feedback, and so on.
2. The leader can actually help the individual develop a higher level of skill through an educational process.
3. The leader can present the individual with activities and tasks that correspond to the individual's current skill level.

In its broadest sense, understanding perception also enables the leader to understand participants' attitudes, values, motives, and, hence, behavior. It is interesting to note that research studies have shown that individuals who are physically attractive are perceived by others to be more intelligent, personable, and kind than their less attractive cohorts. It has also been shown that individuals have a tendency to seek out and relate to individuals with beliefs and values similar to their own. They are also more likely to believe oth-

> Wise men talk because they have something to say; fools, because they have to say something.
>
> *Plato*

ers when they espouse values and beliefs that correspond to their own. These examples demonstrate the pitfalls that the leader should be aware of when attempting to deal with the perceptions of individuals, for such perceptions may not be totally accurate. In the first instance just given, the perception that physical attributes and intelligence correspond to one another is obviously not true. In the latter case, perceptions are likely to be biased and based upon "what a person wants to hear." The point is that perceptions will greatly influence people, although such perceptions may be inaccurate when compared with empirically verified scientific investigation.

Consider the recreation, parks, and leisure services leader whose job is to program for individuals with physical disabilities. If indeed physical beauty is perceived by the community to be associated with desirable attributes (intelligence, kindness, and so on), the leader whose values reflect that societal norm may perceive individuals with physical disfigurement as lacking these qualities or even being more likely to exhibit negative qualities, such as poor temperament, mental lassitude, and so on. These perceptions will affect the leader's expectations and the way that the leader communicates with these individuals. However, the leader who has an understanding of perception will be in a position to communicate more effectively and plan more appropriately for those whom he or she serves.

An entire generation, or cohort, group can establish a certain framework or set of perceptions that are carried throughout their life span. Cohorts are faced with specific sets of life conditions during important and impressionable periods in their lives. In other words, cohorts have lived during the same time period and have experienced the same historical, social, economic, and political conditions during their life span (Edginton, Hudson, Dieser, & Edginton, 2004).

An individual's basic personality is developed by the age of four. Up to the age of seven is the time of imprinting, the human influences and the life events that have occurred have imprinted on and are a permanent part of the individual. Early formation of values and modeling or exhibiting behaviors occurs during the ages of eight to thirteen. The values that were earlier imprinted may at this point be evident in the person's behavior and lifestyle. By the time an individual reaches twenty years of age, his or her value system is strongly in place. A focus on a cohort group infers that major specific societal, cultural, and personal experiences have affected and influenced the lives and development of the individuals in the group in ways unique from other cohort groups (Table 7.1) (Edginton et.al., 2004, p.112).

Kind words can be short and easy to speak, but their echoes are truly endless.

Mother Teresa

Table 7.1

Cohorts and Generational Events

Decades of Cohorts	Historical Events	Business and Technology	Social and Media Events	Music and Dancing	Famous People
Old age 1900–1909	Turn of century; Spanish-American War; McKinley assassinated	Severe unemployment; trolley cars; Model T Ford; electric light bulb	First airplane flight; first radio message; first World Series; yellow fever epidemic	Let Me Call You Sweetheart; Home on the Range; Sweet Adeline; the turkey trot	William McKinley, Teddy Roosevelt, W. H. Taft, Henry Ford, Orville and Wilbur Wright, Charlie Chaplin, Carrie Nation
1910–1919	First woman in Congress; World War I; communism started	Federal income tax; telephone invented; vitamins discovered; use of electricity	Panama Canal opens; Halley's comet; *Titanic* sinks	"Alexander's Ragtime Band"; "When Irish Eyes Are Smiling"; "Over There"; the fox-trot	Susan B. Anthony, W. H. Taft, Woodrow Wilson, Thomas Edison, Buffalo Bill Cody, Jack Dempsey, Jane Addams, Emma Goldman
1920–1929	Prohibition Act; Harding's Teapot Dome Scandal; League of Nations	Child labor laws; oil replacing coal; mechanical cotton picker; Wall Street collapse	Bootlegging; Lindbergh's Atlantic flight; Empire State Building	Vaudeville; "Yes, We Have No Bananas"; "Old Man River"; the Charleston	Woodrow Wilson, Warren Harding, Calvin Coolidge, Herbert Hoover, Babe Ruth, Andrew Carnegie, Margaret Sanger
Later adulthood 1930–1939	Great Depression; New Deal; Social Security Act	Bank panic; WPA—public works; color movies	Amelia Earhart solo across the Atlantic; John Dillinger; public enemy no. 1; Hindenburg explosion	WPA orchestras; "Brother, Can You Spare a Dime?"; "I've Got You Under My Skin"; the big apple	New York Yankees, Bing Crosby, Mickey Mouse, Babe Didrikson, Greta Garbo, Amelia Earhart
1940–1949	World War II; United Nations; GI Bill of Rights	Taft-Hartley Act; 40-hour week; first electric locomotive; first atomic bomb	Pearl Harbor attack; first black major league baseball player—Jackie Robinson; country of Israel	Big band sounds; "In the Mood"; "White Christmas"; "When You Wish Upon a Star"; jitterbug	Franklin D. Roosevelt, Harry Truman, Winston Churchill, Joseph Stalin, Bob Hope, Frank Sinatra, Eleanor Roosevelt, Katharine Hepburn, Clare Booth Luce
Middle adulthood 1950–1959	Korean War; Cold war; Truman fires MacArthur	Minimum wage 75¢ per hour; AFL-CIO merger; first earth-circling satellite; Salk antipolio vaccine	Racial segregation banned; school desegregation; development of television; two monkeys in space	Hit parade; "Rock Around the Clock"; "My Fair Lady"; Twist; rock and roll; Elvis Presley	Harry Truman, Dwight Eisenhower, George Meany, Grace Kelly, Perry Como, Rosa Parks, Julius and Ethel Rosenberg, Marilyn Monroe

Continued

Table 7.1
Cohorts and Generational Events—Continued.

Decades of Cohorts	Historical Events	Business and Technology	Social and Media Events	Music and Dancing	Famous People
1960–1969	Civil Rights Act; assassinations of J. F. Kennedy, Robert Kennedy, Martin Luther King, Jr.; Vietnam War	Minimum wage $1.25 per hour; affluent economy; men on the moon; birth-control pill	Fifty-star flag; beatniks, hippies; Woodstock; student demonstrations; drug culture	Beatles; "Hello, Dolly"; "Moon River"; rock	J. F. Kennedy, Lyndon Johnson, Richard Nixon, Warren Burger, Martin Luther King, Jr., Neil Armstrong, Golda Meir, Jackie Kennedy, Martha Graham, Rachel Carson, Diane Arbus
Young adulthood 1970–1979	End of Vietnam War; Watergate scandal; 19-year-olds vote; Israel-Egypt accord	Minimum wage $2.65 per hour; oil embargo; inflation increases; test-tube baby	Nixon resigns; women's liberation; two popes die within 40 days	Rolling Stones; Country-western; Punk rock; disco dancing: "You Light Up My Life"	Richard Nixon, Gerald Ford, Jimmy Carter, Muhammad Ali, Hank Aaron, Pittsburgh Steelers, Gloria Steinem, Billie Jean King, Barbara Walters, Patty Hurst
Adolescence 1980–1989	Hostage crisis in Iran; President Reagan shot; Israel-PLO war in Lebanon; San Francisco earthquake; Challenger disaster; U.S. military action in Panama; fall of Berlin wall	Major recession; energy crunch subsides; inflation slows down; industry and business in transition; artificial heart; acid rain	Prince Charles marries; Princess Grace dies; home computers are big items; E.T.: The Extra-Terrestrial; Star Wars series; "Batman"; "Teenage Mutant Ninja Turtles;" children in daycare outside of the home	Rock subsiding; country rock; Barry Manilow; Dolly Parton: Flashdance; "Gloria"; Michael Jackson; rap music; "Dirty Dancing"; MTV	Ronald Reagan, Pope John Paul, Sally Field, Jesse Jackson, John McEnroe, Jane Pauley, Geraldine Ferraro, Christa McAuliffe, George Bush, Mikhail Gorbachev, San Francisco 49ers
1990s	Operation Desert Storm; midwest flooding; Oklahoma City bombing; war in Bosnia; Million Man March; U.S. government shutdowns; Atlanta Olympics; Republicans take control of U.S. Senate and House of Representatives; U.S. mili-	Minimum wage $4.25 per hour; VCRs; professional baseball salaries; Nintendo; World Wide Web; Internet; virtual reality; inline skates; murders in the workplace; American female astronaut	Major league hockey strike; O. J. Simpson trial; Major League Baseball strike; Forrest Gump; Lion King; "Bay Watch"; "Friends"; Menendez brothers trial; Prince Charles and Princess Diana divorce; AIDS/HIV; body piercing and tatooing:	Garth Brooks; line dancing; Branson, MO; macarena	Norman Schwarzkopf, Madonna, Boris Yeltsin, Michael Jordan, Bill Clinton, Tom Hanks, Bob Dole, Chicago Bulls, Colin Powell, Cal Ripken, Jr., Hillary Rodham Clinton, Mother Teresa, Newt Gin-

Continued.

Table 7.1
Cohorts and Generational Events—Continued.

	tary in Somalia and Haiti; Los Angeles (Northridge) earthquake	baby boomers turn 50 years old; John F. Kennedy, Jr. marries; George Burns dies; drive-by shootings; coffee bars; blue M & Ms; women at the Citadel; "trash" talk shows; liposuction; cosmetic surgery	grich, Christopher Reeves, Bill Gates, Itzak Rabin, Howard Stern, Rush Limbaugh, Dr. Jack Kevorkian
2000	9/11 Twin Towers; 2000 election; terrorism; sniper attacks; anthrax scare; wild fires; child kidnappings; pipe bomber; First blind man ascends Mt. Everest; Erik W. cloning; North/South Korean exchanges; war with Iraq	Enron scandal; DVDs; .com; instant messages; digital photos; caller I.D.; stock market plunge; electronic marketing and banking; baby boomers retiring; GPS in cars, self-scanning groceries	American Idol; Eminem; boy bands; Britney Spears; Dixie Chicks; Faith Hill; Kid Rock	Kurt Warner, George W. Bush, Barry Bonds, Lance Armstrong, Elizabeth Dole, Venus and Serena Williams, Steve Forbes, Osama bin Laden, Rudy Guiliani, Sammy Sosa

Adapted from *Human Development: The Span of Life*, 3rd edition by Kaluger/Kaluger, © 1984. Reprinted by permission of Prentice-Hall, Inc., Upper Saddle River, NJ.

Cohort differences are influenced by the major events that occurred during significant periods in a person's life.

Bearing in mind the differences in shared experiences that affect the perceptions of each new generation, we can see that communication between generations may be affected. Many individuals who shared the experiences of the 1930s with shortages in jobs and necessities have different perceptions of material possessions, work, and leisure than those who shared the experiences and perceptions of the 1960s, characterized by affluence, freedom, and mass education. Many 1930s individuals cannot understand why others are consumed by a desire for products and are not willing to defer gratification in order to obtain them. They are not able to understand why others do not place a high degree of importance on job security. Many 1960s individuals, on the other hand, really cannot understand how others can tie themselves to a single job for years at the expense of freedom of movement, freedom of thought, and freedom to pursue alternative lifestyles. When these two groups attempt to communicate, they often perceive the environment in two distinctly different ways and, therefore, have great difficulty relating to each other's needs.

Another example of the way that one's generation influences perceptions is related to the perceptions of various age groups toward leisure. Our grandparents often viewed play, recreation, and leisure as frivolous unless work-related (e.g., company picnics, parties, etc.). Our parents' generation often viewed recreation, leisure, and play as a way of restoring or refreshing oneself for work. Recreation was an activity that was conducted during discretionary time in order to help them work more productively. Conversely, the current generation "works to play." In other words, the focus of life tends to be on recreation, parks, and leisure services, and work serves as a vehicle that can be shaped, altered, and modified to facilitate play. Because the values of each generation are different, the relative importance attached to recreation, parks, and leisure services will vary.

Perceptual Selectivity

There are numerous factors or variables in the environment that affect the perceptual process. Our senses do not attend to all the stimuli that exist, but rather select the stimuli that are relevant to our current situation and needs. Right now, the reader may be in an environment in which the radio is playing, cars are going by, people are talking, the dishwasher is running, and so on; however, many of these sounds are not "heard" or perceived. The individual's perceptive process determines the stimuli that are to be selected for attention at any given moment. According to Luthans (1977), some of the environmental variables that influence perception are "intensity, size, contrast, repetition, motion, and novelty and familiarly" (pp. 259–261.) A discussion of these six variables follows.

Intensity. The intensity with which a stimulus is presented will affect the likelihood that it will be attended to. Or the more textural stimuli are, the more attention they will receive. The recreation, parks, and leisure services leader who desires to receive a great deal of attention from participants might consider wearing bright clothes, using a whistle, talking loudly, and so on.

Size. The larger an object is, the more likely it is that it will be perceived. In promoting a program, a large brochure is more likely to attract potential attendees than a small one.

Contrast. Individuals are more likely to perceive things that stand out from their surrounding environment. For example, a sign painted green and placed in a park to warn the public of danger will not be perceived as well as one painted bright yellow or red. The leader who wants to conduct an activity that requires close attention on the part of the participants might want to choose a quiet classroom setting (which would offer a contrast with his or her directions), as opposed to conducting the same activity in a gym or playground (where the noisy surroundings would compete for the participants' attention).

Repetition. The more often a stimulus is repeated, the more likely it is that it will be attended to by the individual. The recreation, parks, and leisure services leader who repeats his or her directions more than once will be "heard" by the participants, and heard more accurately than the leader who states things only once. It should be pointed out, however, that excessive repetition in communication can result in the participants' "tuning out."

Motion. Individuals will pay more attention to things that move than they will to stationary things. According to Luthans, "advertisers capitalize on this principle by creating signs which incorporate moving parts. Las Vegas is an example of advertisement in motion" (Ibid., p. 261). An application of this principle in the recreation, parks, and leisure services field would be the use of demonstrations in instruction.

Novelty and Familiarity. The individual is more likely to notice a novel stimulus in a familiar setting or a familiar stimulus in a novel or new setting. The recreation, parks, and leisure services leader conducting a six-week activity course, who notices a decrease in the interest of participants, may want to use novel stimuli to rebuild interest in the program. For example, a leader conducting a summer

As we must account for every idle word, so must we account for every idle silence.

Benjamin Franklin

playground program may want to bring in a local sports figure one week.

It is important to remember that all these variables are related; that is, events may be characterized by more than one of these variables and correspondingly may receive more attention from the individual as a result. The recreation, parks, and leisure services leader, in establishing communications with participants, needs to keep in mind how each of these variables can relate to the way that individuals perceive the leader, the activity, and the experience as a whole.

Other Physical and Personal Factors Influencing Perceptions

Perceptions are also heavily influenced by both the physical environment and individual characteristics. The following is a brief discussion of these factors.

Environment. The physical environment, geographic location of the participant, or both are major factors influencing his or her perception of a given situation. For example, an individual living in New York City, used to dense spatial relationships, will have a different perception of land use, social interaction, and physical accessibility from an individual residing in Kanosh, Utah, with a population of 350. An individual living in a dense urban population may have a different perception of time use related to travel. To commute 30 miles or more to a cultural event may be commonplace to the New Yorker, whereas the rural dweller might consider this excessive travel for the reward.

Personal Goals. The aspirations, level of achievement, and desires of an individual will greatly influence his or her perception of information being transmitted. An individual who is a high achiever concerned with his or her level of status might, for example, place a higher value on messages that communicate information regarding material possessions, finances, and so on. If an individual's goal in life is to acquire a million dollars, this will in turn affect the way that he or she perceives incoming information and ultimately makes life decisions relating to that goal. On the other hand, if his or her personal goals are altruistic, this will also influence his or her perception of the world.

Values. Societal norms and customs, religious beliefs, and personal values also influence the process of perception. In Eastern cultures, for example, marriages between individuals are often still arranged by their families or societies. On the contrary, Western societal customs and norms suggest that

Men are born with two eyes, but only one tongue, in order that they should see twice as much as they say.

Charles Caleb Colton

this is unacceptable. Obviously, these two different cultural values influence perceptions of the entire dating and courting process. Thus, our personal values greatly influence the process of perception in a very personal way.

Past Experiences. An individual's past experiences will influence how he or she perceives a given situation. If an individual has had a positive or negative past experience, this will color or affect his or her current or future perceptions of leisure opportunities. For example, an individual who has a previous leisure experience in golf that has resulted in a sense of enjoyment, satisfaction, and fun will tend to view similar opportunities favorably in the future. Conversely, an individual who has never been able to drive a golf ball successfully will have a different perception. When an opportunity to play, read about, or watch golf presents itself, the individual may engage in avoidance behavior owing to past second experience.

Personal Evaluation of Hearsay. Often the comments that are made by other individuals about a situation, leisure activity, or even another person will affect an individual's perception. For example, a film critic's judgment of a popular movie may influence an individual's decision to attend or not to attend it. The greater value that one places on the judgment of the other individual or individuals transmitting the information, the greater the likelihood that it will influence ones perception of a given situation (see Figure 7.3)

Fiction is the truth within the lie.

Stephen King

Figure 7.3
Edward C. Cannon, 1981. One view of "John is slow"
Source: Edward C. Cannon, Humbolt State University, 1981. ©edward C. Cannon.
Used by permission.

Social relationships. The individuals with whom we commonly associate, such as our parents, siblings, work associates, and friends, have a direct influence on our perceptive processes. The shared values common to a family unit, for example, will influence an individual's ability to process information and make decisions. Although individuals often have values parallel to those of their immediate family and peer group, there also is a potential for conflict based on differences between family members regarding personal goals, personal values, and perhaps experiences.

It is apparent that perceptions play an important role in the communication process for both the sender and the receiver, communication can be enhanced if one can bridge the differences in perception that occur between individuals.

STYLES OF COMMUNICATION

There are a number of styles of communication that can be employed by the recreation, parks, and leisure services leader. Depending on the situation, the leader may want to consider using one style of communication versus another. For example, if the purpose of the communication is to share ideas with another individual, the style of communication used will be different from what it would be if the purpose of the communication were to persuade another individual. One style of communication might be more direct and forceful, whereas the other style might be more subtle and indirect.

Often, when resolving conflict, the leader will want to draw out the ideas of others. Figure 7.4 presents a model that depicts the various styles of communication that can be used by the recreation, parks, and leisure services leader. There are four basic styles of communication: developmental, controlling, relinquishing, and defensive. Each of these approaches, in turn, can be subdivided into two categories. As an individual moves from the top to the bottom of the model counterclockwise, his or her style of communication becomes increasingly aggressive. Moving clockwise from the top of the model, an individual becomes more submissive as he or she moves toward the behavior at the bottom of the circle.

Developmental Approach. The developmental style of communication is based on sharing information and exploring the ideas of others. It involves a willingness to listen and offers an opportunity to present ideas. No attempt is made to win others to one's point of view. Informing involves the contribution of ideas, stimulation of discussion, and the sharing of information.

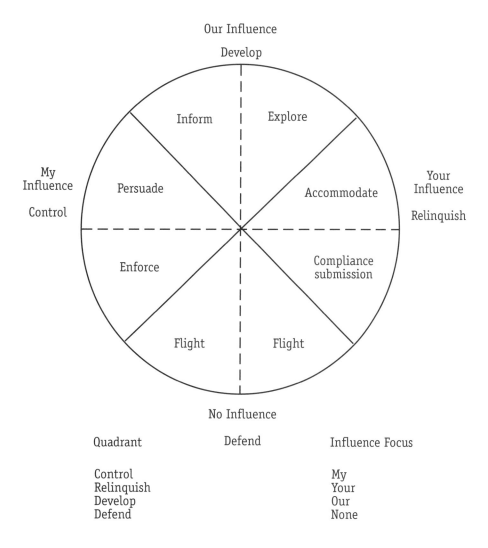

Figure 7.4
A model showing the influence of communication
Source: *Building Team Effectiveness* (Westport, CT: Educational Systems and Design, Inc., 1970), p. 39.

The other portion of the developmental approach, exploring, involves a willingness to listen to the opinions of others. It may also entail probing; that is, asking individuals questions that help them expand on their ideas and thoughts and giving support in the form of verbal and nonverbal feedback. The developmental approach is best employed when there is a need for individuals to share information or build joint commitment, or both.

Controlling Approach. The controlling approach to communication is one of trying to influence, persuade, or dominate others. The sender tries to influence other individuals to act in a manner consistent with the sender's interests or

> I'm all in favor of keeping dangerous weapons out of the hands of fools. Let's start with typewriters.
>
> *Frank Lloyd Wright*

desires. Often we see the controlling approach to communication in the enforcement of rules and regulations in sporting activities. The official uses the power of his or her position to ensure that a game is conducted according to the rules.

Persuasion involves directly selling one's ideas to another individual or individuals. When one is using the enforcing style of communication, authority, superior knowledge, or the threat of undesirable action, or a combination of these, is often employed.

Relinquishing Approach. There are situations where an individual will defer to another's point of view or knowledge of a situation, or both. This approach to communication is known as the relinquishing approach. Often, when the recreation, parks, and leisure services leader is dealing with an issue that is very important to another individual, he or she may defer to the other's wishes. This does not mean that the leader necessarily relinquishes his or her own values or opinions but rather that emotional issues may be better handled using this approach, at least temporarily. Certainly there are many situations in the recreation, parks, and leisure services profession when an individual becomes highly emotional or "charged up." Rather than trying to alter the behavior of the other individual, one may find it more effective to allow the emotional individual to express himself or herself. Two ways or patterns are used in this approach of defirring to another's point of view—accomodate compliance. In the former case, the individual attempts to maintain his or her point of view or integrate it with the other's point of view. In the latter case, the individual completely defers to the other's point of view, interests, or suggestions.

Defensive Approach. There are situations in which an individual will either withdraw from the communication process or strike out in anger. For example, an individual may become so frustrated in discussing an issue that he or she may begin to focus away from the issue and engage in character assassination and "dumping." This style of communication is known as the defensive approach. It is usually viewed as an inappropriate communication style except when there are ethical, legal, or moral implications that force the individual to withdraw. As the individual reaches the bottom of the model, two options are available: flight or fight. Flight involves complete withdrawal from the communication process. Fight occurs when an individual strikes out and attacks the other individual, verbally or physically.

Be a good listener. Your ear will never get you in trouble.

Frank Tyger

ACTIVE LISTENING

A major responsibility of the successful communicator is listening to others. The ability to listen carefully to others is a skill that can be developed. We use the term active listening to stress the importance of learning how to listen to others. This type of listening implies active participation on the part of the listener rather than merely passive absorption of comments made by others. In other words, the communicator actively seeks to understand what another individual is trying to communicate. Active listening is a process that directly affirms or acknowledges an individual's emotional and intellectual needs, interests, and desires. It requires that one give understanding to an individual without necessarily agreeing. It simply offers support for another's point of view. Often, because of poor listening skills, we shut off an individual prior to discovering the basis for his or her point of view. This essentially closes the door to communication as it ignores or rejects the other's thoughts, feelings, and, in a sense, his or her very being. In rejecting other individuals by failing to listen appropriately, we create feelings of mistrust, disloyalty, and lack of confidence.

Active listening allows the communicator to become more sensitive to what he or she hears and, as a result, to become more sensitive to those with whom he or she communicates. The active listener often becomes less argumentative and more willing to incorporate the views of others. In addition, active listening enables those individuals communicated with to feel as though their ideas, suggestions, and comments are worthwhile. As such, it increases the flow of information that can be used in problem-solving.

What Should the Leader Avoid

Often, when listening to an individual, one is more concerned with one's own needs than the needs of the other. We may want the other individual to see things from our viewpoint. In order to achieve this end, we may threaten, cajole, plead, or show contempt for the other's point of view. In short, the listener often tries to change the other's point of view rather than attempting to listen with understanding to the ideas, comments, feelings, and information being transmitted. Usually, poor listening is characterized by behavior such as constant interrupting, avoidance of eye contact, hurrying the speaker, and the use of automatic responses (e.g., "uh huh," "OK," "yeah").

Other characteristics of poor listening are a failure to ask the sender to expand on his or her ideas, a tendency to "put

> No man ever listened himself out of a job.
>
> *Calvin Coolidge*

down" the sender's ideas, and a tendency to ignore the feelings or body language of the sender. Several comments are presented as follows that reflect both poor responses and poor active listening:

Sender's question
"The fees for this program are too high! I'm not getting my money's worth."
"This basketball league is a disgrace. It's poorly organized."
"Don't you think I've improved my baseball skills by hitting and fielding?"

Poor response
"Well, I don't set them. Don't bother me about it!"
"It has always been organized this way. We aren't changing it!"
"Yeah, but you still have a lot that you do wrong, like holding your bat on your shoulder."

Active listening
"It seems to you that the fees should be lower, I take it?"
"You think we need to talk about the league's organization?"
"Sounds as if you feel that you've really improved your baseball skills!"

In each of these situations, the individual responding in the poor response category closed off further communication. Furthermore, telling individuals "Don't bother me," or "You still do a lot wrong," sends a negative message to the individual about his or her worth. It reduces the possibility of additional positive communication and creates barriers between individuals. By failing to deal with the comments and feelings of others in a way that provides understanding without necessarily agreeing with the individual, active support is denied. On the other hand, the active listener does not necessarily agree with the sender, but the way is left open for additional communication. This enables further discussion of the situation, provides an opportunity for the sender to expand his or her feelings or comments, and provides an opportunity for positive interaction.

Interestingly, because the leisure experience is highly personal and individually defined, there must be a rapport between the leader and the participant that enables the participant to reach conclusions about his or her own behavior. The open-ended supportive responses that characterize active listening are conducive to this. In the example given earlier, the active listener who responds "Sounds as if you feel that you've really improved your baseball skills" leads the participant to draw their own conclusion. With this approach, it is up to the participant, rather than the leader, to define and evaluate the success of his or her performance.

Never interrupt me when I am trying to interrupt you.

Winston Churchill

LEADERSHIP: A POINT OF VIEW
FROM THE PROFESSION
Michelle Gholston

 Michelle Gholston is Chief Professional Officer, Boys & Girls Clubs of Black Hawk County, Iowa. A nonprofit organization, the Boys & Girls Club has been in the forefront of youth development, working with young people from disadvantaged economic, social, and family circumstances. Gholston received her Bachelor's and Master's Degrees from Lewis University and has over five years experience working with youth, first in the juvenile detention field and then with the Boys & Girls Clubs of Springfield, Illinois. She started as Chief Professional Officer at the Boys & Girls Clubs of Black Hawk County in May of 2002.

The Boys & Girls Clubs of Black Hawk County are a 501(c)3 non-profit organization that has reached out to youth for more than 36 years. The Boys & Girls Clubs of Black Hawk County have actively sought to enrich the lives of girls and boys whom other youth agencies have had difficulty in reaching. The organization is dedicated to ensuring that the community's disadvantaged youngsters have greater access to quality programs and services that will enhance their lives and shape their futures. There are currently 26 staff positions for this organization.

On leadership. . . .Leaders focus on how to develop quality, character, mind-set, values, principles and courage among their employees. Leaders know that people are an organization's best asset. The best leaders do not use just one style of leadership but are skilled at several and switch easily amongst the styles as circumstances dictate.

Leadership and success. . . . Face-to-face leadership provides direct feedback to a subordinate and maximizes an individual's strengths while helping to develop their areas of weakness. Supervisory leadership provides quality control, ensures day-to-day operational tasks are being completed, ensures policies and procedures are being adhered to and reinforces positive actions by the employees. Recognition of employees is essential to, the flow of the organization. Managerial leadership allows for the incorporation of the three leadership styles: eclectic, democratic and authoritarian. Each style requires the leader to apply skills appropriately to each individual employee. This requires the leader to become acquainted with the staff and to know which style of leadership each individual needs in order to thrive at their job performance. At the community level, a leader brings their experience and expertise to community events, task teams, and committees, and takes a leadership role in those capacities.

The exemplary leader. . . .A leader within my organization demonstrates a passion for their job/role, is dedicated, takes the initiative, and is self-motivated to succeed. They are reliable and are resourceful, which is a necessity in a non-profit organization.

Leadership in action. . . . Organizational skills, be people oriented, good communication, flexibility.

Developing Active Listening Skills

When you have nothing to say, say nothing.

Charles Caleb Colton

There are a number of active listening skills that can be acquired and developed. Following are some of the skills that are conducive to active listening:

Learn to Listen to Yourself. The active listener should be in touch with his or her own feelings, prejudices, values, and needs in order to listen effectively. We all have biases that can influence or even block our ability to listen accurately and effectively. An awareness of these biases can help the listener overcome them when attempting to communicate.

Learn to Listen Accurately and Completely. The active listener lets an individual complete his thoughts and express his thoughts completely before responding. He or she should try to understand what the speaker is trying to convey in his or her message without interrupting or otherwise detracting from the speaker's message.

Learn to Read Body Language. The message that an individual conveys will often be more accurately represented by his or her gestures or other body language. The feeling or intensity with which a person presents his concern, interest, or idea is often more valuable to the listener as an indication of the intent of the message. Reading body language should help increase the listener's sensitivity to others.

Learn to Listen Courteously. Often individuals fail to demonstrate basic courtesy in listening to others. Their own verbal and nonverbal responses may demonstrate disrespect for the speaker. Being abrupt, curt, or disinterested should be avoided by the active listener. Individuals can learn to be tactful in their responses to others. The rule here is treating others as you would expect to be treated. Making eye contact and showing genuine interest in the speaker is essential to active listening.

Learn to Give and Gather Feedback. The way that the listener reacts to the speaker's message will communicate a concern or lack thereof for the views of the speaker. The way that the active listener "listens" to the message being presented can convey support, interest, and empathy. It is important to learn how to give feedback that allows for openness and continued positive communication. Often this will involve learning how to mirror, reflect, or clarify the speaker's queries. In order to clarify the communication that takes place, one can use such phrases as "Now you feel, then, that X is the case?" and "Let me make sure that I understand you correctly. Please tell me if I'm right." Such feedback increases the accurateness and effectiveness of the communication.

Learn to Accept Different Viewpoints. The active listener should learn to respond courteously to the ideas of others even though they may be different from his or her own. In other words, the listener must be willing to accept the ideas of others without necessarily being defensive. Further, the listener should avoid setting up barriers to communication based on personality. Active listening implies that the leader is willing to understand and give support to others. This may involve personal risk on the part of the leader as it requires him or her to be open and willing to be exposed to different views. When open to the views of others, the leader may be forced to reexamine his or her own views, concerns, and ideas.

A yawn is a silent shout.

GK Chesterton

TECHNIQUES OF COMMUNICATION

The recreation, parks, and leisure services leader should be familiar with various techniques of communication. Some of the specific techniques of communication that may be used by the leader are face-to-face, small-group, public speaking, and mass communication. These are detailed as follows.

Face-to-Face Communication

Face-to-face, or interpersonal, communication is a primary technique of communication used by recreation, parks, and leisure services leaders. Face-to-face communication suggests a direct one-to-one interaction between a leader and another individual. This type of communication can involve giving or receiving information, or both, in the form of coaching, lecturing, listening, demonstrating, role playing, and activity involvement, wherein the leader joins the participant in the activity. Interpersonal, or face-to-face, communication can also involve the sharing of emotional expressions, such as love, joy, grief, sorrow, or excitement. Emotional expressions are subjective in nature, but should be recognized as an essential component of the leisure experience.

Face-to-face communication is profoundly affected by the personality characteristics of the leader. The leader actively demonstrates a caring, empathetic attitude toward others will be more successful in face-to-face communication than one who does not. The leader who is comfortable with other people and who enjoys interacting with others on a one-to-one basis will likely be more effective the face-to-face leadership role. The ability of the leader to express his or her own feelings and emotions and listen and respond to the feelings of others is also conducive to effective face-to-face communication. The effective face-to face leader can be characterized as genuine, responsive, and respectful of the needs of others.

In order to increase the quality of face-to-face communication, the leader may disclose his or her feelings, thoughts, beliefs and values, and ideas as they relate to the existing situation. This is a dynamic process that serves to increase the intimacy between individuals and, as a result, facilitates the communication process. It is known as "immediacy," and it is one of the most important factors influencing interpersonal communication. Using this approach to communicate, the leader might express his or her own personal feelings or encourage the participant to do the same in order to create a meaningful dialogue. For example, the leader might state, "I am uneasy. I'm asking myself if I am paying enough attention to you," or "I feel as if we are having fun, but I don't know if I am expressing it well." Such statements open the door for a mutual exchange between the leader and the participant.

Face-to-face communication can also involve confrontation between individuals. The idea of confrontation often conjures up negative feelings. We have all been the subject of irresponsible interpersonal attacks, and perhaps we attempt to avoid such situations in the future. However, confrontation, when handled appropriately, is a useful form of interpersonal communication that can facilitate the communication process. By confrontation we mean that individuals are provided an opportunity to examine their own behavior. By having to account for feelings and ideas and examine these in relation to others, an individual is allowed, by the process of confrontation, to modify or change his or her ideas or behavior, or both.

Small-Group Communication

Much of the work of the recreation leader is carried out in small groups. Whether coaching a girls' basketball team, teaching a knitting class, leading New Games, or discussing contemporary events with friends, one is engaged in small-group communication.

For the recreation, parks, and leisure services leader to be successful in leading small groups, he or she must be able to use communications skill within a group setting.
Regarding the leader's role within groups, Wofford, Gerloff, and Cummins (1977) write:

We are members of many more groups today than at any other time. These groups tend to be less permanent, stable, and enduring in nature. Consequently, communication skill becomes increasingly more important; one must be able to interact quickly and to relate effectively on a limited time basis. The successful (leader) . . . today must become adept at establishing close, open relationships. One who remains guarded and defensive in the group context will be unable to succeed in a wide range of situations. (ibid, 1977, p. 251.) Thus, the ability to communicate effectively in small groups is extremely important.

Whether one is planning or implementing a program, communicating effectively with other individuals is essential to the successful operation of the organization. Effective communication can influence the identity of a group, its social structure, and the extent to which it achieves its goals. Communication within small groups also builds cohesiveness and is a primary vehicle for establishing behavioral norms and patterns.

As indicated in Chapter 5, communication within groups often focuses on three areas: process, task, and relationship. Communication activities focusing on the process orientation of a group are concerned with the vehicles used to transmit and receive information. Information is processed by talking, listening, and acting out or demonstrating. Use of the most appropriate of these vehicles to process information will facilitate communication. The process orientation of a group also refers to the assignment of responsibilities or the establishment of channels of communication, or both. When a group picks a leader, that individual assumes a certain role that, in turn, defines how communication with the group will occur.

Task orientation refers to the content communicated within the group. This might involve an introduction of information, a debate, analysis, decision making, or a combination of these. For example, a leader involved in small-group communication within a basketball team might lecture or demonstrate (process orientation) to teach zone defense (task orientation).

Small-group communication is also concerned with the relationship orientation between members of the group. Often within a group tensions will arise due to differing expectations that can influence the flow of communication. In the basketball example given earlier, the team's relationship orientation might center on the building of a "teamwork" philosophy, building esprit de corps, and attempting to avoid tensions related to individual performances.

Does group communication vary from individual, one-to-one communication? The processes used in individual communi-

No one can whistle a symphony. It takes an orchestra to play it.

H.E. Luccock

cation are basically the same as those employed in group communication; however, predictably, group communication is more complex. The dynamics of interaction that take place in a group usually are more formal or structured than interaction in face-to-face communication. Face-to-face interaction is more amenable to spontaneous change in both the type and style of communication. If the leader communicating individually desires to change from written to verbal to nonverbal communication as the situation demands, he or she may do so and, consequently, is able to respond to the communication needs of the individual more readily. On the other hand, when group consensus must be achieved as to the most appropriate type of communication in a given situation, the flexibility with which the leader can change types or styles of communication may be limited.

Public Speaking

Good public speakers are in demand. The recreation, parks, and leisure services leader who can express himself or herself effectively is an asset to his or her organization. Public speaking can be thought of as the art of moving an audience to belief and action (Gordon, 1978, p. 365). Gordon offers the following description of public speaking and some of its purposes: "A speech may, of course, serve either individual or organizational purposes, be motivated by profit or charity, and be by invitation or self-initiated. The subject matter may be broadly classified as educational, economic, political, spiritual, or recreational. When a speaker addresses an audience he seeks to draw an audience closer to certain ideas, feelings, or actions. . . . Speeches may reinforce established loyalties or promote new ones; they may entertain, inform, impress, convince, or any combination of these that serves the purpose of the speaker to influence the audience" (pp. 206–207).

The development of a speech involves several steps or procedures. The first step in the development of a speech is to identify the audience or intended receivers of the speech. The leader should know the type of audience he or she will be speaking to and its purpose for listening to the presentation. Some audiences represent a casual collection of individuals whereas others may assemble in order to pursue mutual interests. In giving a speech, the leader should ask two basic questions: (1) What do I know about the audience? and (2) What does the audience know about me and my topic? These questions are asked primarily to gauge how information should be presented and how it is likely to be perceived.

The second step in the development of a speech is to state specific goals of the speech. What knowledge or action does the speaker want the audience to exhibit at the conclusion

A speech is a solemn responsibility. The man who makes a bad thirty-minute speech to two hundred people wastes only a half hour of his own time. But he wastes one hundred hours of the audience's time—more than four days—which should be a hanging offense.

Jenkin Lloyd Jones

of the speech? In other words, what is the purpose of the speech? Is it to entertain people? To inform people? Is it to encourage people to join an organization? To influence people to give money to a cause? Is it to encourage people to participate in a recreation, parks, and leisure services activity? The leader should be specific in describing his or her goals, stating precisely "what behavior one want to happen, who should perform it, and when." (ibid., p. 217). Once these first two steps—identifying the audience and the goals of the speach—have been take, the speech may be organized.

Organization of the speech usually follows the same format as a term paper: introduction, body, and summary or conclusion. As a rule of thumb, the speaker wants to inform, entertain, and enlighten the audience. This involves designing a speech that will create interest, provide information, and move individuals to action. Forms of support of a speaker's point of view or topic that can be used in a speech are explanations, illustrations, and evidence. Explanations help the speaker clarify the relationships between ideas, thoughts, and concepts. An idea within a speech can be highlighted by using a story, analogy, metaphor, or simile. Illustrations are often included in a speech to help bring to life an idea, concept, or thought. Both from real life and imagined, illustrations often intensify the interest of the audience and promote the speaker's point of view. Evidence in the form of observable or statistical data is also useful in supporting a person's idea. Also, the use of inductive and deductive reasoning can help sharpen the speaker's argument.

Mass Communications

Mass communication can be thought of as the information that is transmitted in an organized fashion by an agency or institution. We think of mass communication as involved in reporting the news and information via television, newspapers, telecommunications, radio, magazines, books, and so on. In today's society, mass communications has made it possible to instantaneously Americans transmit pictures of people, places, events, and ideas. It is estimated that view an average of six hours and eight minutes of television per day. Over one billion individuals attended movies in 1980, and expenditures for magazines, newspapers, and books are millions of dollars per year. The establishment of home entertainment via cable television or personal computers or both is becoming more popular. Personal computers provide individuals with opportunities for new and instantaneous forms of communication. This type of technology is providing new forms of communication that directly affect the leisure experience and the way in which individuals interact with one another. For example, a semipro football team recently developed an interactive relationship with their fans via cable tel-

The ratio of We's to I's is the best indicator of the development of a team.

Lewis Ergen

evision. A system was established whereby those watching the game on television could vote, from a list of alternative plays, for a particular play to be run. Thus, this vehicle of communication gave these fans direct control over the game.

The possibilities for transactional (two-way) communication using these techniques are growing. Recreation, parks, and leisure services organizations use mass communication to promote and report on activities and services. Certainly, many recreation, parks, and leisure services organizations are involved in newsworthy activities that are reported in newspapers and on television and radio. In addition, mass communication is used to advertise and publicize services. This is done through the preparation of commercial radio and TV spots (or in the case of public recreation, parks, and leisure services agencies, the preparation of public service announcements), news releases, magazine and newspaper advertisements, interviews, photographs, and other media opportunities. In the transmission of information, the leader is communicating information concerning "who, what, when, where, and how." When one is developing copy for radio or television, it is important to recognize that these mediums are personal and direct channels of communication. The communication flow should be more conversational, informal, and casual. On the other hand, when one is writing for newspapers or magazines, communication usually occurs in inverse pyramid style; that is, the body or headline, of the story may be reported first to attract reader interest and the details follow it. In either case, the information communicated to the reader must be streamlined to fit the time or space available.

The recreation, parks, and leisure services leader should provide accurate, complete information to the public served by mass communication. The misrepresentation of a product or service, or inaccuracies due to lack of preparation or poor preparation can adversely affect the credibility of an organization. Knowledge of the various types of mass communication as well as how they can be used is essential to the leader wishing to effectively promote the activities and programs of his or her organization.

BARRIERS TO EFFECTIVE COMMUNICATION

Leaders may become frustrated or discouraged when they fail to communicate effectively. Understanding the barriers to communication can help the leader increase the likelihood that communication will be effective. Barriers are impediments that prevent the recreation, parks, and leisure

Put it before them briefly, so they will read it, clearly so they will appreciate it, picturesquely so they will remember it, and, above all, accurately so they will be guided by its light.

Joseph Pulitzer

services leader from transmitting information, or prevent the participant from understanding the information. As indicated previously, it is important to recognize that communication is a two-way process.

The lack of effective communication can occur as a result of such variables as breakdown, misunderstanding, and lack of empathy between the sender and the receiver. In some cases, failure can be attributed to the sender; in others, it may be the fault of the receiver; or, it may be the fault of both parties. When poor communication occurs the recreation, parks, and leisure services leader should attempt to identify and define barriers. Initially, the leader should analyze his or her own behavior or pattern of communication and ask him or her, "How am I projecting myself?" "Do people understand the meaning of the terms and phrases that I am conveying?"

The second step in the identification of barriers is analyzing the receiver's behavior and its effect on the communication process. The leader cannot initially change the communicative behavior of the participant. The leader can, however, alter his or her own behavior in order to communicate better with the receiver (on the "receiver's terms"). Once communication has been achieved, the leader can facilitate behavioral changes in the participant, including communicative changes, allowing for an easier and more effective two-way exchange. For example, a recreation, parks, and leisure services leader coaching a children's baseball team may need to communicate initially with the children in very simplistic and "non-technical" terms in order to guide the children effectively into a knowledge of the sport. Once the leader has taught the children the rules and technical terms, however, parallel communication can occur based on a shared "language."

Mondy, Holmes, and Flippo (1980) classify communication barriers in three categories: technical, semantic, and psychological.

Technical barriers can be thought of as variables in the environment that influence communication. They include such factors as timing, communications overload, cultural differences, and short-circuiting. Semantic barriers are problems resulting from language and the interpretations applied to various words within one's language. Finally, psychological barriers mainly arise from an individual's perceptions of situations or his or her interpersonal relationships with other people, or both," (pp. 383—387.) A brief discussion of some of the barriers in the communication process as classified by these authors follows.

> Don't use words too big for the subject.
>
> *C.S. Lewis*

▰▰Technical Barriers

Communication Overload. When an individual tries to transmit too much information too fast, a communication overload can occur. Individuals may become bogged down and disinterested and "tune out" when they are presented with more information than they can handle at one time. This problem is rampant in contemporary society, where individuals are constantly bombarded with information from multiple sources at once.

Cultural Differences. Customs and norms may vary from culture to culture, affecting the communication process. One culture may communicate more aggressively and effusively, whereas another culture may communicate in a more reticent and formal manner. Or, one culture may be interested in fast communication and quick results, whereas another culture may tend toward lengthy communication and careful deliberation. Failure to recognize these differences and adjust to them may hinder effective and accurate communication between individuals from two such cultures.

Knowledge of What You Say. Individuals often speak without thinking. As a result, the sender may have an incomplete picture of what he or she is trying to transmit. It is more difficult for the receiver to piece together a complete message if the sender is offering his or her message in a fragmented way. The sender should have an organized mental picture of what he or she is trying to transmit and should avoid such phrases as "you know," "the thing," and so on.

Meanings Associated With Words, Jargon, and Professional Nomenclature. Different meanings can be attached to words by a select group within a society and can affect the communication process. Excessive use of professional jargon when communicating with those unaccustomed to it will create a barrier to communication. For example, terms such as delivery system, planning horizons, proxy goals, and target markets have little meaning to the lay person.

Semantic Language. The level of vocabulary and the knowledge base of the sender and the receiver must be matched for effective communication to take place. Esoteric, problematic, theoretical, and conceptual information transmitted to an individual incapable of dealing in such terms will not be appropriately received. In this case, practical, concrete, and direct communication may produce greater understanding. Use of a vocabulary that consists of many terms that are sophisticated and beyond the grasp of the receiver is a barrier to communication.

He who does not understand your silence will probably not understand your words.

Elbert Hubbard

Short-Circuiting. Often individuals do not allow the sender to complete his or her message. Rather, the sender may be interrupted, or the receiver may form a mental response to communication before it is even complete. The intended message is "short-circuited" and may be misinterpreted or missed entirely. The lack of active listening creates ill will and may lead to mistrust and suspicion.

Timing. The leader must recognize the importance of timing in transmitting information to the participant. How receptive an individual is to a particular idea, concept, or thought may depend on the timing of the message. In teaching, instructors often refer to the "teachable moment." This occurs when the readiness of the students, and the information that is being transmitted, are interrelated and appropriate to one another.

Perception Barriers

Filtering. Related to the manner in which individuals perceive the world, filtering can often become an overt and direct way of manipulating information. Individuals may color information so that it conforms to their desires and wishes, thereby altering the communication that has occurred. This can result in misinformation in the communication process.

Perception Sets. The perceptual set of an individual greatly influences the communication process. This type of barrier to communication may be influenced by one's age, gender, political views, social status, and family orientation, as well as by other life experiences that have molded or shaped an individual's perceptions.

We Hear What We Want to Hear. One of the most common barriers to communication is the tendency to hear or see what one wants. Individuals has a tendency to evaluate information based on predetermined conceptions. For example, an individual may have a negative orientation toward life, and no matter how careful, positive, and joyful the information is that is presented, the individual will "find something wrong with it."

Trust and Openness. If individuals feel that others are not honest or have a hidden agenda, communication can be affected. The need for trust and openness is essential to the communication process. If the receiver lacks confidence in the honesty of the sender, the message may be ignored, devalued, or distorted. In addition, it is difficult to talk about problems or personal experiences when the trust factor is low.

> If you can't dazzle them with brilliance, baffle them with bull.
>
> *W.C. Fields*

SUMMARY

Communication is a process that helps individuals share their thoughts with one another. It is the way in which human feelings and ideas are transmitted. Communication attempts to convey meaning and to assist in understanding between individuals. The communication process consists of a number of interrelated components: the sender-encoder, message, channel, and receiver-decoder. The sender conceptualizes an idea, thought, or feeling. This, in turn, is encoded by using symbols that can be understood and accepted by both the sender and the receiver. The message being transmitted usually intends to inform, persuade, convey social or expressive behavior, or resolve conflict. The channel of communication can be thought of as the type of communication employed. Verbal, nonverbal, written, electronic-technological, and visual symbols are different channels of communication. The last step in the communication process is the receiving-decoding function, wherein the message is received and evaluated by the individual.

The recreation, parks, and leisure services leader is concerned with two-way, or transactional, communication. Transactional communication attempts to ensure that there is adequate feedback to individuals, including the use of listening and observational skills. Listening or active listening is a process in which the sender and receiver seek to understand what the other is attempting to communicate. It involves giving active affirmation or acknowledgment to others' ideas, feelings, or values. As not all communication is verbal or written, the use of observational skills to "read" nonverbal cues is also important.

The way that individuals perceive information that they have received influences the communication process. Perception is a psychological process that assists an individual in selecting, organizing, and interpreting information. It is dependent on both physical senses and complex cognitive processes. There are various factors or variables that influence the way that an individual will perceive a given piece of information or a situation. These include his or her environment, personal goals, values, past experiences, personal evaluation of hearsay, and social relations.

Often the communication process will fail. It is important for the recreation, parks, and leisure services leader to understand the barriers to effective communication that might cause this to occur. Some barriers to the communication process are poor timing, communication overload, short-circuiting, cultural differences, and language. Others include the filtering process, lack of trust or openness, and one's perceptual set.

Discussion Questions

1. Define communication. What is the difference between interpersonal and organizational communication?

2. What is transactional communication? What implications for the leader in recreation, parks, and leisure services settings does this concept have?

3. Identify and define five (5) different types of communication. Give two (2) examples of each.

4. Identify and define four (4) functions of communication.

5. What is the process of communication? What is encoding and decoding?

6. How does one's perceptual set affect the process of communication? What variables influence an individual's perceptions? What environmental variables influence the perceptual process? How?

7. What is active listening? How does one build active support for another individual through the listening process?

8. Identify four (4) techniques of communication and provide examples of the ways that they are used within recreation, parks, and leisure services organizations.

9. Identify ten (10) barriers to effective communication. Suggest solutions to the problems created by these barriers.

10. Discuss how communication influences the recreation, parks, and leisure services experience.

THE CASE FOR LEADERSHIP
Should Insensitivity Charge Be Shrugged Off?

Points of Consideration

Eight months after you were hired to shape up the long-troubled Cedar Center, you are facing many problems of your own. In a four-page letter sent to you this week by the advisory board of the center, you were notified of a charge that you and your staff have misrepresented information to the director and the parks and recreation board. Further, the advisory board states that you and the staff have widened racial divisions at the center, and have been unresponsive and insensitive to the advice of the center's advisory board.

The letter complained that an advisory board memorandum on playgrounds had been "aggressively and falsely characterized as an attempt by white, female outsiders to curtail or eliminate the adult basketball league of predominately African-American players at the center". The letter said the same memorandum was misrepresented to the parks and recreation board.

In addition, this letter claimed that you, as director of the center, have not established good relations with the advisory board, and you have not kept members informed of community meetings and other activities. Advisory board member Chris Edginton, in a published interview with a local journalist, acknowledged that the letter is critical, but it that was meant to help resolve difficulties, not exacerbate them. He said that the full advisory board supported the letter, although only three out of the seven members signed it.

In the letter, Edginton acknowledges there has been a history of communication problems between the advisory board and the center's staff. The relationship between the advisory board and the previous center director had deteriorated considerably before the embattled director resigned last year.

You showed the advisory board's letter to your assistant for her comments, and she replied, "We're following the director's and park and recreation board's orders, which are to clean up the problems at this center. We have nothing to be ashamed of. My thought is that somebody's relative lost a job in the reorganization, and that person is now seeking revenge."

Another member of the advisory board, Kathy Scholl, has also talked to you in private. She said, the letter is "an outreach from the board. I want you to pay attention to these concerns. I'm disappointed that we can't hire a center director who can work with the advisory board.

Questions of Consideration

- What do you say in response to this letter?
- What are the concerns that are overtly expressed in this letter?
- Covertly expressed?
- Through what means should you respond (letter, face to face meeting, ignore the letter)?
- Should a response be immediate, or should you wait a few days?

Suggest ways that communication could be strengthened between the director and the board.
- Which of the parties should be responsible for making sure that good communication exits?

Adapted from: Bannon, J. and Busser, J. (1992). *Problem Solving in Recreation and Parks* (3rd ed.). Champaign, IL.: Sagamore.

REFLECTING ON LEADERSHIP
Value-Laden Words

1. We use value-laden words without realizing what we mean. In addition, these value-laden words are triggers that block the communication process.

On a separate piece of paper, describe the following words in five words or less.

Good	Right	Correct
Bad	Wrong	Incorrect

Try to go a whole day without using one of these words in your conversation with others. Notice how many times the words are used by others and in what context.

References

Berlo, D. K. (1960). *The process of communication*. New York, NY: Holt.

Csikszentimihalyi, M. (1975). *Beyond boredom and anxiety*. San Francisco, CA: Jossey Bass.

Denhardt, R., Denhardt, J. & Aristigueta, M. (2002). *Managing Human Behavior in Public and Nonprofit Organizations*. Thousand Oaks, CA: Sage Publications.

Edginton, C., Hudson, S., Dieser, R, & Edginton, S. (2004). *Leisure programming: A service-centered and benefits approach* (4th ed.). New York, NY: McGraw-Hill.

Edginton, C., Hudson, S., & Ford, P. (1999). *Leadership in recreation and leisure service organizations*. (2nd ed.) Champaign, IL: Sagamore Publications.

Gordon, W. I. (1978). *Communication: Personal and public*. Sherman Oaks, CA: Alfred.

Jordan, D. (1999). *Leadership in leisure services: Making a difference*. State College, PA: Venture Publications.

Luthans, F. (1977). *Organizational behavior* (2nd ed.) New York, NY: McGraw-Hill.

Mondy, R. W., Holmes, R. E., & Flippo, E. B. (1980). *Management concepts and practices*. Boston, MA: Allyn & Bacon.

Nahavandi, A., & Malekzadeh, A. (1999). *Organizational behavior: The person-organization fit*. Upper Saddle River, NJ: Prentice Hall.

Wofford, J. C., Gerioff, E. A., & Cummins, R. C. (1977). *Organizational communication: The keystone to managerial effectiveness*. New York, NY: McGraw-Hill.

CHAPTER

8

Managing
Risks

LEARNING OBJECTIVES

1. To understand the leader's responsibility in managing activity risks.
2. To gain awareness of the elements of negligence as they related to leading leisure and recreation, parks, and leisure services activities.
3. To understand the "standard of care" with regards to supervision practices.
4. To gain knowledge concerning the controlling of risks through good supervision practices.

KEY TERMS

- Risk
- Negligence
- Inherent Risk
- Agreement to Participate
- Legal Liability
- Plaintiff
- Waivers
- Insurance

INTRODUCTION

Who is wise? He who
foresees what is com-
ing.

Jewish proverb

David was fulfilling his summer Internship responsibilities
by serving as the summer playground supervisor at Addams
Community Center Park in Cedar Center. After a half-day orientation to the summer activities, he was expected to run
the program from 8:30 a.m. – 12:00 p.m. and 1:00 p.m. – 4:30
p.m. Since this was a drop-In program, he was never sure
what children would show up on any given day. In addition,
children were free to come and go during the course of the
day. However, while on park premises, he was told he was
responsible for any children who signed up on the daily roster.

One hot summer afternoon, 11-year-old Bill and his pals
decided that they wanted to practice the wrestling moves
they had seen on television. David informed the boys that
this wasn't an acceptable program activity. The boys decided
to leave the park. However, they only went far enough to get
out of the sight of David before resuming their rough play. In
the course of this play, one boy was thrown violently to the
ground and suffered a severe concussion and a broken arm.
David learned of this mishap a month later when a lawsuit
was filed charging him, the department, and city with negligence in the operation of the program.

Unfortunately in today's litigious society, incidences as the
one mentioned above are becoming the norm rather than the
exception. Because of the risk inherent in many recreation,
parks, and leisure services activities, leaders need to understand how to manage risks to protect both the participants
and the agency. This chapter will explore the challenges of
managing risk, the elements of negligence, and the standard
of care expected of leaders as they conduct leisure activities.

WHAT IS RISK

Risk is inherent in any sports or recreation program
(Nonprofit Risk Management Center, 2003, p.1). No recreation, parks, and leisure services leader can insure that a participant will not get hurt as a result of participation in an
activity. It is a generally accepted tenet in most legal jurisdic-
tions that no recreation, parks, and leisure services program
can be 100 percent safe, no matter how well it is run or how
safe it may seem to be. Under certain circumstances the participants in a recreational activity may be expected to
assume responsibility for some of the risks associated with
their participation in that activity. However, it is the responsibility of the leader to try to minimize the consequences of
any foreseeable hazards inherent in either the activity or the

environment. For instance, allowing a person to play hand-ball without safety glasses could be seen as a failure to protect the participant from a foreseeable eye injury. Likewise, allowing children to play on playground equipment that has either broken or missing parts puts them at risk for injury. In both cases, the probability of injury is known and therefore foreseeable.

While there are many definitions of risk, they all contain the ideas of "probability" and "loss." Probability infers the possibility that something might occur. For instance, if a leader takes a group on a canoeing trip and leaves the life vests on the shore, the probability that someone will drown if the canoe overturns is much higher than if the participants were wearing safety vests. The issue in this situation is not one of turning over a canoe but the "probability" that if one landed in the water, wearing a life vest would provide greater protection to the individual for staying afloat.

Loss in the above scenario refers to loss of life. However, other types of loss can take place such as financial loss to the agency if they are sued over the incident, and loss of reputation of the agency.

There are two types of risk that the recreation, parks, and leisure services leader needs to be aware of – inherent risks and negligent behavior.

Inherent Risks

According to van der Smissen (2003), inherent risks are those integral to the activity (p.58). For instance, in the canoeing scenario, because of stability issues, there is a distinct possibility that a canoe may overturn. Factors such as wave action and water current can heighten the instability of the canoe, and even an expert canoeist can end up wet from time to time. Thus, falling into the water is an inherent risk one takes when getting into a canoe. "There is no liability for injury that occurs due to inherent risks of which the injured participant is knowledgeable or should be knowledgeable. The participant assumes such risks" (Ibid. p.58). The role the recreation, parks, and leisure services leader plays with this type of risk is one of helping the participant understand the inherent risks of the activity to help reduce possible injury. Thus, providing instruction about the proper way to use a canoe, information about water currents, etc., as well as checking the swimming ability of each participant, would be important prior to taking individuals out on a lake.

It's too bad that one has to conceive of sports as being the only arena where risks are, [for] all of life is risk exercise. That's the only way to live more freely, and more interestingly.

William Sloane Coffin, Jr.

▰▰▰▰▰ Negligent Behavior

How could youths bet-
ter learn to live than
by at once trying the
experiment of living?

Henry David Thoreau

Opposed to inherent risks, risks arising from negligent behavior on the part of the leader are not assumed by the individual. "Negligent behavior is conduct that is not in accord with the standard of care that a prudent professional should give and, hence, the participant is subject to "unreasonable risk" of injury (Ibid). For instance, a leader who allowed children to leave their life vests on the shore because the children were hot would be opened to a charge of negligent behavior.

If potential incidents can be lessened in both frequency and severity, it follows that there will be fewer lawsuits. With fewer lawsuits being fought, fewer suits will be lost, and less money will be due in damages. One way to lessen incidents is by thinking through and implementing a plan to mange risk for every program that involves the leader. As such every leisure program administrator and leader is advised to consider it mandatory to develop risk management plans for every aspect of the program.

Managing risks as wise fiscal management is, understandably, a valid approach. From a philosophical point of view, however, it may be stated that the primary purpose in managing risks is the concern for the well being of the participants and staff, while the secondary purpose is a concern for fiscal matters. Be that as it may, it is well that all who undertake to lead others in any type of program understand the elements of legal liability.

WHAT CONSTITUTES LEGAL LIABILITY

While programmers and leaders might be concerned with all forms of legal liability, the type of liability most related to leisure programs and the management of associated risks is tort. A tort is a wrongdoing against a person who suffers damages. While there are intentional torts (assault, fraud, slander, misrepresentation, etc.), the concern here is the unintentional tort. Unintentional torts are those where one did not intend to injure an individual, but in fact, an injury did occur (van der Smissen, 2003). The injury may have occurred because of an act of omission (something one did not do) or commission (something one did do) (Ibid. p.56). The wrongdoer to the one who was injured may pay the actual damages.

It is important to note that "negligence law is primarily state law and as such, may vary from state to state" (Colton & Wolohan, 2003, p.55). Thus, what follows are "general rules" that may not be necessarily true in every state.

In a court of law, in order to show that negligence occurred, the plaintiff (person injured and bringing the suit) must prove four elements:

1. A duty was owed. It must be shown first that the person(s) in charge (in this case the administrator and the staff who directed the program) had the duty or responsibility to provide the participant with a safe environment and competent leadership. This duty is based on the relationship between the service provider and the participant. The basic relationship is one that is inherent and obvious.

   Any time a program or service is provided, there usually is an obligation not to expose the participant/user to unreasonable risk of harm (van der Smissen, 2003). This is an inherent relationship recognized by the law, requiring leisure agencies to conform to a certain standard of conduct and protect participants from unreasonable risks. In any recreation, parks, and leisure services program with a designated leader, it is the leader's responsibility to provide a safely operated program. This means a safe environment exists under normal conditions. One can never guarantee that there will not be unforeseen conditions, such as July blizzards in areas normally above freezing, or earthquakes where none have occurred in modern times, but it does assume that the environment or situation will be as safe as is predictable. It can usually be assumed that any organization providing a recreational program owes the participants the duty of providing a safe environment and competent leadership.

   Voluntary assumption is a second type of relationship that might exist. This is when no inherent relationship is present, but a person voluntarily assumes a relationship. For instance, a person who voluntarily renders first aid to an individual in distress has a duty to provide an appropriate standard of care.

   The third relationship may be based on statutes, such as those established for employment, supervisory requirements, or rendering first aid in specified situations. This relationship is a "duty to be proactive in protecting one when the risk is foreseeable by a prudent professional" (van der Smissen 2003, p.57).

2. The duty was breached. (There was a failure to perform this duty.) The plaintiff must show that the duty to provide the safe environment was breached by the leader (or administrator) who did not follow what the courts call standard of care." That is, that through actions (commission) or inactions (omission), the defendant failed to

> The greatest risk you face is the one you don't know about.
>
> *David Mair*

protect the participant from known or foreseeable hazards, or conducted operations without reasonable care.

3. Proximate cause. If it can be shown that there was, in fact, a duty to provide a safe environment and that the duty was breached by the leader or administrator not following a standard of care, the plaintiff must then show that the failure to follow the standard of care was the proximate cause of the injury.

4. The physical or emotional injury was of a nature serious enough to warrant the recovery of funds.

If these four elements (a duty existed, failure to perform this duty, proximate cause, and subsequent need to recover funds) can be proven, a defendant may be found guilty of negligence.

Before discussing the duty (commonly referred to as the standard of care) and the development of the plan to manage activity risks, it is a good idea to consider certain positive elements of risk in recreation, parks, and leisure services activities. There is currently little information on the frequency of accidents in recreation, parks, and leisure services activities of any kind. All available sources tell us that the incidence of these accidents is minimal. In relation to accidents, injuries, and fatalities, four things are known:

1. There is no evidence that recreation, parks, and leisure services activities (even high-adventure outdoor recreation, parks, and leisure services) are inherently dangerous. It is not the activity that causes accidents, it is people who cause the accidents. People in the wrong place, at the wrong time, with the wrong equipment or facilities, and/or making wrong decisions cause accidents.

2. People seek challenges. Individuals desire to test their skills, try new challenges, and have new adventures. Risks can be found in all sorts of situations. There is probably less risk in terms of mental health in a whitewater rafting tour than in accepting a new job. There is probably less physical risk in a learning to dive than in driving a car. Participants in leisure pursuits are like everyone else; they will engage is challenges that might expose them to risk.

Hans Selye, the Canadian psychiatrist, has written much on the aspects of positive stress (eustress). Stress that is self-imposed has a positive effect, as it relieves boredom and increases the joy of living. Participating in a recreational activity may be an example of positive stress. With more opportunity to experience new activities, more people will challenge their abilities for the pure joy of it. The thrill of mastering roller-blades, the excitement of exploring a new area of the country, the joy gained from participating in a guided safari to Africa, the exhilaration of learning to swim, and even the feeling of accomplishment that follows the completion of a complicated craft project are all the results of a natural inclination for challenges and the accompanying positive stress or eustress. Unfortunately, there are times when some participants find that this positive stress turns into negative stress with resulting misadventure, accident, and even death. All leaders need to recognize the value of challenge while doing everything in their power to minimize actual risk.

Because it is recognized that people are challenge takers who will try things without being aware of the risks, it becomes the responsibility of recreation administrators and leaders to conduct activities wherein the risks are minimized and where self-imposed stress remains positive and beneficial. Responsible leaders teach the participants how to manage risks so they can continue to participate in their chosen activities safely. They need skills to keep them from being in the wrong place at the wrong time with the wrong equipment, and/or making wrong decisions long after they leave the sponsored programs.

3. In a recreation program, as in any situation, the leaders are never guarantors or insurers of safety. Unforeseen conditions, improper decisions, and/or improper behaviors on the part of the participants preclude the fact that injuries won't happen.

4. Risk management must not become an excuse for sitting on the sidelines. Effective risk management seeks to find ways to provide for safe participation based on an understanding of the risks, rather than to be a convenient means to refuse to undertake an activity. The exceptions are those situations when the potential loss is so great or the consequences so significant that avoidance is the only prudent course of action. For example, there may be a risk of food contamination associated with a chili cook-off fundraiser; however, that risk is manageable. It is very different from a demolition-derby fundraiser in which racers enter their personal autos (Nonprofit Risk Management Center, p. 4-5).

With the preceding four things in mind, the activity staff can undertake the responsibilities of managing risks and minimizing the possibilities of accidents. Since risk is, by definition, a chance of encountering harm, injury, loss, hazard, or

> Play is a major avenue for learning to manage anxiety. It gives the child a safe space where she can experiment at will, suspending the rules and constraints of physical and social reality....
>
> *Alicia Lieberman*

danger, the management of risks is control of injury, hazard, loss, or danger. A risk management plan is a set of regulations, policies, and procedures for conducting an activity with inherent risk.

Managing risks is the responsibility of the leader of every program. While some activities have more potential for accidents than others and must be planned with extreme caution, potential hazards can be found in nearly every activity. The injury of a participant in the collapse of a broken chair or bench during a training session is of no less significance than the injury of a hiker who breaks a leg in a fall. As a matter of fact, in the former case, the responsibility was probably entirely that of the agency that permitted the use of faulty equipment (a weak chair). In the case of the hiker, it might be claimed that the participant contributed partly to the accident through improper behavior. It may be shown that the hiker was running down a steep hill, contrary to instructions that warned against such behavior. It might be quite difficult to prove that the participant was responsible for the collapse of the broken chair.

The management of risks is based on the premise that people should be able to pursue their natural inclinations toward participation in a wide variety of activities. The possibility of accidents resulting from such activities, however, should be minimized through plans to control them. We might also agree that it is philosophically wrong to deny people the right to participate in activities of potential yet controlled risk. People want to test themselves, to move faster, to try more advanced skills, to explore the unknown, to attempt the unattempted. No program should deny the participant the chance to succeed at what was not previously attempted or performed, as long as the activity is one that the program can offer competently. Every participant has the right to fail without serious physical, mental, or emotional consequences. Also inherent in that right is the right to try again. One goal of the participant is to have a positive experience. If the participant returns home unscathed and able to try again, it is relatively unimportant that the goals of achieving or mastering the skill were not reached immediately.

Preplanning of activities takes into account all aspects or elements of the activity and results in clear, concise policies and directions for dealing with all foreseeable risks. These risks may result from individual elements or from the interaction of these elements. Of concern in a typical recreational activity are lands and facilities, the weather, transportation modes, group and individual equipment, and several categories of people who are directly or indirectly affected by the activity. These people include the public at large (via taxes, insurance rates, associations with individuals directly

Adventure: the pursuit of life.

Daniel Wiarda

A LEGACY OF LEADERSHIP
Betty van der Smissen

As an educator, researcher and author, mentor, and colleague, Dr. Betty van der Smissen has been providing leadership to the Leisure, Park, and Recreation fields for over 50 years. A noted author, especially in the field of legal liability and risk management, Dr. van der Smissen has been elected to membership in the four academies of her profession: Academy of Leisure Sciences (founding fellow); American Academy for Park and Recreation Administration; American Leisure Academy (founding senior fellow), and the North American Society of Health, Physical Education, Recreation, Sport, and Dance Professionals (charter fellow). Dr. van der Smissen's professional involvement with numerous organizations has been essentially as an initiator, a promoter/supporter, a facilitator, and especially as an educator. In addition to her academic teaching and leadership at seven different institutions of higher education, she has given more than 700 presentations (keynotes, educational sessions, and workshops) at the state, regional, national and international levels. She has been recognized for her contributions by the major professional organizations, receiving among other numerous honors the R. Tait McKenzie Award (by the American Association for Health, Physical Education, Recreation and Dance); the Distinguished Fellow Award (by the Society of Park and Recreation Educators); and was invited by the American Association for Leisure and Recreation to be its first Jay B. Nash scholar/lecturer. In 2004, the Sport and Recreation Law Association (SRLA) named its annual Leadership award the Betty van der Smissen Leadership Award.

Dr. van der Smissen has focused her leadership in the field of leisure, recreation and parks in four areas: outdoors, accreditation standards, legal liability/risk management, and research. Her leadership in the outdoor area extends over the years and includes serving as an instructor trainer of the Campcraft program (now the Outdoor Living Skills program), a term as national president of the American Camping Association, and fostering the use of the outdoors in school settings. She also has contributed to the standards program and understanding of legal liability/risk management in the outdoor settings.

Her first work in accreditation came in the 1960s as the Chair of the American Recreation Society's Professional Development Committee, which initiated the academic curriculum accreditation program. About this same time, she began work related to standards for park and recreation agencies, and in 1965 the National Recreation Association published Standards and Evaluative Criteria. These standards stayed in place until the formation of the Commission for Accreditation of Park and Recreation Agencies (CAPRA). She served as a member of the development team for CAPRA and was the Commission's first president. She continues to serve on the Commission and is its Standards chair. In addition, for many years she served on the National Standards Board of the American Camping Association (now the American Camp Association), which administered the organized camping accreditation program, and was co-researcher of the research project that resulted in the first major revision of the standards.

continued on next page

continued from previous page

Dr. van der Smissen is one of those rare individual that holds both a J.D. degree and a Re.D. degree. Receiving her law degree (J.D.) from the University of Kansas (she is a 50-year member of the BAR), Dr. van der Smissen was able early in her career to combine her professional interest in parks and recreation with her background in law. The result was the publication in 1968 of one of the few legal books in the field, titled *Legal Liability of Cities and Schools for Injuries in Parks and Recreation*. A complete three-volume revision was done in 1990 titled *Legal Liability and Risk Management for Public and Private Entities*. In this revision, she broadly covers the fields of parks and recreation, sport and physical education, and camping/adventure programs. Currently, she is co-authoring a text, *Risk Management of Adventure/Challenge Programs* to be published in 2005.

The more you seek security, the less of it you have. But the more you seek opportunity, the more likely it is that you will achieve the security that you desire.

Brian Tracy

involved in the activity, or an obligation to respond to an emergency (i.e., emergency medical teams), the public directly involved (co-users of the area or facility), land or facility managers, administrators and officials of the sponsoring agency, the staff and leaders of the activity, and, of course, the participants.

When people are involved with programs, potential problems are created. The list of these is virtually endless, but most can be contained in three categories: (1) injuries or health problems, (2) damage or loss to property or resources, and (3) failure to meet participant expectations. Accurate identification of potential problems and assessment of risks requires a thorough understanding of the site(s), the facilities and possible weather conditions, the activity to be pursued, and (too often minimized) the goals, objectives, and limitations of the program, the leaders, and the participants. Developing effective policies and procedures for containing and minimizing these risks demands an awareness of applicable management regulations and laws and a sensitivity to social and legal conventions. In order to assure concern for the welfare of the participant, any plan for the management of risks should be developed so that it gives evidence of following the "standard of care" for a given activity.

STANDARD OF CARE

When an individual accepts responsibility for leading a group, he or she is, in effect, declaring competence. Defining the term "competent" may appear to be difficult; however, in the courts of law in the United States, competency is equated with that of a reasonable and prudent professional utilizing the best and most current professional practices. This comparison to the actions of a reasonable and prudent (or careful) professional is known as a standard of care.

Who sets this standard? It may be set forth by statute, ordinance, or regulation; by organizations or agencies; or by the profession. For example, the best professional practice for the design and operation of public playgrounds is set forth in the *Handbook for Public Playground Safety* published by the U.S. Consumer Product Safety Commission. These "guidelines" are given additional authority by the National Playground Safety Institute, a part of the National Recreation and Park Association, who provide a certification program for playground safety inspectors based on the guidelines. The result is that in many state courts around the country, when a recreation, leisure, and park agency has a playground injury incident and it can be shown that the agency personnel disregarded the CPSC guidelines, the agency may be held liable even though the guidelines are not mandatory.

"The professional standard of care does not vary based on the qualifications of the person in charge, whether experienced, older, or certified. If one accepts responsibility for giving leadership to an activity or providing a service, one's performance is measured against the standard of care of a qualified professional for that situation (van der Smissen, p.60-61).

In cases where litigation occurs and the leader(s) or administrator(s) are sued, the defense is made that the standard of care was followed. In other words, in order to be judged as competent, the leader must show that a standard of care comparable with that of the best professional practices was followed.

For example, a handball instructor deciding between two types of eye protectors may have good reason to regard both brand "A" and brand "B" as acceptably safe for the activity. He or she may feel that brand "A" is equal to or slightly better but recommends that brand "B" be purchased because it is less expensive. If an accident occurs to an individual wearing brand "B," the leader could face the additional burden of having to justify his or her recommendation. If the case should go to court, expert witnesses (professional instructors, rule books, and officials familiar with both types of goggles) may be called in, and might designate that brand "A" is not only safer, but the only brand they would approve. This would cast doubt on the performance of the leader and thus on the "standard of care" provided to the participants. Careful and conservative leaders and administrators always consider, at every decision point, both the real risks and the implications of having to justify the decision before a panel of peers. The preceding example is taken from an actual court case where the instructor did recommend the less expensive eye guards and a participant was hit in the eye by a handball. The ball was just soft enough to squeeze between the top and bottom lenses of the goggles, blinding the eye permanently. The instructor was held liable for negligence on

Never measure the height of a mountain until you have reached the top. Then you will see how low it was.

Dag Hammaraskjold

the basis that the goggles recommended were inferior and not the brand approved by the official organization of the sport in question. This example could be applied to many other sports and types of safety equipment recommended or mandated.

The standard of care is not dependent upon the qualifications of whoever happens to be in charge; rather, it is situation-determined. There are three things that define the situation: the nature of the activity, the participants, and the environment.

Nature of the Activity

The leader must be aware of the skill and abilities needed in order to successfully and safely participate in the activity. This means that the leader or instructor must know not only how to demonstrate the skill to be taught, but how to analyze the skill in terms of its component parts in order to help the participant move from the simple to the complex, from the basic to the advanced, along logical progressions that are within his or her ability. For example, a cross-country skiing instructor should teach the participant how to put on the equipment and how to do some "in place" movements, including getting up from a simple fall, before teaching the skills that result in falls. Think of the progression that one teaching woodworking, softball, wrestling, whittling, or swimming might need to follow. Instructors should be familiar with the current literature of their field and attend workshops to keep current with the latest thinking on the teaching of special activity skills. The agency or leader without ready access to reference books on their specific activity may have trouble validating that instructors had adequate information on instructing that activity.

Type of Participants

Not only must the leader be able to teach the skills in logical progression, he or she must be able to modify the plans to meet the age, size, skill, experience, and maturity of the participant. Here maturity refers to both chronological maturity and maturity in terms of knowledge of the activity. The 12-year-old who has participated in a series of diving competitions is probably more mature in diving safety than a 50-year-old who is just starting diving lessons.

In order to understand their participants, the leader must understand the age, size, skill, maturity, and special conditions of every participant. The tall leader needs to realize that the short participant cannot place his or her feet on the same spots that the leader uses. The very young gymnast or soccer player may have much more initial energy than the

I'd just as soon play tennis with the net down.

Robert Frost

older one who may, in turn, have more endurance than the younger one. The words of encouragement used for the seven-year-old will differ from those used for the 17-year-old or the adult of 67. The obese participant may not have the energy to move as rapidly as one who has less body weight to carry. Beginners must be made to feel that they are able to learn new skills, regardless of age. A different plan of instruction is undertaken with the novice and with the expert. The inexperienced do not perform in the same manner as the experienced. The leader is not acting as a reasonable and prudent professional when he or she forgets that the task is to teach people, not activities. Further, the group may include several individuals with either physical or mental disabilities who require modification of the activity and of the instruction.

Environmental Conditions

This term environmental conditions refers to the physical area related to the activity—both the natural and man-made elements found in the area and the layout and design of the area. A brief description of these three elements follows.

Natural Hazards. Natural hazards are those inherent in the environment such as rocks, deep drop-offs in lakes, poisonous plants, high tide, lows rivers, etc. These are all things that one might be expect to encounter on a field trip and should be checked out before the trip.

The suitability of the natural environment depends on the geography of the site, the nature and condition of travel routes, the weather, the proximity of support services such as rescue teams, and the intended activity. An area of gentle rolling hills at moderate elevations, with good trails, may seem implicitly well suited for a beginning hiking course. On one hand, if the area is known for its severe storms and rapid weather changes, or if the area is exceptionally remote, risk levels may be unacceptable for other than highly experienced participants. On the other hand, a rugged and spectacular high alpine region may be reasonable for beginners if the weather is moderate and reasonably predictable, and if the area is not too remote and has good escape routes.

Man-Made Elements. Someone should check the indoor facilities, such as windows, exits, light switches, fire extinguishers, loose or weak boards, electrical cords, and so on on a scheduled, periodic plan. When a condition is reported, it should be noted and cared for at once. If a participant falls down stairs that are covered with loose sand, it may be that the custodial staff knew of the sand but decided to sweep the stairs after the building was closed. Such a decision might not be acceptable in a court of law. The leader who

> Although adults have a role to play in teaching social skills to children, it is often best that they play it unobtrusively.
>
> *Rubin Zick*

finds broken, loose, or weakened equipment should not permit its use.

Layout and Design. Checking out the layout or design means more than an examination of the stairs, emergency exits, lights, and windows. It also means checking the source of emergency help on a trip away from home, locating telephones and sources of aid, and planning emergency routes that may be taken to leave the area. In short, it means checking not only the condition of the area to be used, but checking all surrounding areas for possible use and exit in case of emergency. On trips this means alternate routes to take in the event or fire, flood, storm, or injury. It may mean finding safe shelter also. Consider a tour offered by programmers at a senior citizen center. The bus driver took the wrong dirt road in a forested location and realized his mistake when the bus reached a spot in the road. The road was too narrow for the driver to turn the bus around easily, and too far from the correct road to back the bus up comfortably. The situation occurred because the leader did not check the route before the tour. Fortunately, in this case, the driver was able to turn the bus around, much to the laughter and delight of these senior citizens, none of who were injured and only a few of who were a little frightened. It could have been disastrous!

The material just covered is an explanation of the components of a "standard of care," the legal term on which the defendant makes the case for innocence of negligence. If the defendant in a negligence suit can show that the duty to provide a safe environment and competent leadership was not breached, the plaintiff may have a difficult time proving negligence.

Before describing the steps a leader should follow in planning to mange risk, consider the following actual cases involving questions relative to the "standard of care."

1. During lunch while on a field trip to a forest setting, a group of middle school students were playing "Capture the Flag" with some high school students when one of the younger students bumped into a high school student, fell, and broke her leg. The growth plates of the bone had not finished growing, and the parents sued on the basis that the leg might never heal correctly. They charged that the accident was caused by negligence because the leader permitted high school students, who were relatively large, to play with middle school students, who were relatively small. The plaintiffs claimed that the game was "inappropriate" for a school outing, and the school lawyer called in the services of an "expert witness" in the area of children's games for advice. In this case the expert witness researched the history of

There are few places outside his own play where a child can contribute to the world in which he finds himself.

Viola Spolin

"Capture the Flag" and all its predecessors and was able to document that children had played that or similar games for hundreds of years, usually without any supervision at all. Proving lack of negligence, however, was not so easy. The activity leaders had never developed a risk management plan for their outings and it was deemed that they had not supervised as carefully as they should have.

2. A group of cheerleaders was practicing stunts under the supervision of a gymnastic coach. After the coach left the activity, one of the girls fell and broke her arm near the elbow. It was impossible for the bone to mend without a slight imperfection to the arm. The parents sued on the basis that the girl would never be able to become a ballet dancer with a deformed arm and that their daughter had been subjected to cruel and unusual treatment, as no adult was present to give her first aid or to accompany her to the hospital. This suit was settled in favor of the girl (who, incidentally, as far as is known, had never aspired to be a ballet dancer before the accident).

3. In a recreational campout, a staff member slipped on a flight of stairs and fell, breaking her leg. She sued the owner of the facility for $10,000 in damages of loss to cover time at work, medical expenses, and personal damages. Part of her claim included the fact that the stairs were outside the building and should have been covered. In actuality, an expert witness testified to the fact that no regulation in that state referenced covering any outside stairs. Further, the plaintiff had contributed to her own negligence: she was wearing thongs at the time of the accident, and had, rushed down the stairs, even though she knew it had rained the night before. In this case, the facility owner had not been negligent.

4. Fifteen children from a youth agency program played an activity that consisted of digging up sand as fast as possible to locate a quarter hidden by the staff. A youngster got sand in one eye and had to be sent by emergency vehicle to a hospital to have the sand removed. Fortunately, there was no lasting damage and no ensuing suit. When asked about the purpose of the activity, the staff admitted it was played to "fill in time until the program was over." It is easy to predict what would have happened in a negligence suit relative to supervision.

5. A bus transporting 30 youngsters from a youth agency stalled on a major city freeway during rush hour traffic. Considering the potential for rear end collisions on a major freeway, the leaders followed a pre-designated risk management plan and ushered all children to the grassy

I feel that adolescence has served its purpose when a person arrives at adulthood with a strong sense of self-esteem, the ability to relate intimately, to communicate congruently, to take responsibility, and to take risks.

Virginia Satir

center median, where they were all seated in lines and remained, singing songs and listening to stories, the bus was repaired. Then they finished their trip home, arriving in time to see their activities on the median on the evening television news. Imagine the positive publicity for the program when the parents and others saw the well supervised and well programmed youngsters sitting well away from the bus that was blocking traffic on the freeway.

PLANNING TO MANAGE ACTIVITY RISKS

Up to this point, it may be perceived that trying to plan for risks is a complex and time-consuming task. It is little wonder that many leaders or administrators learn of the foregoing material and decide that programs that entail risk are "not worth the effort" and do not offer them (or worse, offer them without planning to "manage" the risks). Field trips, swimming and boating, gymnastics, backpacking, fencing, gun safety, modern dance, flag football, tee-ball, aerobics for senior citizens, and even group singing all appear to have inherent risks involved. While the topic may be complex, there are ways to manage risks efficiently and practically.

Trying to control risks doesn't mean trying to eliminate all risks, but rather it means creating an environment where the inherent risks within activities and services provided by an organization are minimized without producing a change in the activity itself (Ammon, 2003, p.296). It should be noted at this point that a comprehensive risk management plan for the agency is usually developed at the administrative level, not the face-to-face leadership level. However, face-to-face leaders should have input in the development of the risk management plan and be aware of the elements in it. Rather than look at risk management at the administrative level, what follows is a general framework of the process to provide leaders with an understanding of how they can evaluate activities to micro-manage risks at their level. It should be understood that any plan for managing risk that is created for a specific activity should conform to all policies and procedures of the general risk management plan of the agency. Two steps in managing risks are (1) identifying risks and (2) risk reduction.

Step 1: Identifying Risks

As mentioned previously in this chapter, each event or activity has its own unique risks or areas of potential loss. However, the leader needs to be concerned with three broad areas of risk inherent in any activity: supervision, participants and setting (see Figure 8.1).

Supervision

Supervision is a broad term denoting responsibility for an area and for the activities that take place in that area (Kaiser, 1986). According to Gaskin (2003), supervision also includes coordinating, directing, overseeing, implementing, managing, superintending, and regulating (138). It is a well established fact that leisure, recreation, and park organizations are expected to exercise due care to prevent unreasonable risk of harm to participants, spectators, or others on the premise.

van der Smissen (1990) states that the duty to supervise arises from three sources: (1) a duty inherent in the situation, (2) a voluntary assumption of duty, or (3) a duty mandated by law. In leading an activity as an agent of the organization, a leader is required to exercise reasonable care for the protection of participants in the activity. Any employee or organization volunteer who voluntarily assumes the duty to supervise participants in any activity must meet the same standard as one who has a duty inherent in the situation –that or ordinary care (Gaskin, 2003, p. 139). In some cases, such as with aquatic programs (e.g. requirement of having lifeguards at a public pool) there is a statutory duty to supervise.

A written supervisory plan can help provide directions to the leader as to (1) what type of supervision is needed, (2) ratio of supervisors to participants in a given activity, (3) the responsibility of supervisors within the environment, and (4)

> The greatest risk you face is the one you don't know about.
>
> David Mair

A. Supervision (Leader-oriented)
  1. Types of supervision
  2. Supervision ratio
  3. Supervisors' responsibilities
     in the environment
  4. Qualifications
  5. Emergency planning
  6. Crisis planning

B. Participants (Group-oriented)
  1. Communication
  2. Matching skills and abilities

C. Setting (Activity-oriented)
  1. Conducting the activity
  2. Safety equipment
  3. Physical environment

Figure 8.1 Identifying Risks

the qualifications of the leader. In addition, the plan should address (5) emergency responses and (6) crises management (see Figure 8.2). What follows is a brief discussion of each of these items.

Types of Supervision. A leader may be called upon to provide general, specific, or transitional supervision during the course of an activity.

- General supervision is overseeing individuals or groups involved in an activity and does not require constant, unremitting scrutiny of the activity or facility. General supervision usually is expected for observing participants and activities on the play ground, in the gymnasium, in the weight room, on a baseball field, or in a swimming pool.

- Specific supervision is constant and continuous, the type of supervision that is more appropriate for individuals or small groups receiving instruction, involved in high-risk activities, or using areas that have the potential for serious injury (Ibid. 140).

- Transitional supervision cannot be categorized simply as general or specific, but is transitional in nature—changing from specific, to general, to specific, dependent on such factors as the participants' need for instruction, their ability to perform certain activities, their use of equipment, their involvement with others, and their use of the facility (van der Smissen, 1990).

Regardless of the type of supervision required, all supervisors need to know what and how to observe, where to stand, how to move around the area, when to respond and what action(s) to take if a problem occurs. For instance, if at the end of a heated basketball game (which requires transitional supervision), the referees and supervisory personnel leave the area prior to the players leaving, the risk of a fight breaking out is heightened. In this circumstance, a reasonable and prudent professional (standard of care) would make sure that members of both teams stayed separated until tempers cooled down, even though the activity was ended.

Supervision Ratio for a Given Activity. The younger the child, the greater the supervision ratio. As Gaskin notes, children have a known proclivity to act impulsively and without thought of the possibilities of danger. It is precisely this lack of mature judgment that makes supervision so vital (p.140). To help leaders plan for proper supervision, many professional organizations provide supervision activity ratios (see Table 8.1).

An adventure is only an inconvenience rightly considered. An inconvenience is only an adventure wrongly considered.

G.K. Chesterton

1. Type of supervision required:
   a. General
   b. Specific
   c. Transitional

2. Supervision ratio

3. Supervisors responsibilities
   a. Arrival/departure procedures
   b. Dangerous conditions in the environment
   c. Observation of the activity
   d. Movement through the area
   e. Discipline

4. Qualifications of the leader

5. Emergency plan
   a. Personnel preparation
   b. Facility issues
   c. Emergency equipment issues
   d. Emergency action plan
   e. Accident reports

6. Crisis management plan

Figure 8.2 Elements of a Supervisory Plan

For example, youth overnight trips should have one leader, plus one extra for every eight campers (American Camp Association Standard, for Camp Facilities. ACA: Bradford, Woods.). That means that two leaders are required for eight hikers and three for sixteen. Further, one person (perhaps a participant) should be designated as head of the line and another designated as tail of the line with all the others in between the head and tail.

The American Red Cross standards designate the number of lifeguards and their positions near the swimming area. Swimming, diving, archery, horseback riding, scuba diving and other activities have organizations that recommend leader/participant ratios for their activities as well as placement and qualifications. Activities of a more passive nature usually have experts who can attest to a ratio of leaders to participants.

In the incident cited at the beginning of the chapter, it was evident that the ratio of leader to participant was an ever-changing number. One day, the leader may have had 30 children show up, on another day maybe only 10 were present. Thus, the agency put the leader in a situation where an adequate number was questionable.

When a man points a finger at someone else, he should remember that four of his fingers are pointing to himself.

Louis Nizer

Recommended Staff-Child Ratios Within Group Sizes

AGE OF CHILDREN	GROUP SIZE										
	6	8	10	12	14	16	18	20	22	24	30
Infants (birth–12 months)	1:3	1:4									
Toddlers (12–24 months)	1:3	1:4	1:5	1:4							
2-year-olds (24–30 months)		1:4	1:5	1:6							
2 1/2-year-olds (30–36 months)			1:5	1:6	1:7						
3-year-olds					1:7	1:8	1:9	1:10			
4-year-olds						1:8	1:9	1:10			
5-year-olds						1:8	1:9	1:10			
Kindergartners								1:10	1:11	1:12	
6 to 8-year-olds								1:10	1:11	1:12	1:15
9 to 12-year-olds										1:12	1:15

Source: NAEYC, *Accreditation Criteria and Procedures of the National Association for the Education of Young Children,* 1998 Edition (Washington, DC: Author, 1998, p. 47).

Responsibilities for Supervisors in the Environment. Supervisors are responsible for arrival and departure procedures, awareness of dangerous conditions in the environment, observation of the activity (either using general or specific supervision techniques), movement throughout the area, and any discipline of behavior that might take place.

Arrival/departure procedures involve making sure the participants are safe transitioning in and out of the facility/activity. For instance, in the case of early childhood programs wherein the parents pick the youngsters up after the program is over, how does the leader act when one child is still in the building? At what age does the child become liable for his or her own way home? What is the procedure for locating parents when the child has not been picked up?

Dangerous conditions in the environment means being aware of physical and individual dangers that may be present. The leader or program director must show that, for whatever would be considered "normal" dangerous conditions, there was thought and planning was put into the activity. Is a piece of equipment cracked or broken? Is it tornado season? Is the gym floor slippery? Examples from real cases include a basketball rim falling on a player's head after a slam-dunk and an instructor slipping in some water, falling, and hitting her head on the gym floor. In the first case, no one had checked the bolts holding the basketball rim in place and several were loose, a case of negligence. In the second case, the roof leaked, the staff knew it, and it was felt that the organization did not have the money to repair the leak, especially since it was in Arizona and rain rarely fell. Fortunately, in this situation, the staff member was not injured except for a headache and no suit ensued. All staff must be able to recognize dangerous conditions or signs of trouble and report them correctly.

Returning again to the introductory case, the leader showed an understanding of the potential dangerous conditions of mimicking the actions of television wrestlers in a public park. He did intervene to prevent the boys from pursing what he felt was a dangerous activity.

The leader needs to also be aware of any danger to the participant as a result of engaging in the activity. Fear, fatigue, the onset of heat or chilling, unsafe practices, and skills that are too advanced for the participants are but some of the conditions all leaders are expected to recognize. Plans should be made in advance for frequent rest, early stops, and for checking the condition of any participant. Psychological, physical, and mental conditions often change without warning. The leader should be aware of all possibilities and make plans accordingly, then implement the plans when necessary. On a trip, what does one do when a participant becomes ill? How does the leader act when a leaking canoe soaks all paddlers to the bone? Leaders must anticipate the possibilities

Adventure is worthwhile.

Amelia Earhart

and plan for them. At what point in the day does a leader stop an activity because of darkness or a pending storm?

Observation of the Activity. The leader is more than an disinterested observer of the activity. Watchers of the activity passively observe and do little else. In contrast, an active supervisor frequently scans the area to ensure safety and promote injury prevention.

Supervisors need to look up/down, right/left, and over/under in order to actively view all aspects of the play environment (Bruya, Hudson, Olsen, Thompson and Bruya, 2002). Good scanning also enables the leader to give children "the eye" to prevent conflict and potential injury situations. Many times children will "look before they leap" or engage in behaviors that they know they shouldn't. By maintaining good eye contact with participants, leaders can successfully intervene non-verbally into potential injury-producing situations.

Movement through the Area. As mentioned above, the leader needs to be positioned properly in order to observe the participants in any given activity. Supervisors should not be rooted in one place like trees. Rather, it is important that they actively monitor the activity by changing locations.

Active monitoring means that supervisors are more likely to see hazardous activity or a change in posturing during confrontation (e.g., interpretation of rules of a game). Leaders are better able to respond at the initial stages of a difficulty to prevent injury because they have been moving on the site and have developed a sense or intuition for what needs to be done. Active monitoring can be accomplished by (1) frequent change of position and (2) random pattern movement (Bruya et al., 2002, p.30).

1. Frequent change: When supervisors frequently change location during the activity, views of participants are repeated from different angles. Typically, untrained leaders who have been called upon to supervise tend to stand in only one place. As a result, they can only see a limited amount of participants' play behavior and end up reacting rather than acting when a problem arises. Frequent changes mean that the supervisors should be moving at least one time every fifteen seconds. A supervision training program is essential in teaching leaders how and when to move.

2. Random pattern: Supervisors should be moving constantly during an activity. Their patterns should be unpredictable (Bruya & Wood, 1998) because safety problems increase when participants (especially children) are able to predict a supervisor's location and scanning angle.

Random location change maintains the leader's availability to monitor conflict and generally thwarts intended attempts by some participants to create confrontations.

Discipline. Unsafe behaviors need to be corrected immediately by the leader in order to maintain a safe environment. However, the punishment must fit the crime. In other words, it is imperative that the leader knows ahead of time what action to take for what infractions. For instance, what is the agency's policy about the use of abusive language from participants and spectators during sport league competition? How does a leader in an after school program handle bullying? How is conflict amicably resolved? These things need to be spelled out in the supervision plan so that all leaders maintain consistency in their supervision practices.

Qualifications of the Leader. A good supervisory plan will also list the qualifications expected for the leader of an activity. For instance, it would be expected that a person leading a step aerobics exercise program have certifications from such organizations as from the Aerobics and Fitness Association of America (AFAA), the American Council of Exercise (ACE), or the National Dance-Exercise Instructor's Training Association (NDEITA). The absence of these certifications makes a weaker case for following the standard of care for the agency should a lawsuit arise. As mentioned earlier, the standard of care is based on what a reasonable and prudent professional would follow in terms of best practices. Hiring a person without these certifications places a larger burden on the agency to prove that the standard of care was being followed.

At a minimum, all leisure, recreation, and park personnel in face-to-face leadership capacity should have a knowledge of first aid. No time can be lost looking things up in the book or guessing or hoping to remember. A standard of care assumes that the leader will have immediate recall of first aid needed for situations unique to the activity. The leader who does nothing may be as negligent as the one who acts rapidly but incorrectly. Swimming staff is expected to know CPR; gymnastics leaders are expected to understand how to treat injuries resulting from falls. All leaders are expected to have a current basic first aid card, indicating they have had training in care of simple injuries. Outing trip leaders should also know about cuts, bruises, sprains, burns, insect bites, and most other injuries, as well as emergency care in wilderness situations.

Emergency Plan.
Leaders need to know and understand what steps should be taken in case an emergency takes place during the course of an activity. An effective emergency plan should be tailored to

When written in Chinese, the word crisis is composed of two characters. One represents danger, and the other represents opportunity.

John F. Kennedy

the nature of the organization, personnel, and activity involved (Hall & Gray, 2003, p.128). The plan can be simple or complex depending on the situation. For instance, a more detailed plan might be needed for an overnight hiking trip where help is not easily available than for a possible injury in a golf tournament. Although it is not possible to anticipate all types of accidents that result in injury or that require an emergency response, it is important for the leader of any activity to identify the possible risks present and plan for the "worst case scenario" during a time of non-crisis. Such plans need to include the following:

Personnel Preparation. This involves detailing what actions should be taken by the face-to-face leader in charge of the activity when the crisis occurs. All leaders should be educated as to what immediate steps should be followed (e.g., calling 911) when an emergency arises. The plan should also outline what secondary steps are taken such as aiding police, fire, and other emergency personnel, helping to secure the site for any evidence, and attempting to help secure the safety of the scene before providing any assistance.

Facility Issues. The location of emergency exits and shelters; gas, power, and water shut-off values; alarm systems; back-up power systems, etc. should all be noted. Evacuation procedures should also be developed and understood.

Emergency Equipment Issues. Identify the type of equipment available (e.g., public address and communication equipment, fire fighting equipment, first aid kits, automated external defibrillators, and backboards). Identify where the equipment is stored and who will access it.

Accident Report Forms. It is important that every accident have a written report on file. The report should only record what occurred, not try to give a medical opinion. For instance, one would report that the center fielder dove for a fly ball, landed on his/her shoulder, and immediately started to complain about pain, rather than the center fielder dove for a fly ball, landed on his/her shoulder, and broke the collarbone. A leader is not a medical doctor and therefore should not be making a medical diagnosis.

Further, the accident report should list what steps were taken (i.e., transported to the hospital) and any follow-up that was done (i.e., medical treatment was administered and individual was released). Accident report forms can help pinpoint risks in the environment or in the conduct of an activity that were previously unforeseen. The reports serve as important data to prevent further incidents from occurring.

The best way to deal with a crisis is before it happens.

Anonymous

LEADERSHIP: A POINT OF VIEW FROM THE PROFESSION
James A. "Jim" Donahue

Jim Donahue is Recreation Director, Perinton Recreation & Parks Department, Fairport, New York. The Town of Perinton is a suburb of gently rolling hills located nine miles southeast of Rochester, NY. It is comprised of 48,000 residents in a 35-square-mile area. The town has 17 parks totaling 672 acres with more than 350 acres of open space and miles of trails. Designated "Trail Town USA," the town is proud of its parks, open spaces and, facilities, including a $5.8 million community center and a new $5.9 million indoor aquatics center. The department has a $3.1 million annual operating budget and offers more than 700 recreation programs. Jim is a member of the American Academy of Park and Recreation Administration.

On leadership. . . .The term leadership brings to mind people who possess the ability to envision a goal and effectively motivate people and align resources to accomplish the goal.

Leadership and success. . . . Whether a leader is in a one to one, small group, or large group setting, the ability to work effectively with people and to be consistent and clear in their message is important. Those who lead understand what motivates people and provide rewards consistent with effort.

The exemplary leader. . . .An exemplary leaders is one who understands the mission and dedicates their time and resources to accomplishing the mission. They are able to articulate the needs and desired outcomes and are not afraid to take a risk. A leader must have a passion for their vocation and the empathy to understand those they lead.

Leadership in action. . . .A leader in recreation and parks should be knowledgeable, honest, realistic, consistent, forthright, and possess active listening and problem solving skills.

Crisis Plan.
A crisis is different from an emergency plan in that a "crisis situation" is what occurs after the emergency. For instance, a major riot at a diversity festival can do serious damage to the overall reputation and on-going operations of a leisure, recreation, and park organization long after the police have quelled the disturbance and the emergency crews have left.

A crisis management plan should be created for the organization so that leaders know who, what, when, and how to respond to any crisis situation. Determine who will meet with staff for debriefing. Have plans for dealing with emotional and mental health needs of individuals involved in the crisis (staff, teammates, family members, and friends). Have follow-up procedures for dealing with the media.

After any crisis is over, the agency needs to evaluate the effectiveness of the crisis management plan and make adjustments that protect staff, participants, and the agency from any future crisis situation.

Participants

The second area of identifying risks has to do with identifying the participants engaged in the activity. Risks associated with participants include communication and matching participants' developmental abilities to the activity.

Communication. It is extremely important that a leader communicate at the level and in the language of the participant. This means that the leader must be able to relate to the age, intelligence, and language of the participant. Younger participants, beginners, and those who may be frightened or apprehensive need different explanations than those given to advanced groups. They may need to hear things several times, or they may need a simpler vocabulary. It is the responsibility of the leaders to be sure that everyone in the group understands what is said. It should be so clear that afterward most of the participants in the group would consistently agree upon what was said.

In addition, it is important that participants understand the inherent risks of the activity and adhere to safety practices. This means that the leader must double check that the participants understand what the safety practices are and why they are practiced that way. Clearly, the instructor must not ask the participant to do anything unreasonable and not prudent, or to undertake any unreasonable risk or exposure to foreseeable harm. If the participant is told not to swim at night, the reason for not swimming at night (unless in a lighted pool) must be given. (People can understand that it is difficult to see a swimmer in trouble in the dark but may not realize that depth perception is lost in the darkness and things are further away than they seem to be.) If participants are to adhere to the safety practices, it should be with the understanding of the reasons behind them.

Matching Skills and Abilities. A leader needs to match the activity requirements to the skills and abilities of the participant. When consideration to matching is not given, a situation can arise where a smaller, younger, less skillful, and/or less experienced participant is injured while playing with a larger, older, more skillful, and /or more experienced participant. This is especially true in activities that involve contact (i.e., football and wrestling).

Vision is not enough, it must be combined with venture. It is not enough to stare up the steps, we must step up the stairs.

Vaclav Havel

In addition, the leader must make sure that in directing, teaching, and demonstrating techniques, the leader's size and strength do not cause a hazardous situation. For instance, recently there was a legal case in which a coach, frustrated at the tackling techniques of his Little League players, called them over for a demonstration. Instead of using two players of the same size to demonstrate the skill he was trying to get across, he chose a 90-pound boy as his opponent. He then proceeded to tackle the child in such a manner as to violently throw him to the ground. The child ended up with a broken arm and the family sued the agency and the coach.

Setting

The setting refers to the how the activity is conducted, what equipment and facilities are used, and the physical environment.

Conducting the Activity. When instruction is offered, the recreation leader has a responsibility to ensure that the information provided is adequate, correct, and warns of potential dangers inherent in the activity. As Trichka (2003, p.151) has stated, "appropriate instruction need only be adequate instruction—it does not mean perfect instruction."

What is adequate instruction? The courts have held that adequate instruction includes an explanation of the basic rules and procedures; suggestions for proper performance including feeback; and an identification of the safety rules and regulations (Green v. Orleans Parish School Board, 1979).

Proper orientation to the use of fitness equipment is another aspect of adequate instruction (Trichka, 2003, p.151). Unfortunately, many health clubs and fitness facilities allow participants to use fitness equipment without proper instruction concerning its use. As a result, participants are put at risk when they misuse the equipment because they do not understand how the machine works or how it will affect them physically.

Four elements fall under the broad heading of instruction. They include:

Duty to Warn. Activity leaders have a duty to warn participants of the dangers inherent in the activity, environmental conditions, and non-obvious hazards. Returning to the case of the canoeist, an instructor would have the responsibility to warn the participant about the effect wind conditions and wave action have on the stability of the canoe. Courts have emphasized that the risks must be known, understood, and appreciated by the participant; thus, regular and repeated warnings are important (Ibid.).

Fair Play is a jewell (sic). Give him a chance if you can.

Abraham Lincoln

Coercion. Forcing a person to do something that they feel either physically or psychologically unable to due is known as coercion. Allowing a group of children to "double dare" a timid child into participating in an activity would be a form of coercion. In the leisure, recreation, and park setting, there is little reason to pressure participants to perform beyond their capabilities, since such pressure is the antithesis of the underlying philosophy of a leisure experience.

Dangerous Activities and Conditions. Any game or activity can be dangerous if it is not properly conducted. Thus, the problem may not be with the game itself, but in the manner that it is run without proper supervision or planning. For instance, an agency would have a difficult time defending a time-filler dodgeball game that has eight-year-olds competing against 16-year-olds.

The control of the activity and/or the activity area is basic to properly conducting any activity (Ibid:152). This includes both overlapping use zones and crowding issues. For instance, in the area of playground design, a basic standard is that there be six feet of between stationary equipment. Moving a portable piece of plastic equipment into this "use zone" to give children something extra to play on would be in violation of the standard and put the children at risk for injury. Likewise, playing a game of volleyball with twelve people on a side rather than six on a regulation court could put the participants at risk for injury due to collisions.

Violation of Game Rules. Trichka has written that "one aspect of proper instruction is enforcement of the rules of the game. If a rule has been adopted for safety reasons, lack of enforcement or a permitted violation of such rule will be difficult to defend when the injury occurs. If the activity leader modifies a safety rule, the modification or the rule should be in the direction of making the activity more safe and not less safe" (p.152).

Safety Equipment. Various activities require the use of protective or safety equipment. Certain clothing or protective devices such as seat belts, helmets, personal flotation devices, or rain gear may be required. If the gear is needed for safety, the leader has little choice but to be autocratic, make no exceptions, and refuse to permit those without proper gear to participate. In adhering to a standard of care, no room exists for group decisions related to protective devices and practices. In the interest of performing at an acceptable standard of care, the leader is justified in excluding those without proper equipment from participating in the activity. It is not enough for the leader to suggest the use of equipment that is considered essential for safety; such items must be required, and all participants must be checked to be sure that all such items are present, in good condition, and used properly.

An assessment of equipment would probably begin with a review of the program's written gear requirements list and policies. Every program should have on hand clear and specific lists of the clothing and equipment required of participants in each activity, as well as supplemental lists of gear required for leaders of each activity. While an essential starting point is a well thought-out list, such lists are of little or no value if, in practice, they are not adhered to. In a post-accident review, one of the first things an investigator may do is try to learn exactly what equipment was actually on site.

All too often the leader fails to enforce equipment requirements effectively, leaving the participant less protected and the leader and program in a highly vulnerable position. Equipment lists should be carefully designed, thoughtfully amended in writing on the basis of needs particular to each activity, and then enforced to the letter. When designing the lists of minimum requirements (items without which an individual will not be allowed to participate), such as helmets in bicycling and horseback riding programs, it is wise to seek the advice of administrators and leaders of similar programs. In a case of litigation, one's equipment list might be reviewed by other professionals and compared to equipment lists used by other providers of a similar service. It is prudent when creating minimal gear lists and gear check policies to develop lists that are as complete and specific as those of comparative agencies or institutions.

Physical Environment. The physical environment refers to facilities and areas where the activity will take place. Activity leaders owe a duty to participants to provide safe activity environments. This means that not only must equipment be properly maintained, but facilities and grounds should be inspected regularly for unreasonable risks and such risks should be clearly marked or, if possible, eliminated. One the authors of this text was called on as an expert witness to testify in a case where a woman stepped into a sizable hole in a park. The plaintiff in question was sitting on portable bleachers outside a swimming pool observing her four-year-old, who was disabled, participate in a swim lesson. At the conclusion of the lesson, the woman walked down a grass pathway between the fence and the bleachers. Her focus was on the child, not the pathway. The result was that she stepped in a hole and ruptured a vein in her thigh. When she called the park and recreation department about the incident, the response was "So, what do you want me to do about it? If you have a problem, sue me." So she did. In the course of the investigation of the incident it was shown that: (1) the

Slow, Grandparents at Play

Traffic sign in Orange Harbor, FL mobile-home park

When all around you
people are losing their
heads, learn to hold on
to yours.

*Nonprofit Risk
Management Center*

park and recreation department had moved the bleachers to
the site to give spectators a place to sit for swim events; (2)
the department knew about the hole as park maintenance
personnel regularly mowed and trimmed in the area, thus it
was not the first time that the hole had become known to
the department; (3) the hole had been there for some time;
and (4) the hole was in the natural pathway created by people walking back and forth. Needless to say, the department
settled the issue out of court.

If upon inspection a leader finds a facility/environment
defect, they should cease or modify the activity and not use
the area again until the problem is repaired, retrofitted, or
removed. To simply tell participants to use the facility or area
but watch out for the jagged culvert near the right field line
is insufficient.

Step 2: Risk Reduction

Once the leader has been able to reflect on the risks that
may be present because of supervision, participant, and setting issues, the next step is to seek methods to reduce the
risks. This is a proactive approach whereby the leader
attempts to reduce the chance that an injury will occur or
reduce the severity if it does occur.

As mentioned previously, all risks cannot be eliminated from
an activity, but the probability and severity can be minimized
by providing better training of leaders, matching participants to appropriate activities, and proper maintenance of
facilities and equipment.

Training. Recreation, leisure, and park leaders need to regularly attend training seminars and in-service programs that
help to update their certification and knowledge about the
activities that they are involved with on a day-to-day basis.
In-service trainings also serve to help leaders understand the
importance of the agency's risk management plan and discuss strategies for reducing risks throughout the whole
organization. Risk management plans created by top administrators but never discussed with face-to-face leaders do little
to reduce risks. Any in-service training in the area of risks
should be well planned and held on a regular basis with all
personnel required to attend.

Another topic that can occur in training is the evaluation of
activities so that all members of the staff understand what
actions may lead to risk of injury in conducting the program.
Review of teaching and instructions given to participants is yet
another topic of conversation for these sessions. Rules and regulations should be regularly reviewed and updated, as should
the leader's responsibilities in the enforcement of the rules.

Finally, training can help leaders improve their education, experience, certifications, and general expertise of the field of leisure, recreation, and parks. Training venues include in-house, workshops, seminars, professional conferences, and special meetings.

Matching Participants. As mentioned earlier, the leader needs to know how to make sure participants have the proper skill level and conditioning for activities. For instance, in a swimming program, the skill level and developmental stage of participants must be know to place them in the proper class (Brown, 2003, p.313).

An organization should determine what skill and conditioning level is required for participation in an activity and publicize this information during the registration process. Taking a novice on a twenty-mile hike without any type of pre-notice as to the skill level required puts an agency and the leader at risk.

Maintenance of Facilities and Equipment. One of the most important elements in risk reduction is an on-going and systematic maintenance program for facilities and equipment. Inspection of facilities and equipment is essential in the risk reduction process. Any leisure, recreation, and park agency that does not have a regular inspection process in place can expect to land in court.

If a hazard is found during inspection, a system for addressing the hazard must be implemented. According to Brown (2003), the following steps should be taken:

1. The hazard must be reported to maintenance personnel.
2. The individual overseeing the area where the hazard is located must be notified.
3. The equipment or area must be taken out of service until the repair is made.
4. Once the identified hazard is eliminated, maintenance personnel must inform the manager.
5. There should be established steps to follow in the event the repair has not been made in a reasonable period of time (p.313).

> Play builds the kind of free-and-easy, try-it-out, do-it-yourself character that our future needs.
>
> *James Hymes*

WAIVERS AND AGREEMENT TO PARTICIPATE

Waiver

A waiver is an agreement by which the participant of a leisure, recreation, and park activity agrees to absolve an agency from liability for injury or damage suffered by the participant as a result of the negligence of the leisure, recreation, or park professional (Cotten & Cotten, 2001).

There are many misconceptions about the use of a liability waiver in the leisure, recreation, and parks field. Some people feel that a liability waiver signed by a participant of legal age will preclude that participant suing for negligence. Others feel that a waiver is not worth the paper it is written on. The fact is that waiver law varies from state to state. In addition, many times waivers are not upheld in court due to ambiguous wording.

Injuries to participants result from one of three causes: (1) inherent risks of the activity (which we have previously covered in this chapter), (2) negligence by the service provider or its employees (ordinary negligence), and (3) more extreme acts by the service provider or its employees (i.e., gross negligence, reckless conduct, or willful/wanton conduct). According to Cotton (2003), the waiver is usually meant to protect the service provider from liability for the ordinary negligence of the service provider or its employees (p. 105).

A waiver is a contract, that is, something of value is exchanged between parties. In the case of a leisure, recreation, and park agency, the opportunity to participate in activities of the department constitutes an exchange. Thus, most waivers usually include the language such as "In consideration for being allowed to participate, I hereby waive . . . " (Ibid. 106) (see Figure 8.3). Since a waiver is a contract, two elements are important to remember. First, the party relinquishing rights enters into the agreement without coercion, and second, the party signing the contract has the capacity to do so. The courts have held that certain classes of individuals do not have the capacity to contract. These include individuals lacking mental capacity, those unduly influenced by alcohol, and those who have not reached the age of majority. This last class is an important distinction for the leisure, recreation and park agency since a majority of their services are generally directed at children. Except in certain states (e.g., California, Ohio, and Massachusetts), "a minor cannot be bound by a contract whether it is (1) signed by the minor or (2) signed by a parent or guardian on behalf of the minor"(Ibid. 107).

According to Cotten (2003), waivers can take one of three formats:
1. Stand alone documents in which the only function of the document is to provide liability protection for the service provider.
2. Waiver within another document such as a membership agreement, an entry form, or a rental agreement.

> We cannot swing up on a rope that is attached only to our own belt.
>
> *William Ernest Hocking*

Activity Release and Health Statement Form

This program requires participation in field exercises that are, by their nature, physically demanding. Therefore, all participants must be free of medical or physical conditions, which might create undue risk to themselves or others who depend upon them. You should participate in these outings only if you are free of any physical disability. Physical strength is not necessary, although good condition will increase your enjoyment of the outing activities, and you should have a physical examination.

1. What physical disabilities or conditions do you have which might limit your participation in this activity? ______________________________
2. What else might affect your participation?______________________________
3. What medication are you taking? ______________________________
4. What special dietary restrictions do you have?______________________________
5. Do you have any allergies?_____ If so, please indicate them below:

_____ Penicillin	____ Horses	_____ Dust, hay
_____ Wasps	____ Frostbite	_____ Bees
_____ Foods	____ Others, list ______________	

I have read and understand the nature of the physical demands of this program. I have noted above any medical or physical conditions I have which might affect my activities. I therefore release any and all rights or claims for damages against the University of Oregon and all individuals assisting in instructing and conducting these activities, for any and all injuries, loss or damage suffered by me at, or in any way connected with, these injuries.

Name (PRINT) ______________________________
Signature ______________________________
Date ______________________________Participant's Age__________

Figure 8.3
High-risk management plan—health form

3. A group waiver, which generally includes a waiver at the top of a sheet that several parties sign (e.g., team roster, sign-in sheet, etc.).

All forms have been acceptable in courts, although providers have been encouraged to use the stand-alone waiver.

Many waivers do not hold up in court because of ambiguous wording or missing elements. The following guidelines by Cotten (2003) should help the waiver writer to produce a document that will hold up in court.

- The title of the waiver should be descriptive (e.g., Waiver of Liability).
- Print size should be at least 8-10 point and the waiver language should be conspicuous.
- The waiver should clearly and unambiguously state that the signer is not holding the service provider liable for injuries resulting from the ordinary negligence of the provider.
- Denote consideration within the waiver (e.g., "In consideration for being allowed to participate in . . ., the signer agrees to").

Uncertainty and expectation are the joys of life.

William Congreve

- Specify parties who are relinquishing rights and partiers who are protected by the waiver (p.108).

▰▰▰▰ Agreement to Participate

Many times, agreement to participate forms are confused with waivers. As mentioned in the last section, a waiver is used to protect the service provider against ordinary negligence. Agreement to participate forms, on the other hand, are used to show that the participant was informed on the inherent risks of the activities and chose to participate. Agreement to participate forms establish that the participants knows inherent risks, not that the participant waives any right to sue for negligence. For instance, the canoeist that signs an agreement to participate form is recognizing that they assume the risks if they end up in the water.

As van der Smissen (1990) has pointed out, agreements to participate are used to inform participants of (1) the nature of the activity, (2) the risks to be encountered through participation in the activity, and (3) the behaviors expected of the participant.

Agreement to participate forms protect the agency in that it establishes the primary assumption of risk defense by showing that the participation was voluntary. Furthermore, the form establishes that the participant was aware of the inherent risks of the activity. It also can help in the establishment of a secondary assumption of risk defense (sometimes called contributory fault) by showing that the participant knew the expected participant behaviors and agreed to adhere to them (Cotten 2003, p.117). In other words, the participant has a duty to protect himself or herself from unreasonable risk of foreseeable harm.

Since agreement to participate forms are not contract, there are no "legal phrases" that are universal or required. However, according to Cotten and Cotten (2001), there is certain information that should be contained in an agreement. This information includes:

1. Nature of the activity. A detailed description of the activity.
2. Possibile consequences of injury. This includes the types of accidents associated with the activity, both major and minor.
3. Behavioral expectations of the participant. A listing of rules one expects the participant to adhere to.
4. Condition of the participant. The participant affirms that he/she possesses the physical condition and competency to participate in the activity safely.

5. Concluding statement. This should include a statement by which the participant acknowledges an understanding and appreciation of the inherent risks, enters into the activity voluntarily, assumes risks, and gives emergency notification names.

A place should be provided under the concluding statement for a signature and date.

INSURANCE

Given the nature of leisure pursuits and the tendency of modern-day U.S. citizens to sue, it would seem that every provider of recreational activities would be heavily insured. In fact, many providers carry no insurance at all, others are marginally insured, and a large percentage of public agencies are "self-insured," having, presumably, sufficient financial reserves to cover potential costs.

Generally speaking, it is the smaller organizations and businesses that operate with little or no insurance, and the most frequently cited reason is cost. Insurance rates are soaring, businesses often face intense competition, and other providers may suffer from chronically tight budgets. While not unusual, the practice of operating in an underinsured capacity is not recommended and may be illegal in certain circumstances.

A variety of types of insurance are available to meet the needs of the organization or business, its employees and volunteers, and its participants or clients. The principal areas of concern are liability of the organization or business, employee and volunteer liability and accidents, and participant accidents. The most common pattern seems to be one in which the company or organization pays for a broad liability policy and accident insurance for employees (which in some areas is mandated by law). The company recommends accident and liability insurance to its volunteers, liability insurance to its employees, and accident insurance to its participants or clients, but does not offer to pay for the additional insurance. An argument can be made, however, for the company negotiating a policy (or set of policies) to cover all of those areas. The total expense is likely to be less than the cost of individual policies, everyone is covered, and the costs may be considered, in part, a benefit of employment.

SUMMARY

The management of risks in any recreation program is based on the premise that participants have natural inclinations to

> The greatest glory in living lies not in never failing, but in rising every time we fail.
>
> *Anonymous*

pursue activities involving the potential for accidents. While the sponsors cannot guarantee freedom from accident, risks can be managed so that the likelihood of an accident is lessened. Every recreation leader should perform at the competency of a reasonable and prudent professional following the best and most current professional practices. Such performance is known as practicing a standard of care. A standard of care adheres to specific points related to supervision, conducting the activity, and understanding the environment. One way to practice a standard of care is to develop and follow a risk management plan that identifies potential dangers and outlines how the activity may be managed to lessen the risk.

Waivers and insurance are administrative concerns that require legal advice. It is the responsibility of administrators and leaders to carry adequate insurance and to utilize appropriate documents (statements of risk, assumption of risk, and releases) that have been approved by legal counsel.

Discussion Questions

1. What is risk? Why is risk an important subject for recreation leaders?

2. What is meant by the term inherent risk?

3. What are the four (4) elements of negligence? What are some of the ways that recreation leaders can defend themselves against a charge of negligence?

4. What elements should a leader consider in trying to manage risks?

5. What is meant by the term standard of care? What is involved in proving that one followed a standard of care in working with participants?

6. Describe and discuss leadership situations that might arise where you might feel vulnerable to a charge of negligence.

7. What is the difference between an emergency and a crisis? How would you handle these events?

8. What role do waivers play in managing risks?

9. What role do agreements to participate play in managing risks?

10. Is having insurance a good idea? What kind of insurance should a leader consider?

THE CASE FOR LEADERSHIP
Supervisor Uncovers Liabilty Scam

Points of Consideration

You are the supervisor of lifeguards for Cedar Center Parks and Recreation Department. Even though your pools and beaches have been packed for years without a major liability incident, your insurance premiums have increased greatly over the last five years because of national lawsuits. If your agency had a lawsuit filed against it and lost, your premiums would be likely to increase three to four times more next year.

One day, as you walk along a crowded beach, you overhead four young men plotting to scratch each others' backs until they bleed so they can claim that they have been injured at the beach. One of the young men assures the other three that because of the claims and settlements paid for any type of liability, they can make lots of money quickly. He claims that an out-of-court settlement is likely, and therefore no trial will ever take place.

As you continue to walk by, one of the young men takes off his t-shirt, lays down on a beach towel, and lets his three friends begin to claw at his back.

Questions of Consideration

- What should you do? What duty do you have to intervene in this situation?
- What would the young men have to prove in order to get an out-of-court settlement?
- If the case did go to court, would the young men be likely to win?
- What would the department have to show to defend itself?
- How could liability insurance costs on beaches be reduced?
- How much risk should swimmers assume?
- How much responsibility should a public parks department assume for swimmers' safety?
- Are there some responsibilities that an administrating agency must always assume, and if so, what are they?

From: Bannon, J., and Busser, J. (1992). *Problem solving in recreation and parks* (3rd ed.) (pp. 406-407). Champaign, IL: Sagamore Publishing, Inc.

REFLECTING ON LEADERSHIP
Managing Risks

There is a difference between a moral obligation and a legal obligation. Let's say you are at a beach party with your friends and someone begins to drown in the lake. Even though you are a trained lifeguard, you are under no legal obligation to attempt to rescue the individual. However, you probably will have a sense of moral obligation to do so.

We create laws to try, in part, to regulate human behavior, but the best regulation is an individual's value system based on the premise of "do unto others as we would have those do to you." Laws are based on doing things right; moral behavior is based on doing the right things. What paths will you follow and what decisions will you make?

References

Ammon, R. Jr. (2003). Risk management process. In Cotten, D. & Wolohan J. (Eds.)., *Law for recreation and sports management* (3rd ed.). (pp. 296-307). Kendall/Hunt Publishing.

Black's law dictionary. (5th ed.). (1979) St. Paul, MN: West Publishing Co.

Brown, M. (2003). Risk identification and reduction. In Cotten, D. & Wolohan J. (Eds.), *Law for recreation and sports management* (3rd ed.). (pp. 308-319). Kendall/Hunt Publishing.

Bruya, L. R., Hudson, S., Olsen, H., Thompson, D., & Bruya, L. (2001). *S.A.F.E. Supervision manual.* Cedar Falls, IA: National Program for Playground Safety.

Bruya, L. R., & Woods, G. (1998). Why provide supervision on the playground? In Hudson, S., & Thompson, D. (Eds.)., *The SAFE playground handbook.* (pp. 17-25). Cedar Falls, IA: National Program for Playground Safety.

Cotten, D. (2003). Waivers and releases. In Cotten, D., & Wolohan J. (Eds.)., *Law for recreation and sports management* (3rd.ed.). (pp. 105-113). Kendall/Hunt Publishing.

Cotten, D., & Cotten, M. (2001) *Waivers and releases for the health and fitness club industry* (3rd. ed.). Statesboro, GA: Sports Risk Consulting.

Edginton, C. R., Hudson, S. D., & Ford, P. M. (1999). *Leadership in recreation and leisure services organizations* (2nd ed.). Champaign, IL: Sagamore.

Gaskin, L. (2003). Supervision of participants. In Cotten, D., & Wolohan J. (Eds.)., *Law for recreation and sports management* (3rd ed.). (pp.138-148). Kendall/Hunt Publishing.

Hall, R., & Gray, J. (2003). Emergency care. In Cotten, D., & Wolohan J. (Eds.), *Law for recreation and sports management* (3rd ed.). (pp. 296-307). Kendall/Hunt Publishing.

Head, G., & Herman, M. (2003). *Enlightened risk taking.* Washington, DC: Nonprofit Risk Management Center.

Herman, M., & Oliver, B. (2003). *Vital signs.* Washington DC: Nonprofit Risk Management Center.

Kaiser, R. (1986). *Liability and law in recreation, parks and sports.* Englewood Cliffs, NJ: Prentice-Hall.

Mair, D., & Herman, M. (2003). *Playing to win.* Washington DC: Nonprofit Risk Management Center.

Trichka, R. (2003). Conduct of Activity. In Cotten, D., & Wolohan J. (Eds.), Law for *Recreation and sports management* (3rd ed.). (pp.149 -156). Kendall/Hunt Publishing.

van der Smissen, B. (1990). *Legal liability and risk management for public and private entities* (vol. 2). Cincinnati, OH: Anderson.

van der Smissen, B. (2003) Elements of negligence. In Cotten, D., & Wolohan J. (Eds.)., *Law for recreation and sports management* (3rd ed.). (pp. 296-307). Kendall/Hunt Publishing.

9

Leadership in Outdoor and Aquatic Leisure Settings

LEARNING OBJECTIVES

1. To distinguish the different leadership responsibilities between outdoor skill leaders and
   environmental education leaders.
2. To understand the components of outdoor
   leadership qualifications.
3. To list various leading techniques used by
   environmental educators.
4. To explain the outdoor leader's role in caring
   for the environment in which outdoor recreation activities occur.
5. To identify six leadership roles in aquatic settings.
6. To identify important rules for aquatic safety
   and the various types of aquatic activities.

KEY TERMS

- Outdoor Recreation
- Outdoor Skill Leaders
- Environmental Educators
- Environmental Interpreters
- Naturalists
- Adventure Educators
- Aquatic Activities

INTRODUCTION

Many individual enjoy spending time outdoors participating in all types of activities. Many studies have shown that outdoor recreation experiences can provide opportunities for the development of a positive self-concept, self-satisfaction, self-reflection, and environmental awareness. This chapter will examine leadership roles and competency in both outdoor and aquatic settings.

LEADERSHIP IN THE OUTDOORS

Within a 12-month period (1994-1995), an estimated 189.3 million Americans over the age of 16 went to the woods, oceans, mountains, beaches, lakes, and rivers to participate in myriad activities that depend on natural resources for their success (Cordell, 1999). Americans continue to place a greater demand for outdoor recreation settings and services across an increasing diversity of social groups and recreation interests. Their goals, through participation in such outdoor experiences, are fun, enjoyment, education, and adventure. It is the job of the outdoor leader to help them attain these goals safely. This increase in outdoor recreation users creates a need for outdoor leaders who understand the complex nature of the social, economic, cultural, legal, and environmental effects of the ever growing numbers of Americans involved in recreation that occurs in natural settings.

While there are many definitions of outdoor recreation, we define it as any voluntary leisure activity that involves the use, understanding, or appreciation of natural resources, or a combination of these. In this definition, the emphasis is on natural resources. This first half of this chapter, therefore, will primarily focus on activities conducted outdoors in which the major focus of the activity includes the land, water, plants, or animals in their natural state. Some activities included in the category of outdoor recreation are camping, canoeing, walking, backpacking, ice skating, studying nature, horseback riding, hiking, and picnicking, and there are many more. The scope of outdoor activities is so large that hundreds of books have been written on outdoor-related activities ranging from the very simple viewing- and learning-oriented activities such as walking, bird watching, or picnicking, to very challenging, high-risk activities such as backpacking, kayaking, or skiing. This section will offer leadership techniques that can be applied to most programs in the outdoors. The potential outdoor leader is advised to consult material on specific outdoor activities prior to entertaining the idea of leading any activity involving skill or off-road travel.

In addition there is a demand for leadership in aquatic settings, and this chapter presents the various types of aquatic activities found in recreation, parks, and leisure services organizations. Some of the direct, face-to-face leadership roles found in aquatic settings are the lifeguard, pool manager, waterfront director, instructor, coach, and activity leader. The techniques used in leading aquatic activities are built on an awareness of the capabilities of participants, the development of a plan of action, and effective communication to ensure safety in aquatic settings.

Outdoor Leaders' Roles and Settings

The recreation, parks, and leisure services leader working with participants in the outdoors has a great deal of responsibility. Not only does this type of leader attempt to lead and instruct participants in a way that is meaningful and enjoyable, but he or she must also ensure that participants follow guidelines for their own protection and the protection of the natural environment. The outdoor leader should keep in mind that his or her primary responsibilities are to maintain the quality of natural areas and to ensure that all participants return to their homes both physically and psychologically safe. The necessary amount of skill and experience in leading outdoor recreation activities can vary depending on the activity. A picnic is relatively easy to plan and implement compared to a backpacking trip down into the Grand Canyon of the Colorado River. A nature walk requires fewer technical skills of the leader with less inherent dangers than leading a rafting trip down a swift river.

Although outdoor leaders may be found in any of the roles discussed in Chapter 3, there are three major interrelated categories of outdoor leadership (Miles & Priest, 1999). First, there are outdoor skill leaders whose major functions entail leading or teaching the necessary skills that depend on the natural environment for their performance. These outdoor leaders teach a variety of outdoor skills, such as backpacking, mountain biking, flat and whitewater canoeing, whitewater and sea kayaking, wilderness first aid, rock and ice climbing, mountaineering, caving, and nordic and tele skiing. Second, there are outdoor leaders who teach or lead programs concerned with understanding the environment as it exists in its natural condition. These outdoor leaders are also referred as environmental educators or naturalists whose

I have three rules for leaders in the outdoors: You have to know where the people you're leading are coming from, you have to know what you want to do with them, and you have to love them.

Paul Petzoldt

role is to foster an appreciation, understanding, and responsibility for the environment to their students and program participants. These leaders might teach classes in forest ecology, pond and stream, earth science, insects, water quality, map and compass, Native American history, or hiking and canoeing. Third, there are outdoor leaders who are referred as adventure educators who use outdoor recreation activities and experiences to produce personal growth and development among individual participants and the entire group. An outdoor leader in this position is responsible for designing, managing and implementing experiential learning programs that use outdoor activities to improve team building, group dynamics, and communication skills. These activities may include challenge courses, rafting, or backpacking expeditions.

> The more clearly we can focus our attention on the wonders and realities of the universe about us, the less taste we shall have for destruction.
>
> *Rachel Carson*

Leaders of Outdoor Skills

Outdoor skill leaders and adventure educators who specialize in teaching technical skills or facilitate awareness of individual and group interaction depend on the natural environment for their success. These activities may be seasonal in nature, may be related to specific land-, water-, snow-, or ice-based recreation activity, or may be a combination of two or more types of activity. Though there are many examples of such activities, the following list represents a wide variety of them: downhill or cross-country skiing, winter (snow) camping, fishing, hunting, orienteering (cross-country racing by map and compass), hiking, backpacking, rock climbing, caving, rafting, white water canoeing, sailing, kayaking, and bicycling. Outdoor skill leaders may work in a variety of settings with all ages and abilities. The area in which their duties lie is generally labeled as "outdoor recreation." Examples of programs that typically advertise leadership positions in this area of specialization include the following:

Adventure/wilderness therapy programs
Challenge/ropes courses
Climbing gyms and clubs
College/university outdoor education or recreation
     programs
Commercial outfitters/guide service
Environmental education programs/centers
Military recreation programs
Outdoor skills school (NOLS, Boulder Outdoor
Survival School, Outward Bound)
Summer camp
Wilderness medical trainer

Leaders of Environmental Education Programs

There is a subgroup of outdoor leaders called "environmental educators" or "environmental interpreters." The leaders' success depends not on teaching various technical outdoor skills, but on provoking interest and instilling facts, attitudes, and concepts through firsthand experiences and real objects. Their efforts are aimed at increasing the participants' knowledge of natural or historical resources and whetting their curiosity to learn more about the interdependence of living organisms, such as the web of life or the food chain including key interactions between human society and basic biological concepts (Miles & Priest, 1999). There is an important distinction between environmental educators and environmental interpreters (Knapp, 2001). The environmental educator is usually associated with a formal education setting that requires students to participate in a sequential learning process. The environmental interpreter works among a wide range of people usually organized in informal groups, most of who are on vacation or in a leisure setting and are voluntarily seeking knowledge. The interpretive experience is usually comprised of short term, stand alone experiences rather than a series of educational lessons over an extended period. Both the educator and the interpreter may be specialists or generalists. A leader who is a specialist may have an expertise in a specific area of knowledge such as ornithology (the study of birds), entomology (the study of insects), geology, botany, zoology, forestry, soils, pond life, marine life, fossils, Native Americans, pioneer history, astronomy, or other areas. Leaders may be generalists in broader categories such as ecological studies, environmental concerns, landscape alteration, or general outdoor awareness. Examples of leadership positions necessitating knowledge of natural or historic resources include the following:

> Aquarium, arboretum, or zoo director, docent
> Audubon Society or National Wildlife Federation
> Summer camp instructor
> Camp nature counselor
> Eco-tourism/educational travel guide
> Environmental education camp field instructor
> Historic monument guide
> Interpreter at a living history park
> Museums
> Nature center director, docent, or volunteer
> Ranger naturalist (National Park Service)
> Sight-seeing trip tour guide/field trip leader
> State park trail guide
> Visitor center information specialist (U.S. Forest Service)

There are three ways of trying to win the young. There is persuasion. There is compulsion and there is attraction. You can preach at them; that is a hook without a worm. You can say "You must volunteer." That is the devil. And you can tell them, "You are needed," that hardly ever fails.

Kurt Hahn

A LEGACY OF LEADERSHIP
John Muir (1838-1914)

John Muir, an environmentalist, naturalist, traveler, writer, and scientist, is best remembered as one of the greatest champions of Yosemite natural wonders. He has been called "the father of our national parks," and "protector of the wilds." Muir viewed the need for the public to visit wilderness not for mere escapism from city life, but for the recreation of discovering what makes life most worthwhile for many people—the beauty of the forests, the mountains, the wild places. For Muir, wilderness was not merely a matter of conservation of natural resources, but a matter of human physical and psychic survival. Muir wrote, "I know that our bodies were made to thrive only in pure air, and the scenes in which pure air is found."

Beginning in 1874, Muir wrote a series of articles entitled "Studies in the Sierra" that launched his career as a writer. Muir's writings expressed both a scientific and a poetic voice for preservation of the natural environment. John Muir saw nature as not just a warehouse of raw materials for man's economic needs, but saw man as part of the natural world rather than the center of it. Over the course of his lifetime, John Muir published over 300 articles and 10 major books that recounted his travels, expounded his naturalist philosophy, and beckoned everyone to "Climb the mountains and get their good tidings."

Muir's writings were landmarks in the history of environmental conservation. Written recommendations from two of his articles ("The Treasure of the Yosemite" and "Features of the Proposed National Park"), were influential references to a Congressional bill that would model Yosemite after Yellowstone National Park. Congress passed this bill on September 30, 1890, initially putting Yosemite Valley in state control. Other writings of John Muir led to the establishment of the U.S. National Park System. In 1892, he was the founding president of the Sierra Club. The purpose of the club was to preserve and make accessible the Sierra Nevada, which continues as a leading American grassroots organization for protecting wilderness and the human environment.

John Muir was not always successful, however. After years of national debate that polarized the nation about whether or not to dam the Tuolumne River, president Woodrow Wilson signed a dam bill in 1913 to allow a reservoir to be built in Hetch Hetchy Valley, within Yosemite National Park, for a San Francisco water supply, even though less damaging options existed. This incident inspired conservationists to work to prevent future dams in other national parks, like the Grand Canyon and Dinosaur National Monument.

John Muir remains an inspiration for environmental activists. The John Muir Trail, John Muir Wilderness, and Muir Woods National Monument are named in his honor. An image of John Muir, with the California Condor and Half Dome, will appear on the California state quarter due to be released in 2005. In addition, April 21 is recognized as "John Muir Day," a day to recognize the modern ecological insight that man is a part of Nature, and that our well being, and our very survival, depends upon an ecologically sound natural environment.

Outdoor Leader Qualifications

Regardless of whether the outdoor leader is primarily concerned with teaching technical outdoor recreation skills or with fostering an awareness and knowledge of the complex nature of the natural environment, the prudent outdoor leader must understand and evaluate their abilities in several areas before embarking on any outdoor leadership function. Paul K. Petzoldt (1908-1999), a world-class mountaineer and founder of the National Outdoor Leadership School, is considered one of the early pioneers of American mountaineering and wilderness education. Dedicated to the training of wilderness leaders, many of today's wilderness leadership practices and procedures came from Paul Petzolt. One of his beliefs was that "a leader should not guide others into country beyond his [abid] own abilities (1984 p. 28). Before one can attempt to lead others in outdoor environments, an outdoor leader must be able to honestly self-evaluate their own skills and abilities.

Priest and Gass (1997) identify 12 components or leadership qualifications that are important for effective outdoor leader. These 12 qualifications are arranged into four categories: foundational history, hard skill, soft skill, and meta skills (see Figure 9.1).

First, the outdoor leader's skills and abilities need to be built upon a solid philosophical and theoretical foundation related to leading individuals and groups in outdoor environments. Having a solid foundation of what is known about adventure and environmental programming allows the outdoor leader to develop a strong professional practice. Professional practice is defined by Priest and Gass (1999) "as a set of rules that provide a professional activity with its

> Play is a major avenue for learning to manage anxiety. It gives the child a safe space where she can experiment at will, suspending the rules and constraints of physical and social reality....
>
> *Alicia Lieberman*

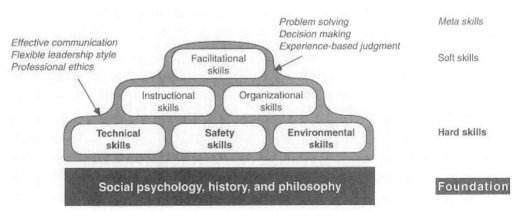

Figure 9.1. Outdoor leadership qualifications

structure of what should be accomplished as well as how this should be done" (p. 13). Second, the outdoor leader must develop technical activity competence, provide safety for group members, and avoid environmental damage when leading a group in the outdoors. These hard skills are considered tangible, and it is easily measured whether the leader has accomplished these compentencies. Third, the leader must be able to effectively organize, instruct, and facilitate the experience. These abilities are considered soft skills for they consist of leadership qualities the are more difficult to assess, such as the ability of the leader to have empathy for first time learners, and whether the leader is approachable, unselfish, and an innovative thinker. Finally, what integrates the leader's philosophical foundations, their hard and soft skill abilities, is what Priest and Gass (1999) define as meta skills. Meta skills include critical leadership competencies such as flexible leadership style, experience-based judgment, problem-solving skills, decision-making skills, effective communication, and professional ethics (pp. 4-5).

In addition to understanding human needs and environmental concerns, it is recommended that all outdoor leaders have experience with groups, first aid specific to the activity, weather, and a degree of biological and physical science. Plants, animals, astronomy, meteorology, geology, and water studies are all useful to the outdoor leader. Certainly, no one can be expected to know all there is about any one subject. It is possible, however, to know basic information about each of the above that will enhance the welfare of the participant and at the same time ensure that the program offers a fulfilling experience.

Techniques for Leading Environmental Education Programs

Various techniques are used by environmental educators and interpreters that can make a difference between an excellent program and one that may be only mediocre. Regnier, Gross, and Zimmerman (1992, p. 74) list a number of interpretation techniques that can be applied to any program.

Arrive early. You should be at the site at least 15 minutes early. First time participants need assurance that "this is the place.

Get to know your participants. Informal conversations go a long way toward building bridges with your audience.

Start on time. You owe it to the people who came on time.

Set expectations. Give the participants details about things like the distance to be covered, what they will see, and length of time the activity will take.

Make your first stop within sight of your starting point. Late arrivals can catch up with the group.

Stay in the lead. It should be more exciting to stay with you than to forge ahead on the trail.

Keep visitors comfortable. Be especially observant of wind and sun in their faces.

Go past the object you wish to talk about, then go back to the middle of the group so all can see the object you are to talk about. This is critical in moving efficiently with large groups.

Use teachable moments. If an osprey dives for fish in view of the group, shift your discussion to focus on the action.

Speak loudly by using inflection. Your voice will not carry as far in the out-of-doors as it would inside.

Return on time. Whenever possible, bring the group back to the beginning point (physically and thematically).

Carry a gimmick bag. This bag would include all the equipment you might need to help "see things better." It also helps to keep a potential "trouble maker" busy assisting you.

Involve the group. Actions are more meaningful than words. Involve the senses. Smell a milkweed flower, don't just talk about it. Remember to use questioning and discussion as much as you use lecture.

Conclude the walk. Don't allow the group to drift away one by one. Tie the walk to the theme, and bring the activity to an end.

Make certain your activity does not destroy the resource.

> It is a wholesome and necessary thing for us to turn again to the earth and in the contemplation of her beauties to know the sense of wonder and humility.
>
> *Rachel Carson*

▩▩▩▩ Care of the Environment

The goal of outdoor leaders is to develop in the participant an attitude of stewardship for the land accompanied by behaviors that demonstrate that attitude. Care of the environment is vital, for if the environment is altered perceptive-ly by human-caused problems such as erosion, litter, fire, human waste, vandalism, etc., the quality of the outdoor activity is lessened. Indeed, in some situations, misuse of the environment means elimination of the recreational activity dependent on that environment. People cannot swim in pol-luted streams or catch fish in polluted water. No one wants to hike or picnic in a burned area. Litter, erosion, and vandal-ism can turn people away.

Care of the environment means that the leader in all outdoor settings must advise participants against picking plants and cutting across the land instead of using trails, and should ensure that they maintain small, wisely located campfires. Leaders in the outdoors should also be leaders of the out-doors. Every outdoor leader can learn basic ecology and help others to be aware of the world around them. It is incumbent on the outdoor leader to learn about weather, poisonous plants and animals, insect pests, and the common plants of the area. It is further a responsibility of the outdoor leader to know and follow the policies and regulations of the agencies managing the land on which activities and programs occur.

LEADING AQUATIC ACTIVITIES

Aquatic activities are among the most popular leisure pas-times of North Americans. As a result, they are an integral component of most recreation, parks, and leisure services organizations. Aquatic activities can involve all age groups, from babies six weeks old to older persons. They contribute not only to the physical well-being of participants, but also provide opportunities for social interaction with others. Furthermore, aquatic programs, when organized and led with the safety of the participants in mind, offer participants activities that are challenging yet enjoyable.

When referring to aquatic activities, we are including activi-ties that occur in and on the water. This can encompass not only swimming, but also scuba diving, water skiing, water shows and pageants, water polo, canoeing, sailing, kayaking, and so on. These activities can occur in swimming pools, on lakes, at ocean beaches, and on rivers. Aquatic programs often involve considerable investment financially by public and commercial recreation, parks, and leisure services organ-izations. Because aquatic activities are often so prominent in these types of agencies, it is important that the leader have an understanding and awareness of the roles, purposes, and activities that contribute to the makeup of an aquatic pro-gram.

Leadership Roles in Aquatics

To be a leader of aquatic activities entails a great deal of responsibility. Individuals who work with participants in this setting have as their primary and essential responsibility the safety of each participant. The goal of a leader, regardless of the type of aquatic activity involved, should be to provide participants with appropriate knowledge, attitudes, and skills to enable them to participate in, on, and around the water safely. Some of the direct, face-to-face leadership roles that can be assumed in the aquatic setting are the following:

Lifeguard. Perhaps one of the most obvious aquatic leadership roles is that of a lifeguard. Lifeguards are found at swimming pools, beaches, and lakes and are responsible for the safety of participants within their jurisdiction. The lifeguard must exercise the greatest care in fulfilling his or her responsibilities. A study reported by the National Swimming Pool Institute has indicated that less than 40 percent of a guard's time is spent surveying swimmers. The lifeguard must not only be diligent in watching participants but must also act with confidence and competence when assisting an individual in distress. Many recreation, parks, and leisure services organizations require all lifeguards to have the following certifications: Community First Aid, CPR for the Professional Rescuer, Automatic External Defribulator (AED), Oxygen Administration for the Professional Rescuer and Prevention of Disease Transmission (http://www.redcross.org).

Pool Manager. A pool manager very often straddles the roles of face-to-face leader and supervisory leader. In his or her face-to-face role, he or she is responsible for greeting the public, ensuring that the swimming area is safe, and resolving problems involving participants. A pool manager will often act in the capacity of a lifeguard, providing rest breaks for staff and filling in for lifeguards who are ill. The pool manager has daily and continuous, direct contact with the public and, therefore, is a type of face-to-face leader.

Waterfront Director. A waterfront director is usually associated with a camp resort or other commercial agency providing aquatic services at a lake, beach, or river area. The waterfront director is responsible for training and supervising his or her staff to provide a wide variety of activities, such as swimming, sailing, canoeing, rafting, and so on. The waterfront director, like the pool manager, has daily and continuous, direct contact with the public and therefore is a face-to-face leader.

Consider the postage stamp. It secures success by sticking to one thing until it gets there.

Josh Billings

Instructor. Aquatic instructors are individuals who teach, instruct, and lead individuals in and around the water with the distinct purpose of increasing participants' knowledge and capabilities in the area of aquatic activities. The most common type of aquatic instructor is one who teaches individuals the basics of swimming. This particular instructor's role often requires that he or she hold an American Red Cross Water Safety Instructor's Certificate or its equivalent. Aquatic instructors are not, however, limited to just teaching the basics of swimming, but also may provide instruction in the areas of scuba diving, skin diving, boating, sailing, canoeing, kayaking, and other water-related activities.

Coach. Many aquatic activities are competitive in nature and involve the leader as a coach. Types of coaches found in aquatic settings are water polo coaches, swimming coaches, rowing coaches, synchronized swimming coaches, and so on. Any team coach is responsible for establishing training programs, teaching new skills, and maintaining team morale. A team coach is also responsible for developing team strategy and maintaining discipline. In addition, this type of coach often fulfills a liaison role with parents of the team members. Parents of team members should be informed of team schedules, goals, and objectives and should also be made to feel a part of the total team effort.

Aquatics Leader. Often the aquatics leader will be involved in the planning of program activities that complement the aquatic activities. An aquatics leader involved in face-to-face leadership of a canoeing club, for example, may be involved in the planning and implementation of program activities to complement the basic function of the club. The leader might want to organize social gatherings such as picnics or barbecues in conjunction with outings; organize workshops or clinics to enhance the participants' canoeing skills; or organize trips to areas with special or unique opportunities for canoeing.

The six leadership roles described represent broad categories of aquatic leadership. There are, however, other direct service roles in which the leader may engage that complement and enhance the provision of selected aquatic activities. For example, the leader may act as an official, judge, maintenance worker, concessionaire, and locker room attendant. Any or all of these auxiliary leadership functions might be necessary to successfully conduct certain aquatic activities.

A challenge to lead instead of being led, to participate instead of watching, to act... instead of waiting with idle hands.

Paul Petzoldt

LEADERSHIP: A POINT OF VIEW
FROM THE PROFESSION

Kala M. Stroup

Kala M. Stroup, Ph.D., is president of American Humanics, a national nonprofit organization connecting 70 universities and colleges with 17 of the largest national nonprofit youth serving organizations American Humanics has a professional staff of nine and annual budget of 1.4 million. American Humanics is the only national organization that prepares undergraduate students for professional careers in the nonprofit sector and for careers with youth and human service organizations. Dr Stroup has served as Missouri's commissioner of higher education, a member of the governor's cabinet, chief executive officer for all of Missouri's higher education with 52 colleges and universities. Dr. Stroup was president of Southeast Missouri State University with 9,500 undergraduate and graduate students, 1,000 faculty members and approximately a 19 million budget from July 1990 until her appointment as commissioner. Before Southeast Missouri State University, she spent seven-year tenure as president of Murray State University in Kentucky with 9,500 undergraduate and graduate students, 1,000 faculty and approximately a $19 million budget (1983-1990). She previously served as a fellow with the American Council on Education (ACE), spent five years as vice president for academic affairs and professor at Emporia State University in Kansas, and was a member of the faculty and held several administrative positions at the University of Kansas for over 18 years.

On leadership. . . .Leadership is the ability to mobilize resources to achieve a goal. Leadership is often attached to a person rather than a concept, leadership is also a term that contains a value judgment we often think of it as a positive term rather than a negative. Leadership can also be exercised to achieve what we consider negative ends. Over the years I have tried to think of leadership dynamics a neutral concept, which enables one to see negative and positive and shades of gray in between.

Leadership and success. . . .I think of face-to-face leadership as interpersonal communication with some persuasive elements. Supervisory leadership is related to the ability to articulate the mission, assist in working through the strategies to accomplish that mission and to mobilize both human and financial resources to achieve that mission. Managerial leadership is more related to organizational skills and the ability to be sensitive to both internal and external barriers, to achieving goals and the ability to effectively implement processes and plans. Community-level leadership involves the ability to work effectively using a team approach.

The exemplary leader. . . . . Effective leaders are able to mobilize resources to achieve a goal. For me, exemplary leaders are those that have been effective over time, with the ability to clearly articulate organizational goals, utilize strategies that move the organization forward and have contributed to the viability of the organization.

Leadership in action. . . . The leadership characteristics that are necessary for these professionals are the same as in the nonprofit organizations. The basic characteristics involve understanding of and commitment to the mission of the organization, inter and intra personal communication skills, and organizational skills for effective planning.

Aquatic Safety

The importance of adequate and comprehensive water safety precautions cannot be overemphasized. Thousands of people drown every year in water accidents that are preventable with proper precautions. The leader cannot be too careful when planning a program to ensure the water safety of participants. These programs often involve not only the aquatics staff, but also the participants themselves. The buddy system, for example, is often used in camp settings involving aquatic activities to supplement the use of lifeguards or waterfront directors. With this system, each participant chooses a friend, and the two of them assume responsibility for one another. They make sure that they enter and leave the water together and attempt to keep an eye on each other while in the water. Although aquatic sites may vary from lakes to beaches to pools, the basic rules of safety are very similar for all these sites. Some of the most important rules that a leader should enforce to ensure safety in aquatic areas are detailed as follows:

1. All aquatic leaders must possess a Red Cross or similarly approved Water Safety Instructor's Certificate.
2. Never permit anyone to swim alone. Constant and responsible supervision is a must.
3. Keep basic rescue and lifesaving equipment always available.
4. Post emergency instructions and telephone numbers conspicuously.
5. Have an aquatic first-aid kit available.
6. Enforce common-sense safety rules at all times. At least one responsible person should know how to administer artificial respiration and give intelligent first aid.
7. Clearly mark deep and shallow sections as well as hazardous swimming areas.
8. Prevent dangerous activities inconsistent with the aquatic activity presented (e.g., running).
9. Do not permit glasses, bottles, or sharp objects in the swimming area.
10. If possible, fence off the swimming areas and secure with a lock to prevent children from gaining unauthorized entry. (Swimming & Water Safety Textbook, 1968., pp. 112–113, 115–116.)
11. All boaters must wear U.S. Coast Guard-approved life jackets, secured completely.

The best possible way to ensure aquatic safety is to make sure that each individual has developed swimming competence and is qualified in terms of skill level to engage in the

> A ship in port is safe, but that is not what a ships are built for.
>
> *Admiral*
> *Grace Murray Hopper*

activities being offered. In addition, each participant should be made aware of, and expected to observe, safety rules. The recreation, parks, and leisure services leader should serve as an advocate in the promotion of safety of aquatic activities.

Types of Aquatic Activities

A wide range of aquatic activities can be planned, organized, and implemented by the recreation, parks, and leisure services aquatics leader. The types of aquatic programs that an agency is able to offer will depend on the man-made facilities and geographical resources that are available. Some of the many types of aquatics activities that may be offered by recreation, parks, and leisure services organizations include learning to swim programs, drown-proofing, lifesaving and water safety instruction, competitive swimming, small-craft programs, skin and scuba diving, recreational or open swimming program, aquatic programs for the disabled, water shows and pageants, swimming fitness activities, and water games. These activities are described as follows.

Learning to Swim Programs. As the name implies, learning to swim programs are involved with teaching individuals to swim. Instructional programs can be held for all age groups and for varying skill levels. The YMCA uses special names to differentiate between beginning swimming groups (pollywog) and progressively more difficult ones (porpoise). The American Red Cross "Learn to Swim" program uses the titles of "beginner, advanced beginner, intermediate, and swimmer." The beginner program focuses on alleviating participants' fears and inhibitions and teaching them how to float and swim a short distance. As individuals progress, they learn breath control, turns, a mastery of various swimming strokes, and how to survive in deep water. Programs directed toward the teaching of diving skills would also be included in the "Learn to Swim" category.

Type of Participants

Drown-Proofing. Drown-proofing is a program that teaches very young children and babies skills that they can use to remain safe in the water. It is based on the notion that a child should be trained to have an automatic reaction when falling into the water that will help him or her survive, and that the child should be able to survive without necessarily knowing how to swim. The child is taught not to be afraid of the water and to relax with water covering his or her face. The child is also taught to tread water and to float to support himself or herself as means of survival.

Accomplishment is when you use your extra strength to help someone else, rather than get to the top first.

Anonymous

Lifesaving and Water Safety Instruction. Lifesaving and water safety programs are conducted by the American Red Cross. In order to complete the lifesaving program, an individual must pass written and practical tests and demonstrate swimming endurance. Furthermore, individuals who advance to the water safety instructor's program must demonstrate various swimming strokes in proper form as well as learn various instructional procedures.

Competitive Swimming. Most communities offer competitive swimming programs. In the United States, swimming competition is sanctioned by several organizations. The National Collegiate Athletic Association (NCAA) and USA Swimming conduct programs in the following divisions: eight years and under, 10 years and under, 11 to 12 years, 13 to 14 years, 15 to 16 years, and 17 to 18 years (USA Swimming, Rules and Regulations, 2004). Age group competition is divided by gender—boys competing against boys, and girls competing against girls. Events for age group categories include freestyle, back stroke, butterfly, individual medley, and relays. One of the more innovative competitive swimming programs established in 1970 is the United States Masters Swimming (USMS) program. USMS provides opportunities for individuals over the age of 18 to participate in competitive swimming activities, including national championship competition. Individual age classifications in the USMS include 19 to 24, 25 to 29, 30 to 34, 35 to 39, and continues in five-year increments up to 100 to 104 years of age. Guidelines for competitive swim programs for all age groups can be found in Figure 9.2.

Small-Craft Programs. The implementation of small-craft programs within recreation, parks, and leisure services agencies will depend on the availability of such geographic resources as lakes, rivers, or oceans. Some of the most popular types of small craft programs include sailing, canoeing, rowing, kayaking, rafting, and windsurfing. Many of these specialized small-craft activities require instructors with a high degree of competence and specialized knowledge. All these types of programs should be conducted with stringent safety considerations in mind. These small-craft programs can vary greatly in the cost to the sponsoring agency and the participant. The recreation, parks, and leisure services organization may want to encourage the formation of small-craft clubs, sponsored by the organization but largely operated and administered by participants.

- Clear time and date for each meet. Plan for the entire season and coordinate with other programs.
- Type of meet.
  (a) Competition open to all age groups.
  (b) Competition between agencies.
- Events for meets.
  (a) Novelty swimming events might include such races as egg and spoon race, balloon race, dry towel race, hot dog race, pajama race, and flutterboard race.
  (b) Swimming races might include individual races and several relays of varying lengths to have more campers in the events.

freestyle	freestyle relays
backstroke	backstroke relays
breastroke	breastroke relays
butterfly stroke	butterfly relays
individual medley	medley relays
synchronized swimming	fancy diving low-board (1 meter)

  The events should be varied as to styles of swimming, as to distances, and as to age classifications. In addition, nonswimmers and beginners in an intramural meet should have some competitive experience, such as nutterboard or innertube races over shallow water. In other words, not all events should be speed events for swimmers. Clothes changing and towel procedures should be worked out if visiting teams are scheduled, and a responsible person should be assigned to them as a hospitality guide.

- Entry blanks for meet. These should be made out early and submitted to coaches in duplicate in order so that they may retain and submit a copy. These blanks should include
  (a) Date and time of meet (or trials).
  (b) Type of meet.
  (c) List or order of events, which will not be altered.
  (d) Awards for meet, if any, and when awards will be presented.
  (e) Point system to be used declaring winners.
  (f) Current records for specific events whenever possible.

- Preparation for meet.
  (a) Publicity should be handled well in advance, and preparation made to submit results of meet to designated persons.
  (b) Program of events should be duplicated and distributed with names of entries, events, records, and so on.
  (c) Appointed officials should be dressed in appropriate uniforms.

- Meet accessories.
  (a) Stopwatches—as many watches as teams.
  (b) Starting revolver and blanks.
  (c) Whistles.
  (d) Score calculation card for diving.
  (e) Diving flash cards.
  (f) Official swimming and diving rule book.
  (g) Awards for presentation ready.
  (h) Running score sheet for meet.
  (i) Team scoreboards.
  (j) Colored place cards for each place winner.
  (k) Lane lines set out (if necessary).
  (l) Numbers on cards (3 by 5) for lane selection by chance method.
  (m) Finish rope if needed.
  (n) Starting platforms if needed.
  (o) Recall rope.
  (p) Megaphone or P.A. system or both.
  (q) Sufficient towels for competitors.
  (r) Seating section reserved.

- Officials for meet.
  (a) Referee (1)—usually acts as the starter and should be most competent.
  (b) Starter (1).
  (c) Five or more finish judges, one as chief judge. Each picks a designated place (i.e., one picks first, two pick second, one picks third, etc.).

Figure 9.2
Steps in organizing a swim meet

(d) Timers—generally one for each team.
(e) Diving judges—referee is generally designated along with two more.
(f) Relay touchoff judges, one for each team.
(g) Recall rope clerks.
(h) Three diving clerks—one to record score, another to compute, and a third to add.
(i) Scorer and a runner to obtain results.
(j) Announcer should be competent, as he or she can make the meet interesting and attractive. An attempt should be made to instruct as well as to entertain. Such announcements direct attention to personalities, suggest records that may be broken, explain scoring of the meet and the scoring of diving, and so forth.

- The actual meet.
  (a) Have equipment ready before meet time.
  (b) Start on time.
  (c) Use some opening ceremony if feasible.
  (d) Make no changes in order of events.
  (e) Run events that require heats first.
  (f) Announce and introduce important guests.
  (g) Present awards after each event.
  (h) Send results to hometown newspaper.
  (i) Send photos, if possible, with suggested captions.

- Postmeet duties.
  (a) Replace auxiliary equipment in proper storage after drying gear.
  (b) Record and post results on bulletin board.
  (c) Add any new swimming records to record board with names, events, date, and swimming time.
  (d) Check on how meet was conducted, and record procedures that will avoid future mistakes.
  (e) If it is a dual or triangular meet, give a copy of the results to the visiting team or teams. This may be done by having a staff member type results as they occur; a few minutes after the conclusion of the last event, the original and carbon copies will then be available for distribution. This is a service much appreciated by all concerned.

Figure 9.2
Steps in organizing a swim meet
Source: Adapted from Richard H. Pohndoff. *Camp Waterfront Programs and Management*.
New York: Association Press, 1960, pp. 106–110.

Skin and Scuba Diving. For those persons who wish to explore new and mysterious surroundings, the recreation, parks, and leisure services agency may wish to provide opportunities for instruction in skin and scuba diving. Skin diving refers to one who, with the aid of a mask, swimming fins, and a breathing tube or snorkel, swims on or below the surface. Scuba diving, which involves oxygen tanks has many applications, including lifesaving, fishing, and commercial and sport applications. Both of these sports should be classified as high-risk activities and should be treated as such when they are being organized and implemented. Instruction in them should be provided only by qualified instructors or trainers with experience in skin diving or scuba diving.

Recreational or Open Swim Program. Most aquatic facilities provide opportunities for recreational or open-swim activity. This is the case whether the program is located at a swimming pool, lakefront, or ocean beach. This type of program requires the provision of appropriate leadership to ensure the safety of participants while they are engaging in unstructured swimming. Sometimes the recreational swim program is organized so that dif-

The worst sin toward our fellow creatures is not to hate them, but to be indifferent to them; that's the essence of humanity.

George Bernard Shaw

ferent age groups have access to the pool at different time periods. For example, in a community pool, adult open-swim may occur from 6:00 to 7:00 p.m., whereas children's open or recreational swim may occur from 1:00 to 5:00 p.m.

Adaptive Aquatic Programs. The leader working with individuals with disabilities is in an excellent position to be able to provide enriching activity via the use of aquatic programming. Aquatic activities often provide a person with physical limitations a greater degree of freedom of movement and greater opportunities for expression than are possible out of the water. Working with persons with special needs requires that the leader possess knowledge about a variety of disabilities. Although the general techniques for instructing participants in water-related activities are effective guidelines for working with individuals with disabilities, some activities and techniques will need to be adapted for those with varying physical, cognitive, or emotional abilities. As with all recreation and leisure programs, the leader should make an effort to include all people into existing aquatic programs. This often means providing training for aquatic instructors who have limited experience in working with the disabled (Anderson & Kress, 2003). The attitude of the aquatics leader providing this type of instruction is the key to providing a positive experience for participants.

Water Shows and Pageants. The fun and excitement that can be generated in a community through the production of a water show or pageant can be of great value to the overall aquatic program. Activities of this type provide many opportunities for community involvement and also provide great visibility for the recreation, parks, and leisure services organization as a whole. Water shows can be very practical in nature, demonstrating lifesaving techniques, fishing techniques, and small crafts; or they can be very festive, entertaining, and colorful, involving dramatic or musical presentations with elaborate costumes. Some of the shows or pageants designed to provide such entertainment are synchronized swimming, water drama, water ballet, water stunts, and fancy and comedy diving. Competitive swim shows may be presented as well that have as their purpose friendly, informal competition. A recreation, parks, and leisure services agency may want to combine all these types of activities (practical demonstrations, dramatic and musical presentations, and informal competition) into an elaborate aquatic pageant that spans several hours or an entire day.

Risk is essential. There is no growth or inspiration in staying within what is safe and comfortable. Once you find out what is best, why not try something else?

Alex Noble

Swimming Fitness Activities. Increasingly, aquatic programs are offered to promote physical fitness. Such programs are often aimed at the adult population. They may range from elaborate aquatics activities to simply reserving time periods during which participants may swim laps at the pool in conjunction with an open-swim or recreational swim program. Swimming fitness activities may focus on certain predetermined goals, such as cardiovascular improvement. A popular activity that has attracted a broad range of audiences is aqua aerobics, whereby patrons enjoy water exercise for fitness purposes.

Water Games and Activities. An aquatics leader may be involved in leading aquatic games, water activities, or auxiliary activities related to aquatic programs. For example, the aquatics leader might organize and teach a water polo team or a synchronized swim team. On another level, the aquatics leader may simply initiate aquatic games that are fun and enjoyable and simple for participants to learn. In community swimming pools, aquatic games may be organized to maintain participant interest and to provide a period of supervised play in which participants are allowed to use game equipment generally not allowed in the pool. In addition, nonaquatic programs that are social in nature may be organized by the aquatics staff to complement aquatic programs. For example, a teenage dance and swim, or an adult barbecue and swim, might be planned, organized, and led by an aquatics staff. These types of nonaquatic programs can complement aquatic activities and extend the use of aquatic facilities.

Miscellaneous Aquatic Activities. Several aquatic activities fall outside of the categories mentioned earlier. Surfing, rafting, and waterskiing are a few of the other aquatic activities that the leader may be called upon to direct in a recreation and leisure setting. As with other types of aquatic activities, the leader should always make a point of researching the safety precautions that should be taken with each type of activity and should then make sure that the participants are aware of, and observe, safety considerations.

SUMMARY

Outdoor recreation consists of programs that involve both physical skills and environmental education. Regardless of the focus of the program, every outdoor leader should understand that safety to the participant and care of the environment are as important as the leadership of the activity itself. Regardless of the activity and how expertly it is led, the ultimate quality of the experience will be diminished without sound environmental practices and recognition of human psychological and physiological needs in natural resource settings. Many responsibilities are inherent in the job of outdoor leader, and it is recommended that further study be undertaken before leading skill- or knowledge-based activities. Outdoor leaders should follow carefully established risk management plans and understand basic concepts of group work, first aid, natural and physical science, and skills specific to the activity being led.

Some of the types of aquatics activities that can be provided by a recreation, parks, and leisure services organization are learning to swim programs, drown-proofing, lifesaving and water safety instruction, competitive swimming, small-craft programs, skin and scuba diving, recreational programs or open-swim programs, aquatic programs for the disabled, aquatic shows and pageants, swimming fitness activities, and water games and activities. It is important to recognize that the location and design of an aquatic facility will determine the range of water experiences that the leader can facilitate, whether that be unstructured water fun and play, water confidence and safety, or fitness, health, or sport training.

Discussion Questions

1. Explain the two (2) primary responsibilities of leaders in the outdoor setting.

2. Explain the four (4) major qualifications of outdoor leaders.

3. What behavior might a participant expect to see in a leader of an outdoor activity?

4. Discuss the psychological needs of people in the outdoors. How does meeting physical needs adequately and appropriately affect psychological needs?

5. Defend the wisdom of a leader who insists on taking extra clothes, water, and food on a day trip.

6. What is the responsibility of the outdoor leader for stewardship of the land?

7. Identify some of the leadership roles that can be assumed in an aquatic setting.

8. Note some of the important safety rules one should follow in leading aquatic activities.

9. Identify and describe the various types of aquatic activities that a recreation, parks, and leisure services organization might offer.

10. Identify the settings in your community in which aquatic programs are offered.

THE CASE FOR LEADERSHIP
A Difficult Participation

Points of Consideration

Sarah has been hired as a youth worker by the Cedar Center Parks and Recreation Department to provide opportunities for the personal and social development of young people ages 13-19. One of her responsibilities is to plan and implement programs such as community/environmental projects, outdoor education, and sports activities. Sarah has a lot of experience leading young children at summer camps and in Girl Scouts groups, but not much experience with teens. One of her first activities with your organization is a weekend river canoe trip for a co-ed group of nine teenagers. Sarah had met interested participants and spoke with them on various aspect of the trip, such as what to bring and what not to bring on the trip, getting permission slips signed by parents, etc.

The trip starts late because Mike is 30 minutes late getting to the meeting point. He doesn't have some of the required equipment that was on the equipment list, and has a bit of an attitude when Sarah hurriedly works to get him outfitted with surplus gear your organization has in the storeroom. In the van ride to the put-in, Mike is very quiet and seems detached from the rest of the group members.

When you arrive at the boat launch and the group is getting ready to put the canoes into the river, Mike misses some of the instructions for the day and paddling information because he wanders off in search of a restroom. When he returns, he continually interrupts Sarah when she is talking to the rest of the group. Once in camp for the night, Mike doesn't participate in the camp chores like setting up tents and cooking dinner. He goes for a walk by himself, eats dinner, and then goes to bed early.

Mike spends much of his free time on the trip by himself, getting up before the rest of the group and going on walks in the area. Sarah doesn't see much of him because he seems to be avoiding her. On the second day of the trip the group wants to paddle through a safe stretch of rapids. When the group gets half way through the rapids, Mike panics. He throws down his paddle, grips the sides of canoe, and weeps to his canoe partner, "I can't do this. If you don't stop this canoe, I'll jump out." Mike is very frightened. He and his partner land their canoe on a small island half way through the rapids and he refuses to go any further. You and the rest of the group are able to land your canoes on the same island.

Questions of Consideration

- How does Mike's behavior affect the group?
- Why is Mike behaving the way he is?
- Why is Sarah behaving the way she is?
- If you were Sarah, what would you do about his disruptive behavior?
- How could Sarah have worked differently with Mike?
- What should Sarah do about Mike and his fear of rapids?
- How would you get Mike to proceed down the river and continue the trip?
- What is your recommendation for a longer-term solution?

Maintaining necessary lifeguards

Recruiting and retaining lifeguards is a nationwide challenge. The need for initial certifications in CPR, First Aid, Automated External Defibrillator (AED), Oxygen Administration, and Preventing Disease Transmission, as well as the maintenance of these certifications and further certification in water safety, instructor, or pool operator cost hundreds of dollars. Life guarding jobs typically pay $8 - $10 per hour. Lifeguards have an enormous responsibility for the life of the swimmers in their environments. At the Cedar Center aquatics facilities there can be numerous rescues over the course of the season. This can be more responsibility than people are willing to take, especially when jobs involving less responsibility are available at the local mall.

You are the aquatics manager of a large recreation facility and were asked by your director to put together a recruitment and retention plan for attracting lifeguards to work at your facility. How is one's leadership style related to attracting and motivating potential lifeguards to apply and stay at your facility? What values must you present to your staff in order retain lifeguards once they are hired and trained? In the last month, one of your lifeguards was tardy three times and yesterday did not report for a scheduled shift. As the lifeguard supervisor, how would you handle this situation?

References

Anderson, L., & Kress, C. (2003). *Inclusion: Including people with disabilities in parks and recreation opportunities*. State College, PA: Venture.

Cordell, K., McDonald, B., Teasley, J., Bergstrom, J., Martin, J., Bason, J., Leeworthy, V. (1999). Outdoor recreation participation trends. In Ken Cordell (Ed.), *Outdoor recreation in American life: A national assessment of demand and supply trends*. Champaign, IL: Sagamore.

Knapp, D. (2001). Environmental education and environmental interpretation: The relationships. In H. Hungerford, W. Bluhm, T. Volk, & J. Ramsey (Eds.), *Essential readings in environmental education* (2nd ed.). Champaign, IL: Stripes.

Miles, J., & Priest, S. (1999). *Adventure programming*. State College, PA: Venture.

Petzoldt, P. (1984). *The new wilderness handbook*. New York, NY: Norton.

Priest, S., & Gass, M. (1997). *Effective leadership in adventure programming*. Champaign, IL: Human Kinetics.

Regnier, K., Gross, M., & Zimmerman R. (1992). *The interpreter's guidebook: Techniques for programs and presentations*. Stevens Point: WI: UW-SP Foundation Press.

Swimming and water safety textbook. (1968). Washington D.C.: The American National Red Cross.

USA Swimming Rules and Regulations Manual. (2004). Colorado Springs, CO: USA Swimming.

CHAPTER

10

Leadership in Social Settings

LEARNING OBJECTIVES

1. To understand the importance of social recreation to the leisure, recreation and parks field.
2. To understand the differences in programming
   for vertical and horizontal groups.
3. To identify the social activities patterns that
   help the leader plan appropriate activities.
4. To understand the importance of follow-up for
   future social gatherings.

KEY TERMS

- Social Recreation
- Vertical Grouping
- Social Activities Patterns
- Socialization
- Horizontal Grouping
- Social Action Curve

INTRODUCTION

Some people weave burlap into the fabric of our lives, and some weave gold thread. Both contribute to make the whole picture beautiful and unique.

Anonymous

People are gregarious by nature. We like to congregate in small or large groups to socialize talk, laugh, observe, or participate. Social recreation, by its simplest definition, is recreation that has interaction with others as its major motivating factor. This means that many recreational activities may be classified as social recreation even though their forms are dissimilar. Activities that can be classified as social recreation include parties, potluck dinners, picnics, banquets, play days, campfires, conventions, class reunions, and many other group-oriented events. Each of these activities often relies on socialization for its success.

Although activities within many social events may appear to have a purpose other than socialization (for example, competition, education, or skill development), an activity can be classified as social recreational if the social factor is of the greater importance. For example, although some children's parties may include competitive activities, the socializing factor is of greater importance than is the winning factor. This is evidenced by the informality of such competition, where simple skills, a few rules, and improvised equipment are substituted for highly developed skills, exacting rules, and precisely built equipment. Also, prizes may be nominal or nonexistent, and fun for fun's sake takes the place of a concerted effort to win.

Picnics and potluck dinners are forms of social recreation, for interaction with others is the primary motivator, not hunger. People who plan picnics or who plan to attend picnics really do so because a picnic is an ideal social event, not because they necessarily anticipate hunger. Eating together in an informal setting is fun. It is more work to prepare a picnic and pack everything up to take outdoors than it is to eat at home. Still, judging by the number of picnics held each year, the socialization is worth the extra work. For many who eat out in restaurants and attend banquets, their meals are motivated more by a desire for socialization than by hunger. A banquet is a lot of work, yet it is an ideal way for people to celebrate a common cause as a group. A play day, although consisting almost entirely of competitive activities, has as its major purpose having fun together. A convention has educational objectives, yet it is through the socialization of the participants at and between educational sessions that the objectives are often attained.

Social recreation events are of short duration, with definite beginnings and endings. The entire event may last one hour, one day, or a few days. Further analysis of social recreation shows that it is a program integrator. In other words, through the social program, the participants are integrated to feel enthusiasm toward a common goal and actually become, for a short while, an integrated unit. Like singing, social recreation can transform a "group of individuals" into an "individual group."

Social recreation events can include both horizontal and vertical groups. A horizontal group is a group that is characterized by personal similarities. The Cub Scouts, a grandmothers' bridge club, or a teen club are examples of horizontal groupings. Vertical groupings are made up of persons of many ages, interests, and abilities. A family reunion is a social event exemplifying a vertical group. Social recreation is probably the best form of recreation for use with vertical groups because of the adaptability of a wide variety of activities to meet the interests and abilities of an equally wide variety of participants.

Social events can be adapted for all people; they require little skill, knowledge, or preparation on the part of participants. Even in a competitive play day or field day, little highly skilled practice is needed prior to the event. Equipment for social recreation may be simple, improvised, or invented. If a picnic planning group wants to play horseshoes and can't locate any horseshoes, then beanbags, flat rocks, wooden blocks, or even pine cones may be substituted. A balloon may become a volleyball. A net may be raised or lowered. Hands may become paddles. There is no end to innovative adaptations for the purpose of socialization. The characteristics of social recreation, then, are socialization, short duration, group integration, horizontal or vertical groupings, little skill, knowledge, or preparation on the part of the participant, and simple equipment.

PURPOSES AND VALUES OF SOCIAL EVENTS

The purposes of social recreation are basically the same for all social events: they get people together to work, play, learn, and have fun together.

Depending on what the event is, parts of these objectives will be emphasized or de-emphasized. For example, in order of emphasis, the objectives of attendees at a professional conference may be working, learning, and having fun, whereas those attending a birthday party for 10-year-olds may be more interested in playing and having fun than in learning.

Be happy while you're living, for you're a long time dead.

Scottish proverb

Everyone is kneaded out of the same dough but not baked in the same oven.

Yiddish proverb

Each person involved in a social event brings to it his or her own personal objectives and goals. The objectives of the leader, the participant, and the sponsoring organization are usually somewhat different, yet they should be compatible. For example, if a YMCA sponsored a one-afternoon camp reunion for boys who attended its summer youth camp, three different objectives might be in play. The main purpose of the event, from the perspective of the sponsoring organization, would be to recruit campers for next summer. The objective of the leader organizing the reunion would be to offer opportunities to renew acquaintances, offer safe and wholesome activities, review camp skills and songs, and provide the participants with a good time. The participants' objectives would probably be to have fun and to do things with their camp friends. These objectives, although dissimilar, would also be compatible and logical.

The values of social recreation are realized primarily through the group process. Social recreation provides opportunities for all program members to participate on an equal basis. Because skill and competition are of negligible importance, the unskilled can participate on an equal basis with the skilled. The skills used in social recreation events may be those that have not been learned or practiced before and that may never be used again.

Another value of social recreation is that group loyalty, solidarity, and a feeling of belonging can be developed through the social process. For example, a community Halloween party, with special activities for all age groups, can contribute to a feeling of community pride, loyalty, friendship, and solidarity. Certain social events can also bring out and encourage the development of latent talents in music, drama, committee organization, and countless other attributes.

Finally, social events can have educational value. The educational value of social recreation can range from the subtle learning of cooperation and fairness that takes place at a children's party to the more obvious learning that takes place at a convention. Perhaps one of the finest forms of adult education is the workshop, conference, or convention that is attended voluntarily for social, educational, professional, and personal reasons. Potlucks with brief business meetings and short lectures or entertainment are popular ways to bring together those who may not ordinarily socialize together, yet who have some common interest or bond. Volunteer organizations honoring outstanding volunteers, service groups awarding annual certificates, retirement centers, and special interest groups can all benefit from the socialization that comes with a potluck dinner at which some business is conducted. Further, the business meeting may never have a quorum without the addition of the social activity.

THE SOCIAL ACTIVITIES PATTERN

Live out your imagination, not your history.

Stephen Covey

Even though social activities vary greatly, all social events can be planned using one format, or a planning pattern. A planning pattern or outline that can be used to plan any social event is detailed in Table 10.1. When used for social recreation, the outline is often called the "social activities pattern" and may be used for either a small social party or for a banquet for 500 people. The task is magnified for the larger group, but the organization is the same.

▬▬ Background Material

Prior to planning the program for any activity of a social nature, it is imperative that background material be developed, for it is the background material that provides the basis for planning the program. Background material includes information regarding the type of activity, its purpose, the participants, the date and time of the activity, and the theme. A discussion of these five factors follows.

Table 10.1
Planning Outline for Social Activities Pattern

I. Background Material
    A. Type of activity, purpose
    B. Participants
    C. Date and time
    D. Theme
II. Details
    A. Operations
        1. Facilities
        2. Promotion, publicity
        3. Decorations
        4. Refreshments
    B. Program
        1. First-comers
        2. Mixers
        3. Active events
        4. Quiet events
        5. Ending
    C. Financial
        1. Expense
        2. Expense
III. Follow-up
    A. Cleanup
    B. Appreciation
    C. Evaluation
    D. Report

Type of Activity. There are many types of activities for which a leader might plan a program. The type of activity will determine some of the program's components. The following is a list of some of these types of recreation and leisure service activities.

- banquet
- campfire
- carnival
- conference
- convention
- fair
- festival
- field trip
- group trip
- orientation party
- picnic or potluck
- progressive party
- reunion
- talent night
- workshop

This list is by no means exhaustive, for other activities may also be classified as social recreation and may follow the same pattern.

Purpose. The purpose of a social event can be simple or complex. The individual or individuals planning a social event should be able to identify what is to be accomplished through the event. The purpose of a banquet might be to recognize a retiring or founding member, to celebrate a victory, or to commemorate an anniversary. The purpose of a carnival might be to involve a large number of participants with a wide range of abilities. Or it might be to coordinate the programs of several community centers, to give recognition to youth achievement, or even to raise money for a group. The planning committee should be able to identify the purpose of the event in order to plan effectively to meet the intended goal.

Participants. As in all other phases of recreation, participants and their needs are of paramount importance and, consequently, must be defined and understood before any planning occurs. In social recreation, because of the fact that the participants socialize and often develop a feeling of togetherness and compatibility, it is extremely important that the persons planning the event know as much as possible about the group in advance. Knowing the age range of the participants is more important than knowing the age of the majority. A family reunion with members ranging in age from six months to 90 years requires a different program from a class reunion with members ranging in age from 40 to 45.

A LEGACY OF LEADERSHIP
Juliette Gordon Low (1860-1927)

Juliette Gordon Low was an individual whose inspirational leadership came later in life. She was born into a prominent southern family; her father was a Confederate Captain in the Civil War. Daisy, as she was known to family and friends, was the second of six children. She spent a happy childhood in Savannah, Georgia, developing a lifetime interest in the arts. She wrote poems, sketched, wrote and acted in plays and later became a skilled painter and sculptor. As was the fashion for girls from well-to-do families in the later 1800s, she attended private schools including a French school in New York City. Upon completion of her formal studies she traveled extensively in the U.S. and Europe to broaden her education. When she was about 25 years old, Juliette had an ear infection that was treated with silver nitrate. This damaged her ear and caused her to lose a great deal of hearing in that ear.

In 1886 she married a wealthy Englishman, William Mackay Low and moved to England. During the ceremony, a grain of wedding rice lodged in her good ear and became infected. When the doctor attempted to remove the rice, it damaged the nerves in her ear and caused total deafness in that ear. For the next 19 years she spent her time traveling around the British Isles and America, and frequented many social events. During the Spanish-American War, she returned to the United States and with her mother helped to organize a convalescent hospital for soldiers in Florida, where her father was stationed there as a General in the U.S. Army. At the end of the war, she returned to England.

Upon William's death in 1905, Juliette spent the next several years globetrotting through Europe and India without much purpose in life. That all changed, one day in 1911, when she attended a luncheon in England and met Sir Robert Baden-Powell, founder of the Boy Scouts and Girl Guides. She immediately became interested in the new youth movement. During that year she organized a troop of Girl Guides among poor girls at her estate at Glenlyon, Scotland, and then founded two more troops in London. In 1912, she returned to Savannah and made an historic phone call to a friend saying, "I've got something for the girls of Savannah, and all America, and all the world, and we're going to start it tonight." Thus, on March 12, 1912, Juliette Low gathered 18 girls together to organize the first two American Girl Guide troops. Daisy Gordon, her niece, was the first registered member.

Through her steadfast promotion and leadership, the movement grew rapidly, becoming the Girl Scouts of America in 1913. The organization was incorporated in 1915 with the national headquarters established in Washington, D.C. She served as president of the organization until 1920, when she was bestowed the rightful title of founder.

Forward-thinking Juliette Low brought girls of all backgrounds into the out-of-doors, giving them opportunity to learn about nature and develop self-reliance and

continued on next page

continued from previous page

resourcefulness. She encouraged girls to prepare themselves not only for traditional homemaking roles, but also for possible future roles as professional women, in
the arts, sciences, and business, and for active citizenship outside the home.
Disabled girls were welcomed into Girl Scouting at a time when they were exclud-
ed from many other activities. This seemed quite natural to Juliette, who never let
her own deafness keep her from full participation in life. Juliette Low died of cancer in 1927, but her legacy of leadership continues as Girl Scouting has grown to
nearly 3.3 million members in the U.S. On December 2, 1983, president Ronald
Reagan signed a bill naming a new Federal Building in Savannah, Georgia for Juliette
Low. It was only the second federal building in history to be named for a woman.

Friends I have had
both old and young,
and ale we drunk and
songs we sung . . .

Charles Webb

It is good to keep in mind certain age traits particularly
applicable to social events. Young children (ages four to
nine) have short attention spans and a great amount of energy. They need more things to do than other age groups, and
they must have things planned for them as they cannot plan
their own activities. They enjoy surprises and are generally in
high spirits. Instructions must be given on their level, and
they must be carefully supervised. In events where young
children are part of a group of a wide age range, it is necessary to assign leaders to be specifically and constantly with
the younger children. At this age, boys and girls will play well
together, but all need to receive rewards, recognition, or
prizes (if possible). The leaders should also plan calm activities to be interspersed among the active ones.

Generally speaking, activities for children should be out of
hearing range but not necessarily out of seeing range of the
adults attending the event. When activities take place in too
close a proximity with adults, conflict can arise with the different socialization patterns that are present. This is especially true if the group is composed of older adults who are not
accustomed to the energy and exuberance of the younger
generations. Depending on the purpose of the event (i.e.,
family reunions), some intergenerational activities may be
planned in the beginning of the socialization, process but
time should also be given for each generation to interact
with each other in activities that provide for conversation
and fellowship.

Preteens, in social situations, may be awkward unless separated from the young children for most of the activities. Boys
and girls are better when separated for some activities, such
as games requiring hard physical contact. Other activities
lend themselves well to coeducational participation.
Teenagers can assume planning responsibilities for many of
their own social events. The function of such planning committees is to encourage feelings of belonging as well as to
formulate a program of action. With careful supervision,
teenagers are capable of planning and executing dances,
conferences, parties, work projects, and many other social
events. In cases where they cannot be involved in much pre-

planning, they can have responsibilities during the function. They also need an opportunity to be with their peers to socialize.

Adults enjoy conversation more than any other means of social interaction. Certain leisure activities serve as icebreakers and can lead to enjoyable conversations. Any adult social program, be it a party, workshop, conference, picnic, or whatever, should balance structured activities with such unstructured activities as conversation. In addition, the activity program should not be crowded, nor should it contain awkward lapses of empty time between activities.

Other factors or variables regarding participants that should be taken into consideration in planning the program include:

Demographics. The sex, age, income, marital status, education, and other attributes of participants are all basic factors that should be considered when planning a program. The leader wants to meet the needs of participants. Individuals of low economic status may be able to participate in programs only if they are free or of minimal cost. Young, single adults might best be served by a program that emphasizes social interaction and provides a large number of mixers. Individuals of different age groups will have different physical capabilities that also should be taken into consideration.

Lifestyles. Lifestyle variables encompass a broad variety of attributes, ranging from the participants' introversion or extroversion, propensity for risk taking, and liberalism or conservatism. Lifestyle is also influenced by the norms, customs, and values of the country or the region within which a participant resides. These norms, customs, and values will influence dress, dance, and other aspects of the participants' relationships with others. Lifestyle variables contribute to the makeup of the personality of the participant. The influence of these lifestyles, therefore, should be considered by the leader involved in program planning. For example, when meals are being planned, the preferences of vegetarians and others with particular dietary wants and needs should be considered.

Purpose in Attending. The reasons that individuals attend social activities vary tremendously. Some individuals have common interests with other members of the group and simply want to share these interests. Other individuals attend a group because of their previous involvement in a leisure opportunity, in order to become involved in a novel experience, or for educational reasons. The reasons that participants seek out a particular program should have an influence on program planning and implementation. If, for example, a participant is attending a program in order to duplicate

> It is a wholesome and necessary thing for us to turn again to the earth and in the contemplation of her beauties to know the sense of wonder and humility.
>
> *Rachel Carson*

an earlier positive experience, program planning will be very different from that for a participant who is attending a program in order to experience novel and unique opportunities for leisure.

> The best way to cheer yourself up is to try to cheer somebody else up.
>
> *Mark Twain*

Date and Time. The length or duration of an activity is an important planning item and should help to determine the program's contents. In turn, the type of group and the purpose of the event should help to determine the length of the event. For example, a Christmas party for children should be about two-and-a-half hours long, at the most. An elaborate dinner party with a medieval theme and entertainment might last four hours or more. Sometimes the duration of a program is determined by external factors such as cost, availability of a facility, and continuity with other events.

A definite starting and ending time should be given for social events, and consideration given to the frequency of occurrence of the event. Some social events are scheduled on a weekly or monthly basis, whereas others occur annually or biannually or, in the case of something like a golden wedding anniversary or 90th birthday, once in a lifetime.

Theme. Regardless of the scope of the program, every social event can be based on a theme, and the use of a theme can enhance the success of the program. World fairs and international exhibitions are based on themes, as are national and local conventions. As a matter of fact, themes are used universally whenever a program is designed to develop a feeling of social identity. A theme is a single idea around which a program is planned. A party may be planned around football, hoboes, the circus, or golden days. A conference generally has a more sophisticated theme, such as challenge, progress, focus, or relevance.

There are two major functions of program themes. First, they help the participant to identify with a common idea. A theme provides direction to a program and motivates participants to think along common lines. Through use of the theme, the participants are unified. The second major function of a theme is to help make planning easier. A theme can be the basis for decorations, invitations, and sometimes refreshments. The theme also assists the leader in planning publicity and maintaining continuity in the coordination of activities.

As mentioned, through proper use of a theme, participants can be encouraged toward a similar frame of mind before the first activity is conducted. A good theme tells the participant in advance what to expect. Too often, when planning parties or programs, social leaders use themes that are too broad and tell too little. A party called "Christmas of Holiday Fun" or something equally broad tells us little. A Christmas program called "A Child Is Born" connotes a serious religious tone, as does "Joy to the World." "Christmas Capers" connotes an entirely different tone than would "Christmas Around the World" or a "Christmas Carol Carnival." Many activities held at Easter time are religious, yet many are not. A theme such as "Easter Celebration" could mean a variety of things to a variety of people. On the other hand, themes such as "Life Eternal," "Spring Eternal," "Easter Bonnet Parade," or Easter Egg-Citement" leave little doubt as to what type of Easter program could be expected. Figure 10.1 is an example of a poster from a Valentine's Day party sponsored by the Willamalane Park and Recreation District in Springfield, Oregon. The theme of this program is a family Valentine's Day.

Effective leadership is putting first things first.

Stephen Covey

Figure 10.1
A poster from a Valentine's Day party

Examples of various other themes that effectively communicate an idea are the following:

- Hobby Fair
- Pioneer Party
- The Year 2020
- Shipwreck
- Rodeo

- Backward Party
- Prophecy Party
- Cupid's Carnival (February)
- Flanagan's Frolic (St. Patrick's Day)
- Fool's Festival (April first)

DETAILS

The details component of the social activities pattern depicted in Table 10.1 (see page 351) is logically divided into the three areas: operations, program, and financial. The breakdown of each of these areas is fundamentally the same for a short party or a long social event, yet because social events can vary widely in duration and complexity, considerable difference may exist between, say, the work of program planning for a two-hour party and that for a Memorial Day weekend family reunion.

Operations

Before an actual program is planned, specific operational details should be worked out. Operational details are all those items that must be decided except for the program itself. Generally, they include facilities, promotion, decorations, and refreshments.

Facilities. After the group is identified and before one goes further with any details but basic planning, the facility where the event will take place should be identified, reserved, and studied. The facility may vary from being a room in a private home to a group of hotels to a convention center in a city.

Prime considerations in determining facility needs include the following:

- Number of rooms needed for lodging, meetings, meals, exhibits
- Sizes of rooms needed
- Utilities and equipment needed and available (electrical outlets, shades for darkening, public address system, projectors, speaker's lecterns, tables, chairs, ventilation, kitchenettes, heat control, soundproofing, exits, water, etc.)
- Restrooms in proximity to major activities
- Drinking fountains
- Parking spaces needed: number, availability, cost
- Accessibility for those participants who have mobility issues

- The availability of transportation to and from the area: bus, private car, train, plane, taxi
- Safety and police protection needs

A facility checklist for special events is found in Table 10.2. This can be used by the leader to ensure that the facility is used safely and effectively. One should develop a risk management plan for the event simultaneously.

Promotion/Publicity. Operational concerns include publicity. Publicity for an event may involve a simple invitation or an elaborate series of announcements, articles, and fliers. Invitations may be in the form of telephone calls, informal notes, e-mails, catchy theme-oriented cards, or formal engraved notices. Publicity releases contain the same information but are intended to reach a greater number of people living at greater distances from the site of the function. In more recent years, the use of a dedicated web site for events has become popular, especially for conventions (see Figure 10.2). The use of such sites can help to not only help publicize the event, but facilitate the process of registration, selecting appropriate housing, and locating transportation to and from the site. Most organizations planning large meetings or conferences now rely heavily on the internet for publicity.

The purposes of publicity are twofold: educational and motivational. Interest in attending the function must be aroused. Here careful selection of the theme may be a deciding factor. Somehow the social event should be made to sound exciting. If personal invitations are mailed out, the leader should attempt to do something different with paper, color, or cutout shapes that will be eye-catching. For instance, invitations to a sack social could be written in crayon on very small paper bags. Invitations to a mystery party could be torn into pieces that have to be reassembled to read the message. If the group of people who will be invited to attend a social event are getting together at an earlier date, an impromptu skit or other novel medium could be used to invite them. Announcements in the form of original limericks delivered by a group from the planning committee often arouse interest purely because of the often inanity of the verse as well as the antics of the speakers.

Decorations. Decorations may be simple or elaborate. They may consist of flowers, centerpieces, colored lights, banners, costumes, and so on. Decorations are generally in keeping with the theme and are used to create a mood. They show that something special is happening and, like the theme, help participants develop a unified spirit.

We create magical moments that last a lifetime.

Camp Adventure ™

Youth Services

Figure 10.2
A web page from CampAdventure.com

Refreshments. Although it not mandatory to serve refreshments, most social recreation leaders plan for refreshments because they add to the socialization. They are looked forward to, and, in most social events, serving refreshments is a good change of pace from other activities. Refreshments may be simple coffee or soft drinks or may be as elaborate as a seven-course dinner. At the party of short duration, they are usually compatible with the theme and may be color coordinated with the decorations as well.

▬▬▬Program

In planning the program for special events, one needs to realize that there is no single program format to follow, for many combinations and arrangements of activities work well. There is, rather than a set format, a curve of action affecting patterns of activity that can be made flexible to meet the objectives of a given program. This is known as the social action curve, shown in Figure 10.3.

Because social activities follow a certain pattern or curve, the leader can select and structure activities that conform to and support the desired pattern of activity. At a rock concert, for example, the leader may want the excitement of the activity to be highest during the finale. Most parties, however, reach the peak of excitement earlier. The pitch of excitement at a typical children's party is at a natural, quiet or low level as participants arrive and begin warming up to the activities and to each other. Through social events and socialization, the leader should build to the high pitch or greatest

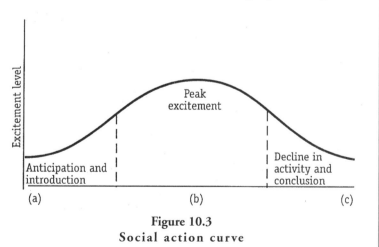

Figure 10.3
Social action curve
(a) The program commences with a low, anticipatory level of excitement. (b) At the middle of the program, excitement reaches its peak. (c) As the program closes, the pitch of excitement is controlled so that the participants leave in an orderly, calm manner, yet with a warm memory of their participation.

LEADERSHIP: A POINT OF VIEW FROM THE PROFESSION

Terry G. Trueblood, CPRP

Terry G. Trueblood, CPRP, is the Director of Parks and Recreation in Iowa City, Iowa. Responsibilites include a wide spectrum of recreation programs and facilities, parkland in excess of 1,400 acres, foresty, cemetery, central business district, and maintenance of government buildings. He formerly served as Director of Parks and Recreation, Director of Recreation and Assistant Director of Recreation for the City of Dubuque, Iowa. He has served two terms on the Board of Trustees of the National Recreation and Park Association; two terms as President of the American Academy for Park and Recreation Administration; President of the American Park and Recreation Society; Chair of the National Forum; Chair of the Great Lakes Regional Council; and President of the Iowa Park and Recreation Association. Honors and awards include the Richard J. Slattery Outstanding Professional Award (Iowa); Great Lakes Region Outstanding Professional Award; American Park and Recreation Society Professional Meritorious Service Award; and the Iowa City Boss of the Year Award.

On leadership. . . .Someone who "shows the way," is always there when needed, is capable of changing people's behavior.

Leadership and success. . . .To me, leadership is probably the single most important factor in the successful operation of a parks and recreation department . . . certainly with regard to recreation programs, but also throughout the entire operation. Good leadership results in trust and confidence, and without this, whether it's on an individual basis or a community-wide basis, our organization cannot be effective, and may not be able to exist.

The exemplary leader. . . . .The exemplary leader within our organization believes in what he/she is doing (i.e., the benefits offered by the profession), is a team player, is flexible in appropriate situations, and exhibits those characteristics as noted below. I am reminded of a statement about leadership from the book *In Search of Excellence*, which has, for some reason, stuck with me over the years . . . "It is being visible when things are going awry, and invisible when they are working well.

Leadership in action. . . . Integrity, service-oriented, honesty, good listener, dedication, good communicator, respect for others, good attitude, acts professionally.

excitement of the event approximately midway through the program. Refreshments are generally served about two-thirds of the way through the program, and these can serve as a quieting event. The events after the refreshments should serve to taper off the excitement completely, culminating in a definite ending activity, when the party ends on a pleasant note. In the case of a child's party, refreshments are fairly noisy and should be served earlier, just past the middle of the party. They should not be served last at a children's party, for they are not calming. With excitable children, a story told after refreshments will often calm their excitement. The leader wants the group to leave the event calmly and quietly to ensure an orderly and safe return home.

It is important that the leader planning a party try to include activities for the first-comers, icebreakers, mixers, active events, and quiet events, and have a definite ending so people will know that the event has ended. Some of these activities are described as follows.

First-comers. First-comers are, as the word suggests, the people who are first to arrive. Because they arrive before everyone has assembled, they may find themselves at a loss as to what to do. While they wait for the arrival of the others, they should be involved in some type of activity.

A first-comer activity must be one that can be entered into at any time by one or more arrivals. It must last until the last person arrives and takes part in it for a short time. It may be competitive or non-competitive; it may require group work or individual participation. It may be a socializing, mixing activity, or it may be solitary. It probably should have written instructions, and after it has ended, a follow-up should give recognition to many participants.

A first-comer activity has a catchy introduction (related to the party theme), clear directions, and a definite ending that is controlled by the leader. In many unstructured social events, the first-comer activity consists of hanging up the coats, being introduced to other people present, and being offered a cocktail or appetizer. In a structured social event, the first-comer activity is more of an active event, with the participants actually engaging in some type of recreation activity.

An example of a first-comer activity for a children's birthday party might be the involvement of guests, as they arrive, in the creation of a memory scrapbook for the guest of honor. Each guest could draw a picture representing a memory of the guest of honor, and these could be assembled in a scrapbook. Another example of a first-comer activity might be the involvement of guests in the creation of something related to the party; for example, place cards, name tags, place mats, and so on.

Icebreakers. Many times in social settings people feel inhibited or shy or insecure. An icebreaker or defroster activity is designed to break down social barriers through a social activity that causes some mutual amusement or mutual fun.

I'm late, I'm late for a very important date.

The White Rabbit hurrying to the tea party in Alice in Wonderland

Activities that help people feel at home with others generally involve all people doing something similar. First-comer activities that are of the mixer type are also icebreaker activities. As the name suggests, icebreaker activities help to thaw the frigid atmosphere that often permeates a group at the beginning of a party.

One example of an icebreaker is the game Initial Impression. In this game, each guest has an 8½ by 11 inch piece of poster board attached to his or her back, and all the guests take turns writing on each other's cards what their initial impressions are of one another. These impressions could be guesses as to type of work, hobbies, marital status, and so on. After a time limit of five minutes or so, the cards are read out loud.

Mixers. A social mixer is designed to encourage participants to move among each other and to socialize. They must converse, question, answer, or communicate with each other somehow. The purpose of the social mixer is to help people to get acquainted informally and to socialize with many others. Some mixers are also first-comer events.

One of the most common and successful mixers that can be used for many age groups is the game termed Human Bingo. Guests involved in this mixer fill out a slip of paper with their name on it as they arrive, and these pieces of paper are collected in a large bowl. Next they are given bingo cards with blank squares. They must mingle among the guests and fill in the blank squares with the names of the others at the party. Following this, the guests play bingo with their cards, as the host or hostess draws the names of guests. The winner, of course, would probably win a prize, and the guests may have learned each other's names.

Active Games. As the name implies, these games are of a physically active nature. Active games are employed more often out-of-doors, unless there is a sufficiently large indoor area to accommodate them. Some examples of active games are volleyball, baseball or softball, horseshoes, kick the can, and so on. Some active games may be sub-classified as stunts, such as pie eating contests, egg throwing contests, or obstacle courses. The leader might think twice before planning to include this type of activity. The controversial purpose, risk management, and cleanup necessitated by these events probably preclude their being good choices.

Quiet Activities. Many quiet games can be enjoyed by a group of guests. Some of these games may be used to begin to tone down the excitement as the end of the party approaches. Some examples of quiet games are concentration and musical charades. As mentioned previously, story-

Games—an activity providing entertainment or amusement; a pastime...

American Heritage

Dictionary

telling is a good way to calm down active children, as is singing. It is not by coincidence that many campfires and other events end with stories and/or a song.

Financial

Though the finances involved in short-term social events are relatively simple, financing a major convention can be quite complicated and usually entails a finance or budget committee. However, the general expenses of a simple social event budget can be broken into the following classifications:

- Invitations
- Decorations
- Equipment, prizes, favors
- Refreshments
- Rentals (if any)
- Transportation (if needed)
- Extra personnel (if needed)
- Total expenses

Funds for such simple social events are usually obtained from organizational monies earmarked for such activities. However, ticket sales, sales of food and drink, donations of sponsors, or income from raffles or drawings may contribute to the total income from small social activities. In some cases a "free-will" donation (anonymous collection of monies) may be asked of the participant. Such monies are used to off-set any expenses occurred in putting on the event with net proceeds then applied to a social cause such as youth scholarships or other programs. Free-will donations are similar to passing the collection plate at church. However, the organizers need to understand that they might not meet expenses if this is the only source of revenue for the event. In many cases, non-profit organizations use the free-will donation method for low cost activities where the expenses can easily be absorbed by the agency if collections are low. However, in most cases, donations cover not only expenses but help to contribute to other worthwhile programs of the organization.

FOLLOW-UP

Four things should be accomplished by the leader before the job of administering the social event is over. First, the facility should be cleaned up; the decorations taken down, the equipment put away, and the leftover refreshments put away. Second, any persons who helped should be thanked. This should be done for both major social events as well as small parties. A letter of appreciation is always in order for those who were volunteers as well as those who were paid for

Every American is entitled to Life, Liberty and the Pursuit of Trivia.

Trivial Pursuit board

games advertisement

their services. Third, even a short social event should be evaluated. Fourth, a report should be developed and filed with the agency regarding the social event.

Evaluation. A major event lasting one or more days should be evaluated on three levels: facilities, personnel, and program. Many events have mediocre or less than desirable programs because of ill-prepared personnel or poor facilities. When these things are evaluated separately, information is obtained that can help in the planning of the next event. Evaluation also allows the leader to assess whether or not his or her program was successful (see Table 10.2 and Table 10.3).

> Although there are not real winners or losers, in games of pretending, children soon learn that the game ends when mutuality ends.
>
> *Joanne Oppenheim*

PLANNING
1. Is there definite evidence of careful planning?
   a. Was the party organized?
   b. Was all equipment readily available?
   c. Were there continuity and variety?
   d. Did the party show unity? Decorations? Activities?
   e. Did the party rise to a peak?
   f. Was there a definite ending?
2. Were the leaders there well in advance of party starting time?
3. Was the party started on time?
4. Was the first-comer planned for and made welcome?
5. Were activities suited to the group?
6. Did the leaders share responsibilities?
7. Were refreshments a chore, a bore, the peak, or just another part of the evening's fun?

PROGRAM
1. Was there unity?
2. Did activities follow the theme?
3. Was the program varied in interest and activity?
4. Did events move smoothly from one event to another?
5. Was there time allowed for "breathers"?
6. Was there a climax?
7. Did guests know when the party was over?

LEADERSHIP
1. Was leader friendly and enthusiastic without losing poise?
2. Was he or she thoroughly versed in the activities he or she was explaining?
3. Were explanations clear and concise?
4. Did the leader stand where he or she could be seen and heard?
5. Was control of the group evident?
6. Was the leader aware of group reactions?
7. Were mistakes handled tactfully?
8. Was the leader a sharer?
9. Did he or she give everyone a chance to participate?
10. Was leadership responsibility shared?

Elements Nicely Handled _____

Elements Poorly Handled _____

Table 10.2
Evaluation of social recreation events

SOCIAL ACTIVITIES EVALUATION

Check each item from 1 (low) to 5 (high):

ITEM	RATING
	5 4 3 2 1

I. Planning
1   Was activity organized well?
2. Was equipment readily available?
3. Were there continuity and variety?

Total

II. Program
1. Use of theme
2. Variety
3. Movement from one activity to another
4. Equipment
5. Suitability of activities to group
6. Beginning/first-comer activities
7. Ending

Total

III. Leadership
1. Enthusiastic and poised
2. Prepared to explain activities
3. Voice clear
4. Position correct
5. Explanations clear and concise
6. Mistakes handled tactfully
7. Responsibilities shared
8. Group control obvious
9. Everyone included in activities
10. Aware of group response

Total
Final Total

Table 10.3
Example of a simple check sheet for rating social events

Report. Personal parties, picnics, and the like rarely entail reports. However, special events conducted at youth camps, playgrounds, community centers, schools, youth agencies, and so on should have reports filed to help subsequent leaders in their planning efforts. In addition, the leader of a special event should also keep copies of all reports to help plan future events. These reports can include information such as that reported in the evaluation worksheets, as well as attendance figures, the program's organizational plan, the names and phone numbers of suppliers of equipment and supplies, advice for improvements in the program, and other recommendations. We firmly believe, based on past professional experience, that such information improves future programs dramatically both in terms of their overall quality and in their ease of preparation.

BASIC SOCIAL ACTIVITIES

Two basic activities usually found within the majority of social recreation settings are games and songs. Both can add a sense of fellowship and interaction to the proceedings and can also serve to quickly bind diverse groups together.

Although leading games and songs is not a difficult task, there are some distinct elements to both that the leader needs to be aware of before initiating either activity. What follows is a brief description of each of these social activity areas and some techniques that a leader should follow as they incorporate games and songs into the social recreation setting.

Games

Social recreation activities, playgrounds, before and after school care programs, camps, church groups, clubs, and special interest groups all make extensive use of games. Games usually have simple rules and lack the strategy and complexity required in sporting activities.

Types of Games

Each book on games seems to use a slightly different method for categorizing them, and each has validity. Games can be classified as active or passive or according to age, type of activity, or program area. Furthermore, games may be classified according to their benefits, such as social development, physical development, and so on. We have chosen to classify games into eight categories of game types, including (1) low organized games, (2) lead-up games, (3) team games, (4) table games, (5) mental games, (6) wide games, (7) simulation games, and (8) New Games. A description of each of these types of games, including brief examples of them where appropriate, follows.

Low Organized Games. Although usually considered children's activities, low organized games are played by all ages. They are characterized by having few rules, demanding very simple skills, and requiring little or no cooperation among the players. Another characteristic of low organized games is that the status of the players (thrower or dodger or runner or chaser) changes frequently, and the games usually can continue until interest wanes or a leader suggests something new.

Lead-up Games. Beginners more easily understand many games requiring highly developed skills, intricate rules, and complex plans for group cooperation if the leader introduces them through lead-up games. A lead-up game is designed to emphasize one or more facets of a more intricate game and allow participants to become familiar with one aspect of the game before going on to the more complex parts of the activity. A game of keep-away may be used as a lead-up game for basketball as it can emphasize team play, throwing, catching, movement, and feinting. The technical skills and rules come later, and the beginners will already have had a successful experience learning an introductory activity.

Team Games. Team games usually bring to mind baseball, basketball, football, and the like, but there may be teams of bridge players, teams for initiative tasks, and so on. Team games may be low organized games such as crows and cranes, in which one group of players chases and catches another (see Figure 10.4). This game meets all the prerequisites for a low organized event; however, it is played by groups of children in teams, of whom one team is the chaser and the other team is the pursued. Team games are characterized by the division of players into groups or teams cooperating together for the good of the group as a whole rather than for each one as an individual. Team games are usually not recommended for the immature or young child, who still displays an egocentricity and has not yet developed a team spirit.

The rules of team games are usually quite complex because such games involve many individual players performing a wide variety of functions according to their roles or positions. For example, baseball has a pitcher, catcher, people on bases, and fielders, all of whom are defensive players when

The Joy of a spirit is the measure of its power.

Ninon de Lenclos

Establish two goals 60 to 80 feet apart, and line up one team behind each goal. One team in known as crows and other as cranes. The leader stands in the middle and give the command, "Forward, march," whereupon the team marches forward. Just after he or she gives the command, the leader calls, "C-r-r-rows" or "C-r-r-rranes," holding the C-r-r sound until the teams are close together. If the call terminates in "crows," the crows dash back to their goal with the cranes in pursuit; if the call is "cranes," the cranes run back. All who are tagged join the other side.

Much of the fun element in the game depends on the cleverness of the leader. The call should be drawn out as long as possible, thus adding to the suspense and uncertainty of the players. Occasionally, after starting the call, the leader terminates it with either "crackers" or "crawfish," to confuse the players momentarily; he or she then immediately calls the proper word.

Figure 10.4
Crows and Cranes

Plans fail for lack of
counsel, but with
many advisors they
succeed.

Proverbs 15:22 (NIV)

in the field and offensive players when at bat. Consequently, there are many rules for each player involving catching, throwing, hitting, and running. Furthermore, team games usually involve advanced and sometimes intricate skills. The lead-up game of keep-away discussed earlier does not resemble the complex game of basketball at all (even though it may be used as an introductory activity). Basketball requires that the participant learn and develop precise and often complicated skills.

Table Games. Table games may be low organized, lead-up, or teams games but are played with a table or small flat surface as the game area. Table games may involve boards, as in checkers, Monopoly, Chinese checkers, and so on; or they may involve paper and pencil, as in tic-tac-toe; or they may use cards, dice or chips. A low organized table game is slapjack or go fish, whereas the game farmer and pig (see Figure 10.5) is a table game played as a lead-up activity for checkers.

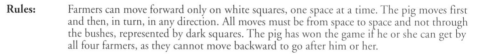

Title:	Farmers and the Pig
Type:	Table game
Participants:	Two to five players
Age, Sex:	Six years and up, either sex
Equipment:	Four discs, one disc of a different color (five total) Game board or chart as for checkers
Formation:	Place four farmers and a pig in the indicated squares (see chart)
Object:	The farmers try to pen the pig in so he cannot get by.

Rules: Farmers can move forward only on white squares, one space at a time. The pig moves first and then, in turn, in any direction. All moves must be from space to space and not through the bushes, represented by dark squares. The pig has won the game if he or she can get by all four farmers, as they cannot move backward to go after him or her.

Figure 10.5
Farmers and the pig

Mental Games. Some activities called mental games may be more correctly categorized as contests, for they do not involve interference or impeding strategy. They do, however, involve much choice. Guessing games are mental games, as are strategy events designed to "trick" or bluff opponents. Charades may be considered mental games by some and mental contests by others. A good example of a true mental game is one known as Our Cook Doesn't Like Peas (see the purpose. If, however, the group is already skilled and is competing to identify its best, elimination games are ideal. In these cases, players can be inspired to perform well and may be motivated to enhance their abilities further.

Low organized elimination games may be modified so that they are played for time, with the game ending as soon as one person has made the "eliminating error" three or four times. Even the old game of musical chairs, which eliminates the one not sitting when the music stops, can be modified. This activity always uses fewer chairs than players. Instead of continually taking away chairs with each eliminating round,

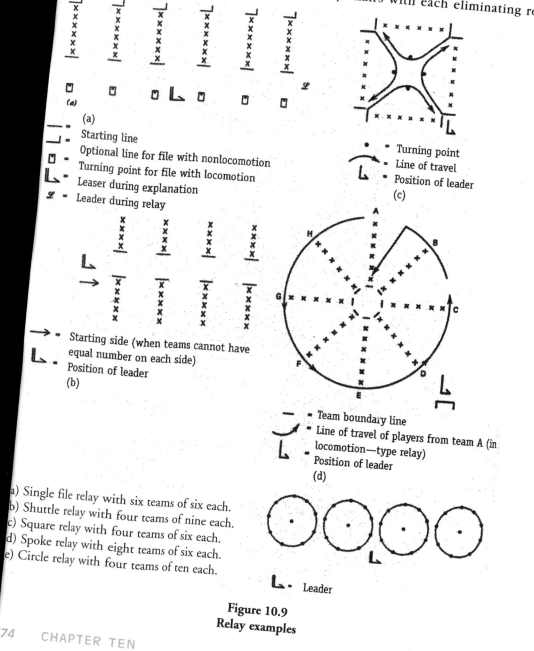

- Starting line
- Optional line for file with nonlocomotion
- Turning point for file with locomotion
- Leaser during explanation
- Leader during relay

(a)

- Turning point
- Line of travel
- Position of leader

(c)

- Starting side (when teams cannot have equal number on each side)
- Position of leader

(b)

- Team boundary line
- Line of travel of players from team A (in locomotion—type relay)
- Position of leader

(d)

- Leader

a) Single file relay with six teams of six each.
b) Shuttle relay with four teams of nine each.
c) Square relay with four teams of six each.
d) Spoke relay with eight teams of six each.
e) Circle relay with four teams of ten each.

Figure 10.9
Relay examples

Figure 10.6), which is a simple game with advanced, complex variations.

> One player starts the game by saying, "Our cook doesn't like peas. What can we have for dinner?" He or she points a finger at some player, who must quickly answer with some article of food. To be acceptable, the article must be one that is spelled without the letter p. Onions, cabbage, chocolate, celery, and the like are accepted; but if the players answers with peas, pumpkin pie, parsnips, or some other word having the letter p, the leader will say, "I am sorry, but our cook will not prepare that." A player who answers incorrectly may be required to pay a forfeit. Or the game may be played until most of the players get the idea.

Figure 10.6
Our Cook Doesn't Like Peas

Wide Games. Called tabloid games by Australians, wide games are actually a series of games or contests for a large group of people in a large (wide) area. In wide game events, participants rotate among several activities made up of individual or small-group skills, contests, quizzes, manual dexterity races, or a combination of these. Wide games activities may consist of knot tying, wood sawing, plant identification, tent pitching, and other similar events. Ten to 15 minutes per event are usually allotted. A group of 200 may be divided into 10 smaller groups, each of which progresses from activity to activity for a total of 20 activities with or without accumulative scores. The activities occur on large fields, in meadows and forests, or in any "wide" area. Suggestions for leading wide games and other such events are found later in the chapter, in the section entitled Task-Oriented Leadership. In wide games, all the activities usually relate to a common theme, such as the Olympics. The events may even be noncompetitive. One of the events in the series may be eating refreshments, thus wide games may be "games" by title only.

Simulation Games. Whenever educational events are designed to involve participants in situations simulating real life, the activities are called simulation games. Many times there is no winner, although there are considerable strategies, choices, and interference. Simulation games may be designed for children or adults and usually are comprised of role-playing, decision making, and necessary trade-offs. We may question the use of the word "game" here, for some simulation games end up as cooperative events. An example of a true game in a simulation model is the freeway planning game seen in Figure 10.7. The freeway planning game was designed for high school students by the California State Department of Education and is reproduced here with their encouragement. This activity was used as a get-acquainted

> Playing games with agreed-upon rules helps children learn to live by rules, establish the delicate balance between competition and cooperation, between fair play and justice, and exploitation and abuse of these for personal gain.
>
> *James Comer*

event and icebreaker on the opening evening of an adult conservation activity workshop, when it lasted over two hours and resulted in comradeship, points of reference, and illustrations for the remainder of the weekend.

New Games. Throughout the world, an interest in New Games has developed as the result of a series of New Games Tournaments, the first of which was held in October 1973 at Gerbode Preserve near San Francisco. The original idea of Stewart Brand, New Games are a concept designed to introduce people to cooperative competition in which the playing is more important than the winning. "Play Hard, Play Fair, Nobody Hurt" soon became the motto of New Games all over the world, and people were reviving and revising old games and inventing new activities, all of which were physical and

had an emphasis on group fun rather than group winning. Most New Games end up not being true "games," as the group competes only against itself, the equipment, or the weather. People pass, planet pass, and the lap sit are three of the most popular New Games (see Figure 10.8).

As mentioned, there are many ways of listing types of games; however, those just described are the types of games generally considered most popular and of greatest current interest.

Title: Freeway Planning Game

Number of Players: Up to 100, preferable even groups of 6

Location: Indoors

Length: One hour or more

Objectives: To learn about trade-offs in planning
To understand factors in planning better

Materials: Paper, pencil for each player;
copies of game for each player;
posterboard or blackboard

● Residential ▲▲▲ Hills ⬭ Digging site
∎∎∎∎ Business ⌂ Historic site
Legend

Procedure

Divide into groups of six. In each group, participants will assume the roles representing various vested interests—city council, taxpayer, and so on.

Each individual will now plan the freeway that will cost the groups he or she represents the least number of penalty points. The freeway must run from the top row of hexagons to the bottom row of hexagons. After all participants have planned their ideal freeway, they should total their penalty points.

The six participants with their assumed interests will now come together as a community and plan for when the freeway to be completed; each participant totals the cost for the group he or she represents. Then these costs are totaled, this represents the community costs.

The community with the lowest cost to the total community wins. The penalties to the city council, taxpayers, university, and so on in the various communities, should also be compared.

Explain scoring very clearly—for example, make sure it is clear that each space costs five points, and when houses or hills are on that space, they increase the value of that space. Penalties are in relation to vested interests.

Figure 10.7
Simulation game

People Pass
Have everyone stand facing the same direction in a double line, as close together as possible. One person at the head of the line leans back and is hoisted up to start a high, overhead, hand-delivered journey on the back over the line, being put down carefully at the other end. As soon as one person is passed, another person is started, and the activity will be self-perpetuating until the group agrees to pass no more.

Planet Pass
Everyone forms two lines, and all lie down on their backs with heads toward the center of the two lines. Raise hands and pass an earthball down the line (if it slips to the side, tap it with the foot). As soon as the "planet" has passed you, get up, run to the end of the line, and lie down again to receive the planet again. How far can the planet be passed?

The Lap Game
Everyone available stands in a circle shoulder to shoulder. Turn to the right. Then everyone slowly sit down on the knees of the person behind you. Put your arms out to the side. Hold it for five seconds.

Figure 10.8
Three new games

Games to Avoid

In spite of the availability of hundreds of activities, the prudent leader is sophisticated enough to scrutinize all activities under consideration to see if they meet the goals of the program. Some activities are not recommended under specific conditions (for example unusually strenuous events for older persons), and some activities are better if modified to fit a theme, season, group, or equipment. Elimination games are those that, as their title suggests, are designed to eliminate players one by one until only one person remains. If the goal of the event is for all people to participate, the elimination activity works to a disadvantage. If the goal is for the unskilled to get added practice, the elimination game defeats

Sandlot – a vac
used especially
dren for unorg
sports and gan

American

D

have those eliminated sit in the chairs, and the remaining players must greet them by name as they pass them. This now becomes a get-acquainted game with the eliminated players serving as a challenge to those who are left.

Other activities to avoid are relays that cause embarrassment, that are offensive, or those that create health problems. For example, passing an orange held between chin and chest to the next player without use of hands or passing a lifesaver from toothpick to toothpick held in the mouth are activities that the leader may want to avoid or modify. A leader who has empathy with the feelings of other individuals can imagine the discomfort caused by shyness when activities involving such close contact are directed. The sensitive leader imagines how people might react and selects activities with great care.

> In the end, it is important to remember that we cannot become what we need to be by remaining what we are.
>
> *Max De Pree*

Leading Games

How do you organize and lead a game? A number of questions need to be asked prior to the implementation of activities. Before attempting to lead or teach a game, one needs to do an assessment of the game and the play area to identify potential risks. The leader must know the various dimensions of the game in order to determine whether or not it can be safely implemented. In other words, one has to know the size of the area required, whether the game is passive or active, and other questions regarding its implementation. Further, the leader must determine the age and individual appropriateness of the game and be able to modify it to fit a given situation (see Figure 10.9).

Camp Adventure™ Youth Services has developed a solid technique for game leadership. This organization encourages the involvement of participants in leadership roles and also approaches their work with children and youth with great zest and energy. Their strategy for game leadership with children and youth is as follows:

1. **Entice.** Children and youth love to play. However, it is often difficult to get their attention and convince them to play the game that you have programmed. You must make them want to play your game. You must entice them. You also must participate. Everyone plays, including staff, as long as safety is not compromised.

2. **Tell a Story.** *Camp Adventure™ Youth Services* uses a story to entice children and youth to play. The presentation of this story is crucial to the success of your game. Children will mirror the counselor. If you are excited about the game and having fun, the children and youth will also be excited. Keys to telling an enticing story are:

a. Maintain a positive attitude.
b. Tell it with enthusiasm and creativity.
c. Make it applicable and creative.
d. Involve the children and youth in your story. Make them the characters or even have them act out the story as you are telling it.
e. Vary your voice and tone.
f. Create a setting the children and youth can visualize in their minds and put themselves in.
g. Be spontaneous. Use your own style no matter how farfetched it is. The crazier you get, the more involved the children will get.

3. **Provide Directions/Explain Rules.** Present simple and easy directions or instructions to follow. Use demonstrations as well as an explanation. Give children and youth one or two directions at a time, and make them fun and exciting. Keep everyone involved at all times. For example, if you need to separate into teams, have everyone with red and yellow shirts on one team and everyone with white and blue, and so on, on the other team. The next step in the process is to explain the rules of the game. This may sound like an easy task; however, when dealing with varying age groups and interests, it can become challenging. In-depth knowledge of the game is required to be able to answer varying questions.

Some things to keep in mind include the following:

a. Never give movement directions until all guidelines are stated.
b. Never let children or youth pick teams to get them into groups.
c. If the rules are complex, have a trial demonstration, then ask for questions.
d. Avoid repetition in your explanation.
e. Avoid making explanations in the middle of a circle. All children and youth should be facing you and you should be facing them.
f. After going over the rules, include the boundaries and tell them all what they can and cannot do.
g. REMEMBER RISK MANAGEMENT!! Explain any cautions or potential risks to the children. Relate it to the original story to motivate them again.
h. The last thing you do is take out the equipment.

4. **Playing.** It is essential to keep everyone involved. If everyone is not actively involved, keep the others busy by singing, playing another game, or refereeing. Try to eliminate having children being "out." Instead, give opposing teams a point, and allow those tagged to continue to play. When the children and youth are not busy, discipline problems can and

will occur. A great way to ensure success is for the leader to be "it" first.

5. **Transitions.** It is imperative that activities are smooth and that there is flow from one game or song to the next. Transitions will keep the children and youth anxiously awaiting the next activity as well as aiding counselors in control and further instructions.

6. **End on a Positive Note.** After the game has been played, end it on a positive note. Refrain from overplaying a game. Give verbal praise for group togetherness, or conclude the game with a story. On completion of a game, solicit feedback about variations or highlights from the campers.

Singing

Many recreation, parks and leisure service settings have singing at their core of social activities. Day camps, before and after school care programs, and senior citizen services emphasize singing as an important part of their effort.

Singing provides for the expression of a great range of human emotions. It can be joyful and filled with positive, zestful energy, conversely it can provide for reflection, contemplation, and a soothing of one's emotion. Great song leaders can bring out a full range of emotional experiences. Songs are used to set the mood, fill in space, promote group unity, and often to create a sense of excitement in recreation, parks and leisure service programs and settings. People often love to sing.

Leading Songs

Song leading is a great art. You don't necessarily have to be a great singer to be a great song leader. Steps in the song leading process are similar to leading other activities. They include:

1. The first step is to get the group's attention.
2. Next, the song leader should introduce himself or herself and the song.
3. The entire song should be sung with actions or motions if a part of the activity.
4. The song should be broken down into the chorus and each individual verse, taught separately to participants.
5. Actions accompanying words should be taught.
6. Each line should be sung with actions, asking for participants to repeat that portion.
7. Finally, the entire song should be sung combining words and actions.

> I am always ready to learn, although I do not always like being taught.
>
> *Winston Churchill*

Many songs are sung in rounds. When leading a round it is often useful to sing a song as many times as you have groups. On the other hand, you may want to divide a large group into two (2) or more smaller groups. The leader would move from one group to the other, assisting them in their portion of the round, singing and adding motions where appropriate.

SUMMARY

Social recreation can be defined as any structured or unstructured event where socialization is the primary motivation. Countless opportunities exist for persons working in face-to-face leadership positions to be involved in social events. A leader can use the social activities pattern as a basis for program planning, with modifications made when needed. This pattern or format can be used for any type or size of social event. Games and songs are two activities that are commonly associated with social recreation. Games can be categorized by type including (1) low organized games, (2) lead-up games, (3) team games, (4) table games, (5) mental games, (6) wide games, (7) simulation games, and (8) New Games. A leader needs to understand that not all games are appropriate for all participants and select games based on their understanding of who is in the group. In addition, singing can be used to bring diverse groups together and provide a common theme. One does not need to be a great singer to lead singing but does need to follow specific steps in order for the group to learn songs.

▓▓▓Discussion Questions

1. How does the motivation of participants for social recreation differ from that for other types of recreation?

2. Explain how age differences will affect the planning for the social recreation event.

3. What is the difference between a horizontal group and a vertical group?

4. In what ways may leader objectives and participant objectives be different for a social event?

5. What is meant by theme in a social event?

6. Explain how a leader might adapt three specific activities to fit a variety of themes .

7. What is a social action curve, and why is it important to consider it when planning a social event?

8. Describe the different types of games that a recreation leader might use with various social groups.

9. What are the various steps one can use to lead a game?

10. What are the various steps to follow when leading singing?

THE CASE FOR LEADERSHIP
General Wants to Fight Pretend War

Points of Consideration

You are director of the Cedar Center Parks and Recreation Department. One afternoon, you are approached by "General" Clyde Drake. Drake, dressed in green and brown camouflaged fatigues, wants you to allow him and his friends to play an "adult version of Steal the Flag." He says that both teams have a flag, and that the object is to move the other team's flag onto your side. He notes that the bullets are round and plastic, the size and color of a gumball, and that they are filled with a sticky red dye that washes out with water. The bullets are shot through pistols powered by CO_2 canisters. He claims that people wear safety goggles and that the most harm the bullets do is sting "like a BB-Gun." If a bullet leaves a red mark the size of a quarter, the victim is considered dead. He assures you that there is no harm in the game.

From your journal readings, though, you know that survival games have been criticized as fostering violence and an unrealistic idea of what combat is like. Drake denies that the war game simulates real combat—"[the players] know [they] aren't going to get killed"—and claims that it is truly a recreation experience. "Although the pistols and bullets are make-believe, the excitement is genuine."

"War may be hell, as General Sherman said, but war-like survival games are just plain fun," said Drake.

Questions of Consideration

- Should you allow this type of game to be sponsored by the department?
- At what age would this be an appropriate activity?
- Why?
- Should the feelings of the community be considered when deciding whether to allow the game to be played?
- What is the purpose of a game?
- What is the purpose of recreation?
- Is the war game both a game and recreation?
- Does "fun" make something "recreation"?
Outline a policy for which games should be accepted in a park.

From: Bannon, J. and Busser, J. (1992). *Problem Solving in Recreation and Parks* (3rd ed.) (pp. 359-360). Champaign, Ill.: Sagamore Publishing, Inc.

REFLECTING ON LEADERSHIP
Leadership and the Play Experience

1. Close your eyes and envision a recent social occasion that you considered to be fun.
    a. Was this occasion spontaneous or planned?
    b. Where was the setting?
    c. Who were the people present?
    d. What type of recreation activities were people doing?

2. Choose five descriptors that made this activity fun.
    a. If you had to give up one of the descriptors, which one would it be? How does this alter the experience?
    b. If you had to give up a second descriptor, which one would it be? How does this alter the experience?
    c. If you had to give up a third descriptor, which one would it be? How does this alter the experience?

3. What role did leadership play (either direct or indirect) in making this experience fun?
    a. How would the absence of leadership have affected this experience?
    b. What could leadership have contributed to this experience to make it even more meaningful?

References

Edginton, S. R., & Edginton, C. R. (1996). *Youth outreach and service excellence*. U.S. Army Youth Services.

Edginton, C. R., Hudson S. D., & Ford, P. M (1999). *Leadership for recreation and leisure programs and settings*. Champaign, Il: Sagamore.

CHAPTER

11

Leadership and Event Management

LEARNING OBJECTIVES

1. Define and identify various types of special events and their value.
2. Outline the planning process for a special event.
3. Explain the importance of recruiting necessary resources for event planning.
4. Explain the importance of evaluating the outcome of a special event.

KEY TERMS

- Festivals
- Pageants
- Conferences and Conventions
- Finance
- Community Involvement
- Committees

INTRODUCTION

Special events occur in a wide variety of locations and settings. Literally every community throughout North America and every type of organization is involved in the management of events. Events are often built around historical, religious, geographical, or cultural themes that reflect the unique social makeup of the community or region. Opportunities for recreation, parks, and leisure services personnel to give leadership to the organization of such events are virtually as unlimited as the themes that might be chosen for such activities. Also, such events often involve many community members with divergent talents and skills in the planning, organization, and implementation of such activities. In other word, such programs are often planned separately or in concert with recreation, parks, and leisure services professionals. In many cases, recreation, parks, and leisure services professionals may be called on to aid in the organization and implementation of events sponsored by other professional organizations, associations, or by amateur community groups.

WHAT ARE SPECIAL EVENTS?

Special events are one-time events that focus on a specific purpose. They can be celebrations in which people gather together to celebrate something of significance to them, such as a grand opening of a new library, an awards banquet, or other meaningful occasion. Special events contribute to community or group cohesiveness, pride and spirit, and can result in increased revenue for a community or organization.

Although special events have many qualities in common, they also have respective qualities that are different from one another. For example, festivals have their roots in primitive societies. Many early civilizations engaged in festivals to ensure continued good fortune and prosperity. These types of events provided opportunities for individuals to express their joy and gratitude. From a historical perspective, festivals were often tied to changes in the seasons or to religious holidays. As a result, they commonly occurred on a regular basis, usually once a year. A festival, therefore, may be defined as a celebration based upon a significant event that occurs with some regularity, usually annually. The settings and themes for these types of events can be very diverse. Some special events, as in festivals and pageants, are oriented toward such themes as historical sites, dates, personalities, or occurrences; cultural or ethnic heritage; art forms, such as dance, drama, music, art, crafts, film, poetry, and photography; sporting events; agricultural products (for example, the

---

Delegating work works, provided the one delegating works, too.

Robert Hall

National Peanut Festival in Dothan, Alabama, or the Hazelnut Festival in Springfield, Oregon); lifestyles (pioneer, farming, and folk); geographic features; time periods (for example, Gay Nineties, colonial, Civil War); international locations, styles, or events (for example, Scandinavian festivals and Oktoberfests); and seasonal phenomena (a rose festival, a cherry blossom festival, or a festival of Christmas lights). Some events are also held just for the fun of it, oriented toward novel, unique, or offbeat themes. All festivals and pageants are considered to be an accepted part of world culture. European Festivals include the Highland Games of Scotland, Holidays of the Colonies in Belgium, Parade of the Cantons in Interlaken, Switzerland, Octoberfest in Germany, and the spectacular Viking Celebration, Up Helly Aa, held each January in Shetland.

Pageants are usually based on legends or history and typically involve elaborate ceremony, exhibition, and display. Participants in pageants often march in procession in colorful costumes. Pageants may also entail elaborate dramatic productions. A pageant, like a festival, is a tremendous source of public entertainment. It celebrates events similar to those of the festival and, in fact, may be a component within a festival celebration. A pageant may be planned and executed by a smaller group of people than a festival. Some festivals (such as a city-sponsored Scandinavian Festival) involve participation in planning and implementation by an entire community. Others may involve most or many of the members of a community organization (such as an arboretum-sponsored Wildflower Festival). In addition, a pageant usually occurs over a short period of time, possibly only a few hours, whereas a festival may occur over an extensive period of time of one or more days to a week or more.

Conferences and conventions are large business and social activities that often last for several days and attract hundreds of individuals. Conferences and meetings are events that provide for a formal interchange of views and are designed to bring people together to learn, exchange information and ideas, make decisions, and enjoy themselves. Go into any hotel, on any day of the week, and you may find many organizations gathering to make professional business contacts. The individuals attending the conference are also there to have a break from the typical work routine and enjoy themselves. There are other terms that are used to define an educational type of gathering, such as meeting, seminar, symposium, colloquium, or workshop. These types of gatherings are usually much smaller in scale than a conference or convention.

> You can't depend on your eyes when your imagination is out of focus.
>
> *Mark Twain*

What is Special Event Management?

Special event management as the name suggests, is the business of managing special events. A recreation, parks, and leisure services professional must take the time to understand all of the planning and management aspects required to ensure that special events are successful. Special events are multifaceted and must be carefully and extensively planned and organized. To successfully manage a special event, the recreation, parks, and leisure services leader should ask a number of preliminary questions related to such basic factors as the type of event dates and times, finances, tourist interest, and so on. These should be considered by the planners of the event, even before any planning committees are organized or, at least, at the first meeting of the planning committee (Seekings,1992). A checklist of questions that should be considered by planners of such events as follows:

- What is the main purpose for staging the event? To celebrate a holiday season or a historical event, to raise funds, to provide a cultural or educational experience, to provide fun and entertainment, or to accomplish some other purpose?
- What type of event would be most in keeping with the community's unique location, history, customs, facilities, and abilities?
- Will the event meet a variety of needs and interests of community residents and perhaps of many visitors as well?
- What time of year should the event be held to best meet the objectives and purposes for which it was organized?
- On what dates will the event conflict least with other local programs or those of nearby communities?
- How long should the event last? Hours? One day? Several days? More?
- What basic types of facilities, equipment, and supplies are needed to conduct the event?
- How many people might attend the event?
- How many planners and workers will be needed?
- How much money will be needed to get the event under way?

Once these questions have been resolved, it is essential that a detailed management plan is developed with the following seven aspects: staffing, scheduling and location of facilities, secured financing including a detailed budget, marketing and media relations, risk management and legal considerations, event production, and evaluation (van der Smissen, Moiseichik, Hartenburg, & Twardzik, 1999).

I've found that luck is quite predictable. If you want more luck, take more chances. Be more active. Show up more often.

Brian Tracy

What Are the Values of Special Events?

Special events have many attributes that are of value to those individuals and communities participating in them. Some of the more important values of these types of events are the following:

Promotion of Community Spirit. Special events often generate a great deal of enthusiasm, interest, and excitement on the part of community residents. This helps to spark community spirit and pride. An example is the Scandinavian Festival held annually in a community with roots and ties to the Scandinavian countries.

Promotion of a Community Identity. Special events, especially if they occur annually, can help to focus attention on a given community, region, or area. Ashland, Oregon, for example, draws intensive media attention from its annual Shakespeare Festival. Another example is the Crisfield Crab Festival in Maryland. Each of these festivals has lent identity to the sponsoring areas.

Promotion of Community Cohesiveness and Involvement. Special events, by virtue of their very magnitude, necessitate the cooperation of a large number of individuals. Often this may entail the cooperation of an entire community. This type of common effort toward a single goal can act to bond individuals together.

Promotion of Historical Heritage, Cultural Heritage, and Rituals. Our cultural values and sense of history are learned and reinforced through participation during special event celebrations. Individuals attending such events learn about, and gain an appreciation for, the theme or topic represented (legends, social customs, historical values, artistic endeavors, and so on). Perhaps the most well-known historical, cultural, and ritualistic event is the Mardi Gras celebrated each spring in New Orleans.

Economic Development. Successful events can be economically rewarding to communities and organizations. Tourists often plan their travel itineraries to attend such events. This can result in increased revenue for a community or the sponsors of the event, or for both. A successful event may also serve as an impetus for increased development within the community in terms of new facilities, renovation of existing buildings, or other efforts that occur in conjunction with festival preparations.

> You can't build a reputation on what you are going to do.
>
> *Henry Ford*

Productive Use of Leisure Time. Special events also provide an excellent opportunity for individuals to enjoy their leisure. Many people may spend a large portion of their leisure time in the creation and production of a festival or pageant. There are also the individuals who participate in the event as consumers. Although their involvement may be less extensive than that of the individuals organizing the event, their participation also represents an important use of their discretionary time.

Types of Special Events

Numerous types of special events exist. Many of these events are based on ethnic and cultural heritage; sporting activities; geographic areas; and regional, national, and international history. Others are based on major holidays such as Christmas, Easter, and Thanksgiving. Some of the most common types of special events are described as follows.

Holiday Celebrations. The term holiday refers to a day or time period of some distinction or significance. A holiday can focus on a secular or non-secular event of local, regional, national, or international importance. For example, the Fourth of July holiday can serve as an impetus for a special event.

Historical Celebrations. The celebration of historical events and historical individuals is common in many communities in the United States and Canada. Some of the most common historical celebrations are based on political events such as Memorial Day, Washington's Birthday, Lincoln's Birthday, Martin Luther King's Birthday, and, in Canada, Boxing Day, Dominion Day, and Queen Victoria's Birthday.

Cultural Arts Celebrations. Cultural arts celebrations are especially popular events. They may focus on the visual arts, performing arts (dance, music, and drama), crafts, and what are termed "the new arts." The new arts are those artistic pursuits that are based on technological innovations such as film, computers, and television. Examples of cultural arts festival include the Peter Britt Music Festival, Mozart Festival, Bach Festival, Shakespearean Festival, and others.

Ethnic Celebrations. Our society contains a large number of ethnic groups. These groups are of many national origins and consist of people who live within specific geographic regions. Ethnic groups can be an excellent theme source in planning festivals or pageants. Ethnic groups are often eager to share their heritage with others, and the general public can benefit from participation in, and observation of, such events. The Cinco de Mayo Celebration in Dallas, Texas, is an example of a well-run and culturally valuable ethnic celebration. Kwaanza is another example of this type of celebration.

Geographical Celebrations. Geographical events highlight the noteworthy features of a given area. They are often planned in conjunction with some occurrence of local interest, bringing attention to a historical remembrance or cultural aspect of the area. Gold Rush Days relate to the past activities of a specific geographical location.

Religious Celebrations. Religious festivals and pageants are among the oldest and most significant celebrations in our society. Individuals of various faiths celebrate prominent religious events. For example, among various faiths such holidays as Easter, Hanukkah, and Christmas are often celebrated with festivals and pageants. Even though public recreation and leisure service agencies may not become involved in the more serious religious aspects of such holidays, they do, of course, engage in activities associated with major holidays, such as tree trimming, Easter egg coloring, caroling, and so on.

Sports Celebrations. Many sporting events may serve as the focus for the organization of a special event. The oldest and most elaborate sports event is the Olympic Games. More recently, the Super Bowl in the United States and the Grey Cup in Canada form the nucleus for special events within the cities in which they are held. These events can spur great economic gain within the communities hosting them and can also provide such communities with recognition and visibility.

Novelty Celebrations. Novelty events are based on innovative and unique ideas that are conceived primarily to "have fun." This type of celebration is exemplified by the beauty pageant, the prettiest baby contest, the Texas chili cook-off and bar-b-que, hot air balloon festival, the jumping frog contest, and so on. These types of celebrations often attract great interest owing to their unique qualities and the opportunity they provide for participants to have fun, and perhaps to laugh at themselves.

The Role of the Leader in Special Events

The recreation, parks, and leisure services leader can assume numerous roles to assist in the planning and implementation of a special event. Some event organizers are professionals

The greatest gifts you can give your children are the roots of responsibility and the wings of independence.

Denis Waitley

whose careers are devoted to such tasks. In general, however, the leader is more likely to work as a facilitator or in a face-to-face role with groups of individuals or committees. The leadership role in this type of setting is one of helping to coordinate the work of groups, encouraging individuals, ensuring that deadlines are met, and acting as a liaison between groups, as well as actually contacting individuals to acquire materials, supplies and equipment, facilities, and space.

When a special event is actually implemented, the leader may serve as a master of ceremonies, a judge, an official, a contact for emergencies or last-minute needs, a host, or a troubleshooter. The leader involved in an arts festival might engage in such activities as introducing himself or herself to all presenters and offering assistance while they set things up. The leader might also identify himself or herself as someone who could be contacted in the event of any questions or needs. Later the leader might greet participants as they arrive. All these activities involve direct, face-to-face contact with people. Even though some of these tasks may appear to be supervisory, they all involve the provision of service directly to people.

PLANNING THE SPECIAL EVENT

The following material may help explain the use of the modified and simplified convention plan as it relates to festivals and pageants.

The Event Theme

Prior to the development of the event, a theme should be considered. This may be done by the sponsoring organization or by the steering or planning committee. The theme of an event provides the idea around which the planning efforts will revolve. The theme will determine, to a large extent, the direction that the planning will take, the types of activities that will be involved, and so on. The theme will also set the tone of the event. It will determine, for example, whether the celebration is to be serious, humorous, educational, or historical.

When attempting to select a theme, a conference or convention planning committee may want to consider the reason for holding the event, what they want to achieve, and who should attend. A festival planning committee may want to consider the history of the community or region within which the celebration is to take place. There may well be historical or cultural attributes of the area that would complement such an event. However, a planning committee that

A mind that is stretched by a new experience can never go back to its old dimensions.

Oliver Wendell Holmes

A LEGACY OF LEADERSHIP
Ernest T. Attwell (1842-1949)

Ernest T. Attwell was a significant voice in the establishment and growth of the recreation movement in the United States, especially as it relates to the provision of services for minority groups. A true pioneer of the recreation, parks, and leisure services movement, Attwell's tireless efforts were eulogized in a resolution adopted by the Board of Directors of the National Recreation Association (a forerunner of the National Recreation and Park Association) noting that his "work carried him to every quarter of the country. He wanted to see more adequate recreation facilities and a larger number of better trained leaders in the field of recreation. Because or their relative economic and educational status, he felt that people of color, even more than the white, needed active help in this field. For this reason, he gave most of his time to the twin objectives of more facilities and a richer program through more and better trained personnel for the public recreation movement, particularly as it relates to minority groups in American."

Attwell was born and raised in Greenwich Village in New York City. His father, the Reverend Stanford Attwell, was the minister of one of Harlem's oldest and largest churches, St. Phillips Protestant Episcopal Church. As a young man, he worked for the Southern Pacific Railroad gaining knowledge of business practices and management methods. He joined the staff of Tuskegee University at the turn of the century working closely with Booker T. Washington. At Tuskegee he was in charge of the business department, coached football, and was involved in the provision of recreation services for students. During WWI, Attwell worked for the U.S. Food Administration in Washington D.C. and was responsible for organizing a nationwide program aimed at minorities for the wartime conservation of food.

In 1919, he joined the staff of the National Recreation Association (NRA). From 1920 until his death in 1949, he was responsible for the Association's Bureau of Colored Work. His basic responsibilities were directed toward the expansion of opportunities, facilities, and leadership for minority groups. He extended himself to numerous community groups throughout the United States, serving as an advocate and leader and encouraging the development of recreation, parks, and leisure services for minority groups. George D. Butler writes in *Pioneers in Public Recreation* that Attwell's "success resulted from his understanding of the point of view of people of both races, his rare gift of diplomacy, his skill in resolving controversial issues, his genuine love of people, and his concern for their well being."

Attwell was sought after to provide advice and counsel. As noted by the Board of Directors of the NRA in their resolution paying tribute to Attwell, "he was in constant demand to make studies for communities and neighborhoods, and to submit recommendations for their guidance. He was called upon to help groups with their initial, fundamental problems of recreation organization and with the organization of membership and financial campaigns for those groups not yet under the support of municipal tax funds. He was frequently consulted by local groups for advice on the planning of buildings . . . was effective in organizing training institutes and conferences. . . and was frequently called into assist with personnel problems."

cannot identify such a focus can base an event on any theme that they believe would attract participants. The wide diversity of special events that exist in any state, for example, are testimony to the creativity and ingenuity of individuals.

Once a theme has been selected, the actual name of the special event should be chosen. An effort should be made to select a name that will have appeal to the participants for whom the event is intended. The theme should also tell participants what to expect if they attend the event. If the special event is intended to encompass a broad variety of activities, the theme should reflect this and should also be broad. If on the other hand, the event will have a narrow focus, the theme should also be specific. In addition, the theme should reflect the nature of the event in terms of the emotions that it is intended to evoke: gaiety, humor, reflection, spiritual awareness, and so on.

Activities within a special event can be adapted to correspond with the particular theme. For example, a simple marathon run can be adapted to a Thanksgiving theme by calling it a "Turkey Trot." Singing and dancing can also be adapted to various themes. A festival with a Scandinavian theme, for example, might have dances, singing, or even dramatic presentations that relate to this theme.

In addition to choosing the theme of a special event, the leader should carefully consider the selection of an appropriate date and time. Careful consideration should be given to the date and time in order to avoid conflicts with other organization or community activities and to attract the type and number of participants desired. Furthermore, adequate planning time must be set aside, depending on the nature and complexity of the activity. The planning for a special event may take an entire year or even longer.

ORGANIZING SPECIAL EVENTS

Although most recreation, parks, and leisure services leaders do not assume ultimate responsibility for the organization of a special event, some leaders will assume this role. Further, all leaders can benefit from knowledge regarding such organizational processes.

In the organizing of any large-scale event, the first step is to identify potential members of a planning, organizing, or steering committee. There is usually an over-all chairperson and chairs of the subcommittees for Operations, Program, and Finance. The Executive Director of a non-profit organization may serve as ex-officio member of the steering committee. The people who serve on the steering committee help to

A leader is best when people barely know he exists, not so good when people obey and acclaim him, worse when they despise him. But of a good leader who talks little when his work is done, his aim fulfilled, they will say: We did it ourselves.

Lao-Tzu

coordinate the work of all other committees. There need not be meetings of everyone involved in planning the event. The steering committee members who chair the subcommittees can hold meetings related solely to their own particular portion of the responsibility and include just their own volunteers. The subcommittees may include individuals with special skills in such areas as drama, music, art, finance, or other skills related to the type of event being planned. It may be the event coordinator's responsibility to recruit individuals to serve on the steering committee. The chair should attempt to create an atmosphere of enthusiasm and excitement as the planning and organizing process evolves. After the organizing or steering committee takes shape, the various subcommittees for planning purposes should be identified and the subcommittee chairpersons can recommend members to perform specific tasks related to their portion of the event. Some of the concerns of the subcommittees may include the following:

Operations. The operations subcommittee may include within its purview the responsibilities for facilities, safety and security, publicity, invitations, hospitality, setting up and taking down the accommodations, and anything related to the overall event.

Facilities. A facilities subcommittee serves to identify appropriate physical facilities necessary to hold the event in an efficient and safe manner. This subcommittee should give consideration to the type of program being planned, the safety of persons attending, the props and sound equipment required, the permits needed for concessions and parades, the accessibility of activities and facilities to all participants, the concerns related to transportation and parking, and (perhaps the most important) the resources necessary for coordinating the set-up and tear down of each of the program components being implemented. An additional concern of this committee is whether arrangements should be made for an alternative site in the event of inclement weather. If an alternate site is not planned, the committee should decide whether or not to schedule an alternative date in the event of inclement weather. The financial ramifications of alternative locations or dates should be determined, as should the safety considerations that might be affected by an alternative location (see Table 11.1 for an example of a facilities checklist).

Safety and Security. Participants should be protected from unsafe conditions from the time they arrive until they depart. The most effective way to ensure this is to formulate a safety and security subcommittee, the purpose of which is the planning for safety prior to the

> Whether adversity be a stumbling block, discipline, or blessing depends altogether on the use made of it.
>
> *Anonymous*

Table 11.1
Facility Checklist for Special Events

Facility _____			
Reserved from _____			
Open when _____	Keys from _____		
Restrooms _____	Open _____		
Fountain _____			
Heat _____	Controls _____		
Lights _____	Controls _____		
Police _____			
Fire _____			
Equipment available _____			
Cleanup _____			
Trash _____			
Parking area _____	Number	Cost	
Refreshment _____			
Store _____	_____	_____	
Heat _____			
Cool _____			
Serve _____			

event. The planning of this committee should be coordinated with local fire and police officials. The officials will be able to advise event planners how to best circumvent possible problems. In addition, fire and police officials can inform the committee of local regulations regarding licensing, permits, and the like. The physical well-being of those attending the special event can be enhanced by the provision of rest areas away from the body of event activities, yet close enough to be easily accessible. In climates that are unusually hot, provisions should be made for a number of drinking stations. Parking is another safety concern. Traffic control must be well-coordinated with local police for smooth traffic flow to and from the event. If the event includes such activities as auto racing, fireworks, or rodeo events, special crowd control provisions may be necessary to protect the spectators.

Publicity. The efforts of the publicity subcommittee may well determine the success or failure of the event. The publicity committee must ensure that all possible sources are exhausted in their efforts to promote the event. An important part of the promotion process is the identification of the audience or target markets for whom the special event is intended. Once the publicity committee has identified the audience that they want to attract, promotional efforts should be directed toward this select group. For example, if the event is being planned for children, an effective promotional method might be the distribution of colorful fliers to schools and youth agencies. The publicity committee must decide what media they will attempt to use to publicize the event: radio, television, newspapers, posters, fliers, billboards, or a combination of all of these. Publicity activi-

Before the Event

News releases and ads	Radio and television coverage
Posters, billboards, and signs	Bumper stickers and buttons
Talks to local groups	Fund drives
Mayor's proclamation	Printing on shopping bags
Parades in neighboring towns	Fliers enclosed with bills
Airplane banners	Youth rallies or walkathons
Event name or slogan contests	Beard-growing contests
Reduced-price ticket sales	Endorsements by local firms
Invitations	Newspaper supplements
Engraved pens, pencils, etc.	Pennants on vehicles
Street banners and marquees	Signs in public transportation

During the Event

Appearances of famous persons	Balloon ascensions
Newspaper picture stories	Fireworks shows
Searchlights	Bumper stickers (I've been to . . .)
Car-top announcements	Parades through business district
Lettered hats, pennants, etc.	Staging of some activities in other towns
Skydiving shows	Guessing contests (beans in a jar, etc.)
Prize drawings for early arrivals, children, senior citizens, etc.	Television and radio coverage

After the Event

News releases	Movies or slide shows
Speeches to civic groups	Volunteer recognition banquets
Post-event parties	Announcement of contest winners
Newspaper ads or letters of thanks	Radio and television interviews

Figure 11.2
Promotional methods for festivals and pageants
Source: Robert P. Humke, *Planning Community Wide Special Events*. Cooperative Extension Service, University of Illinois at Urbana-Champaign, 1976, p. 11.

ties can vary greatly in terms of their degree of complexity and scope. Some of the many vehicles that can be used to increase the public's awareness of special events are included in Figure 11.2. It should be noted that some radio and television stations are required to provide a certain number of hours of free public service announcements and may be eager to help in promotional efforts.

Program

The program subcommittee is responsible for the selection and development of activities and events that will be included in a special event. Its duties may include locating entertainment, exhibitors, speakers, and so forth. The program committee will also formulate the structure of the program, as well as the format for activities. They will determine what event is to take place at what time and where. Often a program committee will establish the scope of the event. This is important, for the scope of the event should be consistent with the available resources for the event, the goals of the event, and the number of participants expected. The program committee is often the committee that has "the big picture" of what the form of the event will be, how it will be implemented, and with what resources. As such, it must maintain close contact with the other subcommittees to ensure that plans are carried out in a coordinated and consistent manner.

Finance

The finance committee plans the budget for the special event. It coordinates the budget needs of each of the planning committees and the event as a whole. In addition, such items as ticket pricing and distribution, revenue collection, and banking should be handled by the budget or finance committee. It is vital that the budget committee keeps scrupulously accurate records of its transactions in terms of banking, bills paid, cash received, checks written, and petty cash. Individuals within the committee should be assigned specific responsibilities regarding these functions. One of the main functions of the finance committee is to coordinate with the chairs of the Operations and Program subcommittees to be sure all groups inform each other of expenses needed and budgeted.

Food or Concessions Operations. The provision of food at a special event can enhance the event tremendously. Food can be theme related, adding to the flair and festivity of the celebration. The planners may desire to take responsibility for food purchasing, preparation, and sales, or they may want to turn this aspect of the operation over to a concessionaire. In either case, it is important that the areas in which food is being served are easily accessible, clean, and logically placed. If a concessionaire is selected, planners should make financial arrangements in advance. There will be local health regulations that pertain to the serving of food. The food or concessions committee should check these local regulations. Often food handlers are required to have a food handlers' permit and proof that certain inoculations are up-to-date, and they must comply with this regulation prior to the event.

It can sometimes be difficult for a food committee to plan how much food they will need to buy for an event. The number of participants that will turn out is almost impossible to predict. The committee can, however, make their "best guess" and buy food from merchants with the understanding that unsold food, still properly packaged, can be returned promptly for a refund. This is not an unusual request to make of local merchants when planning for a large event.

Product sales. Concessions include not only the serving of food, but also the sale of products and services that may contribute to the theme of the special event. Such

LEADERSHIP: A POINT OF VIEW
FROM THE PROFESSION

Ronald Olson

Ronald Olson has served as Associate City Administrator/ Superintendent of Parks and Recreation for 19 years with the City of Ann Arbor Michigan. The park and Recreation system consists of over 2000 acres of park land, including 148 parks and 18 recreation facilities and services, including two 18-hole golf courses, two canoe liveries, 55,000 street trees, Horticultural areas, an innovative environmental center, a Senior Center, community centers, a Farmer's Market, extensive athletic fields, pools, artificial ice arenas, greenways and an extensive Natural Area Preservation program, and over 100 miles of bike trails. The department has a budget of over $16 million with up to 84 full-time and over 300 part-time /temporary employees. Olson is a member of the American Academy of Park and Recreation Administration.

On leadership. . . .The ability to develop a collaborative vision and then aligning human and financial resources to achieve it with clearly defined goals. This is only accomplished with staff and stake holders honestly involved in the process.

Leadership and success. . . .Over the years we have engaged with 11 citizen-based advisory committees and/or commissions to assist in policy development and planning for a quality Park and Recreation system. Staff are encouraged to have their say. Regular staff meetings are a must—along with other team-building oriented activities that occur at all levels of the organization. The goal is to ensure the staff stay connected to the mission so they understand the critical role each of them play in achieving it.

The exemplary leader. . . . . Great listener, honest communicator, genuine, trusting, respect for others, expresses expectations and openly solicits expectations of others, engages all in the visioning process and practices these every day.

Leadership in action. . . . Must be open to ideas and input from others, ensure the staff understand the mission and empowers them to engage with the customers to provide quality services that enhance the quality of life for the community. Must have a sense of humor and engage in recreation themselves. Must genuinely care about why, how, and who we are serving and seek continuous improvement.

concessions might include souvenirs, arts and crafts, parking concessions, amusement rides, and so on.

▰▰▰ Additional Trouble Shooting

Theoretically, the troubleshooting committee examines and scrutinizes the plans and activities of other committees and attempts to identify possible organizational problems and offer solutions to them. Committee members should be independent of the actual planning and decision-making processes, acting in an advisory capacity only. Individuals on this committee also act to solve problems that occur on the day of the event, such as getting last minute supplies, providing extra parking attendants if needed, answering questions, dealing with emergencies, and so on.

Outlining the Plan

There are many challenges to the operation of a successful event. Each challenge appears to have some similarities, but every one is different. Using the previous guidelines an outline of duties may be developed. A local arboretum may outline the plans for both its annual Wildflower and Mushroom Festivals as follows:

I.   Steering Committee
   A. Festival Chair, Operations Chair, Program Chair, Finance Chair
   B. The Executive Director and the Office Manager are ex-officio

II. Operations Committee (Each of the following has a sub-committee chair)
   A. Transportation
      1. Schedule the bus to shuttle participants from the large parking area to the site of the festival.
      2. Arrange for highway signs to designate directions to the shuttle bus parking area, and the site parking area.
      3. Maintain a map of the locations to put up the directional signs.
      4. Procure all signs from storage area; arrange for new or repaired signs.
      5. Put up and take down all signs, then return them to the storage area.
      6. Arrange for parking lot attendants to secure the area at all times.
      7. Schedule extra vans and drivers to transport early arrivals, volunteers, and late exiters, and in case of emergency or unexpected needs.
      8. Keep a list of all volunteers and the times they spent during the festival.
   B. Hospitality
      1. Recruit persons to greet those who enter the site. Explain how to request donations, how to handle the donated money, and the location of events and facilities. Explain how to handle unwelcome guests, such as those bringing dogs.
      2. Arrange for a membership/information booth in which people may learn about the organization,

By believing passionately in something that still does not exist, we create it. The nonexistent is whatever we have not sufficiently desired.

Nikos Kazantzakis

join it, ask questions, and be directed to areas of their interest.

3. Arrange for publicity.
4. Arrange for first aid, including who should administer it. Plan emergency exits.
5. Procure pencils, badges, sign-up sheets for volunteer names, addresses, and hours worked.

C. Set-up
   1. Arrange for the set-up and teardown of the exhibits, including procuring tables, chairs, tents or tarps, electricity, public address system, diagram of locations of booths, and storage of items.

D. Publicity
   1. Contact news media.
   2. Arrange for publicity, posters, and fliers, including distribution.
   3. Plan articles for the newsletter.

E. Evaluation
   1. Supervise the evaluation procedure; collate and tabulate results.

III. Program
   A. Arrange for musical entertainers.
   B. Arrange for the children's program.
   C. Arrange for the nature walks.
   D. Coordinate the plant exhibit with the Native Plant Society.

IV. Finance
   A. Set up a budget for expenses to be allowed and estimated costs for publicity, and so on.
   B. Arrange for commercial vendors.
   C. Arrange for donated baked goods.
   D. Coordinate sale of donated baked goods.
      1. Procure supplies for coffee, tea, hot chocolate, milk, cream, sugar, plates, napkins, latex gloves, food handler licenses.
      2. Set up coffee, and so on.
      3. Price the baked goods; cut and serve baked goods.
      4. Arrange for volunteers to help serve, set up, clean up, take money.
   E. Recruit vendors for hot foods (vegetarian and omnivarian), ethnic if desired, cold drinks, and so on.
   F. Recruit commercial vendors (mushroom sales, bouquets of dried flowers, books, etc. as appropriate)
   G. Recruit nonprofit exhibits such as Audubon, County Extension, and so on.
   H. Coordinate expenditures with all other committees.

> We must accept finite disappointment, but we must never lose infinite hope.
>
> *Martin Luther King Jr.*

I. Pick up money from donations, vendors, member-ship, and so on periodically throughout the festival; count and record income from each booth.
J. Arrange for the poster art, the T-shirt art, T-shirt printing, sizes, and so on.
K. Send bills.

Each committee chair will submit a report on attendance of volunteers, any problems encountered, changes recommend-ed for next year, and comments as desired. Each task listed in the foregoing outline has a time line designated for com-mencing and ending. Publicity must be done well in advance, as must the procuring of vendors and volunteers.

Recruiting for Community Involvement

Special events planning often requires the mobilization of large numbers of individuals, many with special talents and skills. Therefore, the tapping of community resources is an extremely important part of the organization process of fes-tivals and pageants. Communities have many individuals and groups who are eager to provide their skills, talents, and abil-ities for a worthwhile cause. The ability of the leader to locate and use such community resources will increase the likelihood that the event will be a success. Figure 11.3 pro-vides a list of groups and organizations that could be tapped to provide talent and workers for festivals or pageants.

A key factor in the use of community resources is pairing the skills and talents of individuals with the tasks that need to be undertaken. For example, an accountant would make a valu-able addition to a budget or finance committee. Conversely some individuals volunteer their time to work in areas that are unrelated to their vocations. They may view volunteer service as an opportunity to stretch and expand their hori-zons. This feeling should, of course, be accommodated.

> Leadership can be thought of as a capaci-ty to define oneself to others in a way that clarifies and expands a vision of the future.
>
> *Edwin H. Friedman*

Service clubs	Political parties
Civic clubs	Colleges and universities
Youth groups	Chamber of commerce
Businesses	Board of realtors
P.T.A's	Special interest groups
Senior citizen groups	Ethnic groups
Historical societies	Arts organizations
Religious groups	Craft guilds
Media organizations	Governmental agencies
	Fraternal organizations

Figure 11.3
Resource groups for festivals and pageants

When planning or implementing a special event, the recreation and leisure service organization might want to align itself with a civic or service club in the sponsorship of the event. This can provide the recreation and leisure service organization with human resources, finances, and support that might not otherwise be available to conduct the event. The service club, on the other hand, can receive visibility and an opportunity to fulfill its mission of service. This arrangement is not uncommon and, in fact, is often sought by both public agencies and civic and service clubs.

EVALUATING SPECIAL EVENTS

Why evaluate? An evaluation is carried out primarily to provide information that can assist in the planning of similar future events. An evaluation report should impart the knowledge gained through the planning and implementation of the event. The evaluation report should include the support groups involved, the media used, the type of committee organization used, the planning schedule, the merchants that might have contributed merchandise or money or may have offered discounts, and the methods and procedures used in all areas of planning and implementation. Theoretically, an evaluation report for a large event should be so complete that another planning group could implement the same event with similar results just by reading it.

Evaluative data (such as questionnaires and discussion) not only should be gathered at the conclusion of the event, but also throughout the planning and implementation phases of the event. An evaluation report is often concluded with recommendations for similar future programs. Some of the guidelines that can be used in planning for evaluation are:

- Planning for evaluation should be included with all other event planning details.
- Information and opinions gathered in the evaluation process should be as objective as possible. It is just as important to record minor failures as it is to record major successes.
- Input into the evaluation process should be made by planning and evaluation committee members and others involved in the event.
- A variety of evaluation methods should be used with the results combined and compared.

> It is of the utmost importance in the decades ahead to practice ethical business. When you see something wrong, speak up about it. It is the only way to have a clear conscience and sleep at night.
>
> *Roger Boisjoly, one of five Morton Thiokol engineers who argued against the disastrous launch of the space shuttle Challenger*

SUMMARY

Special events provide an exciting format for recreation and leisure activity that captures the interest and enthusiasm of professionals and participants. Themes for festivals and pageants are diverse and can focus on such areas of interest as sports, geography, history, culture, religion, ethnic groups, holidays, and unusual or novel events. A key to the successful implementation of festivals and pageants is the involvement of community members. This type of celebration can be one of the most spectacular of community events.

Discussion Questions

1. What is the difference between a pageant, a festival, and a conference?

2. Identify and discuss some of the values of special events.

3. There are a number of different types of special events. Identify eight (8), and provide examples of each in your own state.

4. What role or roles does a leader play in planning and leading special events?

5. What are the key questions one must ask when planning a special event?

6. Choosing the "theme" of a special event is an important part in the process of planning. How would you select a "theme" for a community festival? Whom would you involve?

7. List some promotional ideas that can be used in special events.

8. Community involvement in festivals and pageants is important. Why? What are some important sources of community assistance?

9. Identify and discuss guidelines that can be used in evaluating special events.

THE CASE FOR LEADERSHIP
Increasing Cultural Diversity

Points of Consideration

Each year, the entire city of Cedar Center celebrates Christmas with a number of events. Churches host basement bazaars; various organizations coordinate Christmas caroling; children involved in youth groups make Christmas tree ornaments to sell as a fundraiser; lights are hung on the homes of many residents of the town; the downtown business decorate their storefront. The city hosts a nighttime parade and tree lighting ceremony and on the night of this event, the local merchants serve hot cider and Christmas cookies to all. This holiday celebration has been a tradition in the town for years.

Over the past five years, a number of Orthodox Jews have moved into the city of Cedar Center. The Jewish faith celebrates Hanukkah this time of year, a celebration of the Jews winning religious freedom from the Syrian-Greeks. Hanukkah is a family time and is also called the Festival of Lights. There are many traditions observed throughout the eight days of Hanukkah, such as the lighting of the menorah the giving of Chanukah gelt to children, and the eating of certain foods such as latkes. Some Jewish residents have voiced their opinions that they don't mind the public display of the Christian traditions, but they would like it to be toned down in order to be more inclusive of other religious and cultural traditions.

You are the director of Cedar City Parks and Recreation Department. In order to recognize and celebrate the increased cultural diversity in Cedar Center, you would like to incorporate Hanukkah traditions with the holiday traditions that have been occurring in the town for years.

Questions of Consideration

- Through your leadership, how would you approach this task?
- Who may need to be informed and educated on differing religious traditions?
- What other cultural and religious traditions occur during this season?
- What problems do you anticipate in trying to incorporate two different traditions into one holiday event?
- Do you think this is a bad idea and feel that Cedar Center should have two distinct holiday events?

REFLECTING ON LEADERSHIP
Evaluating the Success of Your Special Event

You have just been appointed to serve on the steering committee for the Taste of Cedar Center festival local restaurants offer the public a taste of their culinary specialties. At the Taste of Cedar Center there is a wine tasting event, a chili cook-off, a waiter's race, and silent auction. Festival-goers cast their vote for the People's Choice Award, which represents the best tasting food at the festival for that year.

As part of your role as the Festival Chair, you have been asked to evaluate the success of the Taste of Cedar Center festival in the following areas: (a) economic impact, (b) environmental impact, (c) community cohesion, and (d) cultural diversity. How would you go about involving the operations chair, the program chair, and the finance chair in assisting you in this task? What is your approach to leadership? What is your philosophy in motivating and working with groups? How would you empower the committee members to accomplish this task?

References

Seekings, D. (1992). *How to organize effective conferences and meetings* (5th ed.). London: Kogan Page.

van der Smissen, B., Moiseichik, M., Hartenburg, V., & Twardzik, L. (1999). *Management of park and recreation agencies.* Ashburn, VA: National Recreation and Park Association.

Index

type of, 13-14
environmental conditions, 293-96
environmental education programs, 325
equipment, 304, 308-9, 311
ethics, 17, 47-48
ethnic celebrations, 390-91
ethnicity, 129
evaluations, 32, 112, 113, 366
event management. See special events
excellence, striving for, 16
excellence theory, 67
expectancy, 221
expectations, 48-49
experience, 6, 8, 46-47
experiential exercises, 189
exploitive autocratic style, 75
exploration, 51
expressed needs, 204
external forces, 13

face-to-face communication, 265-66
face-to-face leadership, 101-3, 105-7, 109
facilities, 11, 311, 358-59, 361, 395
family structure/patterns, 130
family unity, 52
favorableness, 80
feedback, 247-48, 264
felt needs, 204
festivals, 386-87
Fidler's Contingency Model of Leadership Effectiveness, 79-82, 81
finance committee, 398-99, 401-2
first aid, 303
first-comers, 363
The Flight of the Buffalo, 87
followers, 37-38
empowerment of, 41-42

influence and, 40-41
leaders and, 46-47
foundational history, 327-28
freedom of choice, 41, 208
French, J. R. P., Jr., 46
funding strategies, 11

game rules, 308
games, 364, 368-77
Gaskin, L., 297
general supervision, 298
general task roles, 182-83
generational events, 251-53
geographical celebrations, 391
George, B., 90
Gholston, Michelle, 263
goal-directed activity, 210-11
goals, 12, 13, 50-53, 169
attainment of, 211-12
identifying, 32
leadership and, 38
perception and, 256
when working with older people, 143-44
Godbey, G., 50, 207
Gordon, W. I., 268
"great man" theory, 66, 92
Greenleaf, Robert K., 88-90
groups, 4-5, 5
analyzing interpersonal relationships, 170-72
case study of, 196
characteristics of, 7-8
communication in, 175-77
conflict in, 177-78
definitions of, 162, 164
discussion questions, 195
dynamics of, 102-3
goals, 13
group dynamics, 159-62
group functioning, 178, 180-81
group properties, 168-70
group roles, 181-86
influence of, 166-68
introduction to, 158

leadership of, 173-75
maturity of, 83
primary and secondary groups, 164-65
reasons for joining, 165-66
responsibilities of leaders and, 33
size of, 172-73
summary of, 193-94
youth, 134-36
group symbols, 103
group theory, 66-67
guidance, leadership and, 30
guidelines, for youth development, 132-33

Hall, James R., 223
Hall, R., 304
Hallberg, K. J., 144-45
hallmarks of leadership, 14-17
hard-nosed style, 81
hard skills, 327-28
Haun, Paul, 55
health forms, 313
health/physical competence, 131
health promotion programs, 138
hearsay, 257
Heath, S. B., 134
Henderson, K. A., 29
Hensley, Sara L., 15
heritage, 389
Hersey, P., 83-84
Hesselbein, F., 2, 3-4, 31, 36, 68, 100, 114
Heywood, L. A., 219
historical celebrations, 390
Hitt, W. D., 85-86
Hitt's Dreamer and Doer Model, 71, 85, 85-86
Hjelte, George, 241-42
holiday celebrations, 390
hope, 17
horizontal groups, 348
host/guide/interpreter, 12
huddle method, 188-89
human development, 125
human relations style, 81

USA Swimming, 336

values, perception and,
  256-57
van der Smissen, B., 283,
  284, 285, 289-90, 291,
  297, 314, 388
verbal communication, 239
vertical groups, 348
vision, 16, 32
visual symbols, 242
vocational/career/employ-
  ment, 138-39
vocational competence,
  132
volunteer groups, 161

waivers, 311-14
waterfront directors, 331
water games and activities,
  340
water shows, 339
wide games, 371
Wofford, J. C., 266-68
written communication,
  240

YMCA, 335
youth, 127-29
youth development,
  130-34, 136, 138-39
youth workers, 105-7

Zimbardo, P. G., 166